Identity in
Professional Wrestling

Identity in Professional Wrestling

Essays on Nationality, Race and Gender

Edited by AARON D. HORTON

McFarland & Company, Inc., Publishers
Jefferson, North Carolina

LIBRARY OF CONGRESS CATALOGUING-IN-PUBLICATION DATA

Names: Horton, Aaron D., editor.
Title: Identity in professional wrestling : essays on nationality, race and gender / edited by Aaron D. Horton.
Description: Jefferson, North Carolina : McFarland & Company, Inc., Publishers, 2018. | Includes bibliographical references and index.
Identifiers: LCCN 2018003906 | ISBN 9781476667287 (softcover : acid free paper) ∞
Subjects: LCSH: Wrestling—Social aspects—Cross-cultural studies. | Wrestlers—Social conditions—Cross-cultural studies.
Classification: LCC GV1196.4.S63 I34 2018 | DDC 796.812—dc23
LC record available at https://lccn.loc.gov/2018003906

BRITISH LIBRARY CATALOGUING DATA ARE AVAILABLE

ISBN (print) 978-1-4766-6728-7
ISBN (ebook) 978-1-4766-3141-7

© 2018 Aaron D. Horton. All rights reserved

No part of this book may be reproduced or transmitted in any form or by any means, electronic or mechanical, including photocopying or recording, or by any information storage and retrieval system, without permission in writing from the publisher.

Front cover: Wrestler Mark Henry completes a double body splash in the corner against two wrestlers at a WWE house show in Halifax, Nova Scotia, on September 19, 2009 (Myles McNutt)

Printed in the United States of America

McFarland & Company, Inc., Publishers
 Box 611, Jefferson, North Carolina 28640
  www.mcfarlandpub.com

Table of Contents

Introduction   1

Part I. Race

The Iron Sheik and Public Representation of Iranian National Identity in Professional Wrestling
 ZARA MIRMALEK   11

"They ain't like us": Race, Class and Gender in Smoky Mountain Wrestling
 EDWARD SALO   24

Latin Lords of the Ring: Politics, Nativism and Mexican/Chicano Identity Through Professional Wrestling
 JUSTIN D. GARCÍA   37

"Degenerative sports and dirty tactics": Race and Professional Wrestling in Cape Town, South Africa, c. 1880–1988
 HENDRIK SNYDERS   56

Nazis, Japs and Pearl Harbor Attacks: German and Japanese Stereotypes in American Professional Wrestling
 AARON D. HORTON   76

Deepest, Darkest Africa(, Illinois): Cultural Appropriation in Professional Wrestling
 KEVIN HOGG   92

Part II. Gender

Wrestling with Masculinity: *Exóticos* in Lucha Libre
 XIMENA ROJO DE LA VEGA GUINEA   109

Transformed Bodies and Gender Norms: Gender Identity
of Japanese Women Pro Wrestlers
    Keiko Aiba   120

"A secret fascination": Professional Wrestling, Gender
Non-Conformity and Masculinity
    Elizabeth Catte and Josh Howard   137

Sasha Banks, the Boss of NXT: Media, Gender and
the Evolution of Women's Wrestling in WWE
    Christiana Molldrem Harkulich   148

III. Culture and Modernity

The Beginnings of Wrestling in Brazil: Theatricality, Marketing
and a Colorful Character
    Riqueldi Straub Lise, André Mendes Capraro,
    Natasha Santos and Aaron D. Horton   162

The Transmission of Cultural Values Through Professional
Wrestling: A Cross-Cultural Comparison
    Tyson L. Platt   179

The "Sportification" of Wrestling in France: Strength,
Performance and Regulation (1852–1913)
    Frédéric Loyer and Jean-François Loudcher   199

IV. Wrestling and Media

"I couldn't carry a tune in a bucket": Music in the Memphis
and Mid-South/UWF Professional Wrestling Territories
and the Transformation of Southern Political Culture,
1958–1987
    Christopher L. Stacey   221

Pile Driving the Past: *WWE '13* and Mediating the History
of WWE Through Video Games
    Andrew Baerg   234

Lowland Gorilla Ballerina Acrobat: Brock Lesnar, Sherdog.com
and the Perception of Professional Wrestlers Competing in
Combat Sports
    Evan Karl Nagel   249

Macho Madness and the Mania ("Oh Yeaaaah, Dig It!"):
Mediatization, Masculinities and Affective Memories
of WWF's Halcyon Days (c. 1984–1993)
    DAMION STURM   270

Origins of the *Rock 'n' Wrestling Connection*
    SETH BOVEY   289

About the Contributors   301

Index   305

Introduction

Professional wrestling is a unique business. Part sport, part performance, it defies conventional categorizations. Scholars, including those who consider "real" sports legitimate topics of study, have tended largely to dismiss wrestling due to its "fakeness" or the misconception that it is and has always been full of cartoonish silliness. I would counter, however, that those who acknowledge legitimate sports such as football or soccer as valid subjects because they are competitive athletic contests while disregarding wrestling because its outcomes are predetermined fail to recognize one of their most important similarities: both present athletic displays for the primary purpose of making money. Whether or not the contests are "real," professional wrestling, just like boxing, football, soccer, baseball, hockey, basketball, and various other sports, seeks to maximize profits through live spectators, television viewership, and merchandise sales. In pro wrestling's 150 years (or so) of history, promoters and wrestlers have used a wide array of tactics to attract fans and build their own careers. In the process, they have played to all manner of national, regional, racial, and gender stereotypes in hopes of striking a particular nerve with a particular audience. Wrestling has offered nearly every caricature imaginable: from the turban- or fez-wearing "Terrible Turks" (who were, it should be noted, rarely either terrible or Turkish) that were often featured as foils for top grapplers in the United States in the late 19th and early 20th centuries, to effeminate, prissy villains ("heels") such as "Gorgeous" George Wagner or Gardenia Davis in the 1940s and 1950s, to the slew of "Russian" heels (who were, it should be noted, rarely actual Russians) in the 1960s, 1970s, and 1980s, only to name a few examples, both promoters and performers have intentionally capitalized on popular perceptions of national, regional, racial, or gender identity in hopes of drawing fans and, therefore, profit. Identity is, however, a complex concept that is certainly not limited to the stereotypes and caricatures that often initially draw one's attention in wrestling. Wrestlers have often used their in-ring personas to challenge prevailing narratives of nation, race, and gender, sometimes while appearing to embody or reinforce them. As the essays in this book demonstrate, the issue of identity in professional wrestling is both complex and diverse. From South Africa to Brazil, from Japan to Mexico, from the late 19th to the early 21st centuries, issues of national, regional, racial, and gender identity have featured prominently in professional wrestling. I hope that this book will contribute significantly to the ongoing (albeit still relatively small) academic exploration of these and other themes in professional wrestling.

A Brief Historical Outline

The origins of wrestling, broadly defined as a grappling contest between two competitors, go back thousands of years. Archaeologists have found depictions of wrestling contests in ancient Sumeria and Egypt, and the Greek Olympics featured the style known currently as Greco-Roman wrestling, in which holds below the waist are prohibited and one's primary objective is to throw one's opponent to the ground.[1] The ancient Olympics also featured a contest known as *pankration* in which practically no holds or techniques were barred, including strikes, chokes, submission holds, biting, eye-gouging, and anything else one might use to force his opponent to submit. Minus the more egregiously violent tactics, *pankration* not only resembles the modern sport of mixed martial arts, but also the early days of professional wrestling in the United States.

By the middle of the 19th century, working-class American men often engaged in grappling contests to alleviate boredom and to prove their manliness, and fellow laborers would often wager on the outcomes. During the Civil War, Union soldiers frequently engaged in camp wrestling contests. After the war, professional wrestling developed alongside other popular spectator sports such as baseball.[2] Styles and rules varied significantly across the country, evolving eventually into what came to be known as "catch-as-catch-can," a term derived from the popular grappling techniques in Lancashire, England. Catch wrestling combines elements of Greco-Roman, Irish collar-and-elbow, and Greek *pankration* into a diverse art that incorporates various holds and throws as well as both standing and mat techniques.[3]

Thanks to the prowess and drawing power of early stars such as former Union soldier and camp grappler "The Solid Man" William Muldoon, Martin "Farmer" Burns, and Frank Gotch, wrestling became a popular sport capable of drawing thousands of fans and, more importantly, tens of thousands of dollars. For example, the Frank Gotch–George Hackenschmidt world championship bout in September 1911 drew 30,000 fans to Chicago's Comiskey Park, generating a live gate of $44,000.[4] Given the secretive nature of the business, it is often unclear which, if any, early 20th century bouts were works, though by the 1920s most contests were likely predetermined. By all accounts, legitimate contests often devolved into laborious, hours-long affairs in which grapplers jostled for position on the mat, drawing catcalls from restless spectators. In order to maximize wrestling's profitability, promoters increasingly began incorporating dramatic elements into matches while attempting to maintain an air of legitimacy.

In the 1920s and 1930s, promoters such as Joe "Toots" Mondt and champions such as Ed "Strangler" Lewis and "The Golden Greek" Jim Londos perfected the art of the work, using strategically-timed maneuvers and comebacks to draw heat and keep crowds coming back for more.[5] An occasional job to a top contender, for example, could be used to build interest and hype for a lucrative rematch. Despite modern misconceptions that spectators only began questioning wrestling's legitimacy after World War II, journalists and others speculated as early as the 1930s that the sport was not entirely on the up-and-up. Dan Parker of the *Daily Mirror* (New York City) wrote a slew of articles in the 1930s and 1940s mocking pro wrestling's "fakery," and he regularly (and accurately) predicted the outcomes of matches to prove his point. In 1937, Marcus Griffin wrote a famous exposé, *Fall Guys: The Barnums of Bounce*, in which he detailed many of the inner workings of the wrestling business nearly 50 years before Vincent K. McMahon admitted publicly that wrestling was purely entertainment, largely to avoid oversight by state athletic commissions.

Prior to World War II, promoters and wrestlers fought frequently to establish monopolies over various territories around the country. Vicious arguments about who should hold a particular championship were frequent, punctuated by the occasional in-ring double-cross to snatch a title away, such as in 1925, when Stanislaus Zbyszko "shot" (wrestled for real) against heavyweight champion and former football player "Big" Wayne Munn, forcing him to submit audibly in earshot of spectators, giving the referee no choice but to award him the championship, lest he admit the outcome had been predetermined. In 1948, a group of North America's most influential promoters formed the National Wrestling Alliance (NWA). The NWA established strict rules for its members, including respecting the boundaries of each promoter's territories.[6] NWA promoters would vote to approve all world title changes, and recognized Lou Thesz as their first champion. Thesz, a legitimate shooter, was the perfect choice because he could fend off a rogue promoter's attempts to steal the title in a double-cross.

The rapid expansion of television after World War II went hand-in-hand with a revival of wrestling's popularity. Wrestling was perfect for early stations looking for cheap, first-run programs; all one usually needed was a single camera in the arena, pointed at the ring. By 1949, all four American networks featured prime-time wrestling, and promoters resorted increasingly to flashy gimmicks to draw viewers.⁷ Figures such as "Gorgeous" George Wagner, a bleached-blonde, sequined-robe-wearing performer, thrived in the new medium by cultivating outrageous behaviors such as demanding the ring be sprayed with perfume before he would deign to enter, enraging fans in the process. Gorgeous George mastered the art of the heel promo (interview) by exuding vanity and arrogance while insulting the fans, creating a template not only for future wrestlers such as "Nature Boy" Ric Flair, but for boxers such as Muhammad Ali, who acknowledged Wagner's influence on his own pre-fight hyperbole. As stations expanded their programming in the 1950s, wrestling promoters resorted increasingly to outrageous gimmicks in hopes of competing with sitcoms and variety shows for viewers and with baseball, football, and other sports for live attendance. Promoters could no longer rely merely on wrestlers who appealed to local fanbases, such as Italian or Puerto Rican babyfaces (good guys/heroes) in New York City. Reaching national audiences necessitated using performers who could be universally cheered or despised across the country. This environment was ripe for the use of all manner of stereotypical heels, most notable those of Germans and Japanese, since the memory of World War II remained fresh in the minds of most Americans.

The territorial system prevailed, under the auspices of the NWA, until the early 1980s, when Vince K. McMahon purchased the Northeast-based World Wrestling Federation from his father, Vincent J., and embarked on a national expansion in which he aggressively lured top talent from other promoters (most notably, Hulk Hogan from Verne Gagne's Minneapolis-based American Wrestling Alliance) and featured his product on national cable television. Other promoters saw their business decline, until only Jim Crockett Promotions, the Carolina-based promotion that dominated the NWA, partly due to its nationally-televised programs on Turner Broadcasting System (TBS), remained as any serious competition for the WWF in the United States. Atlanta-based billionaire Ted Turner purchased Crockett's promotion in 1988, renaming it World Championship Wrestling (WCW). Until 2001, the WWF and WCW waged a national war for ratings and fans, particularly from 1995 to 2001, when WCW's *Monday Nitro* program went head-to-head with the WWF's *Monday Night RAW* on a weekly basis. In the end, Vince McMahon purchased WCW after its television shows were canceled following Turner's merger with Time Warner, leaving McMahon with an effective monopoly over mainstream pro wrestling in the United States.

Pro wrestling, known locally as *lucha libre*, was first promoted heavily in Mexico in the 1930s via Salvador Lutteroth's Empresa Mexicana de Lucha Libre (EMLL) promotion.⁸ Though it shares many elements with pro wrestling in other parts of the world, lucha libre came to be characterized by the widespread use of masks among wrestlers, as well as by high-flying, fast-paced matches. Lucha's most famous star, El Santo, became a national cross-media icon, starring in numerous films as well as innumerable high-profile wrestling matches. In 1992, Antonio Peña founded Asistencia Asesoría y Administración (AAA), a promotion that broke with tradition, as embodied by CMLL, by featuring over-the-top gimmicks and characters, strongly influenced by elements of American pro wrestling. Beginning especially in the 1990s, when WCW regularly featured lucha stars (Konnan, Rey Mysterio, Jr., and Psichosis, to name a few) on its programming, American wrestlers began incorporating many of lucha's spectacular maneuvers into their own repertoires, part of a larger "globalization" of wrestling that would also establish strong ties to Japan.

Pro wrestling in Japan, known as *puroresu* (a shortened phonetic *katakana* rendering of "pro wrestling"), was popularized largely through the efforts of Rikidozan, a former sumo, who promoted incredibly successful events in the 1950s that, more often than not, featured him taking on American grapplers such as Lou Thesz. Seeing a "Japanese" (he was actually Korean, a fact he carefully concealed) hero vanquishing Americans was particularly appealing to Japanese fans in the wake of the defeat and humiliation of World War II, and pro wrestling quickly became one of the biggest ratings draws on Japanese television. Japanese wrestling would distinguish itself from its American and Mexican counterparts through a more realistic, hard-hitting presentation that attempted to maintain an air of legitimacy. Among other features, pro wrestling in Japan has tended to treat women's wrestling more seriously than in other parts of the world, where women's matches were often promoted as sideshow attractions where physical beauty mattered as much or more than athletic ability. Japanese women wrestlers undergo the same rigorous dojo training as their male counterparts. Unlike promotions in the United States and Mexico, which usually feature a handful of women's matches in male-dominated cards, entire promotions in Japan, such All Japan Women's Pro-Wrestling, have been built around women's wrestling and stars such as Manami Toyota and Bull Nakano, and have enjoyed a great deal of success over the years. Japanese promotions such as Atsushi Onita's Frontier Martial Arts Wrestling (FMW) pioneered the "hardcore" style of wrestling (with liberal use of weapons, frequent bleeding, and over-the-top match stipulations that included barb-wire and explosions) that would be popularized in the United States by regional promotions such as Extreme Championship Wrestling (ECW) and Combat Zone Wrestling (CZW). Recent years have seen more traditional Japanese promotions such as New Japan Pro Wrestling (NJPW) incorporating more elements from American wrestling, particularly ref bumps (allowing interference while the referee is "unconscious") and frequent outside interference, which represents a seeming departure from the more serious, sport-like presentations throughout most of puroresu history.

Although pro wrestling's three most prominent hotbeds are the United States, Mexico, and Japan, its popularity has few boundaries. Canada has a rich pro wrestling tradition, particularly in Montreal[9] and Calgary, once home to Stu Hart's Stampede Wrestling, a promotion that produced a number of international stars, including Bret "Hit Man" Hart and the Dynamite Kid (Tom Billington). Europe, particularly Great Britain and Germany, has been home to numerous pro wrestling promotions over the years, and has, like Japan, tended to feature more realistic matches based on legitimate holds and maneuvers. France, particularly Paris, featured pro wrestling matches in the "Greco-Roman" (more accurately, "French," as it was a French interpretation of classical Olympic wrestling) style as early as the 1850s, and may have been home to the first-ever masked wrestler, The Masked Marvel, a name and gimmick that would be repeated frequently afterwards. South America has also had its share of pro wrestling promotions. In early 20th century Brazil, for example, many saw wrestling as the embodiment of modernity, a fitting sport for a country attempting to imitate the progress and culture of Paris and London, while others began criticizing its "brutality," as promoters and wrestlers began using increasingly outlandish tactics to draw audiences. In South Africa, black promoters used pro wrestling as an opportunity to promote physical health and articulate a positive self-image in the face of rigid segregation under the white Apartheid regime. These are merely a few of numerous possible examples of pro wrestling's broad appeal and diversity across the globe, as is borne out by this book's essays.

Wrestling with Identity

The essays in this book are chronologically, geographically, and methodologically diverse. The book's contributors represent eight countries across five continents, and a broad range of academic disciplines, including sociology, psychology, communications, kinesiology, history, literature, and theater. The essays deal with a wide array of topics. On the theme of racial identity in wrestling, Zara Mirmalek's contribution ("The Iron Sheik and Public Representation of Iranian National Identity in Professional Wrestling") examines the ways in which the Iron Sheik embodied an alternate public representation of Iranian identity in the 1980s. Although intended to draw heel heat in the wake of the Iran hostage crisis, Mirmalek argues that the Iron Sheik, as a legitimate native of Iran, offered Iranian Americans in particular (and all fans, more generally) a positive public embodiment of Iranian identity, despite the Sheik's seemingly-stereotypical persona. Edward Salo ("'They ain't like us': Race, Class and Gender in Smoky Mountain Wrestling") illustrates how three particular storylines in the Appalachia-based Smoky Mountain Wrestling

(1992–1995) were especially effective at evoking powerful negative reactions from local fans by playing upon their particular attitudes toward race, class, and gender. Justin D. García ("Latin Lords of the Ring: Politics, Nativism and Mexican/Chicano Identity Through Professional Wrestling") examines the complexities of modern portrayals of Mexican and Chicano identity in American pro wrestling as embodied by three performers: Eddie Guerrero, Rey Mysterio, Jr., and Alberto Del Rio. Hendrik Snyders ("'Degenerative sports and dirty tactics': Race and Professional Wrestling in Cape Town, South Africa, c. 1880–1988") offers a fascinating history of black professional wrestling promotion in South Africa. While black promoters and wrestlers used pro wrestling to construct and promote a positive identity for themselves and their communities, white authorities attempted to use regulatory measures and wrestling's "excesses" to hinder or completely prevent black South Africans from organizing events, a situation that endured in part until the official end of Apartheid in 1994. In my essay ("Nazis, Japs and Pearl Harbor Attacks: German and Japanese Stereotypes in American Professional Wrestling"), I explore the history and use of German and Japanese stereotypes in American pro wrestling, demonstrating the lengths to which promoters would go in order to raise fans' ire (along with, it was hoped, revenues) by exploiting basic national and racial prejudices. In his essay, Kevin Hogg ("Deepest, Darkest Africa(, Illinois): Cultural Appropriation in Professional Wrestling") considers the peculiar trend in pro wrestling of individuals regularly portraying characters of different cultures or races, such as Joe Scarpa, an Italian American whose greatest in-ring fame came as Chief Jay Strongbow, an American Indian who utilized "tomahawk" chops and war dances during his matches.

Our essays on gender address several key aspects of pro wrestling in the United States, Mexico, and Japan. Ximena Rojo de la Vega Guinea ("Wrestling with Masculinity: *Exóticos* in Lucha Libre") discusses *exóticos*, Mexican luchadors with gender-bending, effeminate personas that exist outside lucha libre's traditional *téchnico* (good guy) vs. *rudo* (bad guy) dynamic. In her essay, Keiko Aiba ("Transformed Bodies and Gender Norms: Gender Identity of Japanese Women Pro Wrestlers") explains the benefits and challenges Japanese women pro wrestlers experience as a result of their participation in wrestling, from increased physical strength (and confidence) to occasionally being mistaken for men in public, among other issues. Elizabeth Catte and Josh Howard ("'A secret fascination': Professional Wrestling, Gender Non-Conformity and Masculinity") explore the history and evolution of pro wrestling portrayals of gay, queer, or effeminate identity, often exploited to play upon fans' gender prejudices or insecurities to elicit the desired negative reaction from them. Christiana Molldrem Harkulich ("Sasha Banks, the Boss of NXT: Media, Gender and the Evolution of Women's Wrestling in WWE") illustrates the rapidly-changing portrayals of female wrestlers in WWE, beginning with the so-called "Divas Revolution" in 2015, marking a transition away from women's use either as a sideshow or "eye-candy" and toward a more serious treatment as serious athletes.

Next is culture and modernity. The offerings from Riqueldi Straub Lise, André Mendes Capraro, Natasha Santos and myself ("The Beginnings of Wrestling in Brazil: Theatricality, Marketing and a Colorful Character") and from Frédéric Loyer and Jean-François Loudcher ("The 'Sportification' of Wrestling in France: Strength, Performance and Regulation [1852–1913]") examine the early days of pro wrestling in Brazil and France, when some saw wrestling as a means of constructing a positive, thoroughly modern, national identity, and others saw it as a garish, brutal spectacle that represented the antithesis of urban civilization. In the late 19th and early 20th centuries, the lines between sport and performance in pro wrestling were much blurrier than in subsequent eras and, accordingly, state authorities frequently involved themselves in regulatory matters to act against what they saw as wrestling's excessive violence,[10] violence that in reality was usually more performative and intended to enthrall or enrage fans and keep them coming back for more. Tyson L. Platt's essay ("The Transmission of Cultural Values Through Professional Wrestling: A Cross-Cultural Comparison") examines the affinity between national culture and conventional elements in American and Japanese pro wrestling, demonstrating that key performative features of wrestling embody broader social norms and expectations in particular societies.

The final part's essays deal with portrayals of and attitudes toward pro wrestling in various media formats, from video games to social media and websites. Christopher L. Stacey ("'I couldn't carry a tune in a bucket': Music in the Memphis and Mid-South/UWF Professional Wrestling Territories and the Transformation of Southern Political Culture, 1958–1987") discusses the pioneering use of music in wrestling promotion in the Memphis territory, beginning in the late 1950s. Music would become a vital part of national wrestling promotion, through the use of promotional videos and entrance music, and Memphis wrestling was well ahead of the curve. Andrew Baerg ("Pile Driving the Past: *WWE '13* and Mediating the History of WWE Through Video Games") explains how WWE, through its *WWE '13* video game, constructed a playable, "determinist" version of the so-called Attitude Era of the late 1990s that, while appearing to offer players some agency in replaying key moments in a pivotal period in the company's history, actually herds them in a particular direction in order to reinforce the validity of the WWE's official narrative of that era. Evan Karl Nagel ("Lowland Gorilla Ballerina Acrobat: Brock Lesnar, Sherdog.com and the Perception of Professional Wrestlers Competing in Combat Sports") draws from a trove of internet fan and journalist reactions to WWE star Brock Lesnar's foray into mixed martial arts (MMA) to illustrate how their preconceptions of pro wrestling shaped the often-negative reactions to Lesnar's largely successful career in the Ultimate Fighting Championship (UFC). Damion Sturm ("Macho Madness and the Mania ["Oh Yeaaaah, Dig It!"] Mediatization, Masculinities and Affective Memories of WWF's Halcyon Days [c. 1984–1993]") uses modern fan recollections of the WWF's "Hulkamania" era on social media to explore the ways in which nostalgia and memory influence fans' appreciation and understanding of a key period in recent wrestling history. Finally, Seth Bovey ("Origins of the *Rock 'n' Wrestling Connection*") considers the symbiotic relationship between pro wrestling and the music industry, a relationship that arguably reached its zenith with the *Rock 'n' Wrestling Connection* in the mid–1980s, which saw major MTV stars such as Cyndi Lauper involved in pro wrestling, and wrestling events, including a match between Hulk Hogan and "Rowdy" Roddy Piper, featured on MTV.

The essays in this book represent a diverse range of topics and methodologies, and we are confident that this collection will contribute significantly to the academic study of professional wrestling. Pro wrestling has had a profound impact and influence in many parts of the world since the late 19th century. This unique pseudo-sport has been popular, to various degrees, in a wide array of locations and cultures around the world, most of which have tailored pro wrestling to suit their particular aspirations and fears. Because of its widespread global presence and popularity, pro wrestling serves as an useful lens through which to foster a more diverse understanding of numerous cultures and identities, and we hope that these essays will contribute significantly to this process.

I would like to thank Zach Bates at the University of Calgary, a friend and fellow pro wrestling fan with whom I've had many lively discussions, including brainstorming sessions about the possibilities of an edited book dealing with issues of identity in pro wrestling. Although he was unable to take part in the project, I credit him with helping initiate the chain of events that led to the conceptualization and, now, publication of this work. Finally, I want to offer my heartfelt thanks to the contributors, whose amazingly diverse interests, methodology, and perspectives comprise this book.

NOTES

1. Gerald W. Morton and George M. O'Brien, *Wrestling to Rasslin': Ancient Sport to American Spectacle* (Bowling Green, OH: Bowling Green State University Popular Press, 1985), 7–9.
2. Scott M. Beekman, *Ringside: A History of Professional Wrestling in America* (Westport, CT: Praeger, 2006), 7–11.
3. Jake Shannon, *Say Uncle! Catch-as-Catch-Can Wrestling and the Roots of Ultimate Fighting, Pro Wrestling, and Modern Grappling* (Toronto: ECW Press, 2011), 6.
4. Beekman, *Ringside*, 49.

5. David Shoemaker, *The Squared Circle: Life, Death, and Professional Wrestling* (New York: Gotham Books, 2013), 18–23.
6. Tim Hornbaker, *National Wrestling Alliance: The Untold Story of the Monopoly That Strangled Pro Wrestling* (Toronto: ECW Press, 2007), 8.
7. Beekman, *Ringside*, 82.
8. EMLL has since been renamed Consejo Mundial de Lucha Libre (CMLL) and remains the world's oldest continually-operating wrestling promotion.
9. Whose top stars included Yvon Robert and the Vachon brothers, "Mad Dog" (Maurice) and "Butcher" (Paul).
10. By, among other measures, banning certain holds, such as American wrestler Evan "Strangler" Lewis' chokehold in various municipalities in the 1890s. Some authorities went even further, attempting to ban pro wrestling events entirely.

PART I. RACE

The Iron Sheik and Public Representation of Iranian National Identity in Professional Wrestling

ZARA MIRMALEK

Undisputedly, World Wrestling Federation (WWF) wrestlers are part of the late 20th century American zeitgeist. The popularity of professional wrestling surged in the 1980s, putting them everywhere in various forms of media: live performances in sports arenas, pay-per-view television events, action figures and costumes for children and adults, animated cartoons, and a pop music video, "Goonies 'R' Good Enough Part 2," by chart-topping singer Cyndi Lauper, that played in the new media forum of cable television, on MTV. Whether an active spectator cheering for costumed strong men gripping each other's bulging muscles or a person completely uninterested but generally aware of popular culture, everyone had a response to "What is professional wrestling?" It was, as it is now, a form of entertainment and sport discursively affixed in American cultural consciousness. Often it's used as a euphemism for "fake" in the dichotomy of authentic/inauthentic. Writing this essay in August 2016, I heard it used without pause on the local NPR station as a lawyer-turned-news-commentator urged his guest to reveal whether or not a certain television personality's antics are "real or pro wrestling." Indeed, it's easy to see how WWF wrestlers contribute to pro wrestling's status in popular discourse as a standard bearer for fakeness. They loudly give dramatic performances in colorful costumes that are heavy in symbolism and light in fabric. This contrasts strongly with traditional Greco-Roman or freestyle amateur wrestlers who wear plain, uniform singlets, and whose utterances are limited to less articulate grunts during competition.

12 Part I. Race

In the WWF (now WWE),[1] bouts are intentionally framed to be spectacular, carnival-esque performances in which the hero versus villain narrative is as important as the wrestlers' physical contortions. Pro-wrestling has historically used a cast of heroes and villains; the former made more recognizable by their contrast to the latter, who are often stereotypical "bad" guys of identifiably non–American nationality and ethnicity. Case in point—the Iron Sheik—a barrel-chested, handle-bar-mustache-adorned, gold-genie-shoe-kicking, thick-accented-insult-spewing wrestler often draped in the Iranian flag. His signature move, "the camel clutch" couldn't lean more heavily on a popular ethnic stereotype-cum-slur. He presented a cartoon-esque, mish-mash of Middle Eastern stereotypes and in a politically fraught era, declared his allegiance to Ayatollah Khomeini, an Iranian religious leader wrestling with his own set of hero and villain representations. An Iranian immigrant, the Iron Sheik knew well the authentic garb of wrestlers and Iranian men. Who could imagine this "fake" wrestler's performance could have a positive influence on Iranian national identity?

In this essay, I offer an interpretation on the way in which the Iron Sheik's pro-wrestling persona in the 1980s made it possible for alternative images of Iranian national identity to cir-

The Iron Sheik (courtesy Brian Bukantis, Wrestling Revue Archives, www.wrestlingrevue.com).

culate in American culture. I discuss how Iranian identity as performed by the Iron Sheik produced an accessible Iranian ethnicity during a period of grave political events that cast being "Iranian" as synonymous with "villain." I begin this political conversation with a personal account of my relationship with Ali Vaziri, aka the Iron Sheik.

"Is your dad the Iron Sheik?"

In a lifetime of introducing myself to strangers, there are a few recurring exchanges. One usually involves professional wrestling legend the Iron Sheik:

Hi, I'm [insert name of a guy here].
Hi.
What's your name?
Zara.
What? Sarah?
No, Zara. Like Sarah but with a Z.
Ohhh, Zara. What kind of name is that?
Iranian.
Ohh, Is that where you are from? How'd your family come here?
Here and there. My dad came to the U.S. to wrestle.
Is your dad the Iron Sheik?!?

My answer never fails to surprise. "Yes," I respond, "I know the Iron Sheik but no, he's not my dad. He's one of my dad's wrestling friends from Iran." Sometimes I go on to describe a visit that included eating pancakes. I didn't know him as the Iron Sheik but as Ali Vaziri, who picked me up and tossed me so high in the air that I saw myself closer to the telephone lines than to the ground. His *koshtee* (wrestling) abilities, both physical and *zerang* (social), were such that he, like my father, used his wrestling success in Iran (where it is one of the most popular sports) to immigrate to the United States.

To my surprise, this particular exchange continued through the '80s and '90s and into the 21st century. At first I was confounded, but the constancy of "Is your dad the Iron Sheik?" gave me time to reflect and compare. Why was the association seemingly undiscerning? What did it mean that through ongoing conversations, I'd find that most people asking this question were among the least hostile and most easygoing about cultural differences?

The Iron Sheik's career as a wrestler in the WWF was prominent and successful, but not enough to explain the lasting popularity of his persona or his impact beyond the ring. People who bring him up aren't doing so because he was the greatest pro wrestler of all time (though he did hold the WWF heavyweight championship) or a memorable champion for any particular cause (other than the usually-high level of self-promotion common among pro wrestlers). He's talked about for his signature move, his clothing, and the insults he would shout at other wrestlers. These aren't asides, they are goals and accomplishments in pro wrestling. By these standards, Iron Sheik's career in the WWF was quite successful.[2]

The Iron Sheik's lasting hold on American cultural consciousness comes in part from events outside of the ring. His prime years as a WWF wrestler (1979–1987) took place in a politically-charged period; in Fall 1979, the United States' simmering "frenemy" relationship with Iran became unequivocally adversarial when the American embassy in Tehran was seized and its inhabitants held as hostages. Given the political climate, it was a good time to be an Iranian villain in the U.S.

Political Ringsides

Mention the year 1979 and Iran to the average American, and most likely the response will be "hostage crisis!" Another accurate response is "revolution," though the former is the most influential in shaping American perceptions of Iranians in the late 20th century. Indeed, the 1979 hostage crisis remains a common association, a lens through which to consider Iranians (with suspicion). The hostage crisis underscored the prevalent "us versus them" categorization of culture and politics between West and East, between Americans and Middle Easterners. Add the criminal act of taking hostages, of withholding freedom, detaining by force, and commodifying human life by putting a price on release, and most Americans concluded that only villains take hostages, fashioning most, if not all Iranians, as villains in the process. A brief recounting of the turbulent political context of Iran's and America's exchanges follows to familiarize, or remind, readers of their political and cultural clashes beyond the wrestling ring.

On November 4, 1979, Iranian revolutionaries took over the American Embassy in Tehran and held its inhabitants hostage until January 21, 1981. At times, it seemed the clearest aspect of the hostage crisis was the count of how many days the hostages were held against their will. To imagine 444 days of intense media focus, the closest event in recent history was the televised trial of OJ Simpson that seemed to go on forever, but only lasted 135 days.

In fact, it was a shocking and dark turn in an ongoing crisis both among Iranians and between Iran and the United States. In January 1979, the world had watched a revolution years in the making come to a head in Iran. It was preceded by moves and counter moves among political factions in Iran, vying to lead the country. There were those who supported the monarchy of Shah Mohammad Reza Pahlavi and those who wanted it brought down in favor of a system that combined mosque (church) and state. Between these two poles were many categories of people that had no interest in the machinations of political rule and mobilization, no objective other than to make a living, no wish to promote discord that would permanently break up families, either by death or separation.³

On January 17, 1979, Americans reading the *New York Times* saw the following headline: "SHAH LEAVES IRAN FOR INDEFINITE STAY; CROWDS EXULT, MANY EXPECT LONG EXILE." Shah Reza Pahlavi had left his throne of four decades, flying from Tehran, Iran to Egypt en route to the United States. The day's edition included multiple stories about his reign, his immediate family, the crowds exulting in Iran and pulling down his statues, the religious leader Ayatollah Khomeini, who stoked the revolution from exile in Paris, and speculation on where in the world the Shah would live. Given his family's real estate holdings in New York and Beverly Hills, the United States was a strong possibility.

Concern for the Shah's choice of a new domicile was not banal. It was of international interest, because his new country of residence would be designating itself a supporter of the Shah and thus an enemy of the Iranian revolutionaries. An international head of state, even one deposed, can't just fly in, take a cab from the airport and start a new life unnoticed. The host government grants them protection or prosecution (e.g., Manuel Noriega), or a little of both (e.g., Ferdinand Marcos). An April 23 *New York Times* op-ed ("A Home for the Shah") advocated for the U.S. "a haven for the homeless, especially those who are not likely to become public charge," to distinguish itself from other countries that also recognized the "dethroned Shah needs a place to live," but did not grant him access. In making its case, the op-ed unfortunately included a partially accurate prediction of things to come: "A fear of offending the new rulers of Iran is said be one of Mr. [President Jimmy] Carter's reasons for urging the Shah to stay away. That strikes us as too timid. The fear that Iranians might seize Americans and demand the return of the Shah in exchange is probably more substantial, but a determined Administration should be able to establish some ground rules with Tehran for receiving the Shah." A man with many palaces was now fashioned a homeless refugee needing protection from thugs.

Iran's revolution did not end with the Shah's departure. Rather, it broadened the scope as Iranian leaders continued to pursue the Shah. They wanted him to return to stand trial and they wanted access to much of the country's billions of dollars in his possession.⁴ Any country hosting the ex-monarch was seen to be harboring a criminal and impeding Iran's attempts to recover the money. After ten months of speculation and protest by Iranians, in October 1979 President Carter's administration allowed the Shah into the U.S. for "political and humanitarian reasons," despite knowing that it "might endanger Americans at the embassy in Tehran."⁵ A month later, a group of college-age revolutionaries stormed the U.S. embassy in Tehran and took its inhabitants hostage, to be released upon the return of the Shah. A potential theocratic government was on hold—Iranian political leaders opposed the hostage-taking while religious leaders supported the action.[6]

For almost a year and a half, an end to the hostage crisis was unclear given the on-going media reporting of criminal acts, uncertain political stances, pathos, violence, and chaos on both sides. Some things were clear, like the suffering of the hostages' families and communities, and were regularly featured in various media as the crisis carried on through two Christmas holidays, two New Year's Eves, and various other American family celebrations.[7] In contrast, on any given day it was unclear where the two countries stood in their negotiations. Most everyone, whether personally affected or generally aware of developments, knew that people were being held against their will in Iran. The terms of their release were explicit but also vague: would the U.S. government fly the Shah back to Iran and pick up the hostages on a return flight? How would billions be returned to Iran? How would each country's national discourse on the resolution of the event work to repair or further irritate the countries' mutual distrust? During the initial period of negotiations, a couple of maneuvers added to the sense that these very real ordeals were warped political theater too terrible to last another night. Washington lawyers filed a lawsuit in Manhattan on behalf of the government of Iran, against the Shah and his wife for $56 billion in damages in addition to the $20 billion that the Shah and his family allegedly embezzled for personal use.[8] A week earlier, on November 18, 1979, a full page advertisement containing a 3,500 word translation of Ayatollah Khomeini's television address explaining "the position of Moslem people of Iran" to Pope John Paul II and his envoy, ran in the New York Times, paid for by the Iranian Embassy in Washington.[9] How can you hold a country's citizens hostage and then also file a lawsuit in that country or buy advertising space? The 1970s were a period when hostage-taking was not uncommon, from various plane hijackings to heiress Patty Hearst. The long duration of the hostage crisis in Iran could not be explained by lack of political experience. The longer it went on, the more reducible the matter was to "are they all free yet?" What counter-narrative could possibly be drawn to support the demands of revolutionaries wanting money and justice? (None.) There was nothing in national circulation to counter most Americans' identification of Iranians as "the bad guys." Many Iranians found themselves represented by hostage-takers without any voice in the matter.

The American hostages in Tehran were personally no more able to return the Shah and money to Iran than Iranians living in the United States had any ability to release the hostages. But in the court of general public opinion, Iranians in the U.S. were suspect. U.S. agencies took "close looks" into the activities of Iranian college students. Discrimination and distrust of foreigners was easily directed towards people whose personal appearance or speech included symbols of ethnicity and Iranian nationality (e.g., accents, names, hijab). The end of the hostage crisis in late January 1981[10] would see the release of all the hostages but would do little to improve the ongoing tense geopolitical relationship between Iran and the U.S.[11] The episode had created too deep a wound, permanently affecting popular American perceptions of Iranians.[12]

As a person identifiably Middle Eastern, often accompanied by family members who visibly stood out, I put up with racism and discrimination in various forms during the events of 1979–1980 and for years afterwards. There were some "traditional" school bullies, for example, whose shouts of "camel-jockey," "sand n*****s," "go back to where you came from" were hurtful and confusing (I'd wonder where they got the idea we rode camels in Iran or where they could be learning any of the slurs that I knew I'd remember if it had been taught in our classroom). After school one day, a boy from my class threw a rock that landed squarely in the middle of my forehead, drawing blood and an awareness that even a regular acquaintance could be violent. Some adults were not much better. Why would a grown man flip off a short girl in hijab at 8 a.m.? What prompted and entitled random strangers to approach me to ask, "What's your nationality?" "What country are you from?" I was asked these questions so regularly I thought it was a normal feature of social greetings until I learned enough to understand prejudice and the insecure need to put categories before knowledge.

Pro wrestling's rise in popularity meant little to me at the time. Iranians and Iranian wrestlers were not exotic to me. Learning that Vaziri was the Iron Sheik and part of a cultural phenomenon was worth noting mostly because he added to the small number of references (e.g., the ex–Shah and Ayatollah Khomeini) Americans had for Iranian men. Vaziri was one of many immigrants carving out a life in a foreign country. He just happened to be a wrestler who had the opportunity to achieve celebrity by way of the WWF platform.

The Iron Sheik

As a performer in the WWF, the Iron Sheik did not appear as a cultural touchstone for Iranian nationality that one would want to be associated with, unless one wanted to be seen as a hostile enemy in clown shoes. In his appearances he hurled anti–American insults, proclaiming "Iran, Number One" to booing crowds, and enthusiastically waving a post-revolution Iranian flag (the center of the three-color flag no longer had a gold lion holding a sword).

His WWF tag-team partner, Nikolai Volkoff[13] represented the Soviet Union, another U.S. geo-political rival; together they won the tag-team championship against the U.S. Express at the first *Wrestlemania* in 1985.

Even without speaking, the Iron Sheik's costume, an outlandish mixture of Middle Eastern stereotypes, made a powerful impression. He usually wore either tight shorts with a camel appliqué, a reminder of his signature move "the camel clutch," or a traditional wrestling singlet with the Olympic rings logo and "Iran" printed across the stomach. The tips of his gold shoes were long and curled, like every genie ever depicted coming out of a lamp. His scarf (a keffiyeh) and head band (an iqal) are clothing items with no connection to the sport of wrestling; rather, these are among the few clothing items essential to Western depictions of "a man from the Middle East" or "an Arabian sheik" (e.g., Rudolph Valentino, any costume website, Saturday Night Live). Turned up at the ends, his dark thick handle-bar mustache was the preferred facial hair of fictional villains (e.g., villain Snidely Whiplash from a popular American for-adults-cartoon that featured the hero-villain trope with the former played by American animals Rocky and Bullwinkle as well as a Canadian Mountie, Dudley Do-Right, and the latter by Soviet spies Boris and Natasha). When he spoke in his first language, Farsi, there was little to understand. Still, his favorite derogatory term for rivals, "jabroni," became part of trash-talking lexicon, a phrase reinvigorated in the late 90s and early aughts by Dwayne "The Rock" Johnson, another of the most well recognized pro-wrestlers, who made it a part of his character's "Rock-speak."[14]

All told, Vaziri's Iron Sheik outfits were like those of many WWF pro-wrestlers: farcical performance costumes intended to stand out visually and to communicate their status as hero or villain. Interrupting popular discourse on Iranian national identity does not seem to have been a goal of his ensemble. But wrestlers aren't the only ones trained to feel and react to shifts in power. Decoding the Iron Sheik through a lens of camp and post-colonialism brings to light subtextual aspects that may have contributed to his conveying a positive, non-villainous, Iranian national identity.

Camp, Susan Sontag wrote in 1964, is a sensibility, "a consistently aesthetic experience of the world ... that incarnates a victory of 'style' over 'content.'"[15] It's a phenomenon that she ascribes to small cliques which at the time of writing may have been the case. Created by minority communities, camp is a ritual that "neutralizes moral indignation, sponsors playfulness." It employs "mannerisms susceptible of a double interpretation; gestures full of duplicity." It's a theatricalization of experience. It proposes a comic vision of the world (note 44). Later in the 20th century, camp becomes a mainstream descriptor for labeling performances that included exaggerated representations of people, places, actions, language, and emotions.

The Iron Sheik's portrayal of Iranian nationality in pro wrestling is an example of camp. Vaziri, unlike some other wrestlers playing foreign villains in the WWF, was actually an Iranian native, trained as a wrestler in Iran. But for the WWF stage, which involves performing in and out of the ring, the Iron Sheik is a partial exaggeration of Vaziri's personal biography. He came to the U.S. years before the boulevards of Tehran were filled with protestors shouting "up with the Ayatollah" and "down with the Shah." He emerged from his time as wrestler in Minneapolis, Minnesota (an interesting mecca of sorts for Iranian wrestlers), having chosen to develop a character that would capitalize on his ethnic and cultural heritage as well as popular American stereotypes of the "typical" Middle-Easterner. His style was thus fashioned by appropriating stereotypical Orientalist garments and accessories and wearing them non-ironically.

As a camp performer, the Iron Sheik relegated his "real" personality to the background in favor of the persona of a professional Iranian villain that provided an alternative Iranian identity (alternatives to the two popular choices: a member of the community of hostage-taking villains or the wealthy members of the old monarchy). One 1983 interview of The Iron Sheik and his manager "Classy" Freddie Blassie by WWF owner Vince McMahon features the Sheik speaking in Farsi and English.[16] The difference in content is revealing. In his short speech in Farsi, he gives polite and gracious greetings to all Iranians with a brief description of his journey to the U.S. and his intentions to wrestle in U.S. for the enjoyment of all. In the background, his manager makes gibberish noises meant to sound like battle cries, I can only assume in Farsi. The Iron Sheik then switches to English and gives a brief rant meant to incite disgust as he explains that he personally met with Ayatollah Khomeini, who gave his blessing to dub manager Classy Freddie Blassie an "Ayatollah" (a title earned by Islamic clerics).

Masked in camp, the Iron Sheik on the WWF stage was a native crashing into the colonizer's house. Edward Said's groundbreaking work on Orientalism (1978) defines a nomenclature invented by Europeans used to interpret subjects and objects from "the East" (aka pan–Arab, –Jewish, –Muslim cultures located east and southeast of Europe) for dominating, restructuring, and having authority over them.[17] There are many means of domination, including demonization, rendering those against whom you wish to justify violence as "others" undeserving of Western human rights. Others are different because of accents, language, clothing, living habits, food preferences, and gestures.[18] Had Vaziri been called "The Iron Oriental" it would have been too on the nose to be camp.

Among other cultural critiques, Said builds upon the work of Frantz Fanon, a 20th century theorist of revolution, oppression, and decolonization, the violence by which settlers colonize natives and the processes by which the colonized individuals seek to restore their power and displace the colonizers.[19] Granted, Fanon may, at first glance, seem out of place in a discussion about pro wrestling and national identity. The Iron Sheik, however, cannot be separated from the political and cultural contexts that propelled his rise to stardom. Fanon's characterizations of settlers and natives elucidate a subversive subtext of the Iron Sheik. A double interpretation of the Iron Sheik is that, to some, he is a foreign, villainous "other" and, to others, he is a valiant, victorious native.

Fanon names only one item of clothing in his description of the distinctions between settlers and natives: shoes.[20] The settler's feet are always covered and "his feet are protected by strong shoes." The natives are born in towns "starved of bread, of meat, of shoes." Indeed, the Iron Sheik's tall boots with curled toes are among the most distinct ever worn in the ring. Wearing those campy wrestling shoes on a national platform in the midst of heightened tensions between West and East was defiant. Those curly-toed boots were not innocuous; they were weapons. The Iron Sheik often used his boots to cheat by tapping his toe against the mat three times to "load it" (with some heavy object presumably), then kicking and incapacitating his opponent. To the typical American such underhanded move fit the expected depiction of a "foreigner" who had to use tricks to prevail over heroic (American) opponents. But it also reads implicitly as the "native" taking something from the settler and using it to defeat the settlers. His shoes made a statement as part of his costume, offering a possible interpretation in which a native, hailing from the Orient, takes up a position in the forbidden territory of the settler.

Distinct geographic zones, Fanon explains, are used as a tool of domination to separate settlers and natives. Towns are one kind of zone. Settlers live in towns that are "clean," "strong," and "brightly lit," where garbage cans "swallow all the leavings, unseen, unknown and hardly thought about." Natives ("the dirty Arabs in their own town") live in dark, hungry towns "wallowing in mire," which would make one want for shoes all the more. A native transgressing the boundary of the settlers' town is met with violence, and thus can only look on with envy.

The WWF ring serves as a national stage where media lights shine brightly. It is not a territory that can be entered without permission. Even with permission, violence awaits. Standing on the clean white surface is a character whose national identity should preclude him from entry, given the larger political ring in which the WWF community is situated. The Iron Sheik is allowed entry in order to provide heroes a brown-skinned villain to beat.[21] Inside the WWF ring, the Iron Sheik compressed the geographic distance between U.S. and Iran, countries so far apart that 12 p.m. in one place is 12 a.m. in the other. He gave American audiences the opportunity to see an Iranian man up close, cooperating, and to see him trusted to play alongside them inside the lines of their town.

Sitting in the audience of a WWF event in the 1990s, I steeled myself for possible encounters with rabid fans. Though the villains in the bouts that night were not ethnic villains, I expected some unrestrainable prejudice in fan shouts and wrestlers' rallying cries. It was my first time sitting side-by-side with strangers, cheering and booing pro wrestlers. I expected there to be some major aggression, impossible to avoid, like that between fans at a Cleveland Browns–Pittsburgh Steelers football game or among tailgaters at an Oakland Raiders game. They were, after all, staunch enough fans[22] to pay for tickets and sports arena parking. Why shouldn't they get into the full spirit of things?

I was, however, quite wrong. Fans around me were engaged in verbal egging across multiple meanings of the ritual.[23] The atmosphere was charged but not hostile. Watching them on television, fans are mostly heard when they cheer or boo loudly. Now, sitting among them in folding chairs around the ring, I could hear comments and conversations our of microphone range. In addition to talking up their favorite wrestlers, there was chatter about the significance of accessories, costume and prop choices, and the role of the referee. A question about authenticity came up from a kid sitting with his dad, who replied with a description of the technique involved in hitting someone with a ladder. Indeed, participating in the spectacle as a spectator is not, and never has been, akin to being a dupe.

Decoding pro wrestling competition unmasks community. The heroes and villains, "babyfaces" and "heels," appear as diametric opposites seeking to vanquish one another, but they

The Iron Sheik points to his curly-toed boot (courtesy Brian Bukantis Wrestling Revue Archives, www.wrestlingrevue.com).

all work for the same organization and share the same goals. The objectives they share are to perform in a spectacle that values winners and losers on a stage where they (almost) never break the fourth wall to keep their fans happy and returning while, backstage, carrying on camaraderie born from shared trainers, sources of pay, mutual admiration, and competition. Pro wrestlers, unlike actors in a play, don't come out afterwards to bow in acknowledgment of a successful performance of a fictional work. They maintain the reality of their drama through the cheers and boos. Even as they appear to compete for victory, they work to make their competitors look good as well. Their individual successes depend on the community's success, on the well-being of all competitors and their ability to draw emotional responses from spectators in order to keep them coming back for more.

Pro wrestling events are performances that can be entertaining, gratifying, frustrating, and culturally educational. Observers mired in the cliché that "pro-wrestling is fake" can be unable to see villains in the ring normalize the appearance of foreign "others" and demonstrate their humanity. Fortunately, the Iron Sheik's lasting popularity keeps in circulation a cultural touchstone for Iranian national identity that is characterized by cooperation, enthusiasm for jest, and belonging in American community.

NOTES

1. WWF was officially changed to WWE (World Wrestling Entertainment) in 2002 as a result of a lawsuit filed (and settled in U.K. courts) by the World Wildlife Fund (now known as World Wide Fund for Nature) that had been using the WWF acronym since the 1964 (Pinset Masons LLP 2000, 2002).

2. In 2005, the Iron Sheik's induction into the WWE Hall of Fame praised him as "one of the most hated Superstars of all time,"

3. Kader Abdolah, *The House of the Mosque* (Amsterdam: De Gues, 2005), Hamid Dabshi, *Iran: A People Interrupted* (New York: The New Press, 2007), Shirin Ebadi, *Iran Awakening* (New York: Random House, 2006).

4. *New York Times*, March 7, 1979.

5. Bernard Gwertzman, "U.S. Decision to Admit the Shah," *New York Times*, November 17, 1979.

6. Bernard Gwertzman, "Government in Iran Vows to Help in Siege," *he New York Times*, November 5, 1979.

7. David E. Rosenbaum, "Year of Captivity: The Long Frustrating Effort to End a National Humiliation," *The New York Times*, January 19, 1981.

8. Charles Kaiser, "Iran Sues Shah and Wife for $56 Billion in New York," *The New York Times*, November 29, 1979.

9. *New York Times*, November 18, 1979.

10. The Shah would cease to be a figure of contention in the hostage negotiations as he passed away in July 1980 (*New York Times*, 1980). Terms of the resolution were made public (*New York Times*, 1981).

11. Stephen Kinzer, *All the Shah's Men: An American Coup and the Roots of Middle East Terror* (Hoboken, NJ: John Wiley & Sons, 2003).

12. Almost 30 years later, events from the 1979 hostage crisis are informing political negotiations and political agendas in the U.S. and between U.S. and Iran. See "The Fake $400 Million Iran 'Ransom Story," *New York Times*, August 23, 2016.

13. Nikolai Volkoff is a pro wrestling name used by Josip Peruzovich who was not from

Russia but from Croatia (then Yugoslavia). Fashioned as a WWF villain, he wore a red shirt with "USSR" across the front and a black ushanka hat. His signature move was the "Russian Bear Hug," Volkoff also appears with the Iron Sheik in Cyndi Lauper's video "Goonies 'R' Good Enough,"

    14. Johnson credits the Iron Sheik as a mentor. Igal Hecht, *The Sheik*, documentary, 2014; Scott Raab, "The Rock Is Dead. Long Live Dwayne Johnson, American Treasure," *Esquire*, August 2015, http://www.esquire.com/entertainment/interviews/a36037/dwayne-johnson-the-rock-0815/ (accessed September 20, 2016).

    15. Sontag's "Notes on Camp" is written in the form of a list, which explains and explores the form and content of camp. I'm highlighting points 17, 36, 44.

    16. WWF, 1983.

    17. Said's 2000 essay "Jungle Calling" is an interesting read on another former amateur athlete turned popular media celebrity. Said recalls the character of Tarzan from 12 Hollywood films made between 1932 and 1948. Juxtaposing Tarzan from the novels written by Edgar Rice Burroughs with Tarzan of the Hollywood movies, the latter version presides on the big screen almost as mute as if it was the silent film era. His character didn't talk much. Grunts, broad shoulders and a glaring stick-eye was enough to stop rampaging lions and tame them, befriend a chimp, and raise a child. Tarzan's visual presence, his white skin contrasted with the dark skin of the actors in the role of natives, made another juxtaposition. He was living like a native amidst inhabitants native to the wild jungle only by accident. Unlike them, Tarzan could put on suit and travel to Manhattan (e.g., the 1942 film *Tarzan's New York Adventure*). Tarzan produced a culturally acceptable medium for talking about natives and depicting their backward jungle ways and need for a white savior. The Hungarian ethnicity of Hollywood's Tarzan during those years, Johnny Weissmuller, was not recognizable and his personal strengths (three-time Olympic swimmer) were not the central to the films.

    18. Clifford Geertz, *The Interpretation of Cultures* (New York: Basic Books, 1973).

    19. Frantz Fanon, *The Wretched of the Earth*, trans. Constance Farrington (New York: Grove Press, 1963).

    20. Fanon, *Wretched of the Earth*, 39.

    21. Hamid Dabashi, *Brown Skin, White Masks* (New York: Pluto Press, 2011).

    22. Categorizing pro-wrestling fans as dupes, or "inferior beings" (Dallas W. Smythe, "Reality as Presented by Television," *Public Opinion Quarterly* [1954], 143–56), is an example of one of many themes that continue to dominate the discourse, even though it reads as more of a cliché than an attempt to call up critical insight.

    23. James Carey, *Communication as Culture: Essays on Media and Society* (Boston: Unwin Hyman, 1985); Stuart Hall, "The Work of Representations," in Stuart Hall, Jessica Evans, and Sean Nixon, eds., *Representation: Cultural Representations and Signifying Practices* (Thousand Oaks, CA: Sage, 1997), 13–64.

"They ain't like us"
Race, Class and Gender in Smoky Mountain Wrestling

Edward Salo

From 1991 to 1995, Smoky Mountain Wrestling (SMW) was one of the last professional wrestling territories and the last bastion of "old school Southern rasslin'" in sharp contrast to large corporate-based federations like the WWF and WCW. Operating primarily in east Tennessee, eastern Kentucky, and southwest Virginia, the promotion was owned and operated by Jim Cornette, with financial backing from record producer Rick Rubin. Like other territories, SMW held most of its matches at high school gyms and other small venues and focused on regional centers in the Southeast. Cornette, a successful heel (bad guy)[1] manager and booker for promotions in Memphis, the Carolinas, and Georgia, wanted to create an alternative to the large-scale productions and flashy characters of the WWF and WCW. As stated at the beginning of each episode, Smoky Mountain Wrestling was "professional wrestling the way it used to be, and the way you like it." Because the area was a traditional hotbed for professional wrestling, Smoky Mountain Wrestling had a short but successful run before market forces and a "wrestling recession" spelled the end to the promotion. During its four-year run, the promotion utilized many classic professional wrestling storytelling devices as well as older, established talent recognizable to most fans. Smoky Mountain Wrestling also tapped into its Southern fans' fears in the 1990s regarding race, gender roles, and class to create a series of successful villains that would have been unsuccessful in other parts of the country.

While professional wrestling has always used stereotypical foreigners and "rich boys" as heels because they run counter to the blue-collar fan base, Smoky Mountain Wrestling capitalized on contemporary political debates about race and gender roles by embodying liberal views in heels and conservative views in the heroes ("babyfaces" [good guys] such as the "Wild-eyed Southern Boy" Tracy Smothers, who came to the ring with a Confederate battle flag and cap, a gimmick he had used in other promotions, but that was particularly successful in SMW). This essay will examine three heels in the promotion, paying particular attention to how each represented largely hated and vilified sociopolitical ideas among the region's fans. Tammy Fytch, who later reinvented herself as Sunny, the first WWF "diva," was a feminist from the Northeast who idolized Hillary Clinton and threatened sexual discrimination lawsuits against SMW management if she did not get her way. Among other things, she embodied feminism's perceived threat to the traditionally male-dominated public sphere. The Gangstas (New Jack, Mustafa, and "Uptown" D'Lo Brown) were a group of African American wrestlers who dressed in stereotypical "gang-style" clothing, name-dropped civil rights leaders like Malcolm X and Medgar Evers and claimed they only needed a two-count to win a match because of affirmative action. The Gangstas played upon every racial stereotype, drawing boos from the predominately white fans in Appalachia. Finally, SMW offered an unconventional heel in the Dirty White Boy, a stereotypical redneck from Bucksnort, Tennessee, who went from redneck to Yankee when he denounced his Southern roots to claim allegiance to the North, going so far as to be a fan of the New York Yankees baseball team.

Wrestling and Race, Class and Gender Roles

Wrestling, a choreographed form of entertainment that highlights athletic ability with storylines, became extremely popular in the American South during the 20th century.[2] Modern professional wrestling began in the United States in the late 19th century and achieved new heights of popularity after World War II when it gained national exposure through the new medium of television. Wrestling was popular in the 1950s and 1960s and suffered some decline in the 1970s before again being resurrected by the emergence of cable television that again offered national exposure for the promotions. Randall Williams provided a concise description of wrestling in the South when he wrote:

> The small town arenas are drab, barnlike buildings with dirt floors and concrete seats, but their center typically contains a red, white, and blue wrestling ring brilliantly lighted by rows of television lights.... Friday or Saturday night entertainment is part athletic competition and part soap opera. Until recently, professional wrestling was the only sport many of these fans knew, and they have been intensely loyal and enthusiastic. In the wrestling ring, good and evil are distinct, and the fans pour into the arena to cheer the good guys and to jeer and curse the bad ones. Professional wrestling is the morality play of modern sports.[3]

That morality play aspect of wrestling is often described as a "soap opera for males." French scholar and cultural critic Roland Barthes argued that professional wrestling has three elements, suffering, defeat, and justice, and that professional wrestling matches were a battle between good and evil, a moral play. Historian Jessica Friedrichs expanded upon Barthes' critique, contending that

> professional wrestling has always taken cues from current events to create storylines that keep the audience's attention. Many times this has involved negative representations of certain nations or groups.... If minority and foreign characters are featured as the heels, then the message is that because they do not follow the rules of society it is acceptable for them to be ostracized by the fans.[4]

After World War II, wrestling promotions were full of Nazi and Japanese villains, and during the Cold War, Russian "nightmares" battled "real" Americans all over the nation. In a study of how wrestling portrays characters after 9/11, Lucy Nevitt argues that "pro-wrestling characters frequently represent or embody particular ideas, groups, or nations … [and that] the combat encounter between two or more characters in the ring can become a mechanism for what is essentially overt propaganda."[5] While it was easy for wrestling promoters to depict a villain or heel as a foreign enemy, in the 1990s, after the fall of the Soviet Union and the end of the Cold War, some promotions began looking at American society itself for villains. In SMW, the bookers created new heels built upon American concepts of race, class, and gender.

A Short History of Smoky Mountain Wrestling[6]

Smoky Mountain Wrestling was one of the last of the wrestling territories that, since World War II, served as the foundation of the wrestling business in the United States.[7] Former manager Jim Cornette, professional wrestler Tim Horner, and wrestler/booker Sandy Scott formed SMW in 1992. Cornette received funding for the operation from record producer Rick Rubin, who was a fan of "old style Southern wrestling."[8] One of the best descriptions of Smoky Mountain Wrestling came from future WWE superstar Chris Jericho who along with Lance Storm got his start in the United States in SMW. Jericho said:

> SMW offered more of a slower-paced, old-time style of wresting than what the glitzy WWF was selling. To a certain extent the fans in the Southern states preferred Smoky's style to the WWF's, with a lot of them still believing that they were watching a legitimate sport and behaving accordingly. This included automatically cheering or booing a wrestler based solely on whether he came to the ring from the heel or babyface locker room.[9]

SMW ran its shows in high school gyms (in smaller towns) and small arenas (in larger towns). As in wrestling's territorial days, the TV show was used to get fans to attend live events, unlike the WWF or WCW, whose shows were used to sell pay-per-view events. Cornette used a mixture of familiar, veteran wrestlers from the Southern territories (the Armstrong family, Tracy Smothers, Kevin Sullivan, and the Dirty White Boy) as well as young new wrestlers such as Chris Candido, Chris Jericho, the Gangstas, and Brian Lee.

In addition to the mixture of new and veteran talent, Cornette used traditional territorial storylines and booking patterns (i.e., hair vs. hair matches, loser leaves town matches, and TV titles) with new, innovative, and controversial ideas. Many of the ideas and booking concepts would later appear in ECW, WWF, and WCW where they would be heralded as groundbreaking, helping form the foundation of the WWF/WWE's successful "Attitude Era" in the late 1990s and early 2000s.

Tammy Fytch: A Feminist Manager for the 1990s

The use of managers to assist heel wrestlers was a common fixture in professional wrestling; however, the use of female valets was not common. While Gorgeous George, the groundbreaking wrestling star of the 1950s, used his second wife, Cherie Dupré, as a valet, it was only in the 1980s that many territories began using girlfriends or wives as valets for heel wrestlers, most likely as an excuse to place attractive women on TV rather than for storyline purposes.

Traditionally, managers were used by promoters to serve as mouthpieces for heels (and sometimes babyfaces) who were not skilled talkers. The manager also would aid in the heel in cheating and many times serve as the catalyst for the wrestler to turn face after putting up with the heel manager's incompetence or abuse. In most cases, the manager was the dominant partner in a relationship: for example, Mr. Fuji in the WWF, Jim Cornette in the Mid-Atlantic Wrestling, and Gary Hart in World Class Championship Wrestling and Championship Wrestling from Florida would manage their wrestlers, but they always had a dominant role in the relationship, usually serving as the "boss." The female valet's role was totally different. Rather than being dominant over the wrestler, the valet would occasionally assist the wrestler in cheating, but usually served only as "eye candy" for the fans. It was not acceptable for a woman to be ordering a man around or to mastermind evil activities.

This limited role for the female valet changed with the 1993 introduction of Tammy Fytch in SMW. Tammy Fytch (real name Tamara Lynn Sytch; promoter Jim Cornette heard her name wrong on a phone call and began advertising her as Tammy Fytch) was an average 20-year-old from New Jersey who just happened to be dating a professional wrestler, Chris Candido. When Candido received a contract to work at SMW, Tammy joined her boyfriend in east Tennessee. In a 2007 interview, Sytch discussed how she got into the business. A summary of the interview stated that

> she had no intentions of getting into the wrestling business and was only there for Chris (Candido) and that she was studying Pre-Med in Tennessee. Jim Cornette asked her to work for 6 months and get a few bucks and she ended up doing phenomenal and staying in Smoky Mountain with her husband. She also said she missed Smoky Mountain a lot and thought it was great.[10]

Cornette recognized Stych's natural charisma and decided to use her good looks and Northern origins to create a new kind of heel valet/manager. Rather than having her serve as traditional eye candy, Cornette decided to have her be an intelligent, ambitious woman who promoted a type of feminism that would be seen as a threat by the conservative fans in the region.

A similar gimmick had been attempted several years earlier in WCW when Alexandra York (Terri Runnels), who had a laptop computer that supposedly created strategies for victory, advised Michael Wallstreet and others. However, York never dominated the males and never pushed a political ideology (other than "greed is good"). Fytch's portrayal was groundbreaking and played directly upon the fans' fears.

Tammy Fytch debuted on the May 24, 1993, episode of SMW, in an interview segment with Bob Caudle. Caudle explained that the SMW lawyers advised them to allow Fytch to speak because she had filed a lawsuit against the promotion.[11] Fytch immediately pointed out her Northern pedigree as one of "the Fytches from New England," scoffing when Caudle said he was unfamiliar with them. She then declared her admiration for her personal hero, Hillary Clinton, who had been brought into the national spotlight during her husband's successful presidential campaign in 1992. Fytch also commented she was attending Wellesley College, Hillary Clinton's alma mater and an iconic center of the feminist movement.[12] Clinton had polarized many in the nation by not being a traditional candidate's wife; she famously asserted that she would have a role in the her husband's administration that was more than ceremonial. This constituted a disruption in traditional gender roles, and having a woman expressing her desire to be involved in national politics went against many fans' personal and religious beliefs in the South.

To force her way into the male-dominated world of professional wrestling, Fytch had filed a sexual discrimination lawsuit again the promotion because they did not have any women in "prominent positions." She was using the legal system to her advantage, a tactic often portrayed as underhanded in the world of wrestling, where men took care of their disputes in the ring rather than a courtroom. Furthermore, by relying on a judge to get her way, Fytch was forcing the promotion to go against its own code, infuriating the average fan.[13]

When announcer Bob Caudle asked Fytch what role she wanted, Fytch stated she wanted to manage and that wrestlers were "big men that are not too bright [and that] amuses me."[14] Then she said she would work her way up the ladder to commissioner because she had more talent than others there. This exchange highlighted that Fytch saw men as stupid and easily manipulated by women. In this short interview, Fytch established several major reasons for SMW fans to hate her. As a New England Yankee blueblood, she had forced her way into the local promotion, then threated to take over if she did not get her way. While other managers had played similar characters and threatened lawsuits to get their way, this was a female who was threatening the social norms of society. If a male manager had made similar claims, fans would expect a babyface to eventually give him a physical beating in response to his heelish ways. This was, however, not an option for dealing with Fytch, given the strong taboo against physical violence toward women.

To illustrate her disdain for Southern culture and heritage, Fytch attempted to recruit Dixie Dynamite (Scott Armstrong wearing a mask and cape emblazed with the Confederate battle flag) on the May 8, 1993, episode of SMW. Dynamite was a fan favorite who had suffered a series of losses but continued to embody the ideal "Southern gentleman" (even though many parts of the SMW territory, including east Tennessee, actually supported the Union during the Civil War) and exhibit good sportsmanship by saying "Yes, sir" or "Yes ma'am." Fytch said she was emulating her idol, Hillary Clinton, who, Fytch claimed, took a no-talent loser like Bill Clinton and got him elected president of the United States. Fytch also stated that Dixie had little talent, but she could lead him to the top of the wrestling world if he would listen to her and "get rid of all that silly Southern stuff." Dixie responded with a polite "Ma'am" and then with a "hell no" stormed off to a loud ovation. Having been rejected by this inferior wrestler, Fytch commented that it "must take a real man to be led by a woman."[15]

This exchange illustrated the concept of the Southern man being able to maintain his dignity and identity when threated or tempted by the Northern woman Who offered material gains if the Southern man would only renounce his heritage and ideals. Dixie politely but firmly rejected Fytch's tempting offer because it would have gone against his ideals and heritage, placing him under the control of an outsider. While this exchange was on the micro-level, it alluded more broadly to the perceived loss of a distinctly Southern culture in favor of a more homogenous culture defined and exported by the liberal bastions of New York and California.

Even though she was new to wrestling, Fytch made an immediate impact. Cornette stated, "Tammy was scary good at ringside, [and ready for] main event programs after less than six months in the business."[16] Over the next couple of weeks, Fytch continued to look for talent to manage before convincing Prime Time Brian Lee, a babyface, to sign with her. Lee, a 6'7" blond-haired monster, had been the primary face of the company. Fytch recruiting him instantly turned him heel and gave her a wrestler capable of fighting anyone on the roster. She would later be teamed with real-life boyfriend Candido. Fytch was so successful in evoking the ire of SMW fans that some wanted to physically harm her. For example, Cornette remembered a time that a female fan attacked Fytch in Barbourville, Kentucky, and Lee had to make the save to protect her.[17]

By summer 1994, the liberal feminist angle had played out, and Tammy took the role of the standard heel manager, little different from male managers, other than a degree of sexual tension with her charges, Candido and Lee, as they battled for tag team championships. Rather than pursuing the liberal feminist angle, Fytch began using her looks and intelligence to be a "gold digger" character. For example, she tried to gain control of local legend Ron Wright's fortune. Wright, who came to the ring in a wheelchair, was serving as the heel manager of the Dirty White Boy. Fytch's use of her feminine charms to gain control of Wright's money allowed both the Dirty White Boy and Wright to turn face in reaction to being used by a woman.

Cornette considered tapping further into Fytch's sexuality and Southern social taboos and fears in many parts of the south by having Fitch manage an African American wrestler. Rumors suggested that Tony Atlas was the first choice, but that did not materialize. Cornette later wanted to team Fytch with the controversial Gangstas but Fytch refused.[18] Cornette evidently hoped that seeing a pretty, young blonde with an African American (with hints of a sexual relationship) would cause serious "heat" with the promotion's white, Southern male fan base.

In early 1994, Fytch revisited her feminist character during a feud with the Rock N Roll Express, a popular babyface tag team. Ricky Morton, the "teen idol" of the Express, kissed Fytch after a match in what can only be seen as a sexual assault, but the act was depicted as "giving her what she wanted." Fytch appeared on TV and complained that Morton could have given her "cooties" or HIV and threatened to file another sexual harassment suit against SMW. However, this element of the feud was dropped, and no other court cases appeared on the horizon.

Fytch's success in SMW drew the attention of the WWF. In early 1995, the WWF offered contracts to Fytch and Candido, and they left SMW. Fytch, renamed Sunny, had a successful three-year run in the WWF, where she continued to play a headstrong woman manager, but without the obvious feminist or liberal elements that had made her so successful in SMW. As male fans began to see threats to the gender role in society and their lives, it was only natural for them to view a Northern feminist as a heel in the "black and white" world of wrestling. Fytch succeed in portraying a character that depicted the threats to the model of masculinity prevalent in Southern society. Because she was a Yankee, she looked down on Southern fans and culture, and because she was a liberal, she did not mind using unsportsmanlike ways of handling problems (i.e., using lawsuits). Finally, because she was a woman, she could use her feminine charms to get her way.

The Gangstas

The introduction of the Gangstas tag team in 1995 would create the most controversial angle in the history of SMW and represented a return to race-based storylines as a means of antagonizing fans. Historically, African American wrestlers were not widely used in Southern promotions because they were usually not seen as profitable faces. Many promoters avoided putting titles on African Americans for fear of angering white fans. Occasionally, individuals like the Junkyard Dog in Bill Watts' Mid-South Wrestling (operating primarily in Louisiana, Oklahoma, and Arkansas) became immensely popular with Southern fans. However, they were most often depicted in the tradition of the dancing minstrel who would entertain white audiences but was in no way threatening to white audiences' attitudes or masculinity.

The Gangstas were a group of three wrestlers: New Jack, Mustafa Saed, and D'Lo Brown. New Jack and Mustafa had been wrestling in Georgia when Cornette called and asked them to come to SMW. Cornette later provided his reasoning behind the group:

> We ran shows in Marietta, Ga., we'd use some of the local promoter's guys and there was New Jack. He could talk like crazy. Mustafa couldn't say sooey if the hogs had him, but looked like he could break you in half. The OJ car chase had just happened and Rodney King a few years before that, so I came up with The Gangstas from South Central LA.[19]

The Gangstas first appeared on SMW television on July 23, 1994. After beating two jobbers,[20] the two congratulated OJ Simpson for getting rid of two white people and used the term "putting the Reginald Denny" to describe the attacks on the white wrestlers.[21] Wrestling journalist Dave Meltzer stated that

> if a major promotion attempted to do this in a city of any size, they'd either be apologizing for it within a few weeks or be off television.... Expect Cornette, who has been looking for a long time to push black heels to his virtually all-white and he believes borderline KKK–like audience, to give these guys a major push. The only reason it hasn't happened yet is because he hasn't found a black heel who would do it.[22]

The Gangstas immediately feuded with the Rock N Roll Express, the white babyface heroes of the territory, capturing the tag team titles from them. In racially-charged interviews, the Gangstas called the babyfaces and their fans "crackers" and "rednecks." Also, the Gangstas used threats of lawsuits to receive title matches, suggesting that it was no different than lawsuits by groups like the NAACP in the face of civil rights problems.

Other wrestlers easily recognized the racial overtones and stereotypes of the Gangstas. Fellow SMW wrestler Chris Jericho, who entered the promotion at roughly the same time as the Gangstas, said of the controversial team that the Gangstas were making "gang signs, spoke Ebonics, and mockingly ate watermelons and fried chicken to protest the stereotypical 'where all the white women at' portrayal of African Americans by certain segments of society."[23] Jericho added that "Jimmy [Cornette] was hoping to tap in to the racism of the South by making the Gangstas top heels. But instead of the controversy creating cash, it did the opposite. The sponsors, the television executives, and the fans were all offended."[24] Furthermore, the heat caused by the gimmick was evident in the interaction with the white fans. Meltzer reported that "the two needed a police escort out of town after the tapings."[25]

After the feud with the Rock N Roll Express, the Gangstas faced Tracy Smothers and Scott Armstrong, the New Southern Boys, which suggested that only Southern (Confederate) heritage could defeat this African American threat. During the feud the Gangstas confronted Bob Armstrong, the commissioner and patriarch of the Armstrong family, and suggested he favored white wrestlers over African Americans. Because of the threat the Gangstas represented, wrestlers began to form alliances based on their race, regardless of past differences. For example, longtime babyfaces the Rock N Roll Express joined forces with Jim Cornette, a heel manager, to form a united front against the threat of the African American wrestlers. The angles culminated with a battle between the Armstrong family and the Gangstas in a flag match, in which the losers would be covered with the winners' flag. The Armstrongs used the Confederate battle flag and the Gangstas used a Malcolm X flag. The Armstrongs even had WWF superstar (and Texas native) the Undertaker appear on their team. Of course, the faces won, but the heels attacked them after the match and left them covered with the Malcolm X flag. By June 1995, the Gangstas had left SMW for Philadelphia-based Extreme Championship Wrestling (ECW) after a contract dispute. Cornette was angry and quickly erased all mention of them from the promotion.

Dirty White Boy and Tracy Smothers

Because of pro wrestling's enduring popularity in the South, Southern archetypes were often the basis for Southern wrestlers' in-ring personas.

Randall argues that "southern social types portrayed in the ring have reflected the South's changing role in American culture ... [from] the raw, degenerate, *Deliverance*-like mountain man to the more positive simple hillbilly, uncorrupted by modern civilization."[26] During the 1970s, the image of the Southern wrestler began to embrace working-class, redneck culture. This shift to the "good ole boy" face was embodied in Dusty Rhodes (Virgil Runnels, Jr.), the son of a plumber from Texas who fought for the common man and looked more like the average fan, with his chubby frame, than other faces of the day.[27]

While the "good ole boy" face was a popular figure, Cornette also made use of the uncultured, violent redneck, more in the model of the *Deliverance*-like mountain man, with the Dirty White Boy (DWB). DWB was the wrestling persona of Tony Anthony, a journeyman wrestler from Tennessee who had had successful runs in territorial promotions throughout the Southeast, including Memphis in the 1980s. His character was a stereotypical violent redneck that lacked the positive babyface qualities of the good ole boy. DWB embodied those elements of the South that embarrassed many Southerners. Jim Cornette explained that Dirty White Boy "was the perfect villain for the territory from the start. People knew him, he could talk, and knew how to work the style."[28]

In his initial entry into SMW, DWB continued his gimmick of being the violent redneck. He was teamed with Ron Wright, a Tennessee wrestling legend, who performed a crippled manager gimmick by appearing at ringside in a wheelchair. During his first year in the promotion, DWB feuded with Tim Horner, the classic Southern pretty-boy babyface wrestler, as well as Prime Time Brian Lee, babyface SMW champion. These feuds succeeded in drawing crowds, and in August 1992, DWB won the SMW title from Lee, holding the belt until the following April, when he lost it to Tracy Smothers, who was using the Wild-Eyed Southern Boy gimmick.

Losing his title to Smothers opened DWB to a new angle in which he abandoned his Southern heritage for the most un–Southern of places, New York City. Promos in early April 1993 depicted DWB in Central Park, wearing Yankees apparel and declaring that he was now a Yankee. Soon after, DWB attacked Smothers, who said DWB was "just like a Yankee" to jump someone from behind.[29] In another promo, Ron Wright commented that his New York doctors had discovered he was suffering from "asthmatic bronchitis" and said the Southern doctors were all too stupid to diagnose his problem.[30]

Having abandoned his Southern heritage, DWB began to belittle the fans and their culture by asserting the superiority of Northern culture, a message similar to that of the mainstream media, at least in the eyes of many Southern fans. His rejection of the South led DWB into a feud with Tracy Smothers, portrayed as a proud protector of Southern ideals whose ring jacket and tights featured the Confederate battle flag. Over the course of several months, the two battled over whose heritage was better until eventually Smothers and the South stood victorious over DWB and the North. Over the course of the feud, DWB even burned a Confederate flag. Smothers later stated that members of the KKK showed up prior to one match and offered him membership, suggesting they could help against the "Northerners."

Eventually, SMW offered redemption for DWB. After Tammy Fytch began taking advantage of the elderly Ron Wright for his money, DWB saw the evil of the manipulative feminist and turned face to protect Wright. He later formed a tag team with his former enemy Smothers as the THUGS, a team that represented the yin and yang of the South: the violent redneck and the valiant Southern gentleman. They feuded with Fytch's group and also with the Gangstas, who were seen as a threat to Southern values more dangerous than the previous personal problems between DWB and Smothers.

Aftermath

In 1995, SMW closed after a four-year run. Professional wrestling journalists attribute the promotion's demise to a lack of national television exposure, its small regional fan base, and a fraction of the resources that WCW and WWF possessed. Even with a loyal regional fan base, which proved too small, "SMW, though, never reached a consistent level of success that brought profitability for the backers, a humane schedule for the promoters, or a payroll that attracted marquee talent."[31] When SMW closed its doors, Cornette and several of the wrestlers moved to the WWF, while others went to ECW or other small promotions. Although the promotion folded, the three angles discussed above served as models for many of the important angles that drove the Attitude Era in the late 1990s, one of the most profitable periods in wrestling history.

While not as political and blatantly feminist in WWF, Sunny (Tammy Sytch) had a successful run in the WWF managing many tag teams, all the while using her looks and manipulative nature, much like the Fytch character. Her new model of the strong female manager was the model for future women performers in the WWF/WWE. The pioneering nature of her role was acknowledged in 2011, when she was inducted into the WWE Hall of Fame.

While the Gangstas did have a successful run in ECW after leaving SMW, their influence was evident when the WWF created the Nation of Domination in 1996. The group, patterned after the Nation of Islam and the Black Panthers, was a black separatist faction that rebelled against the white-dominated WWF. While not nearly as racially-charged as the Gangstas had been in SMW, the NOD did bring racial politics to wrestling, and, of course, the African

Americans were again seen as the heels. Historian Vaughn May argued "Black Power may have been concerned with personal identity and cultural heritage, [but] traditionalists argued that its advocates posed a dangerous threat to American pluralism and civilized democratic society ... the NOD reinforces the traditionalist view of black power: NOD members engage in thuggish actions, abusing their opponents in and outside the ring."[32] After the late 1990s, African American characters were still occasionally portrayed as criminals (i.e., Cryme Tyme), but these stereotypes are now largely absent from WWE. The African American members of The New Day team have created a new paradigm of fun-loving performers that are not minstrel archetypes. Furthermore, wrestlers like Titus O'Neil, Apollo Cruise, and Darren Young (who was also in the first openly gay pro wrestler) have gimmicks not based on race and are not portrayed in any threatening or stereotypical manner.

The 1990s was a period of change, as the U.S. entered the post–Cold War era. The economy continued to transition from industry to service and information technology, and the ethnic makeup of the nation continued to transform. To reflect these changes, Smoky Mountain Wrestling tapped into its Southern fans' fears in the 1990s regarding the uncertainty of race, gender roles, and class, developing a series of successful heels that spoke to the fears of the fans and offered a fantasy world where those fears could be alleviated by their heroes.

NOTES

1. Professional wrestling, much like the carnivals where it originated, has its own lexicon. For a good review of the special language of the sport, see George E. Kerrick, "The Jargon of Professional Wrestling," *American Speech* 55, no. 2 (1980), 142–45.

2. Randall Williams, "Wrestling," in Harvey H. Jackson and Wilson Charles Reagan, eds., *The New Encyclopedia of Southern Culture, Volume 16: Sports and Recreation* (Chapel Hill: University of North Carolina Press, 2011), 244–48.

3. Williams, "Wrestling," 245–46.

4. Jessica Friedrichs, "Good versus Evil in the Squared Circle: Foreign and Minority Representations in Professional Wrestling," M.S., Middle Tennessee State University, 2014, 9.

5. Lucy Nevitt, "The Spirit of America Lives here: U.S. Pro-Wrestling and the Post-9/11 War on Terror," *Journal of War and Culture Studies* 3, no. 3 (2010).

6. "Fire on the Mountain: The Oral History of Smoky Mountain Wrestling," WWE.com, http://www.wwe.com/classics/oral-history-of-smoky-mountain-wrestling (accessed November 1, 2016).

7. During the 20th century, wrestling promoters operated a territorial system that guaranteed that a certain promoter would have a monopoly over all of the wrestling in that area. In 1948, the territorial system was codified by the founding of the National Wrestling Alliance (NWA), which served as the governing body of the territories until the late 1980s when the system was demolished by WWF and WCW's expanse. The NWA controlled who was the world champion and how that person was used. For a good study of the NWA see, Tim Hornbaker, *National Wrestling Alliance: The Untold Story of the Monopoly That Strangled Pro Wrestling* (Toronto: ECW Press, 2007).

8. Wade Keller, "15 Years Ago—Smoky Mountain Wrestling Closes Its Doors," *Pro Wrestling Torch*, November 29, 2010, http://pwtorch.com/artman2/publish/wadekellerdotcom/45651.shtml.

9. Chris Jericho and Peter Thomas Fornatale, *A Lion's Tale: Around the World in Spandex* (New York: Grand Central, 2007), 180–81.

10. Adam Martin, "Tammy Lynn-Sytch Interview: Talks About Her Career, Michaels, & More," Wrestleview.com, April 20, 2007, http://www.wrestleview.com/news2006/1177056865.shtml.

11. *Professional Wrestling Observer*, April 26, 1993.

12. *Smoky Mountain Wrestling*, Episode #65, April 24, 1993.

13. *Smoky Mountain Wrestling*, Episode #65, April 24, 1993.

14. *Smoky Mountain Wrestling*, Episode #65, April 24, 1993.

15. *Smoky Mountain Wrestling*, Episode #67, May 8, 1993.

16. "The Sad Story of WWE Legend Tammy 'Sunny' Sytch," *Gossip Life*, August 26, 2016, http://www.thegossiplife.com/single-post/2016/08/26/The-Sad-Story-of-WWE-Legend-Tammy-Sunny-Sytch.

17. "Fire on the Mountain: The Oral History of Smoky Mountain Wrestling," WWE.com, http://www.wwe.com/classics/oral-history-of-smoky-mountain-wrestling, (accessed November 1, 2016).

18. *Professional Wrestler Observer*, August 8, 1994.

19. "Fire on the Mountain: The Oral History of Smoky Mountain Wrestling," WWE.com, http://www.wwe.com/classics/oral-history-of-smoky-mountain-wrestling (accessed November 1, 2016).

20. Preliminary wrestlers who usually or always lose.

21. *Smoky Mountain Wrestling*, Episode #130, July 23, 1994.

22. *Professional Wrestling Observer*, July 18, 1994.

23. Jericho and Fornatale, *A Lion's Tale*, 205.

24. Jericho and Fornatale, *A Lion's Tale*, 205.

25. *Professional Wrestling Observer*, July 18, 1994.

26. Williams, "Wrestling," 247.

27. Williams, "Wrestling," 247.

28. "Fire on the Mountain: The Oral History of Smoky Mountain Wrestling," WWE.com, http://www.wwe.com/classics/oral-history-of-smoky-mountain-wrestling (accessed November 1, 2016).

29. "Jim Ross V WCW and Radio Show Hijinx, Wally Karbo Bio, Mania Preview," *Wrestling Observer Newsletter*, April 5, 1993.

30. "Wrestlemania 9, All-Star Dream Slam, Lacey Von Erich Fundraiser," *Wrestling Observer Newsletter*, April 12, 1993.

31. Wade Keller, "15 Years Ago—Smoky Mountain Wrestling Closes Its Doors," *Pro Wrestling Torch*, November 29, 2010, http://pwtorch.com/artman2/publish/wadekellerdotcom/45651.shtml.

32. Vaughn May, "Cultural Politics and Professional Wrestling," *Studies in Popular Culture* 21, no. 3 (1999), 91.

Latin Lords of the Ring
Politics, Nativism and Mexican/Chicano Identity Through Professional Wrestling

JUSTIN D. GARCÍA

> "We are what we are: Black, White, Brown, Yellow. [The] point is don't be ashamed of who you are.... Órale vato, this is who I am! Take me or leave me. You don't like me? Turn around and look the other way. It's that simple."
> —Eddie Guerrero (1967–2005)[1]

This essay examines constructions of masculinity and ethnic identity as embodied by three prominent World Wrestling Entertainment (WWE) stars of Mexican/Chicano[2] heritage during the early 21st century: Eddie Guerrero, Rey Mysterio, and Alberto Del Rio. All three rose to fame during a time in which the Mexican American population was growing rapidly as the United States was becoming an increasingly multicultural society. Although Latino grapplers had performed in U.S. professional wrestling for decades, Mexican/Chicano wrestlers attained unprecedented main event status, visibility, and fame in the United States during the 2000s. Guerrero's, Mysterio's, and Del Rio's emergence as elite WWE superstars coincided with the escalation of U.S. immigration policy, particularly illegal immigration from Mexico, one of the nation's most polarizing political issues. Despite the contrasting versions of Mexican/Chicano masculinity performed by these three men in the ring, the divisiveness of immigration policy in society, along with rising anti–Mexican nativism during this period, shaped the portrayals of each grappler. Ultimately, misfortunes outside the ring ranging from personal tragedies to backstage politics and confrontations with alleged real-life institutional racism within the industry undermined the potential for each to remain main-event, championship-caliber stars within WWE.

Before analyzing these constructions of Mexican/Chicano masculinity, a brief explanation of the terminology used throughout this essay is appropriate. Generally speaking, this essay uses the pan-ethnic label *Latino* rather than *Hispanic*,[3] unless the latter term appears in a quoted source. Wrestlers are referred to by their stage names when discussing their matches, gimmicks, and scripted performances, while those same wrestlers are referred to by their actual names when discussing real-life, non-kayfabe[4] events that have impacted their careers and/or personal lives. Additionally, this essay uses professional wrestling lingo throughout; please refer to the corresponding endnotes for explanations of unfamiliar terminology.

A thorough analysis of each wrestler's stellar career far exceeds the limits of this essay, so primary emphasis is placed on their tenures with Vincent K. McMahon's World Wrestling Entertainment[5] as a standard basis for comparison and contrast. This essay neither attempts to condemn nor defend the Mexican-themed ethnic and immigration gimmicks utilized by these wrestlers. The use of racial and ethnic gimmicks, particularly those rooted in explicit stereotypes, remains controversial and a topic of intense debate among cultural analysts, media critics, and the general public, and such an acrimonious debate will not be resolved here.[6] Any discussion of racism, therefore, focuses specifically on charges of racism that have been raised by these Latino wrestlers concerning the mistreatment they claim to have experienced in the professional wrestling industry.

Wrestling as Staging Ground for Racial/Ethnic Identity Politics

Professional wrestling has long incorporated racial and ethnic themes into the gimmicks of its performers, with the ring representing a metaphorical canvas upon which real-world racial and ethnic dynamics play out theatrically. Despite, or perhaps because of, its scripted nature, certain professional wrestlers have attained status as ethnic icons whose cultural significance transcends their in-ring accomplishments. However, the scripted nature of professional wrestling also enables performers and promoters to carefully and deliberately incorporate racial and ethnic storylines into the action to arouse the emotions of fans and to advance particular narratives. The use of racial and ethnic gimmicks and angles has been a major staple of wrestling since the 1920s and 1930s.[7] Since that time, promoters have used racial and ethnic angles to generate interest, sell tickets, and entice fans to purchase pay-per-view events.[8] Importantly, at different times wrestling has used racial and ethnic angles for two very different purposes: either to build positive fan support among co-ethnics or, conversely, to generate negative reactions and hostility from the crowd and enhance the wrestler's status as a heel (villain).[9] Bruno Sammartino's career as a genuine blue-collar Italian immigrant babyface/face (hero/good guy) is a famous example of the former. Likewise, during the 1950s and 1960s, promoters in the Northeastern United States frequently hired Italian and Puerto Rican wrestlers to capitalize on their respective ethnic fan bases in the region.[10] In contrast, the Iron Sheik's gimmick as an anti–American zealot in the aftermath of the Iran Hostage Crisis serves as one of the most vivid illustrations of using ethnic angles to enrage audiences. As Scott Beekman notes, wrestling "not only adapted to reflect larger social trends but also reinforced national, racial, and political stereotypes through its heel personas."[11]

While not all gimmicks and angles in wrestling center around racial or ethnic identity and conflict, such angles persist and remain common to this day. Given the fluidity of how racial and ethnic storylines can be utilized to advance wrestling narratives, and considering that race and ethnicity can be used creatively to establish wrestlers as either faces or heels, a range of constructed ethnic gimmicks, stemming from a common ethnic or national heritage, may simultaneously exist within wrestling. In other words, two Mexican American wrestlers may exhibit vastly different constructions of Mexican ethnic identity in their gimmicks. The American media and general public frequently essentialize Mexicans (and oftentimes Latinos more broadly) as having a singular and homogenous culture, lifestyle, and identity. However, Mexicans are *not* a monolithic entity. An array of social and cultural identities exist among persons of Mexican descent, based on the tremendous phenotypic, linguistic, cultural, geographic, social class, sexual orientation, generational, and citizenship/immigration status diversity that exists within this population.

Sociologist Pancho McFarland argues that this diversity has produced three basic archetypes of ethnic and masculine identity common among male Chicano rappers: that of the indigenous-minded Chicano who glorifies Mexico's Amerindian heritage, the Mexican nationalist who asserts strong pride in Mexico and Mexican heritage, and the politically conscious inner-city Chicano "street hopper" who identifies primarily with members of other marginalized social groups in his lyrics.[12] Like rappers, professional wrestlers "brand" themselves, constructing distinct identities and personas through the creation of gimmicks, ethnic or otherwise. In keeping with McFarland's analysis of the various constructions of ethnicity and masculinity among Chicano rappers, this essay examines the contrasting versions of Mexican/Chicano masculine identity embodied by Guerrero, Mysterio, and Del Rio through their professional wrestling careers in WWE.

Early Latinidad *in WWE*

The presence of Mexican wrestlers, and Latinos more broadly, in WWE and its forerunners, dates back several decades. Carlos Colón, a native of Puerto Rico, briefly wrestled in the World Wide Wrestling Federation (WWWF) in 1967 and 1968. During the 1970s, Pedro Morales, also a Puerto Rican native, and Mil Máscaras, a Mexican national, both emerged as major stars within the WWWF. Morales became the WWWF's first Latino world heavyweight champion in February 1971, while Mil Máscaras cultivated an intense rivalry with WWWF champion "Superstar" Billy Graham during the late 1970s, although he never captured the title. These stars attained glory at a time when professional wrestling in the United States was still organized into the distinct and relatively autonomous regional territories recognized by the National Wrestling Alliance (NWA). The WWWF ran professional wrestling in the Northeast. Colón and Morales were natural fits for this territory, given the large concentration of Puerto Ricans in New York, New Jersey, and Pennsylvania. However, with only a minuscule Mexican population residing in the Northeast during the 1970s, Mil Máscaras performed in obscurity from the majority of his co-ethnics.

Throughout the 1980s, Tito Santana emerged as the WWF's most high-profile Latino star. A fan favorite renowned for his technical wrestling ability, Santana hailed from Mexico,[13] sported a small emblazoned sombrero on his trunks, and routinely concluded his promos[14] with a loud battle cry of "Arriba!"[15] Santana won the opening match of the first-ever Wrestlemania in 1985, captured the Intercontinental Championship on two separate occasions in 1984 and 1985 (the first wrestler of Mexican descent to win this title), and twice won the tag team championship. Santana's success came after Vincent K. McMahon began broadcasting matches nationwide through syndication and cable television, thus showcasing Santana to fans from coast to coast.

In his analysis of early Latino wrestlers, Phillip Serrato asserts that Morales, Mil Máscaras, and Santana became established as popular babyfaces because of their "ethnic neutrality." Serrato contends that while the WWF acknowledged the Puerto Rican and Mexican heritages of these stars, the three displayed neither overt Latino pride nor criticism of anti–Latino racism in their storylines.[16] Even when white heels hurled ethnic insults at them, Morales, Máscaras, and Santana remained calm and did not verbally respond to such ethnically-tinged indignities. Serrato claims that this reluctance, carefully scripted by the company's creative team, served to comfort its predominantly white audiences by concealing expressions of minority resentment towards racial bigotry in wrestling and, by extension, in American society as a whole.[17]

In the early 1990s, Razor Ramon became the WWF's next significant Latino character. However, Razor Ramon was portrayed by Scott Hall, a non–Latino white wrestler. Razor Ramon exuded a cocky, threatening, macho, and explicitly stereotypical ethnic identity that redefined constructions of Latino masculinity in the WWF, serving as a precursor to future gimmicks adopted by Eddie Guerrero and Alberto Del Rio. A hybridization of characters from the 1983 film *Scarface*, Hall's Razor Ramon gimmick was that of a street-smart, domineering, and chauvinistic Cuban refugee living in Miami. Razor slicked back his jet-black hair and greased it with Vaseline, consistently sported a five o'clock shadow, and exhibited his womanizing ways by declaring that "*chicas*[18] are for fun." He dressed in vibrant, multicolored shirts worn half-unbuttoned to expose his multiple gold chain necklaces, and spoke with a greatly exaggerated Hispanicized accent. Razor Ramon debuted in the summer of 1992, following a series of vignettes filmed at Miami Beach and in Little Havana. One vignette, lifted straight from *Scarface*, featured Razor sitting in a Cadillac convertible as he boasted, "Ninety miles away, they living like pigs. They living in squalor, mang. They eating garbage. People telling them what to do. Nobody telling Razor Ramon what to do, mang. Nobody!"[19] Razor Ramon's gimmick thus amplified the degree of *latinidad* he projected to audiences, albeit through the filter of a menacing villainous character.

In 1996 Ted Turner's World Championship Wrestling (WCW), the WWF's primary competitor at the time, established a Cruiserweight Division, complete with its own title belt.[20] To stock its roster with cruiserweights (wrestlers under 225 pounds), WCW imported scores of wrestlers from promotions in Japan and, especially, Mexico, as well as signing a few wrestlers from the Philadelphia-based promotion Extreme Championship Wrestling (ECW). Numerous Mexican/Chicano wrestlers, trained in the distinctly Mexican lucha libre style, joined WCW, and the company's decision to broadcast cruiserweight matches near the beginning of *WCW Monday Nitro* and *WCW Thunder* exposed millions of American fans to luchadores[21] for the first time. The fast-paced nature of lucha libre, characterized by colorful masks and costumes, constant movement, and frequent high-flying aerial maneuvers, thrilled spectators, quickly becoming some of the most popular matches in WCW.[22] Luchadores such as Eddie Guerrero, Rey Mysterio, Chavo Guerrero, Jr., Juventud Guerrera, and Psichosis energized the division, demonstrating to Vince McMahon the marketability and profitability of Mexican/Chicano wrestlers on U.S. soil.

From "Latino Heat" to the "619": Mexican Masculinity in the 21st Century WWE

Although they were not WWE's only Mexican/Chicano wrestlers during the early 21st century, Eddie Guerrero, Rey Mysterio (real name Oscar

Gutiérrez), and Alberto Del Rio (real name José Alberto Rodríguez) achieved far greater success than other Latino stars working in the company at the time. Each attained main event status, headlined pay-per-view events, and captured the WWE World Championship. Guerrero and Gutiérrez are U.S.-born Mexican Americans, while Rodríguez is a native of Mexico. All three grew up in wrestling families, enabling them to perfect their craft from a young age. As lucha libre scholar Heather Levi notes, both in Mexico and among Mexican American grapplers, professional wrestling is often a family tradition that is passed down from older relatives to the younger generation, and the kinship affiliations of Mexican/Chicano wrestlers frequently factor into the names and gimmicks they adopt when younger grapplers establish their own professional careers.[23] The careers of Guerrero, Gutiérrez, and Rodríguez are linked, insofar as each played a significant role in establishing their immediate successor as an elite WWE superstar. Before joining WWE, each man enhanced his wrestling credentials in Mexico by performing with the respected Asistencia Asesoría y Administración (AAA) promotion.

Despite the vastly different constructions of Mexican/Chicano masculinity embodied through their characters, all three nevertheless found themselves embroiled in angles with various heels who equated their Mexican heritage with illegal immigration. These immigration angles corresponded with contemporary American politics, in which immigration from Mexico emerged as one of the nation's most contentious political issues. Interestingly, the immigration-themed storylines increasingly transcended the worked[24] nature of WWE matches, entering the realm of real-world American political discourse.

Eddie Guerrero was born October 9, 1967, in El Paso, Texas, the youngest of Mexican wrestling legend Salvador "Gory" Guerrero Quesada's four sons. Gory Guerrero was one of the pioneers of professional wrestling in Mexico, wrestling both solo and in a popular tag team with El Santo, the man still revered as the ultimate patriarch of Mexican wrestling.[25] Gory later became a prominent wrestling promoter in the El Paso region and trained his sons in the art of wrestling, establishing the Guerreros, along with the Von Erich (Dallas-based) and Hart (Calgary-based) clans, as professional wrestling's most storied dynasties. By age five, Eddie was already performing dropkicks in his father's backyard ring,[26] and as a child he wrestled with his nephew Chavo Guerrero, Jr. (with whom he would later team with in WWE) during intermissions of the matches his father promoted at the El Paso County Coliseum.[27] Eddie (henceforth referred to simply as "Guerrero") earned a wrestling scholarship from the University of New Mexico,[28] but in 1987 he left college before graduating to turn professional.

Guerrero spent most of his early years as a pro in Mexico where he formed a heel tag team, Los Gringos Locos ("The Crazy Americans") with white fellow American wrestler Art Barr in the early 1990s. This gimmick tapped into Guerrero's real identity as a U.S. citizen, despite his Mexican heritage, in order to establish Guerrero as an arrogant and jingoistic American, analogous to the manner in which foreign wrestlers have traditionally been depicted in the United States. To draw maximum heat,[29] Barr and Guerrero dressed in stars-and-striped patterned attire, defiantly waved oversized American flags, and occasionally made swimming gestures to their Mexican opponents and spectators to insinuate that they were *mojados* (literally, "wetbacks") through mimicking the act of undocumented immigrants swimming across the Rio Grande. Barr died unexpectedly in November 1994, and Guerrero left the Mexican circuit afterwards for a stint in Japan before returning to the United States to perform with ECW and WCW.

In January 2000, Guerrero defected to the WWF from WCW, and his career in the United States began gaining momentum when he reinvented himself as "Latino Heat." A satirical take on the longstanding Latin lover and machismo stereotypes of Latino men in American society, Guerrero's new gimmick portrayed him as a highly confident and overly emotional, yet alluring, ladies' man, brimming with Chicano pride and prone to sudden outbursts of anger. As "Latino Heat," Guerrero emphasized his Mexican heritage like never before, performing promos (interviews) in *caló*, a distinctly Mexican American dialect of Spanglish common in the Southwest. For the remainder of his career, Guerrero inserted common caló slang words and phrases like *Órale!* (All right!/Right on!), *Simón!* (Hell yeah!), *Chale!* (Hell no!), *ese* (man), *ruca* (woman), *vato* (guy/dude) and *homes* (guy), as well as standard Spanish lexicon, into his on-screen performance. Cruising in lowriders, one of the foremost subcultures associated with Chicano youth, likewise became a centerpiece of his gimmick, but this actually reflected Guerrero's real-life passion for customized automobiles.[30] Guerrero's entrance song, "Latino Heat," was a caló rap that hyped up his grappling and romantic skills alike.

Guerrero's first major WWF angle featured him unflinchingly utilizing his romantic "Latino Heat" charisma to successfully woo Chyna, a white female wrestler, whom he affectionately referred to as *mamacita* ("sweetheart" or "baby"). This angle lasted seven months, from the spring until autumn of 2000, when the relationship finally collapsed as a result of Guerrero's on-screen jealousy and hypersexuality. Chyna (real name Joanie Laurer) posed for a nude pictorial in the November 2000 issue of *Playboy*. The WWF's creative team incorporated this development into its programming by depicting Guerrero as an overly jealous and excessively macho Latino enraged at his fiancé's sexual agency and independence. The September 7, 2000, episode of *SmackDown* featured Guerrero, unable to contain his high-octane machismo, driving to the Playboy mansion in his lowrider, futilely confronting Hugh Heffner's security guards in an effort to cease the magazine's distribution.

The Guerrero-Chyna angle finally ended a month later on the October 9, 2000, edition of *Monday Night Raw* when Chyna witnessed undercover surveillance footage of Guerrero cavorting in a shower with two white "hoes,"[31] Mandy and Victoria. As he exits the shower to prepare for his tag team match with Chyna, Victoria peeps out from behind the curtain and seductively exclaims, "Yo quiero Eddie Guerrero!," a sexualized twist on Taco Bell's famous slogan. Heartbroken, Chyna exits the arena and throws her engagement ring on the curb. Shortly thereafter, white wrestler "Bad Ass" Billy Gunn confronts Guerrero in the backstage parking lot and berates him for throwing away Chyna for "two cheap-ass hos" and proceeds to ethnically mock Guerrero by asking him, "Comprende, ese?" in a John Wayne–like, gringo Spanish accent, enraging Guerrero, who smashed a glass bottle over Gunn's head.

Although intended as a heel turn[32] for Guerrero, this segment actually *bolstered* his popularity with fans, as evidenced by spectators' cheers and chants of "Eddie!" after the footage of him with Victoria and Mandy is revealed. In fact, the comedic manner in which Guerrero performed his "Latino Heat" gimmick transformed him into a leading anti-hero in the WWF as his supposedly negative attributes (machismo, sleaziness, feisty temper, sexual avarice) won over fans. Perhaps even more significantly, his Mexican heritage within the context of these qualities *did not* hamper his standing with white fans. As such, Guerrero's pivot towards his new status as a fan-favorite anti-hero among WWF fans in the early 2000s mirrored that of the company's signature star and ultimate anti-hero of the time period, Stone Cold Steve Austin. Originally intended to portray the WWF's lead villain at the dawn of the Attitude Era in the mid-to-late 1990s, Austin's gimmick as a foul-mouthed, anti-authority, beer-guzzling and ass-kicking Texas redneck who deliberately violated all norms of polite decorum (including his revision of a popular Bible verse into his own personal slogan symbolizing rage against the establishment, Austin 3:16) endeared him to WWF audiences. While their ability to transcend their intended heel turns by winning over fans serves as a testament to the tremendous personal charisma of Austin and Guerrero alike, fans' embracing of these qualities may also reflect a shift in professional wrestling's core audience in the late 1990s and early 2000s from young children and their parents towards primarily college-aged males from the tail end of Generation X and the early years of the Millennial generation.

In 2003, WWE paired Guerrero in a tag team, Los Guerreros, with Chavo Guerrero, Jr. Los Guerreros operated under the nihilistic code of "We lie, we cheat, we steal!" which became the opening chorus of their entrance song. This gimmick encompassed virtually every negative Mexican stereotype imaginable, from laziness, hypersexuality, and dishonesty to criminal activity. A series of vignettes depicted Los Guerreros in various scenarios in which they humorously utilize their Chicano street smarts to swindle naïve, threatened, or racist white folks. One vignette featured Eddie and Chavo fraudulently posing as valets in order to steal fancy cars, while another vignette showed the two *vatos locos* ("crazy dudes") cruising through an affluent suburban neighborhood where they encounter two young white couples. Enthralled with their Latin charm, the two females eagerly abandon their boyfriends to accompany Los Guerreros in their lowrider for a night out on the town. With a thick Spanish accent, Eddie asks the ladies if they want to "munch on my burrito?" as their partners look on helplessly.

While the "Latino Heat" and "Los Guerreros" gimmicks proved highly successful with fans, both gimmicks invoked a repertoire of stereotypes that have historically served as a basis for anti–Mexican bigotry and nativism. Not surprisingly, WWE and Guerrero faced sharp criticism for scripting negative stereotypes as virtuous and fan-favorite qualities. Phillip Serrato, for example, asserts, "While Guerrero assumed agency in the crafting and performance of his Latino Heat persona … the exposure of Latino Heat's moral bankruptcy implied that suspicions fans might have had about the moral character of Latino men were, more often than not, justified."[33] Despite such criticism, Guerrero's kin, including his brothers, wife, and daughters, loved the gimmicks and found them hilarious.[34] Guerrero himself disregarded critical judgments and expectations that he use his wrestling fame to articulate socially conscious representations of Mexican/Chicano masculinity. In a July 8, 2001, shoot[35] interview with online wrestling columnist Mike Mooneyham, Guerrero explained.

> I'm a Mexican-American. I am a Hispanic. I talk [in standard English] now, but a lot of guys have that [caló] accent.… I grew up with those guys. They're from the barrio … [and they] talk like that.… The only time [non–Chicanos hear caló] is with Cheech Marin … and you do think it's stereotyping, but go up to California, go up to Texas, even Chicago, and you'll see it's not really stereotyping. Let's face it. America is a melting pot. If you want to say who the true Americans are, it's the native Indians. I crossed a river. You [white] guys crossed an ocean.[36]

Guerrero raises some crucial points regarding the fluid and dynamic nature of ethnic identity. He points out that speaking caló and living a barrio lifestyle are not *universal* attributes of Mexican American culture, but nevertheless constitute real and important lived experiences and markers of identity for *certain segments* of the Mexican American population in some urban communities. Guerrero concedes that non–Latinos on the East Coast may not be familiar with this nuanced understanding of the complex and multifaceted nature of Mexican/Chicano identity, while also challenging nativist perceptions of Mexican Americans as allegedly "not American enough." Questioning the hegemonic notion of "Americanness," Guerrero inverts nativist logic by pointing out that geographically, Mexico is much closer to the United States than is Europe and, therefore, in discourses of national belonging and the meaning of American identity, citizens of Mexican descent could lay stronger claim to "being American" than persons whose ancestors migrated from the other side of the Atlantic.

Despite being a U.S. citizen, Guerrero's white opponents increasingly characterized him as an illegal immigrant, purely because of his ethnic heritage, as the 2000s proceeded. A heated feud with John Cena, the self-proclaimed "Doctor of Thug-a-nomics" who utilized a Marky Mark/Eminem-like rapper gimmick, upped the immigration ante during the August 28, 2003, episode of *SmackDown*. Emerging from backstage to confront Guerrero in front of his hometown fans in El Paso, Cena rapped,

> Yo, you don't belong here. I heard about that green card that you stole.
> You better start runnin' south before I call Border Patrol!
> You know what? I'm lookin' at this picture, and there's something that's not fittin' in.
> You got the U.S. title, but you not even a citizen!
> Go ahead, get deported. For me, that's not a setback.
> I'll pin you in the Gulf of Mexico and leave you with a broken wet back.
> I'm 'bout to punk you out in front of your family here in El Paso.
> I'll break you open like a piñata, stick my foot right up your [avoids saying "asshole"].[37]

On February 15, 2004, Guerrero defeated Brock Lesnar to win the WWE World Championship, becoming the first Latino to capture the company's most prestigious title since Morales in 1971. That spring Guerrero entered a feud with John Bradshaw Layfield (JBL), whose persona was that of an arrogant Texas millionaire. JBL earned a title shot against Guerrero after the airing of a vignette in April 2004 depicting him along the Texas-Mexico border searching for and single-handedly kicking (literally) undocumented migrants out of the United States as part of his alleged patriotic duties. In the buildup to the Guerrero-JBL showdown, JBL continually referred to Guerrero and his relatives as "illegal immigrants" and, at an event in El Paso (a city where Latinos comprise more than 80 percent of the population) on April 29, 2004, threatened to "get all these Mexicans out of here" in reference to the spectators.

Tragically, Eddie Guerrero died on November 13, 2005, in Minneapolis, Minnesota, of arteriosclerotic cardiovascular disease,[38] which causes a hardening and narrowing of the arteries. Following the loss of its most high-profile Latino superstar, WWE began pushing Rey Mysterio as a main event competitor and heir apparent to Guerrero's legacy. However, while Guerrero relied on self-directed stereotyping and comic relief to construct his version of Chicano masculinity, Rey Mysterio embodied the identity of a hip-hop-oriented Mexican American nationalist, equally rooted in U.S. urban youth street culture and the working-class cultural traditions of Mexico. Rey

Mysterio represented the ultimate good guy, almost on par with comic book heroes. His gimmick was that of a hardscrabble, never-say-die bilingual and bicultural homeboy whose perseverance against all odds (visually amplified by his short height and small frame) stood as a metaphor for the struggles of Mexican Americans and could serve as inspiration for underdogs of all backgrounds. This gimmick, in certain respects, mirrored Oscar Gutiérrez's life story. In his autobiography, Gutiérrez notes that his 5'3" stature ensured his status as a face throughout his career. Gutiérrez's height immediately established him as a huge underdog and, thus, a sympathetic favorite among fans, particularly children. This, combined with his tremendous speed and high-flying abilities, guaranteed that he would remain a fan favorite for years.[39]

Gutiérrez was born on December 11, 1974, in Chula Vista, California, the son of Mexican immigrants and the first member of his family to be born in the United States.[40] During his early teenage years, his family moved to Tijuana, and Gutiérrez began to study wrestling more intently under his maternal uncle, Miguel Ángel López Díaz, a professional wrestler in Mexico during the 1970s and 1980s who went by the name Rey Mysterio (Spanish for "King of Mystery").[41] A few years after turning pro in Mexico, Gutiérrez adopted the name Rey Mysterio, Jr., as an homage to his uncle, in keeping with lucha libre tradition in which younger relatives of wrestlers acknowledge their kin through their stage names. While wrestling in Mexico's AAA promotion, Gutiérrez met Guerrero and the two became close, lifelong friends.[42] After performing in AAA, ECW, and WCW, Rey Mysterio joined WWE in the summer of 2002 and wrestled on the company's *SmackDown* program.

Having spent his formative years living on both sides of the border, Gutiérrez deliberately weaved his own transnational cultural identity into Rey Mysterio's character. "I've tried to take the best of Mexican wrestling, the dives, the high flying, and incorporate it into a logical [American] match. I hope it makes Americans appreciate lucha libre better," he acknowledges.[43] Gutiérrez also uses his own flesh, as well as his specialized wrestling moves, to pay tribute to his hybrid identity. Equally proud of his current hometown of San Diego and Tijuana, Mysterio named his signature moves the "619" (pronounced "six-one-nine") after San Diego's telephone area code, the "West Coast Pop" as a tribute to California and Baja California, and the "TJ Drop" in honor of Tijuana.[44] Numerous tattoos cover Gutiérrez's body, with some of the most notable including that of a rosary to acknowledge his deep Roman Catholic faith,[45] a cross and tombstone with Eddie Guerrero's initials as a tribute to his fallen friend on his left forearm, and "MEXICAN," written in large Old English calligraphy, across his abdomen. Regarding this latter tattoo, Gutiérrez explains that it "is to show my pride, my culture ... and it's very important to me. That's who I am."[46] Rey Mysterio's luchador mask is his most distinct characteristic, and the mask itself serves as a salute to Gutiérrez's Mexican heritage and early wrestling years in Mexico. However, the significance of lucha libre masks transcends wrestling, as masked luchadores have emerged as iconic symbols of social and political justice among working-class Mexican citizens since the 1980s.[47]

Immediately following Guerrero's passing, Rey Mysterio emerged as a sentimental favorite among WWE fans. Gutiérrez referred to the day he learned of Guerrero's death as the worst day of his life[48] and reflects in his autobiography, "God gifted me by allowing me to work with Eddie all those months, letting me get to know him a lot better.... I thank God I had a chance to work with him so closely before he died."[49] Aware of the strong personal friendship between the two and blurring the boundary between kayfabe and real life, fans erupted into thunderous chants of "Eddie!" during Rey Mysterio's matches in late 2005 and throughout 2006. WWE management took note of the fans' embracing of Rey Mysterio and quickly elevated him to main event status and a championship run, thus establishing him as the public face of the company. Rey Mysterio won the 30-man battle royal at the 2006 Royal Rumble, setting a WWE record that still stands for longest duration in the match at one hour, two minutes, 12 seconds.[50] At Wrestlemania XXII, held on April 2, 2006, he defeated Kurt Angle and Randy Orton in a triple-threat match to capture the World Heavyweight Championship (the WWE's premier title for wrestlers who perform on its *SmackDown* brand television program).

As Rey Mysterio ascended the ranks throughout the winter and spring of 2006, the United States found itself embroiled in a bitter national debate over immigration policy. The Republican-controlled U.S. House of Representatives passed H.R. 4437 along highly partisan lines in December 2005. Among other provisions, the bill called for the construction of 700 miles of fencing along the U.S.-Mexico border and sought to change undocumented presence from its current legal classification as a *civil infraction* (a non-criminal violation) to a *felony* (the most serious category of criminal violations). This bill sparked massive demonstrations, staged in cities nationwide throughout the spring of 2006, by immigrants' rights supporters who found H.R. 4437 excessively punitive towards undocumented aliens. At the same time, armed citizens' groups, referring to themselves as the "Minuteman Project," conducted private patrols along the U.S.-Mexico border in search of undocumented immigrants.[51] On May 1, 2006, pro-immigration supporters organized "A Day Without Immigrants" which called for undocumented immigrants and their allies to stay home from their jobs as a peaceful protest to demonstrate the economic value of migrant workers to the U.S. economy.[52]

Against this backdrop, immigration angles reentered WWE programming.

After Rey Mysterio captured the championship, JBL began a long feud with the Mexican American titleholder, escalating his anti–Mexican and nativist rhetoric to a new level. On the May 5, 2006, edition of *SmackDown*, JBL accosted Rey Mysterio in the ring and delivered a scathing rant that merged current events, ethnic insults, and wrestling entertainment:

> Last Monday, one million [illegal aliens] went on strike. Your people, Rey, went on strike.... You shut down businesses all across the United States.... Illegals have a place in my America.... I'm not gonna take out my own garbage! I'm not gonna mow my own yard ... we need you and your kind for rich people like me! ... I respect the Hispanic culture.... You're not a dog, Rey. You're a Mexican. And Mexicans have problems...[53]

Although scripted, JBL's diatribe is telling within the context of larger societal anti–Mexican nativism. Aside from viewing undocumented immigrants as having no redeeming value other than their manual labor, this rhetoric rigidly conflates "the Hispanic culture" with "illegal immigration," even though Hispanics/Latinos comprise a wide range of ethno-national heritages, as well as citizenship, immigration, and refugee statuses. Like Guerrero, Rey Mysterio is a U.S. citizen. As a white Texan, JBL's comments about Mexicans being lower than dogs is even more pointed. Such a comparison alludes to Jim Crow segregationist policies in Texas that were common up until the 1960s, in which white-owned public establishments commonly posted signs declaring, "No Dogs, Negroes, or Mexicans Allowed."

The Rey Mysterio–JBL rivalry persisted for years and continued after Layfield retired from wrestling to become a color commentator on WWE programming. WWE incorporated such shrill anti–Mexican and anti-immigrant rhetoric that the satirical website The Onion ran its own hilarious parody of the company that contended that Vince McMahon relied on undocumented Mexicans to take jobs Americans refuse, such as being hit in the face with steel chairs.[54] The Onion parody also claimed that undocumented wrestlers wear lucha libre masks to conceal their true identity and evade the Border Patrol after matches.[55]

WWE's third major Mexican/Latino superstar of the 21st century, Alberto Del Rio embodied a vastly different construction of ethnic identity than Guerrero or Rey Mysterio. At 6'3" tall and 240 pounds, José Rodríguez's physique approximates that of the large-bodied grapplers who have historically dominated American professional wrestling. The son and nephew, respectively, of Mexican professional wrestling legends Dos Caras and Mil Máscaras, Rodríguez was born May 25, 1977, in San Luis Potosí, Mexico.[56] Rodríguez attended Universidad Autónoma de San Luis Potosí and excelled at amateur wrestling during his youth, winning the gold medal in Greco-Roman wrestling at the 1999 Pan American Games.[57] Unfortunately for

Rodríguez, however, Mexico declined to send a wrestling team to the 2000 Summer Olympics. Rodríguez turned pro in Mexico, adopting the name Dos Caras, Jr., to acknowledge his parentage in keeping with Mexican wrestling tradition. In 2010 Rodríguez joined WWE, who believed he had potential to become both an ethnic icon and a crossover star with his heavyweight size, technical wrestling skills, fluency in both Spanish and English, and soap opera actor-like handsome looks.[58] WWE's "long-term goal was to introduce him as a villain, but eventually have him flip and stand up for Mexican Americans, and then become one of the company's signature stars."[59]

Rodríguez adopted the name Alberto Del Rio in WWE and performed the gimmick of an arrogant Mexican aristocrat overflowing with honor, integrity, and pride, who boasted continually about his athletic prowess, wealth, intelligence, fashion, and elegant lifestyle. Del Rio's opulence led him to feature his own flashy entrance and a personal ring announcer. Whereas Guerrero drove to the ring in lowriders, Del Rio entered arenas in various exotic luxury cars, such as Rolls Royces and Maseratis. Debuting on *Smack-Down* in August 2010, Del Rio immediately entered into a feud with Rey Mysterio by interrupting the masked luchador's monologue and berating his background:

> I'm a millionaire.... I'm admired in my country ... and you know, Rey, my blood line comes from kings, from [Spain's King] Fernando and [Queen] Isabella ... and you also know that your blood ... is from the horrible streets of Tijuana ... you're just like the little worm in the bottle of my tequila.... Just look at me—I'm handsome. I'm rich. I'm powerful.[60]

Here, Del Rio plays up the sharp social class divisions that exist in Mexico and among Mexican Americans. The reference to Fernando and Isabella denotes the two monarchs whose marriage unified Spain during the Middle Ages, thus implying that Del Rio is of pure Castilian-European stock, unlike the vast majority of Mexico's population, which is of mixed European, Indigenous, and, to a lesser extent, African ancestry. Del Rio's ability to infuriate fans as a heel enabled him to quickly rise through WWE's ranks, and he emerged as the winner of the 2011 Royal Rumble.

However, by early 2013, Del Rio turned face, and WWE capitalized on his Mexican heritage to reintroduce an immigration angle fueled by the right-wing political gimmick espoused by two white stars, Jack Swagger and his middle-aged manager Zeb Colter.[61] Calling themselves "the real Americans," Swagger and Colter appeared in several vignettes where they bemoaned multiculturalism, immigration, the federal government, and "political correctness." Colter dressed in survivalist gear, while the vignettes depicted the two standing beside the Gadsden flag.[62] Colter's invective particularly singled out Del Rio as an alleged illegal immigrant and an example of what Colter viewed as the "problem with America." Colter explained this "problem" on a February 2013 episode of *Monday Night Raw*:

> I look around and I see a country I don't even recognize. I see people with faces unlike mine. I see people that I don't even know what they're saying. They can't even talk to me [in English].... I think, "How do we get rid of 'em?" ... Because this is the land of the free and the home of the brave, not the land of the free and the home to whomever wants to cross our borders![63]

This angle culminated in a showdown at Wrestlemania XXIX that saw Del Rio defeat Swagger to retain the World Heavyweight Championship. However, the significance of this angle transcended wrestling and entered real political discourse. Right-wing talk radio hosts Alex Jones and Glenn Beck took exception to commentators Michael Cole and Jerry "The King" Lawler joking on air that Colter and Swagger received fan mail from Jones, Beck, and Rush Limbaugh, and they retaliated by openly criticizing WWE and the McMahon family. Jones declared that most wrestling fans are "borderline mentally retarded,"[64] while Beck characterized WWE as "stupid wrestling people."[65] Jones' website Infowars.com accused WWE of developing the Colter and Swagger characters to deliberately and unfairly caricature Tea Party activists as simple-minded racists.[66] Both Jones and Beck alleged that the McMahons, known in political circles as moderate New England Republicans, invented the gimmick out of spite towards the Tea Party Movement and to ridicule conservative-leaning Americans after Linda McMahon, Vince's wife and former WWE Chief Executive Officer, failed to win her 2012 Senate campaign in Connecticut. WWE openly invited Beck to attend an episode of *Monday Night Raw*, which Beck angrily rejected. In response, WWE aired a promo in which Colter (real name Wayne Keown) and Swagger (real name Jake Hager) broke with their gimmick and spoke directly to Beck, pointing out that wrestling is scripted entertainment not intended for literal interpretation.[67]

Beyond the Ring: Wrestling with Real Racism

While wrestling often incorporates racial and anti-immigrant bigotry into its angles, real accusations of racism within the industry are not uncommon. In August 2014, WWE unexpectedly fired José Rodríguez.[68] Over the next few months, various accounts of the incident confirmed that Rodríguez confronted Cody Barbierri, a WWE web page designer, over an anti–Mexican and allegedly racist joke.[69] When asked to clean off his plate after a catered meal, Barbierri made an off-the-cuff remark that it was Alberto Del Rio's and other Mexican wrestlers' duty to clean the dishes because they are Mexican.[70] Rodríguez confronted Barbierri and expressed his disgust. Barbierri smirked at Rodríguez and refused to apologize, at which point Rodríguez slapped him out of frustration. Rodríguez later revealed that he had a similar experience with Barbierri previously. Rodríguez's blow nearly knocked out Barbierri,[71] and WWE increased Rodríguez's punishment from a brief suspension to a firing when Barbierri threatened to sue the company.

In a November 2014 interview with Britain's *Fighting Spirit Magazine*, Rodríguez indicated that WWE's racial problems ran far deeper than his personal issues with Barbierri. Rodríguez claimed that he often overheard WWE employees making disparaging remarks about African Americans and Latinos, only to downplay such comments as mere jokes when challenged. Rodríguez further disclosed that Paul Levesque (known onscreen as Triple H), who also serves as WWE's Executive Vice President in addition to his role as a wrestler, is among the company's most frequent culprits of making openly racist jokes. According to Rodríguez, Levesque's high standing within WWE's front office established an atmosphere whereby lower-ranking white employees felt empowered to express racist sentiments and make racial jokes to blacks and Latinos within the company.[72] In this regard, WWE finds itself in a racial paradox not unlike other American institutions, such as higher education and the corporate workforce, that publicly express commitments to diversity while struggling to ensure an inclusive environment for their students and employees.

During the fall of 2015, for example, several colleges and universities erupted with student-led protests against campus climates that fostered unwelcoming or inhospitable environments for members of racial and ethnic minority groups. Protestors at the University of Missouri, Yale University, Claremont McKenna College, Ithaca College and others specifically claimed that students of color routinely experienced racism on campus (ranging from casual microaggressions to more overt displays of bigotry) and that campus administrators had failed to adequately address such concerns. Campus conflicts over racial tensions are escalating at a time in which most colleges and universities have publicly embraced multiculturalism, openly express support for diversity, and have established diversity-themed courses as part of their general education curricula requirements. In a similar nod towards publicly embracing multiculturalism, WWE aired a series of vignettes on its programming from mid–September to mid–October in 2016 to celebrate Hispanic Heritage Month. These vignettes consisted of brief biographies of key historic figures such as labor leader César Chávez, as well as wrestlers such as Eddie Guerrero, Pedro Morales, and Mil Máscaras. Yet given the experiences described by black and Latino students and wrestlers, a burning question remains: Are official expressions of support for diversity akin to a luchador's mask, presenting a vibrant, colorful public image to onlookers while concealing the true identity beneath it?

Notes

1. "Eddie Guerrero Quotes," AZQuotes.com, 2016, http://www.azquotes.com/author/30339-Eddie_Guerrero (accessed August 22, 2016).
2. The author uses the phrase "Mexican/Chicano" (and its plural version) to refer collectively to Mexican nationals and U.S. citizens of Mexican ancestry. The label "Chicano" became popular during the 1960s among younger social activists as a term for U.S. citizens of Mexican descent. Although its usage remains controversial among Mexican Americans, "Chicano" is used in this essay due to Eddie Guerrero's usage of the term.
3. The U.S. Census Bureau officially considers "Hispanic" and "Latino" interchangeable, as both terms are defined in the same manner. Any preference for one term over the other is purely subjective.
4. "Kayfabe" refers to the fictional/staged/scripted dimensions of professional wrestling.
5. WWE has undergone several name changes throughout its history. Originally known as Capitol Wrestling Corporation, the company changed its name to Worldwide Wrestling Federation (WWWF) in 1963. This was shortened to World Wrestling Federation (WWF) in 1979. In 2002, the company changed to its current name, World Wrestling Entertainment (WWE). This essay uses the company name that was contemporary with the specific time period being discussed.
6. Henry Jenkins, "Afterword, Part II: Growing Up, and Growing More Risqué," in Nicholas Sammond, ed., *Steel Chair to the Head: The Pleasure and Pain of Professional Wrestling* (Durham: Duke University Press, 2005), 323; Alexander Zubatov, "Professional Wrestling, Racism, Transracial Identity, and Why We All Need to Lighten Up," *PopMatters.com*, August 19, 2015, http://www.popmatters.com/feature/196558-professional-wrestling-racism-transracial-identity-hulk-hogan-rachel/ (accessed August 1, 2016).
7. Scott M. Beekman, *Ringside: A History of Professional Wrestling in America* (Westport, CT: Praeger, 2006), 64–66.
8. Beekman, 74–76.
9. Beekman, 91–92.
10. Beekman, 90.
11. Beekman, 92.
12. Pancho McFarland, *The Chican Hip Hop Nation: Politics of a New Millenial Mestizaje* (East Lansing: Michigan State University Press, 2013), xiii–xvi.
13. In reality, Merced Solis (the wrestler who portrayed Tito Santana) is a U.S.-born citizen of Mexican descent.
14. A "promo" is an interview or speech given by a wrestler in alignment with their gimmick.
15. As an exclamation, "Arriba!" loosely translates as "I'm on the way up!" (as in up the rankings and on the road to success).
16. Phillip Serrato, "Not Quite Heroes: Race, Masculinity, and Latino Professional Wrestling," in Nicholas Sammond, ed., *Steel Chair to the Head: The Pleasure and Pain of Professional Wrestling* (Durham: Duke University Press, 2005), 239–40.
17. Serrato, "Not Quite Heroes," 239–40.
18. "Chicas" is Spanish for "girls."
19. Championship Channel, "Razor Ramon Debut Vignette—WWF—June 1992," YouTube.com, April 18, 2016, https://www.youtube.com/watch?v=-H89nxSnNa8 (accessed August 16, 2016).
20. Serrato, "Not Quite Heroes," 245–47.
21. "Luchadores" is Spanish for "wrestlers," particularly those who wrestle in the lucha libre style.
22. Serrato, "Not Quite Heroes," 245–47.
23. Heather Levi, "On Mexican Pro Wrestling: Sport as Melodrama," in Randy Martin and Toby Miller, eds., *Sportcult* (Minneapolis: University of Minnesota Press, 1999), 173–88.
24. "Worked" is pro wrestling jargon for "planned and scripted events."
25. David Shoemaker, *The Squared Circle: Life, Death, and Professional Wrestling* (New York: Gotham Books, 2013), 352.

54   Part I. Race

26. *Cheating Life, Stealing Death: The Eddie Guerrero Story*, directed by Hosam Ibrahim (World Wrestling Entertainment, 2004), DVD.
27. Shoemaker, *The Squared Circle*, 352.
28. Shoemaker, *The Squared Circle*, 352.
29. "Heat" refers to the level of reaction wrestlers generate from the audience, either positively through cheers and negatively through jeers, depending on whether their gimmick is that of a face or heel.
30. *Cheating Life, Stealing Death: The Eddie Guerrero Story*, 2004.
31. This was the height of the WWF's Attitude Era, which was known for its extensive use of sexual innuendo in its content. WWF programming referred to Mandy and Victoria as "hoes" who were under the auspices of the Godfather, an African American wrestler with a pimp gimmick.
32. A heel turn occurs when a face wrestler transforms into a villain.
33. Serrato, "Not Quite Heroes," 252–53.
34. *Cheating Life, Stealing Death: The Eddie Guerrero Story*, 2004.
35. Unscripted, genuine, legitimate.
36. Mike Mooneyham, "Eddie Guerrero—Q&A," MikeMooneyham.com, July 8, 2001, http://www.mikemooneyham.com/2001/07/08/eddie-guerrero-qa (accessed July 21, 2016).
37. "John Cena Raps on Eddie Guerrero: Smackdown, August 28, 2003," YouTube.com, uploaded on April 13, 2016, https://www.youtube.com/watch?v=-3dwo8XZO1I (accessed August 16, 2016).
38. Shoemaker, *The Squared Circle*, 362–63.
39. Rey Mysterio and Jeremy Roberts, *Rey Mysterio: Behind the Mask* (New York: Pocket Books, 2009), 51.
40. Mysterio and Roberts, *Rey Mysterio*, 6.
41. Mysterio and Roberts, *Rey Mysterio*, 6–7.
42. Mysterio and Roberts, *Rey Mysterio*, 77–79.
43. Mysterio and Roberts, *Rey Mysterio*, 117.
44. Mysterio and Roberts, *Rey Mysterio*, 249.
45. Mysterio and Roberts, *Rey Mysterio*, 121–22.
46. Zack Zeigler, "Rey Mysterio: A Made Man," WWE.com, November 1, 2007, http://www.wwe.com/inside/superstarink/articles/reymysterio (accessed August 21, 2016).
47. Levi, "On Mexican Pro Wrestling," 184–85.
48. Mysterio and Roberts, *Rey Mysterio*, 279.
49. Mysterio and Roberts, *Rey Mysterio*, 300.
50. "WWE Royal Rumble Statistics, Records, Trivia & Facts," SmarkOutMoment.com, 2016, http://www.smarkoutmoment.com/p/wwe-royal-rumble-statistics-records.html (accessed August 23, 2016).
51. Lourdes Medrano, "What Happened to Minuteman Project? It's Still Roiling Immigration Reform," *Christian Science Monitor*, April 30, 2014, http://www.csmonitor.com/USA/2014/0430/What-happened-to-Minuteman-Project-It-s-still-roiling-immigration-reform (accessed August 23, 2016).
52. Anita Hamilton, "A Day Without Immigrants: Making a Statement," Time.com, May 1, 2006, http://content.time.com/time/nation/article/0,8599,1189899,00.html (accessed August 23, 2016).
53. F.A., "Rey Mysterio Confront JBL 5.5.06," DailyMotion.com, November 9, 2008, http://www.dailymotion.com/video/x7cghe_rey-mysterio-confront-jbl-5-5-06_sport (accessed August 23, 2016).
54. "WWE: Illegal Mexican Wrestlers Taking Smackdowns American Wrestlers Don't Want," *The Onion*, March 29, 2006, http://www.theonion.com/article/wwe-illegal-mexican-wrestlers-taking-smackdowns-am-1926 (accessed August 23, 2016).
55. "WWE: Illegal Mexican Wrestlers Taking Smackdowns American Wrestlers Don't Want," accessed August 23, 2016.
56. "WWE Profile—Alberto Del Rio," ESPN.co.uk, August 11, 2016, http://www.espn.co.uk/american-fb/story/_/id/17372634/null (accessed August 23, 2016).
57. "WWE Profile—Alberto Del Rio," accessed August 23, 2016.

58. Dave Meltzer, "Why Alberto Del Rio Has Suddenly Become a Sought-After MMA Fighter," MMAFighting.com, December 31, 2014, http://www.mmafighting.com/2014/12/31/7459853/why-alberto-del-rio-has-suddenly-become-a-sought-after-mma-fighter (accessed August 23, 2016).

59. Meltzer, "Alberto Del Rio" (accessed August 23, 2016).

60. WWE, "Alberto Del Rio's WWE Debut," YouTube.com, October 4, 2013, https://www.youtube.com/watch?v=sPGo2n9LRpw (accessed August 23, 2016).

61. The name "Zeb Colter" may very well be a reference to right-wing author and pundit Ann Coulter, one of the nation's most outspoken opponents of both legal and illegal immigration.

62. The Gadsden flag is the infamous yellow flag with a coiled rattlesnake in its center, atop a caption that reads "Don't Tread on Me." The flag dates to the Revolutionary War era but reemerged as a popular emblem at rallies staged by Tea Party activists during the early 2010s.

63. WeThePeopleZeb, "Zeb Colter Educates the WWE Universe," YouTube.com, February 17, 2013, https://www.youtube.com/watch?v=34T2L1hzUKI (accessed August 23, 2016).

64. The Alex Jones Channel, "Alex Jones Body Slams WWE for Demonizing Tea Party," YouTube.com, February 19, 2013, https://www.youtube.com/watch?v=WapIWTm-3ps (accessed August 23, 2016).

65. David Shoemaker, "Survivalist Series: WWE vs. Glenn Beck," Grantland.com, February 28, 2013, http://grantland.com/features/dissecting-wwe-feud-tea-party-glenn-beck/ (accessed August 23, 2016).

66. Paul Joseph Watson, "WWE Creates Racist Wrestler to Demonize Tea Party," infowars.com, February 19, 2013, http://www.infowars.com/wwe-creates-racist-wrestler-to-demonize-tea-party (accessed August 23, 2016).

67. Shoemaker, "Survivalist Series," 2013.

68. Marissa Payne, "WWE Fires Superstar Alberto del Rio For Reportedly Slapping Employee Who Allegedly Told a Racist Joke," *Washington Post*, August 9, 2014, https://www.washingtonpost.com/news/early-lead/wp/2014/08/09/wwe-fires-superstar-alberto-del-rio-for-reportedly-slapping-employee-who-allegedly-told-a-racist-joke/ (accessed August 23, 2016).

69. Alastair Davidson, "WWE: Alberto Del Rio Reveals New Details Concerning WWE Firing," GiveMeSport.com, November 6, 2014, http://www.givemesport.com/519687-wwe-alberto-del-rio-reveals-new-details-concerning-wwe-firing (accessed August 23, 2016).

70. Payne, "WWE Fires Superstar," 2016.

71. Brandon Stroud, "The WWE Employee Who Made a Racist Joke and Got Alberto Del Rio Fired Has Left the Company," Uproxx.com, October 14, 2014, http://uproxx.com/prowrestling/the-wwe-employee-who-made-a-racist-joke-and-got-alberto-del-rio-fired-has-left-the-company (accessed August 23, 2016).

72. Bill Pritchard, "Alberto Del Rio on Racist Remarks in WWE," WrestleZone.com, November 5, 2014, http://www.wrestlezone.com/news/524753-alberto-del-rio-on-racist-remarks-in-wwe-says-top-executives-also-made-comments-in-front-of-talent-including-the-person-who-informed-him-of-his-release (accessed August 23, 2016).

"Degenerative sports and dirty tactics"
Race and Professional Wrestling in Cape Town, South Africa, c. 1880–1988

Hendrik Snyders

Wrestling in Africa predates the advent of colonialism where it "played a crucial role in consolidating gender roles, the social structure, and the initiation of young people into values of patriotism, courage, and solidarity."[1] Greco-Roman and Cornish styles arrived in South African mining towns Kimberley and Johannesburg during the mid- to late 19th century. Out of the various contests for medals, belts, and side-stakes emerged South Africa's first known wrestling champion in the Cornish style in 1886.[2] This laid the foundation for the development of a strong wrestling tradition in both the Black and White communities during the 20th century.

Towards a South African Professional Wrestling Tradition

Professional wrestlers from all over the world visited South Africa in the late 19th century in pursuit of fame and fortune. While prize-fighting in boxing required prior police permission, prize-wrestling was unregulated.[3] Frank Fillis, entertainment entrepreneur and circus-boss with an international reputation of his own, utilized this space to host a wrestling "world championship" between Tom Cannon ("Champion of the world")[4] and Fritz Thiedman (the so-called "South African champion"), on May 20, 1897, in

Cape Town.[5] As an added attraction, the bout for a £100 purse featured both the Greco-Roman and catch-as-catch-can styles.[6] This event coincided with the touring shows of J.W. Sutherland (New Zealand), George Boganski (Russia), Fritz Wehlau, and George Rasso (both German).[7]

Despite the international reputation of some of the visiting wrestlers, attendance numbers varied significantly. A key factor was the reputations of both the promoter and the wrestlers involved. While fight attendances could be "poor and depressing" on one occasion, it could attract "an immense gathering of people" at another.[8] Contemporary newspaper reports generally failed to give specific attendance figures. Based on reports of spectator attendance at wrestling and boxing contests during this period, figures varied between 100[9] and 1500 paying clients.[10] The financial incentive and reputational prospects associated with the sport also continued to attract talented White amateur wrestlers into the paid ranks.[11] Despite the existence of a significant Black South African sporting tradition in various English sports that developed during the late 19th century, wrestling was not part of it.[12]

The black colonial elite (both players and administrators) were ardent supporters of the idea that "good sport, manliness and love of 'fair play' should be promoted amongst all classes of society."[13] They therefore attempted to use sport and the demonstration of prowess as well as the values of fair play and sportsmanship as indicators of their "fitness to be accepted as full citizens in Cape society."[14] Social segregation, which was the prevailing social custom, blocked their advancement, however. Indeed *The Cape Argus*, one of the city's oldest newspapers, noted that "the races are best socially apart, each good in their own way, but a terribly bad mixture."[15]

When famous grappler George Hackenschmidt visited South Africa in 1910, there were no black wrestling professionals (promoters, officials, or wrestlers) anywhere in the country. The only visible amateur wrestling activity in Cape Town was confined to the Young Men's Christian Association (YMCA), which was established the previous year.[16] Anecdotal reports indicated that Hackenschmidt "wrestled" and defeated at least one black individual while on a visit to Durban. From the available evidence, it is clear that his opponent was not a professional wrestler. Indeed, the *Poverty Bay Herald* suggested that this event retarded rather than advanced the cause of black wrestling.[17]

The African Political Organisation (APO, est. 1902), the most prominent campaigner for race equality in South Africa before the First World War, supported sport as a tool of social advancement. "Sport," wrote the winner of the APO's essay competition in 1919, "would help the male and the female to grow up into strong, healthy men and women. It will also crush hooliganism which so much abounds amongst the Coloured race. No more silliness and vulgarity."[18] Boxing, however, was viewed by the APO as the one sport that "will not elevate the Coloured people."[19] Proving black equality or superiority and physically shattering the myth of white invincibility therefore had to be achieved through other means.[20] Physical cultural activities, inclusive of amateur wrestling, therefore inadvertently became the focus of the APO's attention.

Using its party newspaper, the APO in Cape Town highlighted the activities of organizations such as the YMCA and the Ottoman Physical Culture Club (OPCC) and individuals such as George Stewart, who was involved in the teaching of "scientific physical culture."[21] Stewart was particularly lauded for promoting the establishment of "scientific physical culture clubs" as a means of preparing the "parents for our future race."[22] This effectively made physical culture inclusive of amateur wrestling, with the goal of building a non-racial and non-sectarian masculinity. This intimate relationship between physical culture and wrestling in Cape Town mirrored developments elsewhere in the world. Griffiths indeed suggested that the "fitness craze" was essentially a reaction "to fears of physical and moral degeneration associated with modernity."[23]

As Cape Town entered the 1930s, more physical culture clubs than dedicated black wrestling clubs were established.[24] Although this created a larger pool of amateur wrestlers, there were no ethnic promoters to guide them into the professional ranks. The establishment of a local control board in 1934, however, placed the further development of black wrestling on a different trajectory.

Protecting Municipal Property: The CBOCPW

Both the White Western Province Amateur Wrestling Association and the Black Western Province Amateur Boxing & Physical Culture Union, established in 1929, practiced Greco-Roman style in their championship and interclub trophy tournaments held on municipal premises. As a result of their strict regulation of holds, most events lacked spectacle and failed to attract significant spectator support, resulting in slow growth.[25] This again mirrored the international trend, as fans increasingly supported the more exciting catch-as-catch-can.[26]

For most of the 20th century, South African sports controlling bodies aggressively promoted amateurism. The South African Rugby Football Board in particular banned its players and officials from participating in a range of professional sports, wrestling included.[27] With the support of government departments, municipalities, and police and defense authorities, some codes were even criminalized.[28] Rugby-playing wrestlers therefore had to assume false names or wore masks in the ring. With little real resistance to the practice, the status quo remained.[29]

Due to the large number of bouts hosted on municipal premises, Cape Town witnessed an evolution of the different styles. It therefore became one of the first to push for some form of regulation. Following a near-riot by fans at a bout involving George Boganski and Tom Alley at the City Hall in August 1934, City Councilor Aaron Berman demanded a ban on wrestling at all municipal premises.

Berman, a campaigner for racial equality, argued that municipal facilities were built "for edification and decent recreation."[30] Professional wrestling, he suggested, was "undignified" and "barbarous" and the characteristic bloodiness of the sport defeated the objectives behind the provision of public facilities. Similar views by anti-wrestling activists in the United Kingdom resulted in the sport's banning in the Greater London area by the London City Council.[31] Berman was supported by fellow councilor Jasper Smith, who denounced all-in-wrestling for its "corrupting and degenerating effect on the Black community." These sentiments, however, were not supported by the city's Improvements & Parks Committee (IPC).[32]

The anti-wrestling lobby was, however, strongly supported by the Dutch Reformed Church (DRC), Anglican, and Wesleyan churches. All shared the view that wrestling brutalized both spectators and participants and that it was a disgraceful "outlet for the animal responses of the more uncivilized section of our population."[33] This places the White DRC, a staunch opponent of racial equality through its mouthpiece the *Kerkbode*, in sync with Berman, a campaigner for a non-racial, socialist, and democratic South Africa. The ability of this issue to unite sworn ideological and political enemies, proved disturbing to some.

In response, various anonymous individuals wrote to the *Cape Times* and *Cape Argus* newspapers, questioning both the proposed ban and Berman's integrity. They also mocked the actions of the City Council. Calling the proposed ban a ridiculous over-reaction, one writer calling himself "Catch-as-catch can," described the Berman proposal as one that "could not be more of a burlesque than 'Alice in Wonderland' rewritten by P.G. Wodehouse." Another, "Jessie," attacked the proposal as a sanctimonious act of selective morality given the equally violent nature of other sports. The collective problem from their perspective was, firstly, Berman's "lack of humour" and secondly, the council's own proceedings that allegedly sometimes mirrored that of a wrestling circus.[34] The city administration's view was simply that a blanket ban was financially illogical and would represent a sizeable loss of income.

As responsible corporate citizens, the *Cape Times* and *Cape Argus* urged the opposing groups to search for a mutually beneficial solution. Both were of the view that wrestlers' misbehavior, particularly their unwillingness to adhere to the rules and their disregard for the referees, were the key problem.[35] Given the politically sensitive nature of the matter, they also encouraged politicians to abstain and allow the sport's practitioners (administrators, promoters and wrestlers) to find a lasting solution. In addition the *Cape Argus* called for the drafting of one set of national rules.[36]

Given the public interest in the matter, the town clerk recommended a meeting between all stakeholders. The Transvaal National Sporting Club (TNSC), which assisted with the establishment of the Transvaal Board of Control for Professional Wrestling (TBCPW) five months earlier, supported this approach.[37] It also volunteered its assistance in setting up a provincial oversight body able to liaise with the City Council. The initiative also received the support of the Cape Province National Sporting Club, a sister club to the TNSC.[38]

The gathering on October 11, 1934, was a whites-only affair, representative of the wrestling fraternity and the city's political and administrative leadership including the mayor and the chairman of the IPC.[39] The matter of black representation never made the agenda.[40] The meeting, one of "interested" and "competent persons" as it was framed, then proceeded to elect an executive from a list of 13 nominees.[41]

After its recognition by the Cape Town City Council on October 12, 1934, the Cape Board of Control for Professional Wrestling (CBOCPW) submitted its constitution to the TNSC and the TBCPW. This was aimed at ensuring reciprocity and uniformity between the two boards.[42] Furthermore, key members of the aforementioned bodies were also influential national administrators in a range of fraternal national amateur sports organizations who often acted as gatekeepers between the two codes.[43]

To signal its break with the status quo, the CBOCPW adopted catch-as-catch-can as its official rules and banned all references to *"All-in-Wrestling."* Cape Townians were acquainted with the different styles from the outset thanks to the frequent visits by overseas grapplers and the long-term presence and permanent residence of former overseas wrestlers like J.W. Sutherland and George Boganski in South Africa. Whereas Sutherland arrived in the country around 1889,[44] Boganski's presence was noted from the 1920s onwards.[45] By the time Sutherland retired in 1903, he was acclaimed as the middle-weight champion of both Australasia and South Africa. In addition, the new body's executive members were wrestling promoters in their own right and due to their regular interaction with visiting overseas wrestlers, seconds and managers were able to clearly distinguish between the different styles.

Although the CBOCPW constitution contained no racial references, prospective office-bearers had to obtain formal police clearance and endorsement by the national police commissioner. This requirement excluded all "undesirable elements" and those who failed the test of being "citizens of good standing."[46] In addition to obtaining all manner of permits for wrestling, promotion, and officiating at a prescribed fee, promoters had to submit a copy of their articles of constitution and had to register all contracts. They also had to keep proper balance sheets and submit audited post-event statements to the Board for compliance with the Provincial Amusements Tax Act of 1913.[47] This matter was regarded as "a great hardship" by both amateur and professional administrators.[48] Entry into the professional ranks for all prospective promoters or wrestlers became much harder.

With few alternative venue options, the professional wrestling fraternity adapted to the new regulations. Black physical culture clubs, with their mix of boxing, wrestling, and weightlifting, continued to have limited access. This, noted the *Cape Standard* newspaper, undermined the ongoing effort to use wrestling as a tool to build "weaklings into strong, robust men."[49] The only consolation was that black wrestling fans could see reputable local and overseas wrestlers in action in their home cities.[50]

After two years of operation, the CBOCPW was notified on November 17, 1937, of the city council's intentions to terminate its tenure. The official reason was that the body had outlived its usefulness. Despite an appeal to continue, it was disbanded by the end of December.[51] This situation followed a renewed attempt by the Transvaal National Sports Club to monopolize the sport and to secure international recognition in order to enhance the sport's profitability.[52] This fight originated in Johannesburg where the TNSC and the Union Sports Club, were at loggerheads about jurisdiction, wrestlers, and bouts.[53] Cape Town promoters on this board, in defense of their economic interests, refused to issue a promoter's license to the Cape Town National Sports Club, the TNSC's local chapter.[54] Amidst threats of legal action, the municipality of Cape Town stepped aside since their only concern was the protection of its public property. As the CBOCPW left the scene, media reports noted a growing pool of black wrestlers competing in tournaments organized by an emergent group of non-white promoters.[55] It also coincided with the first national initiative to extend the provisions of the Boxing Act (1923) to wrestling.

Wrestling Crowds and Apartheid, 1939–1954

During the period 1934–1940 and the reign of Johannes Van der Walt ("The Masked Marvel"), a renewed public focus was placed on the persistence of disorder at wrestling bouts.[56] The "Marvel's" fiercely partisan fan base frequently used violence against his opponents, match officials, and the police in reaction to negative match results. On at least four occasions matters got totally out of hand, leaving visiting wrestlers injured. Amongst these were Whiskers Blake, who was injured by fans after his attempt to unmask Van der Walt on March 2, 1935, in Durban, "The Golden Greek" Jim Londos on March 10, 1937, in Cape Town, John Spellman on October 8, 1838, and Paul "Texas Thunderbolt" Jones on March 29, 1939. In all cases the police had to intervene, which set in motion a series of campaigns for the total banning of the sport.⁵⁷ As a result, the Justice Ministry introduced a bill in February 1939 to formally regulate the sport. The Rev. Miles Cadman (M.P. for Durban North) in particular urged the enactment of measures that would not only give the police sufficient powers to act decisively but that would contribute to stopping the "inhuman exhibition."⁵⁸ With no objections, the Wrestling Regulation Act (Act 10 of 1939) was promulgated on March 27, 1939. The police therefore became the sole authority for approval of events and rules. The start of the Second World War, however, effectively prevented the proper testing of the new dispensation.

In the immediate aftermath of the war, Bill Forgus, a former black professional boxer and Alex Blassoples of the Liberman Institute, hosted a "super show of wrestling" involving "professional wrestlers" in December 1948.⁵⁹ A year later, M.A. Gierdien, businessman and chairman of the anti-apartheid Azzavia Study Group hosted a similar tournament in the Cape Town City Hall.⁶⁰ These events, which introduced more than 20 new mat personalities, launched the careers of the pioneers of black wrestling promotion.⁶¹ For the *Sun*, a publication supportive of black social advancement, this represented a new season of hope. Nailing its colors to the mast, the paper noted: "Coloured wrestling is equal to the best anywhere else and the standard of wrestling is very high indeed."⁶² Given the existing racial divide, this claim could, however, hardly be substantiated.

Following the electoral victory of the National Party in 1948, the government of D.F. Malan promulgated various laws to institutionalize segregation. Chief amongst these were the Population Registration Act (Act 30 of 1950), the Prohibition of Mix Marriages Act (Act 55 of 1949), the Group Areas (Act 41 of 1951), and the Reservation of Separate Amenities Act (Act 49 of 1953). Sport in general therefore officially became a segregated affair with the right to represent South Africa internationally reserved for white athletes.

In reaction, the black community embarked on a civil disobedience movement, the "Defiance of Unjust Laws Campaign" in 1952. Sports organizations in turn established the Coordinating Committee for International Recognition (CCIR) in 1955 to push for the institution of non-racial sport and for the granting of international recognition. Against this challenge, the South African government enacted new legislation to establish state control over professional boxing and wrestling.

National Control, Defiance and Protest, 1955–1970

On February 12, 1955, the South African National Wrestling Control Board (SANWCB) came into being following the promulgation of the Boxing and Wrestling Control Act (No. 39 of 1954). Beyond establishing a regulatory regime in conjunction with the Departments of Justice and Police, it empowered four provincial boards to control professional wrestling at the grassroots level while the national body acted as a supervisory authority.[63]

From the outset, the national board placed new restrictions on the activities of both wrestlers and promoters. In addition to a ban of certain unorthodox grips/ holds, masked wrestling was prohibited. The prohibited grips or holds, among others, included strangling or any hold that impedes breathing, biting, gouging, or deliberate kicking with foot or knee, hitting with a closed fist, forearm, or elbow, and spitting at an opponent. None of these, according to the National Board, "are anywhere regarded as a wrestling grip and thus constituted foul play and dirty fighting."[64] As far as masked wrestling, other than those with an established reputation who were allowed a 12-month extension, no new applicants were allowed. This order was motivated by the fact that more than one masked wrestler were performing under the same ring name. This, in the view of the Board, constituted a form of public fraud. The public, it therefore asserted, should not be misled "by showmen who are, in fact, imposters in so far as the sport of wrestling is concerned."[65] As before, the police were granted full powers to intervene at events. Another unwelcome measure was the mandatory payment of an entertainment tax or levy of 3.75 percent on gross income. Promoters and wrestlers, irrespective of race, were therefore placed at a distinct disadvantage.

The new system was designed by a small group of bureaucrats from the former amateur provincial boards. They were not only opposed to the democratic election of officials, but also against giving blacks and promoters or wrestlers of all races representation in the new system. The general consensus was that fighting men and their promoters lacked "the executive ability which is essential on a board of control" and that blacks were children "who has to be ruled by a firm hand."[66] In direct response to the CCIR's efforts to secure recognition for black sportspersons—an action that many white administrators resented—future representation was to be reserved for "broadminded" persons rather than extremists, i.e., anti-apartheid activists.[67] As expected, Regulation 4 of the Act explicitly forbade interracial competition.[68]

During the first years of its existence, the SANWCB actively ignored black wrestling. No statistics in this regard were reflected in any of its annual reports or audited financial statements.[69] In the absence of a national register of all licensed wrestlers, officials, and promoters, black wrestling was regarded as non-existent as it entered the 1960s. Developments within black sports, however soon changed this dismissive attitude.

Upon the failure of the CCIR to achieve its objectives, black sports bodies established the South African Sports Association (SASA) in 1958 to campaign for the inclusion of their athletes into representative South African teams. Representative of an estimated 70,000 sportsmen and women across the ethnic divide, SASA attempted to negotiate with its white counterparts. This, however, failed, forcing the organization to directly lobby international control bodies in hopes of enacting change.[70] It also tried to pressure sponsors of white events to make change a precondition for financial support.[71] In retaliation, the apartheid government refused travel documents to SASA representatives in the hope of curtailing their activities.

On March 29, 1961, the Nationalist government declared to the world that it would not allow the country to be represented by integrated teams in international sports. To add insult to injury, the same declaration announced that no mixed teams from abroad were to be allowed to visit and compete. Government institutions were also placed under strict orders to enforce the applicable legislation and to prevent any undermining of the system.[72] As a result, various upcoming tours of international teams were cancelled, which equally deprived white sportsmen and -women of foreign competition.

More attuned to political developments, the SANWCB's annual reports indicated a growth in the number of black participants from 10 in 1960 and 21 in 1962. Only two officials were, however, registered.[73] Official reports generally failed to record any and created the impression that none were hosted. Newspaper reports, however, indicated that at least one major event was hosted in March 1963 by black promoters.[74] This came at a time when SASA, having evolved into the South African Non-Racial Olympic Committee (SANROC), replaced the demand for desegregation with a new vision of society and called for an international boycott and the destruction of segregated sport.[75]

During 1964, the Cape Provincial Board notified its national counterpart of the participation of a group of black wrestlers and promoters in a number of unsanctioned events. When confronted by the police, the offenders pleaded innocence and indicated that they were offering their services for free. This prevented the police from any further action.[76] At the same time reports emerged of the existence of a radical grouping that threatened to end the control of the all-white boards.[77] This was an ominous development as it represented a direct challenge to the status quo. A review of the regulations therefore became an urgent priority.

The task of reviewing the regulations was delegated to the national police commissioner and the state law advisor. As a temporary measure, the issuing of permits to blacks was suspended.[78] On the other side of the political spectrum, the SA Amateur Karate Association, a sister organization of the SANWCB, lobbied the authorities to promulgate legislation to ban non-whites from learning karate. This, it was hoped, would pave the way for black exclusion from other sports such as wrestling.[79]

Faced with suspended permits, black administrators and grapplers formed Western Province Wrestling Promotions (WPWP) on May 30, 1965. The organization's ultimate objective was to fully control all non-white wrestling. Realizing the strength of the establishment, the WPWP decided to choose the path of cooperation and formally applied for a promoter's license.[80] This was a victory for the wrestling establishment. The provincial board in turn offered them its support and access to its training facilities.[81] Twelve months later these promises, however, remained unfulfilled.

With the promulgation of the Separate Amenities Act (Act 49 of 1953), mixed race audiences at events were effectively outlawed. This directly impacted on the profitability of featured events. Although some promoters wanted to host mixed audiences, most public indoor venues were too small for the installation of segregated seating. This forced event organizers to use open-air venues, a situation which was wholly unfavorable for wrestling. In addition, promoters had to negotiate with the Department of Community Development for permission to open events to all races. Such applications were frequently delayed, withheld, or even cancelled at the last minute.[82] Even hosting events at fit-for-purpose venues, with separate entrances for the different groups, were no guarantee that approval would be granted. This left promoters, wrestlers, and black fans frustrated.[83] Excluded from equal participation, black wrestlers resorted to emigration in pursuit of a proper professional career. This was a common phenomenon in other sports such as weightlifting, cricket, and rugby. Wrestler Cecil February, who emigrated to the USA and became known abroad as the "African Lion" and "Champion of Africa," established a record of 53 wins, four draws, and only three losses.[84]

By June 1967, new concerns about the decline in the number of new wrestlers joining the profession arose within the white ranks. While the debate about interventions in this regard continued, a three-person Commission of Inquiry from the International Amateur Wrestling Federation (IAWF) arrived to investigate racial discrimination in South African sport in October 1968. In a classic case of mistiming, the national board had recently implemented its first all-white grading system for championship fights, which did not help their cause.[85]

Ensuring black compliance was easy; reigning-in the recalcitrant among the white wrestling establishment was less so. White wrestler and promoter Bull Hefer in particular was a thorn in the flesh of national authorities. Following the introduction of the regulations, Hefer lobbied the Ministry of Justice for either an exemption or the total withdrawal of the regulations.[86] This call was strongly resisted by the national board for whom the tax levy was their main source of income. They also resisted attempts to change any of the other regulations. Faced with a conflict that could derail the regulatory regime, the SANWCB was ordered to resolve the differences. Upon their failure, the Ministry temporarily suspended implementation pending reconsideration of all submitted representations.[87]

In defiance of the regulations, Hefer refused to submit the mandatory documentation detailing his operations. In addition, he moved his tournaments from the urban centers to far-off country towns such as Kimberley where police and regulatory control was less strict. The distance of these venues from the major population centers, also turned oversight into an expensive undertaking. While others were convicted, Hefer merely received warnings and temporary suspensions.[88] This open bias was motivated by the Board's desire to secure Hefer's buy-in for the launch of a system of national and provincial champions. Hefer resented the fact that the board would have absolute control over finances derived from these events while all the leading wrestlers were under contract with him. He could, therefore bargain from a position of strength.[89]

When Hefer appeared for his disciplinary hearing on March 23, 1968, he was unrepentant. He demanded the scrapping of the regulations and the board's weight limits on overseas wrestlers. He also made his participation conditional pending amendments to the regulation. The board relented and granted exemption from the weight limits but refused to scrap the levy.[90] Among the wrestlers imported under this dispensation were the likes of Wladek "Killer" Kowalski (a star for Vince McMahon Sr.'s WWWF), Tarzan Taborda, and Samson Burke. Black wrestling featured nowhere in this debate.

From Multi-National Sport to Multi-Racial Racial Wrestling, 1970–1988

Upon South Africa's suspension from the IAWF in July 1970 as a result of its racial policies, wrestling authorities had to revise their game plan.[91] This came in the form of the announcement of a new government sport policy, the so-called "multi-national sports policy" announced on April 3, 1971. In comparison to strict apartheid sport, the new policy allowed for limited inter-racial mixing.[92] The authorities were, however, adamant that the new direction did not constitute a move towards integrated sport.[93] In line with these developments, the National Board appealed to provinces to "try to put non-white wrestling on a sound footing."[94]

Headed by a conservative executive, the first acts of the controlling body were of a minimalist nature. When Dalla Desai, an Indian wrestler, died of a heart attack after a contest in Durban on December 1, 1970, the national Board voted a donation of R30 to the widow.[95] This allocation was, however, never cashed by the family and by March 1971 had to be reclaimed by the Board. Stuck in the past, its grading lists, continued to exclude black wrestlers.⁹⁶ Adherence to the apartheid blueprint therefore undermined even the smallest of reconciliatory gestures.

Despite efforts by the national board, the number of multi-national wrestling events remained low. Key pieces of legislation, such as the Separate Amenities Act, that outlawed shared facilities ensured that wrestling events remained segregated affairs. By the end of 1972, eight non-white events in comparison to 142 exclusively white ones were held. Twelve months later, the number of registered black wrestlers and promoters in Cape Town dropped to one. This was in contrast with the previous year when the figure stood at 14 wrestlers, eight officials, and two promoters, respectively. Furthermore, tournaments remained split along racial lines. The national report thus noted: "It seems that the sport and specifically tournaments are not supported by the non-white public when it is organised by their own people. In the few cases where non-whites were allowed to attend White tournaments, the events were well-supported."⁹⁷ This notwithstanding, Bull Hefer's request in March 1974 to be allowed to host professional and exhibition wrestling matches in Johannesburg's black township, Soweto, was refused.⁹⁸ Similarly, participation lists remained all-white, and no blacks were invited to a roundtable discussion between the authorities and wrestlers in June 1974 aimed at forging a better working relationship.⁹⁹

Realizing the importance of black wrestling role models for the further growth of the sport, the SACBPW licensed the importation of high-profile wrestlers of Indian descent for local contests. The first to be imported under this scheme was Madjit (or Majid) or Ackra (or Akra), the son of 1936 Olympic wrestler and professional icon Karam Rasul Kashmiri or Accra or Great Accra as he was known in the 1940s and 50s.¹⁰⁰ In addition, the first non-white championship fight was approved for the SA Welterweight title. At the end of 1974, the annual report noted the registration of 28 black wrestlers, three promoters, and 12 officials in the Cape Province as well as five tournaments hosted. The authorities ascribed this "much improved" situation, to the visit of Ackra ("the foreign non-white" as it was termed) in the country.¹⁰¹ A year later, the numbers showed an unprecedented 56 registered wrestlers, four promoters, and 22 officials, respectively, and 17 tournaments. Although inter-racial matches were not yet in the cards, the Department of Sport & Recreation saw fit to appeal to administrators to unite against "the communist onslaught," i.e., anti-apartheid forces.¹⁰²

On June 16, 1976, the country exploded in an orgy of violence following a protest march of black students against political exclusion and inferior education in Soweto, Johannesburg. As a result of a police clampdown and the declaration of a State of Emergency, a significant number of people were killed, detained, or exiled. Under the emergency regulations, mass gatherings in black areas, including sports events, were subjected to strict security controls. Unsurprisingly, the number of non-whites in professional wrestling, both wrestlers and promoters, dropped to 16. As the result of suspended licenses, only two non-white events were hosted.[103]

Realizing the futility of maintaining segregated sport, political authorities permitted sporting codes to run their own affairs from the beginning of 1977. This allowed mostly-foreign black professionals and whites to compete at the same venues. Professional wrestling was one of the first to benefit from this concession. From five events in its first year, it increased to 49 by the end of the decade. This dealt a mortal blow to exclusively black wrestling and pushed the remaining four black promoters into a struggle for economic survival. Cape Town, once the center of domestic black wrestling, ceased hosting events. For their own purposes, the board found it convenient to ascribe the demise of black wrestling to poor organization.[104] In light of rapidly changing political circumstances and changes made by sister sports organizations, the question of black representation on its national and provincial committees reached the agenda.[105]

Black representation, however, posed its own challenges. Left largely to their own devices, black promoters struggled to comply with the board's regulations. More often than not, they remained in breach, which automatically led to the suspension of their licenses. By April 1982, it stripped Ringsport Promotions of its license for "flagrant flouting of the rules and regulations, as well as his unfavourable record."[106] In addition, a new agency, Mia Promotions, following a chaotic tournament and a near diplomatic incident, in the independent but politically controversial homeland of the Republic of Transkei, led the establishment to adopt a wait-and-see attitude as far as representation was concerned.[107] Fearing that these "bad tendencies may spread to the rest of the country"; the SANWCB accepted no non-white nominations for new executives.[108] Similarly, championship challenges continued to exclude black wrestlers. By the end of 1983, the official reports indicated that no black promoters were left in either the Cape Province or Transvaal. Only one Durban-based promoter, PJ Maharaj, was left to carry the flag for black professional wrestling. Without acknowledging its own complicity, the board yet again blamed this situation on black promoters' poor organizational abilities.

Following the introduction of the Tri-cameral parliamentary system in 1984, granting "Coloureds" and Indians representation in public decision-making, wrestling authorities, like all others, were confronted by a new set of dynamics. Blacks now also had to be included in its affairs. In addition, a new militancy amongst white promoters led to a call for "meaningful, ventilative dialogue" between the "two constitutive parts of wrestling; the promotors and the professional wrestlers."[109] Sensing the new winds of political change, Hefer and Kohne & Cohen Promotions, the two leading white promoters, opportunistically, questioned the whites-only grading system.[110]

Sensing an ulterior motive and some opportunism, given the silence of all the white promoters over an extended period about the need for change and the inclusion of blacks, Alwyn Burger, chairman of the Board, questioned their motives and in a fit of rage even resorted to name-calling.[111] Change was therefore temporarily delayed until 1985.

On February 24, 1985, black wrestler Abdul Kader issued a challenge to hold a bout for the vacant SA Middleweight title. This was apparently a repeat of a former application which was ignored for more than 12 months. Upon receipt of the third application, the Cape Provincial Board resolved to "write a letter to wrestler A. Kader commending him for his continued state of fitness and general exemplary high standard of wrestling in this province."[112] Despite a number of further requests to have a match for the title, the matter remained unsolved. When the issue could not be skirted any more, the national board informed its provincial counterpart in May that the matter was referred to a special sub-committee for investigation. Four further requests followed, none of which were supported by the Cape board. Pushed by the ongoing refiguring of the South African political system, the sub-committee, however, had no real choice but to accept and therefore recommended that the challenge be accepted. A meeting with all the registered promoters was therefore set for September 21, 1985, to plot a way forward for professional wrestling in South Africa.[113]

Amongst those present at the meeting were Essack Allie of Ringsport Promotions, Willie Kohne, and PJ Maharaj, known for his Natal operations. At the meeting the promoters argued and defended their right as businessmen with common objectives, not as representatives of particular racial groups. The issues on the agenda thus concerned the profitability of their operations. Among these were the scrapping of all racial references in tournament applications, revocation of the ban on Sunday wrestling, and control over wrestler poaching.[114] Most of these changes were readily accepted. It was, however, still far from the full deregulation of the sport. When Abdul Kader became the first black South African national champion on December 2, 1985, after defeating Gert Strydom, professional wrestling was set on the path of total integration. This was followed by the merger of the promotional agencies of Cohen, Maharaj and Kohne on January 14, 1986, to form World Wide Wrestling Promotions. Integration therefore became irreversible. Fifteen months later, on March 22, 1988, the SANWCB was formally abolished and the sport deregulated.

Conclusion

Professional wrestling was a late development within Cape Town's black community and was directly linked with the activities of local physical culture clubs. These clubs were primarily geared towards the building of an alternative masculinity through men whose skills transcended sectarian and racial divides, allowing them to integrate effortlessly into white-dominated society. Its growth as a form of sport/entertainment was, however, severely constrained by legalized racial discrimination and strict regulatory regimes that made entry into the profession extremely difficult.

During the first phase of pro wrestling's development in Cape Town, the regime used the WPBOCPW to protect municipal property and to curb violence in order to protect the public from professional wrestling's "brutalising" effects. In this situation, the practical imperative aligned seamlessly with the moral one. This regulatory regime was, however, short-lived and faltered at the hands of profit-driven entrepreneurs. This inaugurated a short period of limited control which aided the further development of black participation in pro wrestling.

With the formal promulgation of apartheid in 1948, Cape Town boasted both a new pool of black wrestlers and the debut of its first three promoters of color. This positive development was soon reversed by the promulgation of the Professional Wrestling Act (1954) and the concomitant establishment of the SA National Wrestling Control Board in 1955 to enforce national compliance with the law aimed at bringing order. From the start, the board exercised tight control over the profession as a whole. As a result, promoters across the racial divide resisted by refusing to comply with the statutory regulations through the hosting of unauthorized bouts and deliberate withholding of audited financial statements on which the payment of a special entertainment tax was based. Such organized resistance, was, however, of short duration, with black promoters facing police action, the withholding of operating and tournament permits, and exclusion from the Wrestlers' Benevolent Fund. In contrast, white promoters such as Bull Hefer, due to their access to the political authorities and control over the best wrestlers, got away with a mere slap on the wrist. Political developments in the 1970s, particularly the international sports boycott which led to the country's exclusion from a number of international sports bodies, forced fundamental changes. With the changes in the political system in 1984 that gave black people direct representation in parliament, blacks had to be fully included into the system. When Abdul Kader became the first black all-South Africa welterweight champion in 1985, the old system crumbled, and three years later professional wrestling was deregulated.

NOTES

1. For a scholarly overview of traditional wrestling in Africa, see Scott T. Carroll, "Wrestling in Ancient Nubia," *Journal of Sport History* 15, no. 2 (Summer 1988), 121–37; Mahaman L. Sériba, "Traditional Wrestling in Niger: Between State Voluntarism and Ancestral Symbolism," *Tydskrif vir Letterkunde* 42, no. 2 (2005), 18–32; Patricia Louw, "Games,

Tradition and 'Being Human' in Ayi Kwei Armah's *The Healers*," *Inkanyiso: Journal of Human and Social Sciences* 4, no. 2 (2012); Matthew Carotenuto, "Crafting Sport History Behind Bars: Wrestling with State Patronage and Colonial Confinement in Kenya," *History in Africa*, August 2015, 1–33; and Cheikh Tidiane Lo, "Wrestling in Senegal: A Historical and Ethnographic Study," unpublished Research paper, Department of Folklore & Ethnomusicology, Indiana University Bloomington, 2014, 4–5, https://www.researchgate.net/profile/Cheikh_Lo/publication/260481208_Cheikh_Tidiane_Lo_Wrestling_in_Senegal_A_Historical_and_Ethnographic_Study/links/0c9605316bd79b91b0000000.pdf (accessed April 19, 2016).

2. Michael Tripp, *Persistence of Difference: A History of Cornish Wrestling*, unpublished PhD dissertation, University of Exeter, May 2009, 208–210.

3. KAB, SRP 1/1/17: Union of South Africa Votes and Proceedings of the House of Assembly and Questions and Replies: Third Session, Fourth Parliament, 1923, 63.

4. "Tom Cannon—Champion Wrestler of the World," *The Referee* (Sydney), May 28 1887, 7.

5. "Wrestling in South Africa," *The Referee*, July 14, 1897, 6.

6. These styles are grouped under the "loose" or "free styles" of wrestling "that allow fighters to seize almost any grip they can find." The difference between the two, however, is that in Greco-Roman "any holds below the waist are forbidden in addition to other prohibited grips and attacks." See Donald Sayenga, "The Problem of Wrestling 'Styles' in the Modern Olympic Games: A Failure of Olympic Philosophy," *Citius, Altuis, Fortius* 3, no. 3 (Autumn 1995), 23.

7. "Personal Notes," *The Otago Daily Times* (Otago, NZ), September 5, 1903, 8.

8. "Anglo-American League," *Western Star and Roma Advertiser* (Toowoomba, Queensland), July 16, 1898, 2.

9. Tripp, *Persistence of Difference*, 208.

10. Chris Greyvenstein, *The Fighters: A Pictorial History of SA Boxing from 1881* (Cape Town: Don Nelson, 1981), 27.

11. Within these ranks were the likes of W. McKenzie, Jim McMurdo (the "Scottish South African boxer"), and Peter Nogert (the "Boer wrestler"), all of whom ventured into prize-fighting overseas at the start of the first decade of the 20th century. See "Which Is the Better Means of Self-Defense?" *The Referee* (Sydney, NSW), May 3, 1911, 8.

12. The key sports in which significant developments took place were cricket, association football, rugby football and field hockey.

13. See "Sport on the 'Fields,'" *The Cape Monthly Magazine* 11 (November 1873), 120 and "Health and Happiness: A Lay Sermon," *The Cape Monthly Magazine* 11 (November 1873), 305.

14. Andre Odendaal, "South Africa's Black Victorians: Sport and Society in South Africa in the Nineteenth Century," in J.A. Mangan, ed., *Pleasure, Profit, Proselytism: British Culture and Sport at Home and Abroad, 1700–1914* (London: Frank Cass, 1988), 199–200.

15. V. Bickford-Smith, *Ethnic Pride and Racial Prejudice in Victorian Cape Town: Group Identity and Social Practice, 1875–1902* (Cambridge: Cambridge University Press, 1995), 149.

16. Francois Cleophas, "The African Political Organisation's Contribution to South African Sport, 1909–1914," *African Journal for Physical, Health Education, Recreation and Dance* 16, no. 1 (March 2010), 174.

17. See "Hackenschmidt's Visit," *Poverty Bay Herald* (Gisborne, NZ), January 21, 1910, 2, and "Hackenschmidt Amongst the Zulus," 4.

18. *A.P.O. Official Organ of the African People's Organisation* 6, no. 177 (December 20, 1919), 9.

19. *A.P.O. Official Organ of the African People's Organisation* 4, no. 95 (January 25, 1913).

20. Cody Perkins, "Coloured Champions: Wrestling with the Color Bar and Competing Ideals of Masculinity in South African Athletics, 1936–1960," unpublished conference paper, presented April 12, 2014, at the Sport in Africa and the Global South: Ten Years—What's Next? Conference, Ohio University, Athens, Ohio, 3.

21. See *A.P.O. Official Organ of the African People's Organisation* 5, no. 114 (October 16, 1913), 10, and the edition of January 10, 1914, 11.

22. See *A.P.O. Official Organ of the African People's Organisation* 5, no. 129 (March 21, 1914), 10, and the edition of January 10, 1914, 11.

72 Part I. Race

23. John Griffiths, "All the World's a Stage: Transnationalism and Adaptation in Professional Wrestling Style c. 1930–1945," *Social History* 40, no. 1 (2015), 40.
24. "Why Not Wrestling?" *The Sun*, October 14, 1932.
25. "Amateur Wrestling for Charity: Tourney in Drill Hall," *The Cape Argus*, November 1935.
26. Griffiths, "All the World's a Stage," 41.
27. This information was gleaned from various minute and correspondence books of the South African Rugby Football Board currently in and available from the museum collection of the South African Rugby Union, the successor body to the first mentioned organization.
28. Hendrik Snyders, "Preventing Huddersfield: The Rise and Decline of Rugby League in South Africa, c. 1957–1965," *The International Journal of the History of Sport* 28, no. 1 (2011), 9–31.
29. "Inside Transvaal National Sporting Club: Strictly Amateur Organization," *The Referee*, June 22, 1930, 13.
30. "All-in-Wrestling Not Banned: City Council Agrees to Investigate Control," *The Cape Times*, August 31, 1934.
31. G. Kent, *A Pictorial History of Wrestling* (Feltham: Spring Books, 1968), 193.
32. "All-in-Wrestling Not Banned: City Council Agrees to Investigate Control," *The Cape Times*, August 31, 1934.
33. "All-in-Wrestling," *The Cape Argus*, August 30, 1934.
34. See "In Defence of All-in-Wrestling: Mr. Berman's Idea Is Ridiculous," *The Cape Argus*, August 30, 1934, and "All-In Wrestling to Be Banned? Readers Tilt at City Council," *The Cape Argus*, August 29, 1934.
35. "All In," *The Cape Times*, August 29, 1934.
36. "Unsatisfactory End to All-In Wrestling—Who Won?" *The Cape Argus*, August 27, 1934.
37. The founding organizations represented on the Transvaal Board of Control for Professional Wrestling were the South African Amateur Wrestling Union, the South African Olympic and British Commonwealth and Empire Games Association, the Transvaal National Sporting Club, and the *Rand Daily Mail* newspaper. This body secured an agreement with the City of Johannesburg and the Wanderers Sports Club in the city to use its facilities for the hosting of professional wrestling bouts.
38. KAB, Municipality of Cape Town (forthwith 3/CT): Wrestling in Municipal Premises, 4/1/5/123: Extract from minutes of meeting of the Improvements and Parks Committee held on September 17, 1934; See also letter D.W. Hopkirk, Esq.: Cape Province National Sporting Club—The Town Clerk, City of Cape Town, September 12, 1934.
39. KAB, 3/CT: Wrestling in Municipal Premises, 4/1/5/123, Town Clerk—ER Bartlett, Esq., October 12, 1934.
40. KAB, 3/CT: Wrestling in Municipal Premises, 4/1/5/123: The Western Province Board of Control for Professional Wrestling. Amongst the nominations was Tromp van Diggelen, proprietor of the Tom Van Diggelen Institute of Scientific Physical Culture.
41. KAB, 3/CT: Wrestling in Municipal Premises, 4/1/5/123: Nominations for the Proposed Board of Control for Professional Wrestling in the Cape Province. The first executive consisted of Ronald Miller, W. Sudell, B.F. Jearey and Dr. H. Cohen with E.R. Bartlett as secretary.
42. KAB, 3/CT: Wrestling in Municipal Premises, 4/1/5/123, Transvaal Board of Control for Professional Wrestling—The Town Clerk, Cape Town, February 8, 1935.
43. The Executive Committee of the Transvaal Board of Control for Professional Wrestling was JF Vercuil, President of the SA Amateur Wrestling Union; G. Twomey, Life Member, SA National Amateur Boxing Association, and Vice Chairman, S.A. Olympic and British Empire Games Association; H. Carter, Chairman of the Transvaal National Sporting Club; Ludwig Japhet, Vice-Chairman of the Transvaal Sporting Club; and J. Sacks, Sporting Editor, *Rand Daily Mail*.
44. "Miscellaneous Notes," *The Newcastle Morning Herald and Miners' Advocate* (New South Wales), November 16, 1889, 1.

45. "Wrestling: Sutherland and Dinnie—Wrestling in South Africa," *The Referee*, June 22, 1898, 6.
46. KAB3/CT: Wrestling in Municipal Premises, 4/1/5/123: The Western Province Board of Control for Professional Wrestling—Constitution.
47. SARFB Letter Book, 1913–22: Secretary—The Hon. Sir Frederick de Waal: Administrator of the Cape Province, February 9, 1920.
48. KAB, 3/CT: Wrestling in Municipal Premises, 4/1/5/123: The Western Province Board of Control for Professional Wrestling—By-Laws Governing Professional Wrestling Contests in the Western Province.
49. "'We, too, have our mat men': Wrestlers Who Train to Excel," *The Cape Standard*, May 18, 1936, 10.
50. Sam Sterling, "The Masked Marvel: The Professional Life Story of Johannes Van der Walt," *Fight*, October 1948, 28–32.
51. "City Council and Wrestling: Control No Longer Necessary—Board Chairman's Letter," *The Cape Argus*, November 17, 1937.
52. "Advantages of a Sporting Club: Interview with Mr. L. Japhet—Special Mission to Cape Town," *Cape Times*, March 15, 1937.
53. Sam Sterling, *Die Gemaskerde Wonder* (Johannesburg: Die Goeie Hoop Uitgewers, 1948), 45–46.
54. KAB, 3/CT: Wrestling in Municipal Premises, 4/1/5/123: B574/5: Memorandum of Interview with the Chairman and Secretary of the Transvaal National Sporting Club, Monday, March 15, 1937. Also see Letter Honorary Secretary: Board of Control for Professional Wrestling—Messrs Ashmead & Gragan, 17 February 1937.
55. Cleophas, "The African Political Organisation's Contribution to South African Sport, 1909–1914," 212.
56. Van der Walt, formerly a Johannesburg municipal tram operator, was discovered by Henry Irslinger. Between 1934 and 1960, as a wrestling professional, both masked and unmasked, he scored 111 wins, 21 defeats and 52 draws, having fought in Europe, the United States, the United Kingdom, and Asia. During this time he scored victories against some of the world's foremost heavyweight wrestlers. In April 1938 he became the British Empire heavyweight champion after defeating George Penchoff in Johannesburg.
57. Sam Sterling, *Die Gemaskerde Wonder* (Johannesburg: Die Goeie Hoop Uitgewers, 1948), 25, 46, 91, 93.
58. KAB, SRP 1/3/50: Union of South Africa: Debates of the House of Assembly (Hansard): Second Session—Eight Parliament, February 3–June 16 1939; Columns 385–91, February 15, 1939.
59. "Professional Wrestling: Jim Battle in Hectic Battle with the 'Tiger,'" *The Sun*, December 10, 1948.
60. "No Tears for Malan," *New Age*, November 4, 1954, 3.
61. Among the new entrants were Mat ("The Incomparable") October, "Young" Hussein Enus ("The Black Masked Marvel"), "Terrible" Turner, and "Flash" Rademeyer.
62. "Main Bout to Be Broadcast by S.A.B.C.," *The Sun*, July 29, 1949.
63. KAB, Accessions A 2446; SA Wrestling Board of Control: Minutes, February 12, 1955.
64. KAB, Accessions A 2446; SA Wrestling Board of Control: Minutes, February 4, 1960.
65. KAB, Accessions A 2446; SA Wrestling Board of Control: Minutes, April 7, 1961.
66. KAB: SRP 1/4/143: Union of South Africa: Report of the Select Committee on the Subject of the Professional Boxing and Wrestling Control Bill [S.C. 5 –'54], 3.
67. KAB: SRP 1/4/143: Union of South Africa: Report of the Select Committee on the Subject of the Professional Boxing and Wrestling Control Bill [S.C. 5 – '54], 9–11.
68. KAB, Accessions A 2446; South African National Wrestling Control Board: Constituting Act and Regulations (Act No. 39 of 1954).
69. KAB, Accessions A 2446; SA Wrestling Board of Control: Minutes, September 5, 1960.
70. University of the Witwatersrand Historical Papers Archive, South African Institute

74   Part I. Race

of Race Relations Collection, AD 1715: D.A. Brutus, South African Sports Association—Appeal to All Olympic Councils, January 1, 1962.

71. University of the Witwatersrand Historical Papers Archive, South African Institute of Race Relations Collection, AD 1715: D.A. Brutus, South African Sports Association—The Manager: Hullett's Sugar Refinery, July 16, 1962.

72. Marc Keech, "The Ties That Bind: South Africa and Sports Diplomacy 1958-1963," *The Sports Historian* 21, no. 1, 75-76.

73. See KAB, Accessions: Verslag van die SA Nasionale Stoeibeheerraad en Finansiele state vir die tydperk 1 Januarie 1960-30 Junie 1960; as well as Memorandum from the SA National Wrestling Control Board SA Police Service, September 22, 1960.

74. "Wrestling Comeback," *The Cape Argus*, March 20, 1969.

75. Douglas Booth, "Hitting Apartheid for Six? The Politics of the South African Sports Boycott," *Journal of Contemporary History* 38, no. 3 (July 2003), 482.

76. KAB, Accessions A 2446; SA Wrestling Board of Control: Minutes, Minutes: April 19, 1963.

77. KAB, Accessions A 2446, Verslag van die SA Nasionale Stoeibeheerraad en Finansiele state vir die tydperk 1 Januarie 1964-30 Junie 1964; as well as Memorandum from the SA National Wrestling Control Board SA Police Service, September 22, 1964.

78. KAB, Accessions Verslag van die SA Nasionale Stoeibeheerraad en Finansiele state vir die tydperk 1 Januarie 1965-30 Junie 1965; as well as Memorandum from the SA National Wrestling Control Board SA Police Service, September 22, 1965.

79. "Attempt to Bar Coloureds from Karate Under Fierce Attack," *The Cape Argus*, May 5, 1965.

80. The Executive Committee of Western Province Wrestling Promotions consisted of the following office bearers: President: Richard Pieterse; Chairman: Sid Rule; Vice Chairman: Ron Eland; Secretary-Treasurer: E.D. Hellenberg; Assistant Secretary: Les Langenhoven; Match & Registration Secretary: Charlie Chan; Trustees: Keith Arendse and Enver Matthews; Additional Exco Members: Matt October and George Jacobs.

81. "New Wrestling Body Is Formed," *The Cape Argus*, May 31, 1965.

82. "New Venue for Mat Tourney," *The Cape Argus*, November 21, 1967.

83. "Still Waiting for News on Wrestling Ban," *The Cape Argus*, September 2, 1966.

84. "Coloured Wrestler Excels Overseas," *The Cape Argus*, August 19, 1967.

85. KAB, Accessions A 2446; SA Wrestling Board of Control: Minutes: October 18, 1969.

86. KAB, Accessions A 2446; SA Wrestling Board of Control: Minutes, April 7, 1961.

87. KAB, Accessions A 2446; SA Wrestling Board of Control: Minutes, February 4, 1960.

88. KAB, Accessions A 2446; SA Wrestling Board of Control: Minutes, April 7, 1961.

89. At the time that the idea of national championships was discussed, Hefer had control the largest number of high profile wrestlers including Manie Maritz, Percy Hall, Tarzan Jacobs and Jan Wilkens, all of who dominated the South African pro wrestling scene in the 1960s.

90. KAB, Accessions A 2446; SA Wrestling Board of Control: Minutes, March 23, 1968.

91. "S.A. Out of Wrestling," *The Cape Argus*, July 4, 1970.

92. Juan Klee, "Multinational Sport Participation Replaces Apartheid Sport in South Africa—1967-1978: The Role of BJ Vorster and PGJ Koornhof," *New Contree* 64 (July 2012), 165.

93. "Clarity on Mixed Sport," *The Cape Argus*, June 8, 1971.

94. KAB, Accessions A 2446; SA Wrestling Board of Control: Minutes: April 15, 1972.

95. "Wrestler Had Heart Attack," *The Cape Argus*, December 1, 1970.

96. KAB, Accessions A 2446; SA Wrestling Board of Control: Minutes: March 6, 1971.

97. KAB, Accessions A 2446: Die Suid Afrikaanse Nasionale Stoei Beheerraad: Jaarverslag January 1, 1973-December 31, 1973.

98. KAB, Accessions A 2446; SA Wrestling Board of Control: Minutes: March 9, 1974.

99. KAB, Accessions A 2446: Minutes of the Special Meeting of the SA National Wrestling Control Board, June 1, 1974. The invited wrestlers were provincial and national champions Percy Hall, Jan Wilkens, Percy Hall, Apollo, and Frikkie Alberts.

100. See biographical profile on http://www.wrestlingheritage.co.uk/wrestlersa.htm. The wrestler is also referred to as Mazid Akra of Pakistan (accessed May 20, 2016).
101. KAB, Accessions A 2446: Die Suid Afrikaanse Nasionale Stoei Beheerraad: January 1 1974–31 December 31, 1974.
102. KAB, Accessions A 2446: Minutes of the Special Meeting of the SA National Wrestling Control Board, October 24, 1975.
103. KAB, Accessions A 2446: Minutes of the Special Meeting of the SA National Wrestling Control Board, March 5, 1977.
104. KAB, Accessions A 2446; SA Wrestling Board of Control: Minutes: December 31, 1981.
105. KAB, Accessions: A.2446; SA Wrestling Board of Control: Minutes: March 29, 1980.
106. KAB, Accessions: A. 2446: Minutes of the Cape Provincial Wrestling Control Board, April 22, 1982.
107. The matter, which was discussed based on a verbal report from the Orange Free State-based member of the executive committee, was supposed to be followed up by a formal written report to the Department of Foreign Affairs for further handling through diplomatic channels. The official records of the national Board, however, contained no follow-up report or further discussion about the matter in subsequent meetings. The only logic deduction therefore is that Mia Promotions has generally failed to adhere to the standard regulations concerning the conduct of tournaments.
108. KAB, Accessions A 2446; SA Wrestling Board of Control: Minutes: Special meeting at Jan Smuts Airport, Johannesburg, June 18, 1983.
109. KAB Accessions A 2446; SA Wrestling Board of Control: Minutes: Letter of Savage, Jooste & Adams Inc.—The Secretary: SA National Wrestling Control Board, November 13, 1984.
110. KAB, Accessions A 2446; SA Wrestling Board of Control: Minutes: Letter Hefer, Kohne & Cohen Promotions—The Secretary: SA National Wrestling Control Board, May 5, 1981.
111. KAB, Accessions A 2446; SA Wrestling Board of Control: Minutes: Brig. AF Burger to the Chairmen: Provincial Wrestling Control Boards, August 30, 1984.
112. KAB, Accessions A 2446; Cape Provincial Control Board: Minutes of Meeting held on February 26, 1985.
113. KAB, Accessions A 2446; SA Wrestling Board of Control: Minutes of the Annual General Meeting, Pretoria, March 30, 1985.
114. KAB, Accessions A 2446; SA Wrestling Board of Control: Minutes: Meeting with Promoters September 21, 1985.

Nazis, Japs and Pearl Harbor Attacks
German and Japanese Stereotypes in American Professional Wrestling

AARON D. HORTON

This essay will examine the use of German and Japanese villains in American professional wrestling after World War II as a means of drawing crowds and money. More often than not, these characters played upon prevailing stereotypes in hopes of eliciting strong negative reactions and convincing spectators to spend money to see these villains get their comeuppance. While German stereotypes of the goose-stepping Nazi began to fade in the 1960s and 1970s, stereotypes of the sneaky and cowardly Japanese villain continued to manifest into the 1990s and beyond. This trend is due partly to divergent perceptions of the United States' primary antagonists of World War II, evident in wartime propaganda. More often than not, Americans tended to view Germans as essentially good people misled by Hitler and Nazi ideology. Japanese, on the other hand, were depicted through racist caricatures as an inherently untrustworthy and savage people. This paper will explore several decades of German and Japanese stereotypes in American pro wrestling to arrive at a better understanding of how promoters and performers willingly played upon lingering American prejudices in the interest of attracting spectators.

"Nazis"

Ethnic stereotypes go back to wrestling's early days, when European immigrants such as "The Golden Greek" Jim Londos were top babyfaces, while foreign attractions such as "The Terrible Turk" Youssuf Ishmaelo or Indian grappler The Great Gama served as exotic foils for crowd favorites, drawing heel heat by playing on contemporary American racial prejudices.[1] In this regard, post–World War II German and Japanese stereotypes in wrestling were simply the latest manifestations of an old promotional tactic, one that would also utilize evil Russian, Iranian, and Arab heels in the future. This comparison is especially interesting, however, because what began as an exploitation of lingering World War II animosities toward stereotypical German and Japanese "unrepentant" villains ultimately revealed underlying ethnic and racial prejudices as the memory of the war faded further into the past. Beginning in the 1970s, German wrestlers gradually abandoned Nazi gimmicks in favor either of more generalized heel personas or, most notably in the case of Fritz von Erich, became beloved babyface icons. Japanese wrestlers in America would, however, continue largely to embody base stereotypes into the 1990s.

After World War II, "The Teuton Terror" Hans Schmidt was the first of many German heels to capitalize on lingering animosities among North American fans. Born Guy Larose in Quebec, the aspiring wrestler failed to achieve much success under his own name. A fateful 1951 encounter with Boston promoter Paul Bowser would transform Schmidt into one of the most hated men in wrestling. According to Bowser, Larose "looked like a German," and thus became Hans Schmidt, an arrogant, villainous heel who wrestled across North America against the top stars of his era, including Lou Thesz and Verne Gagne.[2] While Schmidt did not usually engage in the goose-stepping, Nazi-saluting antics of later German heels, he played the role of an arrogant, ruthless, and temperamental foreigner perfectly, drawing the ire of fans everywhere. As one of numerous examples, in a bout against Verne Gagne from the early 1950s, the television commentator refereed to Schmidt's tendency to lose his temper, a "Teutonic trait."[3] Despite his heel tactics and "Teutonic" behavior, Schmitt did not fit the Nazi stereotype performed by later wrestlers.

Karl von Hess was one of the first postwar wrestlers to fully embrace the Nazi gimmick, complete with goose-stepping and "Sieg Heil" salutes.[4] Born Frank Faketty to Hungarian immigrants in Michigan, Hess was inspired to adopt the gimmick in 1955 after encountering Kurt von Poppenheim (Jake Poppenheim), a local performer in the Pacific Northwest territory who played the role of an arrogant, monocle-wearing Prussian noble, but never that of a full-blown Nazi.[5] Thus, World War II United States Navy veteran Frank Faketty became the reviled Nazi Karl von Hess. The newly-dubbed Hess took the role of the unrepentant Nazi to new heights by yelling at crowds in German and appearing in doctored photos with Adolf Hitler and Martin Bormann. In an era known for violent fan reactions, Hess was assaulted numerous times by angry spectators, forcing Vincent J. McMahon, promoter in the DC-Baltimore territory, to admit to *The Washington Post* that Hess was "no Nazi" but simply used his persona to emphasize his role as a villain.[6] Such an admission was rare in the 1950s, and a clear indication of Hess' ability to rile crowds to the point of risking his personal safety.

No one embodies the changing presentations of German wrestlers in the United States better than Fritz von Erich. In 1953, Jack Adkisson was a struggling former college football player looking to make a living in professional wrestling. A German American from Texas, Adkisson began wrestling under his own name as a preliminary performer with little success. Desperate to distinguish himself and move up the cards, Adkisson changed his name to Fritz von Erich and began goose-stepping and "Sieg-heiling" his way across North America, infuriating crowds in the process.[7] His dreaded "Iron Claw" finishing hold, which involved clasping his opponent's forehead with his palm in a vice grip, not only displayed his heelish ruthlessness, but also evoked classical German imagery of "blood and iron" and iron crosses. Von Erich soon began teaming with his "brother" Waldo, a German-Canadian named Walter Sieber, and the two drew packed houses across the country both as singles and tag-team competitors. Waldo's finishing maneuver was, appropriately enough, called the "blitzkrieg," a kneedrop from the top rope. On September 23, 1966, von Erich founded his own wrestling company, Southwest Promotions, based out of Dallas, and promptly turned babyface by engaging in a feud with heel manager Gary Hart's stable of wrestlers.[8] Veteran wrestler Johnny Valentine explained the fans' willingness to accept the former Nazi as a hero, stating that "he was the people's bad guy ... if you're mean enough and tough enough, they ... respect you for that."[9] While Adkisson kept the "Fritz von Erich" name, he abandoned all pretense of being from Germany, instead embracing his Texas roots. Von Erich became a successful and popular promoter in the Dallas territory, and his company, rechristened World Class Championship Wrestling (WCCW), thrived throughout the 1970s and early to mid–1980s, largely through his use of sons David, Kerry, and Kevin von Erich as his top babyfaces. Thus the former Nazi and his handsome, athletic sons became iconic heroes, drawing thousands of spectators to regular cards at the Dallas Sportatorium and, periodically, at Texas Stadium, then-home of the Dallas Cowboys.

From the 1970s onward, German heels were no longer goose-stepping Nazis, but villains rather by virtue of a much vaguer foreign "otherness." Baron von Raschke was a prominent heel throughout North America, facing top stars such as the World Wide Wrestling Federation (WWWF) champion Bruno Sammartino, while utilizing von Erich's "iron claw" finisher. Like the German heels discussed above, the Baron was not actually German, but rather a Nebraska schoolteacher of German descent named Jim Raschke. Originally an unsuccessful babyface, Raschke adopted the "Baron" persona at the suggestion of Montreal heel performer Maurice "Mad Dog" Vachon. Almost immediately, Raschke saw his drawing power and paydays increase. Although Raschke did his fair share of goose-stepping, he never embraced the Nazi persona as Hess or von Erich had, drawing heat instead through his unique look (bald and constantly-grimacing, usually clad in sinister red-and-black robes), menacing promos, and in-ring viciousness.[10]

By the 1990s, German wrestlers (real or otherwise) were no longer compelled to play the roles of reviled villains in American pro wrestling. German bodybuilder Achim Albrecht, known in the ring as Brakus, was a minor star in American independent promotion Extreme Championship Wrestling (ECW), after briefly appearing in the World Wrestling Federation (WWF). In 1996, WWF television ran a series of promos featuring the heavily-muscled and -oiled Brakus growling, in German, that he was from Germany, weighed 300 pounds, and was coming to the WWF to destroy Vader, a top heel at the time.[11] Brakus was therefore being promoted as a powerful, manly babyface that would run rampant over the bad guys. As Fritz von Erich had demonstrated, American fans had largely become inured to the notion of the German "Nazi" heel, forcing promoters to find new ways to push German performers. Brakus failed to catch on, and his career in mainstream American wrestling was brief. This was not necessarily because American fans were unwilling to cheer for a German, but rather due to his lack of in-ring ability. Brakus' star potential was further, and perhaps irreparably, damaged in 1998 by his loss to the decidedly un-muscular Puerto Rican grappler Savio Vega in the ill-conceived WWF Brawl for All, a real boxing competition among mid-card wrestlers.[12]

"Das Wunderkind" Alex Wright, son of British wrestler Steve Wright and a German mother, began wrestling in World Championship Wrestling (WCW) in 1994 as a typical handsome babyface who danced to techno music before and after his matches. While relatively popular due to his good looks and athleticism, Wright failed to catch on as a top star, leading to a progression of unusual gimmicks including membership in the "Dancing Fools" trio with Disco Inferno and Japanese wrestler Magnum Tokyo and a stint as Berlyn, a Mohawk-sporting, sunglasses-wearing character who spoke at length in German about the superiority of his culture. The Berlyn character seems to have been inspired by the German industrial techno music scene, but it largely failed to evoke any significant response from fans.

Understandably, the vast majority of "German" wrestlers in America were not, in fact, German. One finds it difficult to imagine a native of Germany willing to feign support of the Nazi regime after 1945, especially because the lines between reality and fiction in professional wrestling tended to be highly blurred. The individuals, nearly all of them American or Canadian, who developed Nazi personas in the 1950s and 1960s drew tremendous heel heat and enjoyed great financial and professional success as a result of their willingness to play upon lingering resentments and prejudices among American fans. By the 1970s, however, decades of changing American perceptions of Germans and Germany in the postwar era had finally rendered the Nazi heel obsolete and unviable. From the 1970s until the end of the Cold War, promoters turned increasingly to Russian heels as their European villains of choice,[13] featuring a slew of sickle-and-hammer-sporting wrestlers such as Ivan and Nikita Koloff, Krusher Khrushchev, Nikolai Volkoff, and Boris Zhukov. The evolution of Japanese heels would, however, take a much different path.

"Japs" and Pearl Harbor Attacks

Prior to World War II, the first and most notable Japanese professional wrestler was Sorakichi Matsuda. Trained in sumo, Sorakichi immigrated to New York City in 1883, and soon thereafter began competing in the various wrestling styles popular in the United States. He became a feature attraction, wrestling against a wide array of opponents across the country. Contemporary periodicals such as *National Police Gazette* and the *San Francisco Chronicle* provided numerous match accounts, almost always referring to Sorakichi as "the Jap." Matches were often contested in several falls, usually a mixture of styles such as catch-as-catch-can, Greco-Roman, and "Japanese," meaning sumo. Most references to Sorakichi were complimentary of his athletic prowess and willingness to face much larger opponents (Sorakichi was said to weigh approximately 175 pounds), though there are frequent references to his tendency to rely on headbutts as well as "biting and scratching." Fans seemed largely sympathetic to the Japanese competitor, especially because he was normally smaller than his opponents. For example, in a notorious February 15, 1886, match in New York City, catch wrestler Evan "Strangler" Lewis applied a vicious leglock to Sorakichi, appearing to break the latter's leg (it was merely a pull or sprain, as it turned out), nearly causing a riot in the process.[14] Shocked by Lewis' brutality, fans booed, hissed, and, according to one account, demanded that "The Strangler" be hanged for injuring Sorakichi.[15] Such an outpouring of rage on behalf of "the Jap" is a particularly compelling indication that spectators did not always necessarily or unquestioningly support Americans against foreigners, even those who, like Sorakichi, were visibly "other." Contemporary accounts also employed racist terms and questionable quotations. For example, one account refers to Sorakichi as "the Celestial," a racial slur used in reference to Chinese immigrants, and supposed direct quotes from "the Jap" often have him speaking in stereotypical pidgin English: "You twistee my leggee, I twistee your leggee, too,"[16] "I makee a match,"[17] "You too muchee fightee ... you no likee a wrestler,"[18] and so on. Sorakichi died in 1888 of a sudden illness at the age of 32, but had left such an impression that one former opponent, Jack Carkeek, said of him in a 1902 interview with *Mirror of Life*, a British sports paper, that "the plucky little Jap" was "probably the cleverest man in the world at his weight."[19] William Muldoon, who had expressed opposition to boxing and wrestling bouts between black and white competitors, befriended Sorakichi after a series of bouts against him and later served as his second, a clear sign of the former's admiration for a man he continually referred to as "the Jap."[20] Despite the prejudices evident in media coverage of Sorakichi, he had clearly earned the respect of many of his peers and was far removed from later Japanese stereotypes in wrestling.

The first of many successful post–World War II Japanese heels was Mr. Moto, who debuted in 1950. Portrayed by Hawai'ian-born Masaru "Charlie" Iwamoto, a former sumo wrestler, the heel persona was based loosely on the crime-solving Mr. Moto character from a series of novels, radio plays, and films (starring the decidedly non–Asian Peter Lorre). The fictional Mr. Moto was inspired by another literary Asian detective, Charlie Chan, and both characters thoroughly embodied contemporary stereotypes.[21] Mr. Moto, the wrestler, would come to the ring wearing a traditional kimono, clog sandals, and small round glasses suggestive of those worn by former Japanese Defense Minister Hideki Tojo. Normally accompanied by a manservant named Suji Fuji, Mr. Moto performed elaborate pre-match rituals with the fastidiousness of legendary heel Gorgeous George, which both amused and infuriated spectators. He carried a traditional Japanese fan and often painted his nails, emphasizing his "otherness" to American audiences.[22] Most importantly for future Japanese heels, he performed a version of the traditional sumo salt-throwing ritual and would sometimes resort to throwing salt into opponents' eyes to gain an unfair advantage. In interviews, Moto spoke in broken English, a trope that would be repeated again and again by American-born Japanese heels. For example, in an interview on Los Angeles' "Hollywood Wrestling" in the 1950s, Moto proclaimed that "Japanese sumo exercise number one, I think." Later in the same series of interviews, "Classy" Freddie Blassie stated that he'd never heard such "vain, conceit [sic] talk like I heard outta that Jap."[23] Los Angeles promoter Mike LeBell explained his rationale for pushing the Moto heel character: "When he first started, we all hated the Japanese because of the war ... it was just great being able to root against the Japanese. It was mainly the Anglo population that we were asking, 'Come on down and let's kill this Jap.'"[24] Moto struck a chord with fans, and suffered numerous attacks both in and out of arenas. He was assaulted by a World War II veteran at a drugstore in Florida, slashed with broken glass by a female spectator during a March 1955 match in Washington, D.C., and even whacked in the toe with a hammer by The Destroyer (Dick Beyer)'s young son, sitting ringside and upset that his father was taking a beating from the heel. Internally, Moto was well-liked among his peers, and even served as booker (matchmaker/planner) for the Los Angeles territory after retiring from the ring.

A slew of Japanese heels followed in the footsteps of Mr. Moto. Toshiyuki "Harold" Sakata, a Japanese American born in Hawai'i, became the villainous, salt-throwing Tosh Togo in the early 1950s. Sakata would go on to much greater fame as an actor, known especially for his role as indestructible henchman Oddjob in the James Bond film *Goldfinger*. In the 1970s, a new generation of Japanese heels, almost all from Hawai'i, continued the ongoing tradition in American wrestling of the devious, salt-throwing, broken English-speaking Asiatic villain. Tor Kamata (McRonald Kamata) terrorized Calgary's Stampede Wrestling and numerous other territories,[25] while Mr. Fuji (Harry Fujiwara) and Professor Toru Tanaka (Charlie Kalani) became a successful tag team, especially in Vincent J. McMahon's WWWF. While Fujiwara was Japanese American, Kalani was, according to his wife Doris, "almost full-blooded Hawai'ian." In 1967, San Francisco promoter Roy Shire convinced Kalani that he could be far more successful as a Japanese villain. The newly-dubbed Toru Tanaka donned a kimono and began resorting to salt-throwing chicanery, propelling him to success alongside Fuji as two of the most successful Japanese heels of the 1970s and early 1980s. Kalani parlayed his in-ring fame into a film career, appearing in movies such as *The Running Man* and *Pee-Wee's Big Adventure*.[26] As one of countless possible examples of the persistence of the stereotype of the sneaky, deceitful Japanese heel, Vincent K. McMahon, working as a commentator for his father's WWWF, remarked at the beginning of a 1974 match between champion Bruno Sammartino and Mr. Fuji that the referee "better check [Fuji] over good," reminding viewers that the latter would most likely be in possession of an illegal weapon, probably salt for throwing in Sammartino's eyes.[27] Tojo Yamamoto (Harold Watanabe, a Japanese American from Hawai'i) was yet another notorious Japanese heel, working largely in the Memphis territory. His name was taken from World War II-era Japanese defense minister Hideki Tojo and Imperial Navy admiral Isoroku Yamamoto, and throughout the 1960s and early 1970s, he was one of the region's top heels. He later worked as a manager, and even turned babyface for a brief period, a rarity for "Japanese" heels in American wrestling, but likely a function of his long tenure in Memphis and familiarity to the territory's fanbase.[28]

In the 1970s and 1980s, one individual in particular bucked the trend of the evil Japanese heel, but only by making no mention of his Japanese heritage. Richard Blood from Florida, son of an American father and a Japanese mother, became popular babyface Ricky Steamboat in 1976. Florida promoter

Eddie Graham decided that Steamboat's good looks, friendly demeanor, and excellent in-ring work would make him a top star, and began billing him as the nephew of Hawai'ian star Sammy Steamboat.[29] Given the ongoing negative stereotypes surrounding Japanese wrestlers, Graham recognized that fans would be far more likely to accept Steamboat as a Hawai'ian hero, the inverse of native Hawai'ian Charlie Kalani's transformation into the dastardly Toru Tanaka. In both instances, the individual's appearance and charisma played key roles in the development of their personas. Tanaka was bulky and imposing, and far more suited to the role of a heel, hence he "became" Japanese to maximize his drawing power. Steamboat, on the other hand, with his muscular physique and good looks, "became" Hawai'ian to ensure that fans would accept him as a babyface.

It is important to note that while Japanese stereotypes prevailed in American wrestling, the development of pro wrestling in Japan, known as *puroresu* (an abbreviated *katakana* rendering of "pro wrestling"), followed a much different course. After World War II, former sumo Rikidozan (Mitsuo Momota) traveled to the United States and learned the art of American professional wrestling from Lou Thesz and Karl Gotch. Rikidozan founded the Japan Wrestling Alliance (JWA) in 1953, and wrestling became an overnight sensation as virtuous Japanese wrestlers battled nefarious American heels. Rikidozan became a national icon, an embodiment of Japanese pride and identity through his courageous struggles against cheating American opponents. In other words, Japanese wrestling employed the same tactics as American promoters, but in reverse.[30] Ironically, Rikidozan was a Korean adopted by a Japanese family, a fact that he carefully concealed to avoid Japanese racial prejudices. At its heart, wrestling is about maximizing revenues. American promoters knew that German and Japanese villains would draw crowds hoping to see them get their comeuppance, and Japanese promoters, beginning with Rikidozan, capitalized on postwar Japanese humiliation by providing spectacles in which virtuous Japanese heroes triumphed over arrogant and villainous American heels. American and other "gaijin" heels in Japan, from Lou Thesz in the 1950s, to brash, burly Texas brawler Stan "The Lariat" Hansen (arguably the most successful foreigner in the history of *puroresu*) in the 1980s and 1990s, to members of the Bullet Club faction running rampant in New Japan Pro Wrestling as of this writing, played to stereotypes of loud, brash, disrespectful Americans in the same manner as the sneaky, deceitful, salt-throwing Japanese heels in American wrestling.

Although Japan produced a slew of talented and successful wrestlers, few have achieved much success in the United States. Major Japanese stars such as Antonio Inoki and Shohei "Giant" Baba, both protégés of Rikidozan and founders of New Japan Pro Wrestling and All Japan Pro Wrestling, respectively, made periodic appearances in the United States. Interestingly, these native Japanese performers typically did not perform conventional Japanese heel stereotypes, but rather were promoted as competent and respectable foreign competitors. Both Inoki (WWWF Championship) and Baba (NWA World Championship) won major U.S. titles, though their reigns were brief. Such relatively fair treatment is due partly to the fact that both Inoki and Baba were successful and respected promoters, and in any case it is doubtful that they would have been willing to perform the roles of stereotypical Japanese heels.

In the 1970s and 1980s, two notable Japanese-born performers offered a new type of Japanese heel in American wrestling: the exotic Oriental mystic. Akihisa Mera began his career in the JWA, but came to the United States in the 1970s and achieved great success as The Great Kabuki. The Great Kabuki entered the ring wearing a large kabuki mask and robe, and painted his face in the style of an *oni*, a traditional Japanese demon. Kabuki's heel character stemmed from his exotic and mysterious "otherness" rather than the performance of the more conventional Japanese stereotypes mentioned above. Instead of throwing salt, Kabuki would often spew green mist into opponents' faces to gain the upper hand.[31]

In 1988, former Japanese amateur standout and emerging *puroresu* star Keiji Muto came to the United States, where he soon became The Great Muta, the "son" of Great Kabuki. Like Kabuki, Muta wore *oni* face paint and spewed green mist at opponents. Muta was featured frequently in main event matches, and became highly regarded among both fans and fellow wrestlers for his colorful, unusual mannerisms and high-flying in-ring style, which featured his "moonsault" finisher, a backflip from the top turnbuckle onto a prone opponent. Muto introduced the Muta character in Japan, and would often alternate between wrestling there as clean-cut Keiji Muto and the exotic and villainous Great Muta, who utilized his green mist as well as foreign objects to gain an advantage against opponents. While both Kabuki and Muta portrayed Japanese heels, they were villains by virtue of the exotic, mysterious "Oriental" personas rather than as typical salt-throwing Japanese antagonists.

After World War II, the term "Pearl Harbor" became widely used in wrestling as a verb describing *any* sneak attack by one wrestler against another. For example, when Canadian wrestler Earthquake (John Tenta) assaulted Hulk Hogan on *The Brother Love Show* (a spoof of popular contemporary televangelist programs such as those of Jimmy Swaggart and Jim Bakker) in 1990, frequent references were made to the former's "Pearl Harboring" of the popular hero. Beginning in the late 1990s, the usage of "Pearl Harboring" declined, especially with World Wrestling Entertainment's attempts to sanitize its presentation after becoming a publicly traded company in 1999.[32] On the surface, "Pearl Harboring" could be read as a highly racist usage, but I contend that the phrase became divorced from its original meaning, especially because it became a catch-all description of a villainous sneak attack, regardless of the heel's ethnicity. Although the usage could be considered inappropriate (likely the main reason the phrase fell out of use in the 1990s), there were far more egregious examples of negative Japanese stereotypes in the 1990s, just as "Pearl Harboring" was being phased out.

In the mid–1990s, the WWF was in a period of creative and financial decline. Hulk Hogan, the megastar of the 1980s and early 1990s, had left to pursue a largely unsuccessful acting career in 1993, only to sign with Ted Turner's World Championship Wrestling (WCW) in 1994. Vince McMahon sought to create another "Hulk Hogan" in Lex Luger, a former WCW star with a bodybuilder's physique, by appealing to American jingoism as ethnic stereotypes. In June 1993, Yokozuna defeated Hogan for the WWF championship in the latter's final match for the company until 2002. Yokozuna, portrayed by Samoan American Rodney Anoa'i, was a 550-pound monster with a sumo gimmick, complete with a traditional *mawashi* worn over tights. Yokozuna (the Japanese term for the highest rank in sumo) was managed by none other than former wrestler Mr. Fuji, who accompanied his charge wearing a traditional kimono and clog sandals, carrying a Japanese flag. WWF commentators were inconsistent when discussing Yokozuna's origins; early in his career, they referred to him as Japanese, but later began to claim he was a Samoan who had become a sumo champion in Japan (this was not, in fact, the case).

On July 4, 1993, Yokozuna held a bodyslam challenge aboard the USS Intrepid, an aircraft carrier. Both WWF stars and other professional athletes attempted to slam the massive champion, while Mr. Fuji gloated about American weakness.[33] Lex Luger, who began his career in the WWF as "The Narcissist," a self-absorbed vain heel, became "Made in the USA" when he arrived aboard the Intrepid via helicopter and successfully slammed Yokozuna to a massive pop (outburst of cheers) from the fans.[34] Luger then proceeded to feud with Yokozuna off and on for nearly a year. That McMahon believed a "Japanese" heel would be the perfect foil to make Luger into a patriotic babyface in 1993 is a clear indication of the enduring impact of Japanese stereotypes in American wrestling, nearly 50 years after World War II.

The 1990s saw several other stereotypical Japanese performers. In WCW, Kazuo "Sonny" Onoo served as manager for various heels, including wrestlers from New Japan Pro Wrestling, which had an exchange deal with Turner's organization. Since many of the Japanese performers spoke little or no English, Onoo was responsible for cutting promos (giving interviews) in which he denigrated American wrestlers and boasted of Japanese superiority (in broken English, of course). Most notoriously, at WCW's Hog Wild pay-per-view in 1996, a motorcycle-themed event in Sturgis, South Dakota, Onoo claimed he would ride his Kawasaki bike "like a Kamikaze" prior to his wrestler Bull Nakano's match against Madusa Miceli. Ironically, Onoo was a lead plaintiff in a November 1999 racial discrimination lawsuit against WCW, along with various other minority performers, claiming that new head of creative Vince Russo and various other company officials made racist statements and treated minority performers poorly.[35]

Possibly the most egregious and last notable Japanese stereotypes in American wrestling involved Kaientai, a group of wrestlers from the small Michinoku Pro promotion in Japan. In Japan, the various members of Kaientai were heels due to their brash, disrespectful behavior, an act copied later by Team No Respect in Atsushi Onita's Frontier Martial Arts Wrestling (FMW) promotion. Kaientai debuted in the WWF in 1998, and feuded with popular light heavyweight star Taka Michinoku, who had been a member of the group back in Japan. Initially, the storyline was fairly simple: Kaientai wanted Michinoku to join, and he refused, leading to a series of entertaining, high-flying bouts. Although the matches were athletically sound, American fans struggled to relate to a feud between Japanese wrestlers who spoke little English. Soon afterward, the group feuded with Val Venis (Sean Morley), who had a porn star gimmick. The group's manager and mouthpiece, Wally Yamaguchi, began bringing his "wife" and Taka's "sister," model Shian-Li Tsang, to the ring. Venis soon seduced her, leading Taka to join the heels and Yamaguchi to demonstrate how he planned to retaliate by slicing a sausage with a samurai sword while yelling, "I choppy-choppy your pee-pee!" on the August 3, 1998, edition of RAW.[36] Shortly thereafter, all but Taka Michinoku and Shoichi "Sho" Funaki left the company, and the two soon began performing a comedy gimmick in which they would cut promos overdubbed in English in the style of 1970s kung-fu movies, the latest iteration in a long series of Japanese stereotypes in American professional wrestling. Funaki was later known as "Kung Fu Naki," a *gi*-wearing conflation of Japanese and Chinese stereotypes, and used largely as a comedy performer until his release in 2010.[37] Funaki, whose lifelong dream was to wrestle in America, played the comedy roles with gusto. In 2011, he founded a wrestling school, Funaki dojo, in San Antonio, and is also now a trainer for NXT, World Wrestling Entertainment (WWE, formerly WWF)'s developmental promotion for up-and-coming performers.[38] Nonetheless, the case of Kaientai is a perfect example of the long shelf-life of Japanese stereotypes in American pro wrestling. When the Kaientai-Taka Michinoku feud failed to get over (generate sufficient fan interest) as a simple athletic feud between rivals, WWF's writers returned once again to base stereotypes in hopes of drawing more heat and ratings. The fact that the various angles involving Kaientai were more often than not played for laughs suggests that in the eyes both of promoters and fans, the Japanese no longer posed a serious threat, but were rather a harmless, comical "other."

Until recently, attempts by Japanese wrestlers to succeed in the United States have largely ended in failure, partly due to ongoing reliance by American promotions on stereotypes. In 2004, former Japanese international rugby player Kenzo Suzuki, who had been wrestling for New Japan Pro Wrestling (NJPW), signed with WWE along with his wife, model Hiroko Suzuki, for a reported $280,000 per year apiece, remarkably lucrative contracts for new signees. The apparent motivation behind the duo's signing was to make inroads into the Japanese market, but Suzuki's original, aborted gimmick suggests a complete ignorance of Japanese sensibilities. Prior to Suzuki's in-ring debut, weekly vignettes began airing on WWE programs promoting the impending arrival of "Hirohito," a name that many Americans still associated with World War II. According to some reports, Hiroko convinced Vince McMahon that the name would not be received well in Japan, so "Hirohito" was dropped and Suzuki debuted using his real name.[39] While Suzuki himself appeared as a more-or-less "average" wrestler, Hiroko accompanied him in full geisha garb, concealing her model's face and body under thick white makeup and an elaborate kimono, demonstrating once again the tendency in American pro wrestling to play up the most basic Japanese stereotypes in lieu of more nuanced portrayals. The two failed to "get over" with the fans, and left the company in 2005.

Other American promotions have been guilty in recent years of resorting to base stereotypes for Japanese performers. Total Nonstop Action (TNA) had a working arrangement with New Japan from 2008 to 2011 in which the promotions would send talent to appear on each other's shows. The deal eventually fell through partly due to TNA's questionable use of Kazuchika Okada, one of New Japan's most promising young talents. After briefly wrestling as a serious competitor under his own name, Okada was rechristened "Okato," and began dressing like Bruce Lee's Kato character from *The Green Hornet* television series. Okato became TNA star Samoa Joe's (who, unlike most Samoan wrestlers in the past, did not wear a grass skirt or wrestle barefoot) sidekick and was played largely for laughs. Along with several other grievances, this perceived misuse of Okada led to New Japan's decision to end their relationship with TNA in 2011.[40]

A New Direction?

A new generation of Japanese-born stars now performing in the United States suggests that the traditional hindrances of base stereotypes have, finally, been abandoned by WWE, the world's foremost wrestling promotion. In 2014, the company signed Kenta Kobayashi (who wrestled in Japan for Pro Wrestling NOAH as KENTA, to avoid name confusion with veteran star

Kenta Kobashi), who, as "Hideo Itami," has become a popular performer for NXT. In 2015, veteran women's wrestler Kana Urai signed with WWE as "Asuka" (a reference to legendary Japanese women's wrestler Lioness Asuka), and has since become NXT Women's Champion.[41] Asuka's colorful garb and entrance attire contrasts strongly with her hard-hitting, vicious in-ring style, and the company has promoted her as an unstoppable, fearsome competitor en route to her becoming one of WWE/NXT's top stars. In 2016, the company signed top New Japan star Shinsuke Nakamura,[42] a charismatic grappler known for his "stiff" (making real contact) strikes and flamboyant, unorthodox persona and look (inspired by Michael Jackson and Freddie Mercury of Queen, among others). Competing under his real name, an oddity in WWE, which often assigns new, trademarked names to its signees, Nakamura quickly rose through the NXT ranks to become the promotion's heavyweight champion. Nakamura's popularity is evident in fan reactions; from the moment his entrance music begins, most fans cheer wildly and hum along to his theme. WWE also recently signed Kota Ibushi, another former New Japan star, to take part in its Cruiserweight Classic tournament in the summer of 2016. All four Japanese stars have been consistently presented to fans as serious, highly-skilled competitors (with colorful personas, especially in the cases of Asuka and Nakamura), and given serious "pushes" (a series of wins and/or being featured heavily on television in order to promote someone as a top performer). Asuka and Nakamura, in particular, appear poised (as of this writing) to transition to the main WWE roster, where they will likely receive major pushes as top stars, like various other NXT men's (Kevin Owens, Finn Balor) and women's (Sasha Banks, Bayley) champions in the recent past. Fans have responded favorably to this new wave of decidedly un-stereotypical Japanese stars, embracing these performers as they have many other babyface grapplers throughout the history of pro wrestling in America.

This relatively new direction for promoting Japanese wrestlers in America is likely shaped by several factors, most importantly the fact that WWE, a publicly-traded company since 1999, has in recent years attempted to sanitize its image and build a more diverse and inclusive public profile that abandons the more glaring elements of stereotyping common throughout most of pro wrestling's history. Independent promotions such as Extreme Championship Wrestling (ECW) in the 1990s and Ring of Honor (ROH) in the 2000s had often featured foreign stars from Japan and elsewhere as non-stereotypical faces and heels who distinguished themselves through their impressive in-ring work (despite a frequent inability to speak English fluently), and were thus ahead of the curve, so to speak. Of course, the ECW and ROH audiences tended to include a much higher percentage of "smart" or "hardcore" fans who followed, or were at least aware of, non–WWF/WWE wrestling promotions around the world, particularly in Japan and Mexico, and would therefore be expected to have a greater appreciation for foreign stars than the average "mark" (mainstream fan). Many modern smart fans follow NXT more closely than WWE's main programs, particularly because of its more serious, sport-like presentation and focus on in-ring action over interviews and backstage skits. This may also account for the Japanese wrestlers' overwhelmingly positive reception in NXT, though there are countless historical examples to suggest that all fans tend, more often than not, to respond favorably to wrestlers pushed and promoted as serious, successful competitors, even in the absence of cutting many promos (though both Asuka and Nakamura speak decent English). The formula has worked in the past for individuals such as former NFL player Bill Goldberg (WCW, late 1990s) and amateur and UFC standout Brock Lesnar (WWF/WWE, early 2000s and 2011-present), who gave few interviews, instead allowing their dominant in-ring performances to form the core of their personas. Through their colorful (and usually non-verbal) personas and consistently high-quality in-ring performances, Asuka and Nakamura have become popular stars for NXT, and have perhaps permanently shattered the "glass ceiling" created by stereotypes that have traditionally prevented Japanese (actual or presented as such) wrestlers from being promoted as top babyfaces in the United States.

Conclusion

From faces such as Antonino "Argentina" Rocca, Bruno Sammartino, and "Polish Power" Ivan Putski to heels such as the boastful Iranian and supposed Ayatollah Khomeini devotee The Iron Sheik (Khosrow Vazieri) and current Russian-sympathizing Bulgarian Alexander Rusev who frequently proclaims his love for Vladimir Putin, stereotypes in American wrestling tell us much about prevailing popular attitudes in the United States at any given time. After World War II, wrestling promoters and performers willingly played upon lingering animosities through the use of German and Japanese stereotypes. The vast majority of German and Japanese heels in American wrestling were not, in reality, German or Japanese, but embraced their personas in hopes of achieving greater career and financial success. At its core, wrestling is about convincing fans to spend time and money to cheer their favorites against heels. Usually, promoters quickly abandon gimmicks and angles that fail to get over with fans, so the frequent and effective use of German and especially Japanese stereotypes in wrestling is a clear indication of their lasting ability to incite fans. German stereotypes began to fade in the 1970s, as Americans came increasingly to view Germans as sympathetic rather than sinister figures, but Japanese stereotypes endured even beyond 2000, though they transitioned from dastardly, villainous heels to outright goofy

90   Part I. Race

comedic figures. German and Japanese stereotypes were far from unique in wrestling, as promoters have used countless other racial, ethnic, and national stereotypes throughout the history of the pseudo-sport, but they demonstrate that popular wartime attitudes had a lengthy shelf-life in the decades following the war. The recent successes of several Japanese wrestlers in NXT suggest, however, that American promoters' usual reliance on stereotypes when promoting Japanese stars may finally have been abandoned in favor of increasingly positive, serious portrayals more in keeping with our increasingly diverse and globalized society.

Notes

1. Jake Shannon, *Say Uncle! Catch-as-Catch-Can: Wrestling and the Roots of Ultimate Fighting, Pro Wrestling, and Modern Grappling* (Toronto: ECW Press, 2011), 30–32.
2. Greg Oliver, *The Pro Wrestling Hall of Fame: The Canadians* (Toronto: ECW Press, 2003), 194.
3. "Hans Schmidt vs. Verne Gagne," *Chicago Film Archives Presents "Wrestling from Chicago,"* early 1950s, https://www.youtube.com/channel/UCWXxP_rvXryBPpjIw7Dl9Tg/about (accessed May 8, 2015).
4. Greg Oliver, *The Pro Wrestling Hall of Fame: The Heels* (Toronto: ECW Press, 2007), 387.
5. Oliver, *The Heels*, 389–91.
6. Oliver, *The Heels*, 388.
7. Hornbaker, *National Wrestling Alliance*, 242.
8. Hornbaker, *National Wrestling Alliance*, 243.
9. Oliver, *The Heels*, 384.
10. Oliver, *The Heels*, 392–393.
11. Brakus Promotional Vignette. *WWF Raw*, August 19, 1996, https://www.youtube.com/watch?v=xbrEbWNl39E (accessed May 8, 2015).
12. Jonathan Snowden, *Shooters: The Toughest Men in Professional Wrestling* (Toronto: ECW Press, 2012), 239.
13. Beekman, *Ringside*, 91.
14. "Sorakichi's Leg Broken," *New York Times*, February 16, 1886.
15. Nat Fleischer, *From Milo to Londos: The Story of Wrestling Through the Ages* (New York: C.J. O'Brien, 1936), 53.
16. Fleischer, *From Milo to Londos*, 53.
17. "A Giant from Hamburg," *New York Times*, March 21, 1885.
18. "Too Much Like a Fight," *New York Times*, June 9, 1885.
19. Joseph R. Svinth, "Japanese Wrestling Pioneer: Sorakichi Matsuda," *Yo: Journal of Alternative Perspectives on the Martial Arts and Sciences*, January 2005, http://ejmas.com/jalt/jaltart_Svinth1_1100.htm (accessed May 8, 2015).
20. Beekman, *Ringside*, 29–30.
21. James S. Koga, "The Mr. Moto Novels of John P. Marquand," http://www.cpp.edu/~jskoga/moto (accessed May 11, 2015).
22. Oliver, *The Heels*, 373–74.
23. "1950s Wrestling Interviews from Hollywood Wrestling," https://www.youtube.com/watch?v=FGv3bPQ7qTg (accessed May 11, 2015).
24. Oliver, *The Heels*, 374.
25. Greg Oliver, "Tor Kamata: Mean but Nice," *Slam! Sports*, July 7, 2004, http://slam.canoe.com/Slam/Wrestling/2004/06/26/515637.html (accessed May 11, 2015).
26. Oliver, *The Heels*, 375–77.
27. "Bruno Sammartino vs. Mr. Fuji," *WWWF All-Star Wrestling*, 1974, https://www.youtube.com/watch?v=1SCgKpx6nCI (accessed May 11, 2015).

28. Oliver, *The Heels*, 394–96.
29. Steven Johnson and Greg Oliver, *The Pro Wrestling Hall of Fame: Heroes and Icons* (Toronto: ECW Press, 2012), 70.
30. Yoshikuni Igarashi, *Bodies of Memory: Narratives of Postwar Japanese Culture, 1945–1970* (Princeton: Princeton University Press, 2000), 122–24.
31. Morton and O'Brien, *Wrestling to Rasslin,'* 112–13.
32. "WWF Pins IPO," *CNN Money*, August 3, 1999, http://money.cnn.com/1999/08/03/companies/wrestling (accessed May 12, 2015).
33. Sharon Mazer, *Professional Wrestling: Sport and Spectacle* (Jackson: University of Mississippi Press, 1998), 47.
34. "Yokozuna's Bodyslam Challenge," *Monday Night Raw*, July 5, 1993, http://www.wwe.com/videos/yokozunas-bodyslam-challenge-raw-july-5-1993-26016987 (accessed May 12, 2015).
35. Mike Altamura, "Kazuo 'Sonny' Onoo Speaks Out," *Slam! Sports*, April 4, 2002, http://slam.canoe.com/SlamWrestlingArchive2001/apr4_onoo-can.html (accessed May 12, 2015).
36. Ryan Dilbert, "WWE's 15 Most Tasteless and Offensive Storylines Ever," *The Bleacher Report*, December 9, 2011, http://bleacherreport.com/articles/975285-wwes-15-most-tasteless-offensive-storylines-ever/page/2 (accessed May 12, 2015).
37. Nick Paglino, "Details Behind Funaki's Release," *Wrestlezone*, April 26, 2010, http://www.wrestlezone.com/news/180179-details-behind-funakis-release-more-on-mysterios-attacker (accessed May 12, 2015).
38. Bobby Melok, "Where Are They Now? Kaientai," WWE.com, January 16, 2013, http://www.wwe.com/classics/wherearetheynow/where-are-they-now-kaientai-26084603 (accessed May 12, 2015).
39. Dusty Giebink, "Where in the World Has Rikishi Been Lately?" *Pro Wrestling Torch*, May 26, 2004, http://pwtorch.com/artman2/publish/font_color_770000_TPFKATL_font_24/article_8358.shtml#.Vc3iifmCiSp (accessed August 14, 2015).
40. Mike Johnson, "TNA News and Notes," *PWInsider*, July 6, 2015, http://www.pwinsider.com/article/94917/tna-news-and-notes.html?p=1 (accessed August 14, 2015).
41. "WWE Officially Announces the Signing of Kana," *Wrestling Observer-Figure Four Weekly Online*, September 8, 2015, http://www2.f4wonline.com/wwe-news/wwe-officially-announces-signing-kana-160051 (accessed October 14, 2016).
42. Bobby Melok, "Shinsuke Nakamura Signs with WWE NXT," WWE.com, February 21, 2016, http://www.wwe.com/shows/wwenxt/article/shinsuke-nakamura-signs-wwe-nxt (accessed October 14, 2016).

Deepest, Darkest Africa(, Illinois)
Cultural Appropriation in Professional Wrestling

Kevin Hogg

Professional wrestling, like any other business, exists for the primary purpose of making money. Its predetermined nature sets it apart from other sports or athletic competitions, which is both a negative and a positive. It limits the potential audience, as many people will not watch something that is "fake," but it also gives promoters flexibility to determine which wrestlers will be featured to maximize attendance and viewership. Whether fans want to see a favorite wrestler win or a hated wrestler lose, the goal is to get them interested enough to buy tickets or pay-per-views. This is done by creating characters for them to portray, and promotions like World Wrestling Entertainment (WWE, formerly the World Wide Wrestling Federation, then the World Wrestling Federation) often give prominent roles to people of specific races and cultures that resonate with fans, whether in a positive or negative way. At times, however, promotions will give these roles to people outside of the group in question, leading to a form of cultural appropriation.

While other sports feature teams with which fans can connect, wrestling focuses mainly on individuals.[1] Therefore, it is particularly important that the individuals are memorable. Historically, wrestlers' identities, or gimmicks, have been designed to allow the audience to make quick judgments about a character. In *Professional Wrestling as Ritual Drama in American Popular Culture*, Michael Ball identifies "physical disabilities, race, ethnicity, or perhaps political labels" as the easiest ways to make decisions about people, often based on stereotypes.[2] Many promotions have built storylines around racial stereotypes, prejudices, and conflicts. Although WWE is certainly not alone in this, it is both the most well-known federation and also the one that wrestling journalist Dave Meltzer claims has utilized stereotypes more than any other promotion.[3] This essay will trace several examples of borrowed national or cultural identity in a roughly chronological fashion to reflect the rise and fall of wrestling's popularity as well how the business has responded to global events.

Ball states that American history has been characterized in part by negative interactions between races, quoting Robert Blauner's 1972 book *Racial Oppression in America*: "The United States was founded on the principle that it was and would be a white man's country."[4] This belief carries with it the need to defend power in the face of threats, whether real or perceived. Professional wrestling has catered to this belief by portraying foreign wrestlers, as well as visible minorities, in a negative light. Ball cites Victor Turner's 1974 *Dramas, Fields and Metaphors: Symbolic Action in Human Society*, stating that "flat" stereotypes are effective in communicating information about a character quickly.[5] This has been shown consistently in professional wrestling, as characters are often underdeveloped and have only a few characteristics that stand out. For example, Nazi sympathizer characters often wear an Iron Cross or swastika, speak in a German accent, and goosestep. Soviet wrestlers often wear red, sport an ushanka, and carry a hammer-and-sickle flag. Likewise, both groups were known for their violent tactics and penchant for cheating. With little expense or thought, American wrestlers could be transformed into a German, a Soviet, or a member of any other race that would elicit a reaction from the crowd.

Tracing the popularity of professional wrestling over the 20th century reveals that these created identities played a role in generating fan interest during several key points. In an essay titled "The Politics of Professional Wrestling," Jeffrey J. Mondak identifies three peak periods for professional wrestling in the United States: the early 1930s, early 1950s, and 1980s. To this, we can add the rise of the New World Order and Attitude Era of the late 1990s, which came after Mondak's essay was published. The first three are linked by the fact that they came during times that created a sense of American pride or protectionism. The first boom period came, counterintuitively, during the pervasive poverty of the Great Depression. During this time, the United States isolated itself while pursuing a solution to domestic problems.[6] The second came at the beginning of the television era, although it was also fueled by the beginning of the Cold War, when Red Scare paranoia was at its peak.[7] The 1980s brought a renewed sense of patriotism, as the United States exercised its strength in foreign policy disputes around the globe.[8] Wrestling promotions have been quick to capitalize on these pro–America feelings by establishing national heroes and foreign villains to replicate world events.

During the first surge in popularity, many of the top foreign wrestlers were billed from their birth countries, allowing fans to cheer for people with whom they can identify as well as to witness a microcosm of real world affairs. This helped build the popularity of American wrestlers like Ed "Strangler" Lewis as they faced foreign invaders. Others, like the "Golden Greek" Jim Londos were able to gain a following in part due to the appeal they held for fellow immigrants from their homelands.[9] Fan feelings toward Eastern European wrestlers were mixed. They represented the group responsible for the majority of immigration in the previous decades.[10] Some people appreciated the rural values they brought,[11] while others identified with them because of the shared ethnicity. Conversely, they were also treated with suspicion due to feelings of American protectionism or feared because of their size and perceived brutality.

Ali Baba was a key player in changing the practice of creating false identities for wrestlers. Born Arteen Ekizian in Samsun, he was ethnically Armenian. He lived in the Ottoman Empire during the Armenian genocide in 1915; his father, who had received American citizenship, was among those killed. Ekizian resettled in the United States and served in the United States Navy for eight years.[12] Despite his family's history under the Turkish government, when he began wrestling, he took the name Ali Baba, "The Terrible Turk," although he was also said to be from Kurdistan.[13] In 1936, Ali Baba won the World Heavyweight Wrestling Championship; Scott Beekman identifies this as a strong inspiration for other wrestlers and promotions to build personas to capture the interest of the fans.[14] Even during Ekizian's reign as world champion, his true name was common knowledge. Newspapers referred to him as Arteen Ekizian,[15] indicating that, even in the early years of gimmicks, it was understood that Ekizian was portraying a character.

The ability to transform a wrestler into a completely new character solved two major problems for promoters. First, it gave them a marketing strategy that allowed them to differentiate between wrestlers and make the fans care enough to spend their meager Depression-era incomes to watch national, ethnic, or religious rivalries play out in the ring.[16] It also limited the impact of new immigration restrictions, which were added several times during the interwar period and made it difficult for foreign-born wrestlers to come to the United States.[17] The success of wrestlers like Ali Baba showed that a person's ability to portray a character was more important than his true identity. Although he was not the first wrestler to use a false identity, he used his gimmick to gain enough of a following to be given the top prize in the business. Other wrestlers, such as Paul Boesch, a Lutheran, used a similar strategy; Boesch was a top star in matches for the Jewish Heavyweight Championship.[18] Over time, the success of artificial identities and nationalities proved so successful that it became a common practice when promoters wanted to create a rivalry, even if no true foreigners were available.

Mondak identifies the early 1950s, specifically 1952, as the peak of wrestling's second boom period. This is clearly linked to the popularization of television, which took wrestling beyond the local level and forced promoters to create characters that would engage a larger audience.[19] The popularity of flamboyant and effeminate Gorgeous George in the 1940s helped popularize bigger and more outlandish gimmicks, which was ideal for the television era. The gimmick made George the highest-paid athlete in the world, taking home a reported $100,000 per year,[20] and many wrestlers would also have been eager to follow his example. Several promoters combined this idea with America's international conflicts, making World War II and Cold War enemies prime candidates to raise the anger and animosity of wrestling fans.

In the aftermath of World War II, German wrestlers were obvious heels, especially when they professed to be Nazis or Nazi sympathizers, although many were not actually from Germany. Kurt Von Poppenheim, an American who served in the U.S. Navy during World War II,[21] has been referred to as the originator of the fake Nazi persona.[22] He inspired many others, including Frank Faketty of Michigan (who wrestled as Karl Von Hess), Jack Adkisson of Jewett, Texas (Fritz Von Erich),[23] Walter Sieber of Kitchener, Ontario (Waldo Von Erich),[24] and Guy Larose of Joliette, Quebec (Hans Schmidt).[25] Fred Altinger discovered how effective his gimmick was when he was forced to hide for safety until the ring announcer informed the crowd that Altinger was actually born in Milwaukee. Following this, he identified as American to avoid the crowd's wrath.[26]

The 1950s also saw the rise of Japanese wrestlers like Harold Sakata. Sakata had Japanese ancestry but was born and raised in Hawaii.[27] To emphasize his ancestry, he was billed as being from Japan, going by the exotic name Tosh Togo.[28] The history of German and Japanese wrestlers is discussed in more detail in the essay by Aaron D. Horton in this book.

Following World War II, the United States became more involved in international politics and conflicts. Relations with the Arab world were strained after America recognized Israel's statehood in 1948 and sided with Israel in the 1956 Suez Crisis. Wrestlers like Edward Farhat and Lawrence Shreve were able to capitalize on American sentiment, which has historically been supportive of Israel. This created the perfect opportunity for promoters to take advantage of a fear of Arabic countries gaining strength in the 1950s and 1960s. Edward Farhat, a wrestler from Michigan, began wrestling in 1949 as The Sheik. Although his parents were Lebanese, he billed himself from "The Syrian Desert" and spoke phony Arabic.[29] He combined an imaginary aristocratic background with such savagery that he has been called the originator of "hardcore" wrestling.[30] Because of his alleged inability to speak English, he was paired with a manager to help him communicate. Curiously, the man chosen was Ernie Roth, a Jewish man from Ohio. Roth took on the role of Abdullah Farouk, claiming to be a fellow Muslim hired by The Sheik's parents to take care of their son.[31] Farhat and Roth's gimmicks played into the fear felt by many Americans as Arab countries gained political strength and made moves toward pan-Arabic unity in the 1950s.[32] Syria was a particularly effective choice of nationality, as the country had recently gained independence and shown support for its Arabic neighbors by joining them in the 1948 Arab-Israeli war.

Lawrence Shreve, an Afro-Canadian born in Windsor, Ontario, used several gimmicks before he was convinced by a promoter of the financial benefits of becoming Abdullah the Butcher, "The Madman from the Sudan."[33] Abdullah was a brutally violent wrestler who supposedly could only speak Arabic, making him a hated and feared villain. To help his character communicate with fans, he was given a series of managers. One of these managers was Skandor Akbar, who was billed as being from various Middle Eastern countries. In reality, he was Jimmy Wehba from Wichita Falls, Texas. He was encouraged to take on this Arabic gimmick by fellow Texan Fritz Von Erich.[34] Promoters recognized Farhat and Shreve's natural talent but knew they needed an extra touch to differentiate themselves from other villains and generate hatred among fans. Assigning them origins that created a sense of mystery and suspicion helped build careers that kept them active in the business for decades. Like Farhat, the creation of the gimmick took little work—Shreve's skin color helped set him apart, and Wehba simply put on a keffiyeh to look the part. Silence from the wrestlers and fake accents from the managers created believable characters that drew crowds and made money both for the promotions and the performers.

The late 1950s also saw the debut of Robert Marella, an Italian American from Rochester, New York, wrestling under the name Gino Marella. Four years into his career, he decided to take on a new identity as Gorilla Monsoon. He stopped speaking English, claiming, through manager Bobby Davis, to be from Manchuria. He was supposedly raised by gypsies and wrestled bears for a living before coming to America, where he ate raw meat and drank human blood.[35] Davis claimed to have discovered him bathing naked in a Manchurian stream.[36] He gained notoriety under this new gimmick, terrifying fans but contributing to bigger crowds. He was quickly given a match against WWWF champion Bruno Sammartino, and had two runs with the WWWF United States Tag Team Championship. Several years later, he faced Andre the Giant and even had an in-ring confrontation with Muhammad Ali. He also leveraged his position to gain part-ownership of the company, later working as a television announcer and being inducted into the WWF Hall of Fame.[37] By contrast, Antonio Pugliese, an Italian wrestler, debuted two years after Marella. He also capitalized on his Italian ancestry by singing before matches.[38] Although he held several championships, his success never approached Marella's, who recognized and took advantage of the potential of a terrifying and exotic persona.

The Cold War rivalry between the United States and Soviet Union had a pervasive impact on culture in the second half of the 20th century. After World War II, Soviet wrestlers were featured prominently, becoming common villains in many promotions. Fear of communism extended far beyond the political realm, including stereotypes of "political radicalism, illogical and irrational thought processes, aggression, perversion, etc."[39] It should come as little surprise that many of these roles were played by Americans and Canadians, as it stands to reason that legitimate Soviets would not want to be associated with such ideas. It should also be noted that this is not unique to professional wrestling. Omar Sharif, star of the film *Doctor Zhivago*, was Egyptian,[40] and many Russian villains in James Bond movies were portrayed by actors and actresses with no ties to Russia.[41]

Wrestlers like Hyman Fishman had taken on fake Soviet identities even before the Cold War. Fishman was the son of Ukrainian immigrants, was born in Chelsea, Massachusetts, in 1912, and began wrestling in 1935. Soon after his debut, he was told that he could make more money by creating a gimmick, and he and a promoter developed the character of Ivan Rasputin.[42] The WWWF also saw the value in this tactic and, in 1969, hired Orreal Perras, a French-Canadian wrestler from the Ottawa Valley in Ontario who had formerly portrayed an Irishman and was then competing as Ivan Koloff.[43] He faced the top wrestlers in the promotion and won the WWWF Championship on January 18, 1971, ending Bruno Sammartino's reign of over seven and a half years. The win secured him a spot in wrestling history and gave him name recognition for his career after the WWWF that would have been much more difficult to obtain wrestling as a French Canadian.

Perras later wrestled for Jim Crockett Promotions, where he was teamed up with Nelson Scott Simpson, who was said to be his nephew, Nikita Koloff. Although Simpson was from Minneapolis,[44] he took the character to heart, legally changing his name, learning to speak Russian, and even, after the collapse of the Soviet Union, giving his birthplace as Lithuania on his daughter's birth certificate.[45] They were later joined by Barry Darsow, another Minneapolis native,[46] as Krusher Khruschev, an apparent reference to former Soviet leader Nikita Khrushchev. Together, the Koloffs and Khruschev won the NWA World Six-Man Tag Team Championship. Although none of the team's three members was actually Russian, they played their roles convincingly enough to excite crowds and be given a prestigious title.

One of the most famous Cold War–like Soviets was actually billed as Mongolian early in his career.[47] Josip Peruzovic was born in Croatian Yugoslavia but first found success in the WWWF as Bepo Mongol[48]; teaming with Geto Mongol (portrayed by Newton Tattrie from Springhill, Nova Scotia),[49] they held the promotion's tag team championship twice.[50] Peruzovic then became Nikolai Volkoff, although he initially did not want to portray a communist wrestler because he grew up in Yugoslavia and disliked the country's communist system.[51] Peruzovic ultimately embraced the role, angering fans by singing the Soviet anthem prior to matches. He teamed with Iranian wrestler The Iron Sheik, bringing together two countries with negative relationships with the United States. Their notoriety gained them a shot at the WWF Tag Team Championship at the first WrestleMania event, where they captured the belts.

The following year, at WrestleMania 2, Volkoff faced Corporal Kirchner, who had a legitimate background as a U.S. Army paratrooper. Kirchner won the match and, because of the stipulation, got to assert American superiority by waving his country's flag.[52] Volkoff and The Iron Shiek competed again at WrestleMania III, solidifying Volkoff's role as a key player in the WWF's rapidly-growing popularity in the 1980s. He was then teamed with James Harrell of Roanoke, Virginia, who wrestled as Boris Zhukov.[53] They called themselves The Bolsheviks and later appeared in a tag team match at WrestleMania VI. The Bolsheviks' decline is a prime example of the power of a foreign villain gimmick. They were featured at some of the WWF's biggest shows, but fan interest dwindled after the opening of the Berlin Wall in 1989. Volkoff later embarked on a solo career, competing as a fan favorite, since the United States and Russia had friendlier relations, and eventually gained a place in the WWE Hall of Fame.

At times, promotions do not even need to look outside their national borders to find a culture to exploit. Ball lists the "Red Indian" as a popular stereotype exploited by wrestling promotions. Native Americans usually played fan favorites, although they had gestures and abilities to set themselves apart.[54] Although professional wrestling has seen many legitimate Native American wrestlers, including Jack Brisco, Edward "Wahoo" McDaniel, and Tatanka (Chris Chavis), other wrestlers have assumed Native identities to evoke a strong connection to historical America, or endow them with the persona of a fierce warrior. Luke Joseph Scarpa is one of the best-known examples. Using his Italian American skin-tone, he was able to pass as Chief Jay Strongbow for many years. He wore a headdress to the ring and inspired fans to cheer his stereotypical Native American mannerisms.[55] Fittingly, he was paired up with Iraqi wrestler Adnan Al-Kaissie, who was then competing as Billy White Wolf,[56] to form a "Native American" tag team. The WWWF was not the only organization using people of other races in this way—for example, Iron Eyes Cody, the "Crying Indian" from the 1971 "Keep America Beautiful" commercial, was an Italian American named Espera Oscar DeCorti.[57] Images of Native American wrestlers have been used to evoke national pride, and gestures like a "tomahawk chop" give fans a common means to show their support, as seen at Atlanta Braves baseball or Florida State University football games. Because costumes and mannerisms are such strong indications of character, it has not always mattered that they were used by true Native Americans.

African American wrestlers have factored heavily into cultural appropriation, both portraying the African "savage" and as a people imitated through clothing, speech, and mannerisms. James Harris, born in Senatobia, Mississippi,[58] is a prime example of the first type. He competed for several years under various nicknames and saw only modest success. His rise to fame began in 1982 when Jerry Lawler and Jerry Jarrett gave him the identity of Kamala, a Ugandan cannibal, in the Memphis-based United States Wrestling Association (USWA). Wearing a loincloth and mask, with his appearance modeled after a Frank Frazetta painting,[59] Harris' character generated enough interest to win multiple championships and sign with the WWF. Playing upon the tie between Harris' ancestry and North American perceptions of tribal Africa, Kamala terrified younger fans and worked his way into high-profile matches with Hulk Hogan and The Undertaker, among others. Even after becoming a fan favorite years later, he continued with the persona, acting confused about American culture and supposedly forgetting how to pin an opponent.

It is worth noting that, during his time in Memphis, Harris was briefly joined by Kamala #2. In one of the most blatant attempts to co-opt African American culture, white wrestler Stan Frazier, best known for portraying 450-pound hillbilly Uncle Elmer,[60] went through a series of deliberately transparent gimmicks in an attempt to reinvent himself, one of which saw him don Kamala's loincloth and face and body paint. Rather than being taken seriously (the announcers stated, even before the match started, that Kamala #2 was really "Plowboy" Frazier), the short-lived gimmick is remembered for the laughter it generated. Nevertheless, the attempt to pass Frazier off as an African headhunter is another demonstration of how promotions have exploited and misused imagery and stereotypes of African Americans.

The 1980s saw the WWF combine sports and entertainment to a far greater degree than ever before. Wrestlers like Hulk Hogan and André the Giant became household names based on their work in the WWF. Roderick Toombs, better known as Rowdy Roddy Piper, is one of the best-remembered villains of this era because of the identity he created in part through a false claim of citizenship. Born in Saskatoon, Saskatchewan, he had Scottish ancestry but was not a native of Scotland, as he later claimed. He learned to play the bagpipes and used this ability to create a gimmick that gained him worldwide fame both as a hated rulebreaker and as a beloved fan favorite. He headlined the first WrestleMania in a tag-team match against Hulk Hogan and Mr. T in 1985. His feud with Hogan was so memorable that they faced each other 11 years later in the main event of Starrcade 1996, WCW's primary pay-per-view, drawing massive numbers. His image of the "Rowdy Scot," whose Scottish temper and kilt often featured in storylines, made him a memorable character, even though he was born nowhere near Glasgow.

Even in the era of kayfabe, or keeping the secrets of the industry away from fans, the WWF at times made no effort to hide that wrestlers were taking on false identities, even going so far as to draw attention to the fact. A prime example is George Gray, a white man born in Chicago and raised in South Carolina.[61] He competed in the WWF for a year and a half as the One Man Gang, a biker.[62] He was then "reborn" in fall 1988 during a ceremony involving African dancers and a flaming garbage can in an alleyway,[63] after which he took the name Akeem, claiming to be from "Deepest, Darkest Africa." Under his new persona, he spoke in "jive," wore a dashiki, and danced in the ring. Although the character has been described as racially insensitive,[64] it rejuvenated Gray's career, and he was paired in a tag team with the Big Boss Man as "The Twin Towers" and featured at that year's Survivor Series pay-per-view.[65] Gray's transformation was one of the few times the WWF acknowledged that a wrestler was changing identities, further breaking down some of the closely guarded secrets of the business.

Such a transformation is not unique, although it is among the more extreme examples. Another change was a deliberate attempt to anger the audience and build ratings. Robert Remus, who had served in the United States Marine Corps, had competed in the WWF for years as Sgt. Slaughter, a patriotic drill sergeant.[66] He left the company after a falling-out but returned in 1990. However, the returning character had turned against the United States, siding with Iraq in the Gulf War conflict. Slaughter's newfound allegiance to Iraq and Saddam Hussein shocked audiences and was one of the WWF's biggest storylines of 1991. The response was so powerful that Remus needed bodyguards to protect him from threats, and the FBI met with him to discuss his safety.[67] Sgt. Slaughter was accompanied to the ring by Colonel Mustafa, portrayed by Hossein Khosrow Ali Vaziri, known previously to fans as The Iron Sheik. Originally from Iran, Ali Vaziri was one of the most hated villains of the 1980s. In 1983, Hulk Hogan defeated him to win his first WWF Championship and launch the Hulkamania era. The WWF used Ali Vaziri in his new role despite the recent Iran-Iraq conflict and the fact that there was almost no change in his appearance or persona. This was one of the company's most powerful indications that wrestlers are nothing more than characters whose identities can be changed at will. With that understanding, it made sense to use someone with a Middle Eastern appearance to fill the role, even if it defied logic and contradicted the decades-old tradition of pretending that wrestling was a legitimate series of feuds and fights. This was in keeping, however, with McMahon's admission in 1989 that his product was not a true sport, but rather "sports entertainment."[68]

After many of its stars from the 1980s had moved on, the WWF rebranded its product the "New Generation" in the mid–1990s. Although it was far less successful financially, it continued to demonstrate the effectiveness of borrowed identities. When Scott Hall was pursuing a WWF contract in 1992, McMahon asked him to propose a gimmick. Hall suggested a knock-off of Tony Montana from the 1983 movie *Scarface*. McMahon had not seen the movie but was enthusiastic about the idea.[69] Hall, a Caucasian originally from Miami,[70] was billed as Razor Ramon, a Cuban immigrant. The gimmick was successful, and Hall was given main event spots at two pay-per-views shortly after his debut with the company. He stayed with the company until 1996, winning four Intercontinental Championships. The appeal of his character was evident when he maintained the fake accent even after leaving for World Championship Wrestling, where he competed under his real name and continued to enjoy the successful career that had been jumpstarted by the Cuban character he had copied from a movie.

One of the most unlikely forms of appropriation was a Croatian playing the role of a Japanese wrestler. In early 1990, Mr. Fuji introduced a new tag team, The Orient Express, to the WWF. The team was composed of Akio Sato and Pat Tanaka. Sato was born in Japan, while Tanaka was born in Hawai'i but had Japanese ancestry. Later that year, Sato left the team, creating a void. Paul Diamond, a Croatian-born wrestler who had moved to Canada as a teenager, had previously teamed with Tanaka in the AWA. He was selected to fill the role, so he was given a mask, renamed Kato, and billed from Japan.[71] A similar issue arose in 1994 when a new member was needed for The Headshrinkers. Samula Anoa'i and Solofa Fatu, wrestling as Samu and Fatu, both had legitimate Samoan ancestry, although Fatu was born in San Francisco. When Samu left the team in 1994, the WWF did not want to disband one of its top teams. They had recently rehired Sione Vailahi, who had previously competed as The Barbarian. Vailahi was Tongan,[72] which was deemed close enough to Samoan to allow him to compete without a disguise. He was renamed Sionne and competed as a Samoan until leaving the WWF. In both cases, the WWF decided to continue with plans for tag teams but did not have anyone of the same ancestry to take the place of the departed member. Thanks to his mask, Diamond passed as Japanese with no real problem. Likewise, the WWF could count on the average fan not being able to tell the difference in appearance between residents of two different South Pacific islands. As with Colonel Mustafa and Akeem, there was no real attempt to hide the fact that Sionne had portrayed The Barbarian. The company appeared to believe that anyone who recognized him would be aware of the nature of the business anyway, and owner/commentator Vince McMahon even made an inside joke that he was "barbaric."[73]

In the mid–1990s, the fake Japanese role was reprised twice, with varying degrees of success. Rodney Anoa'i, a Samoan wrestler born in San Francisco, portrayed sumo wrestler Yokozuna despite not having Japanese ancestry or sumo experience.[74] He defeated major stars, including Hulk Hogan, and had two runs as WWF Champion. Several years later, Yokozuna became a fan favorite and spoke English in interviews,[75] effectively acknowledging that his Japanese character was a fabrication. In 1994, another wrestler from "The Orient" debuted in the WWF. Juan Rivera, a Puerto Rican wrestler, competed under a mask as Kwang. He was portrayed as a ninja who breathed green mist on opponents, a trait associated with legit Japanese wrestlers such as The Great Kabuki or The Great Muta. He lacked the size and presence of Yokozuna, however, and his manager, Harvey Wippleman, did little to build up the character. The gimmick was dropped after a little over a year, although he later removed the mask and competed as Savio Vega, a Puerto Rican gimmick in keeping with his true nationality.

Wrestling's popularity was on the upswing again in 1996. Steve Austin shed his unsuccessful Ringmaster persona, launching the early stages of the Attitude Era at the WWF's King of the Ring 1996 event with his "Austin 3:16" speech. Two weeks later, Hulk Hogan turned on his longtime fans and christened his new group the New World Order in World Championship Wrestling (WCW). Both the WWF and WCW saw a rise in popularity for their heel, or rulebreaking, wrestlers. With the press coverage of the New World Order giving WCW extensive exposure, the WWF launched its own anti-establishment group by borrowing an idea from the United States Wrestling Association (USWA). Ron Simmons, known in the WWF as Faarooq Asad, led the Nation of Domination, which brought together elements of the Nation of Islam and the Black Panther Party. The group fought under the slogan "by any means necessary," popularized by Malcolm X, and used the closed fist salute popularized by the Black Panthers. Some members wore African colors and kufi caps, and took on new names in a manner similar to the Nation of Islam.[76] Several members of the group were not, however, African American. Crush, portrayed by Brian Adams, was a Caucasian from Hawaii, and the group's rappers, J.C. Ice (James Cruikshanks) and Wolfie D (Kelly Wolfe), were Caucasians from Australia and Tennessee, respectively. Juan Rivera, who had been repackaged as Savio Vega, was another early member. The USWA had white Tennessean Tracy Smothers take on the name Shaquille Ali when he joined the company's version of the group.

Eventually, Asad removed these other members from the group in order to create a "blacker" version. However, white Canadian grappler Owen Hart was brought into the group as a co-leader after Asad was removed.[77] D–Generation X, a group led by Shawn Michaels and Triple H, later performed a parody of the Nation in which D–Generation X members appeared in blackface imitating the mannerisms of Nation members. The WWF's attempt to replicate the success of the New World Order was not successful, as wrestling fans were more excited by the hostile takeover storyline in WCW than racially-driven storylines. The Nation of Domination did gain exposure for the WWF, however, even if the African American gang was not exclusively African American. Rap music, traditional clothing, and references to the civil rights movement made for a memorable storyline, possibly even more so when used by people outside the African American community.

Nineteen ninety-six also brought the return of the Middle Eastern gimmick. Fatu, a Samoan American who had formerly competed as part of The Headshrinkers, began competing as The Sultan. Co-managed by The Iron Sheik and Bob Backlund, he came to the ring under the Iranian flag. To conceal his previous identity, he wrestled under a mask, and a story was created that his tongue had been cut out. At the beginning of his first match, Jerry Lawler reminded viewers that the United States had resumed bombing operations in Iraq two weeks earlier. This seems to indicate that the WWF remembered its previous successes in exploiting real-world conflicts and hoped to capitalize on renewed tensions in the Middle East. The Sultan was given a shot at Rocky Maivia's Intercontinental Championship at WrestleMania 13 in 1997, but interest in the character, like American interest in the Iraq conflict, was inconsistent and insufficient to create a major following.

The following year, a key feud in the WWF was Canada against the United States. Waving Canadian flags and criticizing American culture, the Hart Foundation galvanized American fans, who united behind Shawn Michaels, Steve Austin, and The Patriot (Del Wilkes). The Canadian faction was, however, composed mostly of non–Canadians. "The British Bulldog" Davey Boy Smith and American wrestlers Brian Pillman and Jim Neidhart had connections with the Calgary, Alberta-based Hart family, but they were brought in to give additional name recognition to the Canadian side. This is in keeping with Sigmund Freud's theory of narcissism of minor differences, in which he suggested that people will unite to protect their group or identity when faced with a common enemy, especially if the second group lives in close proximity to the first.[78] This "othering" of a population is particularly effective, as both countries represented are important parts of WWE's target market. This helped increase revenue on both sides of the border, even setting the stage for a pay-per-view event hosted in Calgary. Rather than creating new stars or bringing back lesser-known members of the Hart family (as they had done for Survivor Series 1993), it made sense to find wrestlers with connections to the Harts and have them fight on behalf of Canada, even if their true American nationality was well known. In fact, this can generate even more emotion, as Pillman and Neidhart could be viewed as traitors, much like Sgt. Slaughter during the Gulf War.

In the years that have followed, WWE and other companies have continued to use artificial identities, including racial and cultural identities, to create and develop characters. For example, Kofi Sarkodie-Mensah was born in Ghana but debuted in WWE as Kofi Kingston of Jamaica,[79] likely to connect more closely with the audience, who would have more knowledge of Jamaican culture than of West Africa. Marc Copani, who was born in Syracuse, New York, and identifies as "100 per cent Italian," wrestled as Muhammad Hassan and spoke out against discrimination he had received for being an Arab American.[80] The WWF had wanted someone to play the role and selected Copani, in part, because he would be able to speak about prejudice based on color (while oiled up to enhance his skin tone).

Although cultural appropriation was originally partly due to necessity because of the lack of ethnic diversity in wrestling, it has become a commonly-accepted part of the business. While the idea has not always led to main event payoffs, it has played a role in each of wrestling's four boom periods and shows no signs of disappearing. Even in an age of political correctness, ticket sales, merchandise, and pay-per-view buys are the bottom line. When a feud can be built around race, promotions are likely to jump at the opportunity, even if they have to lie about nationality to make it happen.

Notes

1. Michael R. Ball, *Professional Wrestling as Ritual Drama in American Popular Culture* (Lewiston, NY: Edwin Mellen, 1990), 3.
2. Ball, *Professional Wrestling*, 24.
3. Patrice A. Oppliger, *Wrestling and Hypermasculinity* (Jefferson, NC: McFarland, 2004), 117–18.
4. Ball, *Professional Wrestling*, 27.
5. Ball, *Professional Wrestling*, 84.
6. Jeffery J. Mondak, "The Politics of Professional Wrestling," *Journal of Popular Culture* 23, no. 2 (Fall 1989), 144.
7. Mondak, "Politics of Professional Wrestling," 143.
8. Mondak, "Politics of Professional Wrestling," 141.
9. Barry Moreno, *Ellis Island's Famous Immigrants* (Charleston, SC: Arcadia, 2008), 54.
10. George Brown Tindall and David E. Shi, *America: A Narrative History, Volume Two* (New York: W. W. Norton, 1999), 939.
11. Scott M. Beekman, *Ringside: A History of Professional Wrestling in America* (Westport, CT: Praeger, 2006), 76.
12. Liana Aghajanian, "The Legend of Ali Baba: The Incredible Story of Armenian Genocide Survivor & World Wrestling Champ Harry Ekizian," *Ianyan*, April 21, 2014, http://www.ianyanmag.com/the-legend-of-ali-baba-the-incredible-story-of-armenian-genocide-survivor-world-wrestling-champ-harry-ekizian.
13. "Shikat Thrown Second Time by Terrible Turk," *The Evening News* (Harrisburg, PA), May 6, 1936.
14. Beekman, *Ringside*, 74.
15. Dale Harrison, "Ali Baba Throws Dick Shikat Again for 'Title,'" *The Fresno Bee* (Fresno, CA), May 6, 1936.
16. Beekman, *Ringside*, 65.
17. Tindall and Shi, *America*, 939; Beekman, *Ringside*, 64.
18. Beekman, *Ringside*, 65; "Odds on Louis Soar to 9–5; 'Man Mountain' Defies 2 Oppo-

nents," *Santa Ana Daily Register* (Santa Ana, CA), September 23, 1935; "Rassle Show in Reverse," *The Abilene Reporter-News* (Abilene, TX), February 12, 1942.

19. Beekman, *Ringside*, 82.
20. John F. Molinaro, Dave Meltzer, and Jeff Marek, *Top 100 Pro Wrestlers of All Time* (Toronto: Winding Stair Press, 2002), 74.
21. Sherrie Stahl, "RUS-Samara-Brennental-L Archives: Obituary: Kurt von Poppenheim," Ancestry.com, last modified July 18, 2005, http://archiver.rootsweb.ancestry.com/th/read/RUS-SAMARA-BRUNNENTAL/2005-07/1121700610; "Kurt von Poppenheim," *The Center for Volga Studies at Concordia University*, September 8, 2014, http://cvgs.cu-portland.edu/history/biographies/bio.cfm?id=544.
22. Pat Laprade and Bertrand Hébert, *Mad Dogs, Midgets and Screw Jobs: The Untold Story of How Montreal Shaped the World of Wrestling* (Toronto: ECW Press, 2013), 53.
23. John Grasso, *Historical Dictionary of Wrestling* (Lanham, MD: Scarecrow Press, 2014), 315; Bill Harvey, *Texas Cemeteries: The Resting Places of Famous, Infamous, and Just Plain Interesting Texans* (Austin: University of Texas Press, 2010), 102.
24. Harris M. Lentz III, *Obituaries in the Performing Arts, 2009: Film, Television, Radio, Theatre, Dance, Music, Cartoons and Pop Culture* (Jefferson, NC: McFarland, 2010), 550.
25. Tim Hornbaker, *Legends of Pro Wrestling: 150 Years of Headlocks, Body Slams, and Piledrivers* (New York: Skyhorse Publishing, 2012), 157.
26. Greg Oliver and Steven Johnson, *The Professional Wrestling Hall of Fame: The Heels* (Toronto: ECW Press, 2007), 157.
27. Brent Massey, *Culture Shock! Hawaii: A Survival Guide to Customs and Etiquette* (Singapore: Marshall Cavendish, 2007), 246.
28. Grasso, *Historical Dictionary of Wrestling*, 315.
29. "The Sheik," *WWE*, http://www.wwe.com/superstars/thesheik (accessed June 16, 2016); Michael Kaufman, "Edward Farhat, 78, Dies; 'The Sheik' of Pro Wrestling," *New York Times*, February 5, 2003, http://www.nytimes.com/2003/01/26/sports/edward-farhat-78-dies-the-sheik-of-pro-wrestling.html.
30. Kaufman, "Edward Farhat."
31. Brian Solomon, *WWE Legends* (New York: Pocket Books, 2006), 45.
32. Mordechai Abir, *Oil, Power and Politics: Conflict of Asian and African Studies, Hebrew University of Jerusalem* (London: Routledge, 2005), 95.
33. Tim Baines, "Man or Madman? Abdullah in Hull," *Canadian Online Explorer*, October 31, 2003, http://slam.canoe.com/Slam/Wrestling/2003/10/31/242993.html.
34. Marshall Ward, "General Skandor Akbar Still Has Heat," *Canadian Online Explorer*, July 26, 2010, http://slam.canoe.com/Slam/Wrestling/2010/07/26/14826941.html.
35. John Allen, "'Gorilla Monsoon' a Pussycat Outside Ring," *Today's News-Herald* (Lake Havasu City, AZ), October 14, 1999.
36. Freddie Blassie and Keith Greenberg, *Listen, You Pencil Neck Geeks* (New York: Pocket Books, 2010), 127.
37. "Gorilla Monsoon," *WWE*, http://www.wwe.com/superstars/gorillamonsoon (accessed June 18, 2016).
38. Greg Oliver, "Tony Parisi," *Canadian Online Explorer*, http://www.canoe.ca/SlamWrestlingBiosP/parisi_tony.html (accessed June 30, 2016).
39. Ball, 25.
40. "Omar Sharif," *A & E Television Networks*, http://www.biography.com/people/omar-sharif-9480603 (accessed June 28, 2016).
41. Tino Künzel, "Bond's Top 12 Russian Characters," *Rossiyskaya Gazeta*, October 6, 2012, http://rbth.com/articles/2012/10/06/12_russians_vs_james_bond_18885.html.
42. Oliver and Johnson, *Professional Wrestling Hall of Fame: The Heels*, 154–55.
43. Solomon, *WWE Legends*, 156; Hornbaker, *Legends of Pro Wrestling*, 276.
44. Dave Meltzer, *Tributes II: Remembering More of the World's Greatest Professional Wrestlers* (Champaign, IL: Sports Publishing, 2004), 141.
45. Matthew Asher, "Koloff's Book More Historical Than Autobiographical," *Canadian Online Explorer*, March 26, 2012, http://slam.canoe.com/Slam/Wrestling/Reviews/2012/03/26/19548791.html.

46. Meltzer, 141.
47. Ric Russo, "Whatever Happened to Nikolai Volkoff?" *Orlando Sentinel*, November 24, 2000, http://articles.orlandosentinel.com/2000-11-24/entertainment/0011240077_1_mongol-sammartino-nikolai–volkoff.
48. Solomon, *WWE Legends*, 163.
49. Greg Oliver, "Geto Mongol," *Canadian Online Explorer*, http://slam.canoe.com/SlamWrestlingBiosM/mongol_geto.html (accessed June 17, 2016).
50. Solomon, *WWE Legends*, 164.
51. Solomon, *WWE Legends*, 164.
52. Ryan Murphy, "Where Are They Now? Corporal Kirchner," *WWE*, June 22, 2011, http://www.wwe.com/classics/wherearetheynow/where-are-they-now-kirchner.
53. Mason Adams, "Wrestling with Identity," *The Roanoke Times* (Roanoke, VA), September 22, 2005, http://www.roanoke.com/webmin/news/wrestling-with-identity/article_11bf08d6-89aa-5956-b6ea-5a07c90332cc.html (accessed July 13, 2016).
54. Ball, *Professional Wrestling*, 66–67.
55. Solomon, *WWE Legends*, 63–64.
56. Meltzer, *Tributes II*, 177.
57. Robert Baird, "Cries with Indians: 'Going Indian' with the Ecological Indian from Rousseau to *Avatar*," in Elizabeth DeLaney Hoffman, ed., *American Indians and Popular Culture: Media, Sports, and Politics* (Santa Barbara, CA: ABC-CLIO, 2012), 72.
58. Jerry Lawler, *It's Good to Be the King ... Sometimes* (New York: Simon & Schuster, 2002), 221.
59. Lawler, *It's Good to the King*, 222.
60. Kurt Nielsen, "Singing the Praises of the Underappreciated Stan 'Uncle Elmer' Frazier," *Canadian Online Explorer*, April 14, 2008, http://slam.canoe.com/Slam/Wrestling/2008/04/14/5284451.html.
61. Greg Oliver, "One Man Gang Still Going Strong," *Canadian Online Explorer*, http://www.canoe.ca/SlamWrestlingArchive/oct5_omg.html (accessed July 7, 2016).
62. Ernest Wilkins, "5 Pretty Racist Storyline Moments Still on the WWE Network," *Rolling Stone*, July 24, 2015. http://www.rollingstone.com/sports/features/5-pretty-racist-moments-you-can-still-find-on-wwe-network-20150724.
63. "Akeem," *WWE*, http://www.wwe.com/superstars/akeem (accessed June 24, 2016).
64. David Shoemaker, *The Squared Circle: Life, Death, and Professional Wrestling* (New York: Penguin, 2013), 299.
65. Wilkins, "5 Pretty Racist Storyline Moments."
66. "Sgt. Slaughter," *WWE*, http://www.wwe.com/superstars/sgt-slaughter (accessed July 7, 2016.
67. Kevin Sullivan, *The WWE Championship: A Look Back at the Rich History of the WWE Championship* (New York: Gallery Books, 2010), 70.
68. Oppliger, *Wrestling and Hypermasculinity*, 15.
69. Jim Ross, "How Scott Hall Became the Legendary Razor Ramon Character," *Fox Sports*, September 1, 2015, http://www.foxsports.com/buzzer/story/how-scott-hall-became-the-legendary-razor-ramon-character-090115.
70. Grasso, *Historical Dictionary of Wrestling*, 142.
71. Greg Oliver, "Paul Diamond," *Canadian Online Explorer*, http://slam.canoe.com/SlamWrestlingBios/boric_tom.html (accessed July 6, 2016).
72. Marshall Ward, "The Warlord Was the Right Body at the Right Time," *Canadian Online Explorer*, January 14, 2011, http://slam.canoe.com/Slam/Wrestling/2011/01/14/16895046.html.
73. *Monday Night Raw*, USA Network, October 10, 1994.
74. Grasso, *Historical Dictionary of Wrestling*, 329.
75. Chris Schramm, "Yokozuna: From the AWA to the Top," *Canadian Online Explorer*, http://www.canoe.ca/SlamWrestlingBiosXYZ/yokozuna_bio-can.html (accessed July 9, 2016).
76. Bob Kapur, "Chillin' in the Godfather's Office," *Canadian Online Explorer*, February 28, 2008, http://slam.canoe.com/Slam/Wrestling/2008/02/26/pf-4878793.html; Elizabeth Newman, "WWE's Sordid History of Racism Makes Its Swift Justice vs. Hulk Hogan Ring

Hollow," *Sports Illustrated*, June 26, 2015, http://www.si.com/more-sports/2015/07/26/wwe-hulk-hogan-racism-vince-mcmahon; Mike Abitabile, "Monday Night Raw: 1/27/97," *The History of WWE*, October 3, 2007, http://www.thehistoryofwwe.com/raw1-27-97review.htm.

77. Sergio Robali, "Top Fifteen Stables in Wrestling—Five That Missed the Cut," *ESPN*, August 13, 2014, http://krod.com/top-fifteen-stables-in-wrestling-five-that-missed-the-cut.

78. Sigmund Freud, *Civilization and Its Discontents* (New York: W. W. Norton, 1962), 61.

79. Grasso, *Historical Dictionary of Wrestling*, 164.

80. Colin Hunter, "Muhammad Hassan Is Back, Sort of," *Canadian Online Explorer*, March 27, 2011, http://slam.canoe.com/Slam/Wrestling/2011/03/27/17775686.html.

PART II. GENDER

Wrestling with Masculinity
Exóticos *in Lucha Libre*

XIMENA ROJO DE LA VEGA GUINEA

Pink and black. The phrase "Kiss me" printed in pink on black cotton t-shirt glistens in the Arena México. A young boy is wearing it. I'm not sure he's aware of the message; he wears it just like a rock and roll fan would at a concert. He is a fan of Máximo, currently the most popular *exótico*. A Mexican teenage boy wearing a pink shirt outside of the biggest wrestling arena in one of the most dangerous neighborhoods of the city? Lucha libre makes this possible.

Understanding Lucha Libre

Mexican History Is Lucha Libre History

After the Mexican Revolution (1910–1920), Mexico built a new political regime. Political struggles combined with national growth as Mexico sought modernity. Mexican modernization had to be re-structured in order to match with ideology from the Revolution. The Mexican Revolution was fought on many fronts, and one of the most important was agriculture. Many lives were lost and the country entered an economic crisis (worsened by the U.S. stock market crash in 1929).[1] After the second decade of the 20th century, industrialization was the one and only aim government had. Civil presidencies and syndicalism began and became the norm, and workers, fighting for their rights, formed unions.

Mexico City had been the heart of the country since its foundation, and centralism fed the capital with riches and institutions. After the 1910 revolution the urbanization process began. Until 1919, urban citizens were only 11.7

percent of the population; by 1930, the percentage was 17.5 percent.[2] Millions migrated from the countryside to the city; those who were rich before the war became richer, while poor former peasants moved to the city looking for new opportunities, and became cheap labor for the emerging new industries.

Popular culture emerged and flourished in working-class barrios. Elements of this barrio pop culture are complex, and fundamental for understanding lucha libre. First, "pop" in this context means two things; it denotes "popular," as in folk or common people, and second, it is pop because it is commercial. Lucha libre lives between the spheres. Other components of barrio pop culture are movies, radio shows, circuses and boxing. Movies glorified pre-revolution Mexican past history, an era of *haciendas* and patrons. Movie heroes were usually local cowboys, "rancheros," who sang, seduced young ladies, and saved the people of the *haciendas*. Through such characters, machismo became key component of Mexican culture.[3] Binary narratives featured the good guy, a brave macho vs. the bad guy, a violent cheater.

Origins

Lucha libre was a barrio spectacle, made for and by working classes. The urbanization process in Mexico City is reflected in different cultural products, especially movies, radio shows, and sports. Lucha libre began as small improvised shows in different locations. The hegemonic political party PRI (Institutionalized Revolution Party) insisted on bringing modernity to Mexico to every aspect of life and sports fit perfectly into their modernization plan.[4] Although Lucha libre had to compete with the popularity of soccer and baseball, a few years after its debut in Mexico, it became a cultural phenomenon.

Lucha libre began with small improvised shows in different locations. By the 1920s, some theaters in downtown Mexico City were used as venues. By 1925, it was often presented during intermissions at some movie theaters[5] and it gradually gained fame and moved to specialized places. Businessman Salvador Lutteroth saw the possibilities of a proper, full-time wrestling company and began promoting wrestling in 1933 at the Arena Mexico in the Doctores neighborhood. In 1943, the Arena Coliseo (Coliseum) among many others, such as the arenas Revolución and Libertad, among many others, also regularly featured pro wrestling.[6]

Sport/Spectacle

Lucha was never merely a sport or show. Lucha libre embraces a complex universe of meaning that reaches beyond the ring, embracing many different cultural manifestations. Roland Barthes compares wrestling to ancient solar rites, Greek theater, and bull fighting.[7] These wrestling spectacles are excessive displays of strength and masculinity. Lucha libre, then, probably derives from an ancient ritual. These ancient rituals embody primal, dualistic struggles between good and evil or day and night; thousands of years later, lucha is still significant and sacred. It now is the good guys vs. the bad guys, that is, *técnicos* vs. *rudos*.

Traditional lucha libre is the spectacle/sport of masks. Traditional lucha libre is the spectacle/sport of the masks. This feature is not originally Mexican, but just like wrestling, incorporated perfectly into a set of cultural practices. One most trace back the origin of masks in lucha libre back to 1915 when an American wrestler named "The Masked Marvel," who was the first wrestler to wear a mask on the ring. The anthropologist Heather Levi insists that this was not part of a character developed for wrestling (like a luchador), but instead was "a gimmick."[8]

Masks were introduced to lucha libre in 1934 when an American wrestler, Cyclone MacKay, was working in Mexico and wanted to try the Masked Marvel act in the ring. McKay went to a shoemaker expert looking for help in creating his mask. A year later, Murciélago Velázquez began wearing a mask and it soon became an important motif in lucha libre.

Luchadors quickly made this trend their own; masks could hide their faces, allowing them both to maintain their privacy and portray memorable characters. Masks have a rich history in Mexican culture. The minute they appeared in the wrestling ring, they assumed a deeper meaning, building upon the rich traditions of masks in Mexico's indigenous and mestizo cultures. For example, almost every region in the country features traditional folk dances involving masks. The act of becoming another while remaining oneself is extremely important in our culture.

One of the traditional folk dances with which I'm very familiar is the *Danza de los huehues* (Dance of the elders), from the cultural and geographic region of the Huasteca, close to the Gulf of Mexico. During Xantolo, a celebration similar to the Day of the Dead, people dance while wearing large masks in order to trick the devil. During the dance, masked dancers approach and taunt others, saying, "You don't know me," creating a pact with their fellow dancers in the process. They are anonymous dancers, tricking the Devil with their masks, but at the same time, they are one's friends or neighbors. That is why they repeat the phrase "You don't know me": to remind each other that they are "others," and one should act differently around them. Masking and becoming "other" is a cultural practice and Mexicans see it frequently in many facets of life. Without knowing it, masked luchadors were establishing continuity with prehispanic and colonial dance rituals.

Roland Barthes emphasized wrestlers' gestures and facial expressions,[9] but with masked luchadors, we must consider the notion of a "paused" gesture. The mask essentially "pauses" the face, both protecting it and consolidating a luchador's distinct identity. Blood, sweat, shine and sparkle fall under Roland Barthes' categorization of wrestling as a "spectacle of excess." When exóticos appear without masks, in feminine dress and make-up, they innovate and defy tradition.

Binary Is Never Enough

The essence of the *exóticos* is that of artifice and exaggeration, the same characteristics Susan Sontag ascribes to camp.[10] To speak of Mexican camp is, to some extent, to apply an artificial category. Although glitter, sequins, and feather boas are definitely part of camp aesthetics, they are also part of the iconography of the Catrinas (famous female skeleton figures from the Day of the Dead) and the baroque and colorful nature of various other Mexican traditions. Camp aesthetics feature heavily in lucha libre, and not just among *exóticos*. Glitter and color are essential components of most luchadors' costumes, regardless of whether they identify as macho or queer. The *exótico* aesthetic, however, combines queer, camp, and drag. Drag, we must remember, is always political because it destabilizes gender structures shared by society. *Exóticos* shatter (or attempt to shatter) binary narratives of lucha libre. Being an *exótico* represents a departure from the typical *rudo/técnico* dynamic embraced by most luchadors.

Who Is an *Exótico*?

The *exóticos* were initially referred to in the press as *"raritos"* (little weirdos). The exotic nature of the *exóticos* comes from to different meanings. It is true, as Heather Levi states, that the term *"exótico"* is hardly ever used in any context other than lucha libre.[11] Originally, the term was used to describe wrestlers who resembled exotic dancers. *Los exóticos* was the name the press and promoters gave wrestlers such as Gardenia Davis, Lalo el exótico, and Bello Califa. The term was also used to describe the cabaret dancers who performed on the stage at the Tivoli Theater before a *lucha libre* presentation.[12] The *cabareteras* are a special kind of Mexican dancer that are part burlesque and part stripper. Cabarets were elegant and classy performance stages. The best musicians of the time played alongside the best dancers. Cabaret and *lucha libre* shared much in common, and luchador movies commonly featured scenes of cabaret dinners.

Exóticos made possible a flirtatious and potentially erotic reading of lucha libre. In the ring, interactions between male wrestlers, watched by largely-male audiences, is rarely read as a homoerotic display. Wrestling fans rarely associate desire or sexual tension with the in-ring performance, though wrestling features various degrees of domination and could easily be read that way. On the other hand, the *exótico* represented a strange new element whose performances were nothing like Mexican audiences had ever seen. Before *exóticos*, the moral alignments in lucha were either *rudo* or *técnico*, and those wrestlers avoided the elements of femininity that *exóticos* would embrace: according to conventional wrestling wisdom, perfume, flowers, pastel colors, and fancy, feminine hairdos were never meant for the arenas.

The mystical ritual of putting the mask on before wrestling, is instead a ritual of embellishment for *exóticos*. Make-up, wigs, and headpieces replace traditional luchador masks. This is particularly interesting because an *exótico* applies his make-up on his own, while a traditional masked wrestler needs help tying the back lace. With the help of make-up and wigs, the *exótico* is transformed. The paused gesture that is signified by a mask now becomes a gesture overlapped by color and glitter. The body of the *exótico* is different from that of a traditional luchador. They are allowed to move in ways other *luchadores* aren't. When Cassandro knocks down a wrestler and wins a fall, he can dance and shake his hips. They can also act playfully in the ring. If they knock down another wrestler they fan themselves and fake exhaustion while showing a perfectly-applied nail polish. While a traditional wrestler calls his companion "*güey*" (dude) and celebrates his triumphs with high-fives, an *exótico* typically calls his companion a "*mana*" (an apocope of "*hermana*": "sister"); in other words, the *exóticos* create family-like relations in the ring.

In *El Luchador fenómeno* (*The Phenomenonal Wrestler*, 1952), one of the very first Mexican movies about lucha libre, the main character wrestles an *exótico*: Lalo el *exótico*. This movie appearance makes clear that these kinds of wrestlers were very popular. Lalo el *exótico* steps into the ring and is both cheered and booed by the audience; the booing then becomes louder until it becomes a unified catcall. Once the catcalling begins, he sprays himself with perfume and fixes his hair; as he does that, the arena whistles and mocks him. Whether fans boo, cheer or catcall, *exóticos* always elicit a strong response when they enter an arena.

Gardenia Davis, Dandy in the Ring (Debuted 1941–1942)

Dizzy Gardenia Davis became famous during the 1940s. Lucha libre had never seen a character like this before. He handed out flowers to the ladies and was accompanied by a personal assistant, bringing a refined touch and radically new character to the sport. Before his debut, lucha libre was exclusively a sport for machos. Dizzy Davis brought a classy elegance to lucha libre, and that sort of thing was definitely not for machos. Elegance, understood by the hegemonic masculinity of luchadores, was for the weak.

Dizzy began the wrestling spectacle the instant he emerged from the dressing room. He was followed by an entourage with a gardenia bouquet (which is how he got his nickname). He would give gardenias to the ladies in the front row, then step into the ring. Once in the ring, his personal assistant would perfume him, fix his hair, and pamper him. The audience was very bothered by these episodes, so they booed and insulted him. During matches, he would become angry if his adversary messed up his hair, causing him to run to his assistant, who would fix his hair again. Such *prima donna* behavior served to further infuriate fans.

Davis was also known for his *rudo* technique. Although he was a *rudo*, he wrestled against *rudos* as well; the *exótico* is a different category and can wrestle either *técnicos* or *rudos*. In fact, one of his most emblematic matches was against Charro Aguayo, a famous *rudo* during the period. Davis would spray deodorant on his opponent, then hand him a bouquet of onions before wrestling him with his tougher technique (this act happened frequently).[13] Davis' act would not only inspire future *exóticos*, but the legendary American wrestler "Gorgeous" George Wagner, who drew (and infuriated) massive crowds and television ratings with his prissy, flamboyant persona throughout the 1940s, 1950s, and early 1960s.[14]

The Lilac Wave and the Fine Line Between Dandy and Drag

The '70s were a lively decade of success among *exóticos*, including Mario el Exótico, Divino Roy, Glamuroso [sic] Frolán, Perfumado Reyna, and Hermoso Hércules. Exóticos' names were as glamourous and campy as the wrestlers themselves. This bothered most of the lucha libre press (including *Box y lucha*, a famous periodical) who were scandalized by such displays of queer identity. In 1978, *Lucha Libre* magazine featured an article, "¡Basta ya de jotos!" ("Enough with the fags!"), written by a scandalized lucha libre expert who argued that *exóticos* have made a circus out of that sport and, he states with disgust, they even kiss each other and dress in women's clothes.[15] Fourteen years later, the same outrage towards *exóticos* was still prevalent. In 1992, Kid Vanegas, a *rudo*, declared in an interview that "now our partners go out all dolled-up, and that's not even a men's sport, like one can say, it is *vedetteism* now." Despite Vanegas' disapproval of the *exótico* style, he identifies the glam wrestlers with vedettes, the cabaret dancers featured frequently alongside early lucha shows.

Exóticos gained popular momentum when they began teaming together. In 1976, Sergio El Hermoso from Mexico City joined El Bello Greco of the northern city of Tampico. This pair won several championships during the 1970s and 1980s. They even claimed a historical link with La Maravilla

Enmascarada, the legendary wrestler who began the tradition of mask-wearing in lucha libre, despite the fact that *exóticos* do not wear them.

Why did they trace their origins to La Maravilla Enmascarada? It is a statement on performance. They defy the conventional expectations in lucha libre that a wrestler's body (the face in particular) was, more often than not, obscured. In contrast, *exóticos* emphasized their bodies both through their costumes and makeup as well as their "scandalous" behavior in the ring. The *exótico* represented a new, exotic masculinity in lucha libre that managed to break the binary dynamic of *rudos* and *técnicos* by offering a third, alternative moral alignment/persona.

Modern Exóticos

Cassandro (Debuted 1988, Plans to Retire 2017)

"We [the exóticos] are elegant, extravagant. I like to enter [the ring] in bathing suits. Of course! I love to put on make-up, it makes me whole.... I am myself and all my partners … we not only dress like this for work or to amuse the audience; the character you see in the ring is how I [really] feel."[16]

Cassandro is blond and wears a Farrah Fawcett–like hairstyle, the same he has worn for 27 years. He sews his own leotards, which he calls "bathing suits." He learned to cut, sew, and decorate each of his outfits to satisfy his own fashion taste; he learned these skills from a dress maker in Guadalajara. His fashion sense sets him apart from other *exóticos* because he is usually the best and most elaborately dressed.

Cassandro debuted in 1989. He was born in the northern city of Ciudad Juárez, Chihuahua, a city now famous because of its widespread murder and violence. It is a city of violence, drugs, and machismo. Being openly gay in Juárez is something not every wrestler nor every *norteño* (Mexican from the north, one of the most conservative and catholic regions of the country) can do, but Cassandro has managed to live openly as a gay luchador and a *norteño*. After a spread in *The New Yorker* in 2014, Cassandro became famous internationally, but in Mexico his fame goes back his 1992 match against Hijo del Santo,[17] son of El Santo, the most famous and legendary wrestler in the history of lucha libre.

May Flowers (Debuted 1986, No Date Set for Retirement)

May Flowers talks about how *exóticos* like to spice things up in lucha libre, "we spice things up in our lucha … we rub up on the referee, kiss him, pinch him, scratch our adversary and make the audience part of what we are doing"[18] Born in the northern city of Torreón, Coahuila, May Flowers is an *exótico* who was working at a gay bar when friends invited him to join a gymnasium that taught lucha libre; soon after, he began training to become a wrestler. His name is a reference to the famous *Mayflower* ship that brought the Pilgrim settlers to America, and was suggested to him by a lucha promoter because he could "conquer the audience."[19] "May Flowers" instead of Mayflower puts a campy spin on the nickname.

I met May Flowers during a special lucha libre event: *Exóticos* and *Extremos* (extreme wrestlers who are ultra-violent; they fight with chairs, baseball bats, lamps), held at the Colonia Guerrero, a small gymnasium in one of the most dangerous neighborhoods in Mexico City. He wore an all-black flamenco-like outfit, strategically exposing the chest. May Flowers told me he made that outfit himself. In lucha libre it is not strange for a wrestler's chest to be bare, and many conventional wrestlers show even more flesh than he was. Because Flowers is an *exótico*, the exposure of his chest becomes sexualized as provocative. The moment he exited the dressing room, the audience cheers and yells about his chest. As an *exótico*, his breasts are thought of as feminine and are immediately erotized. Someone in the audience yelled "¡Qué bonitas chichis!" (That's some beautiful boobs!); in response, May Flowers blew him a kiss.

Máximo (Debuted in 2000)

Sporting a pink Mohawk and a purple gladiator robe with a miniskirt, Máximo is the most beloved modern *exótico* in Mexico. He wrestles for *Consejo Mundial de Lucha Libre* (CMLL, Lucha Libre World Council, the world's oldest continually-operating wrestling promotion), whereas most *exóticos* are independent, not under contract to any specific wrestling promotion. He is both an *exótico* and a *técnico*. Unlike Cassandro or May Flowers, Máximo is part of an important wrestling dynasty, the Brazos (Arms); his father, Brazo de Plata (Silver Arm) is one of the most legendary wrestlers from the 80s. Máximo is the only *exótico* in his family.

When Máximo is in the ring, he performs as an *exótico* flirting with men, grabbing and kissing them. Out of the ring, even if he is still dressed in his *exótico* clothes, he acts gallantly with the ladies; once I had the opportunity to talk to Máximo and he called me "nena" (baby) and was very flirty. He has declared in interviews that he acts gay in the ring, and that it comes naturally, despite the fact that he is actually heterosexual.[20] Acting out a sexual preference is a performative act, the same as wearing a mask or make-up in *lucha libre*.

Miss Gaviota (Debuted 2010)

Miss Gaviota embodies many aspects of an outsider to *lucha libre*. Miss Gaviota is a trans woman but wrestles with men and is herself thought of as a man by many fans. But because she is queer and "other," she is considered an *exótico*. She belongs to one of Mexico City's most important working-class barrios, the Lagunilla, were she is a stylist. Miss Gaviota is also a devotee of the Santa Muerte (Holy Death), a controversial folk saint frowned upon by religious authorities. Catholic faith is rather common in lucha libre; El Santo, for example, was known for being a devotee of the Virgin of Guadalupe, the most popular Catholic icon in Mexico. Devotees of the Santa Muerte, however, are considered part of an underground cult, associated with criminals and the LGBT community; outsiders, figures like Miss Gaviota.

When Miss Gaviota enters the ring, she says her signature phrase "*Quiúbole*" (barrio slang for "what's up"). The question is both an invitation and a confrontation. Trans communities in Mexico often endure discrimination and violence. When she enters the ring and confronts men, the gesture resonates far beyond the ring, defying ongoing negativity and misconceptions of transgendered individuals. The very presence of a trans female body in the ring is a powerful statement on the exoticness of the *exóticos*, and she emphasizes her gender identity in her dress, wearing fancy bustiers to show off her ample bosom.[21] Heather Levi talks about how *lucha libre* is able to connect contradictory domains[22] and with Miss Gaviota this is no exception.

During a match in November 2016, Miss Gaviota teamed with May Flawers against Tinieblas Jr., and Anibal Jr. (a técnico team). Both *exóticos* began the match with colorful antics, pretending they didn't know how to wrestle and falling constantly. When the action became more serious, Miss Gaviota challenged Tinieblas Jr.: "let's wrestle man to man."[23] Miss Gaviota's verbal challenge is especially meaningful. In the ring, an *exótico* can be teased because of his (or in this case her) queerness, allowing *rudos* or *ténicos* to mock the "other." In this case, Miss Gavota wanted to set things straight: while she wrestles as an *exótico*, she is the equal of any man. *Exóticos* are thought of as men, not machos, but *maricones* (fags, as they call them in the arenas).

Miss Gaviota has stated that her signature move is the "*quebradora* against homophobia." The "*quebradora*" (back-breaker) is a common wrestling move popularized in Mexico by luchadores such as Santo and Blue Demon, and therefore is performed as a fundamental element in many matches. Miss Gaviota's move works the same as the classic back-breaker, but the great difference here is who is executing it. By making it her own and calling it a "back-breaker against homophobia," Miss Gaviota is wrestling for representation and resistance, publicly challenging and defying ongoing negativity toward the Mexican LGBT community.

It Ends with a Kiss

"From the moment the audience sees that we are about to go up the ring, they start screaming "Kiss!, kiss!, kiss!" because they know our way of being."[24]

"If people ask for a kiss, why wouldn't we indulge them?"[25]

The *exótico's* boldest and most emblematic move is a kiss. They often kiss their opponents on the lips while holding their head with both hands. A man kissing another man in the middle of a lucha libre arena is a statement on power and gender relations. The first *exóticos* did not kiss their opponents, but rather sprayed them with perfume; decades later, direct contact became the norm. Both perfuming and kissing are soft interventions on an opponent's body. Unlike conventional wrestling holds, a kiss is a gesture that can be read as tender or loving, but given the context of in-ring performance, it is deemed as a violent violation. A kiss can hurt the other wrestler more than a strong, open-hand blow. *Exóticos* are literally fighting against heterosexual masculinity, and win or lose, they compete not only against their in-ring opponents, but also against binary constructions of masculinity. Just as there is no a single, monolithic construction of a "man," there is no uniform definition of a luchador. *Exóticos* bring diversity to lucha libre and while they entertain, they literally fight for a place among the more conventional heroes and villains forged in the arenas, challenging traditional notions of gender and masculinity in the process.

Notes

1. Centro de Estudios Históricos, *Historia general de México* (México: El Colegio de México, 2002), 825.
2. Centro de Estudios Históricos, *Historia general de México*, 836.
3. Centro de Estudios Históricos, *Historia general de México*, 1054.
4. Heather Levi, *The World of Lucha libre* (Durham: Duke University Press, 2008), 10.
5. Álvaro Fernández, *Santo, el enmascarado de plata. Mito y realidad de un héroe mexicano moderno* (Guadalajara: Universidad de Guadalajara, 2012), 44.
6. Fernández, *Santo*, 47.
7. Roland Barthes, "El mundo del catch," in Barthes, *Mitologías* (México, D.F.: Siglo XXI, 1999), 8.
8. Levi, *The World of Lucha libre*, 109–10.
9. Roland Barthes, "El mundo del catch," in Barthes, *Mitologías* (México, D.F.: Siglo XXI, 1999), 8.
10. Susan Sontag, *Against Interpretation and Other Essays* (London: Penguin, 2009), 275.
11. Heather Levi, *The World of Lucha Libre* (Durham: Duke University Press, 2008), 153.

12. Juan Cervera, "El bello Greco y Sergio el hermoso. La fragancia sobre el ring," in Alfonso Morales Carillo, ed., *Espectacular de lucha libre* (México, D.F.: Trilce, 2008), 38.

13. "Dizzy Gardenia Davis, un gran exótico," *Box y Lucha*, last modified November 14, 2009, http://boxylucha.com/dizzy-gardenia-davis-un-gran-exotico/.

14. Joe Jares, "George was Villainous, Gutsy, and Gorgeous," *Sports Illustrated*, March 17, 1969.

15. "Gardenia y los exóticos," in *Luna Córnea* 27 (September/November, 2003), 149.

16. *Sin máscara ni cabellera. Lucha libre en México hoy*, ed. Lola Miranda Fascinetto (México, D.F.: Marc Ediciones, 1992), 194.

17. William Finnegan, "The Man Without a Mask: How the Drag Queen Cassandro Became a Star of Mexican Wrestling," *The New Yorker*, September 1, 2014, http://www.newyorker.com/magazine/2014/09/01/man-without-mask.

18. "Exóticos," in Lola Miranda Fascinetto, ed., *Sin máscara ni cabellera. Lucha libre en México hoy* (México, D.F.: Marc Ediciones, 1992), 184.

19. "Exóticos," 186.

20. Caitlin Donohue, "Welcome to My World: El Máximo, Exótico," *The Hairpin*, last modified December 2, 2014, https://thehairpin.com/welcome-to-my-world-el-m%C3%A1ximo-ex%C3%B3tico-304238ef57f3#.gsj11po4n.

21. Chema Artero, "Miss Gaviota: la única luchadora trans mexicana," *Vice Mexico*, last modified March 20, 2015, https://www.vice.com/es_mx/article/miss-gaviota.

22. Levi, *The World of Lucha libre*, xiii.

23. Wrestling Carnival Entertainment Channel, "Exóticos May Flowers Miss Gaviota VS Tinieblas Anibal, Jr.," *YouTube*, November 29, 2016. YouTube, 8:02 minutes, https://www.youtube.com/watch?v=se5KCKadUfE&vl=es-419.

24. Lola Miranda Fascinetto, ed., *Sin máscara ni cabellera. Lucha libre en México hoy* (México, D.F.: Marc Ediciones, 1992), 195.

25. "Exóticos," 189.

Transformed Bodies and Gender Norms
Gender Identity of Japanese Women Pro Wrestlers[1]

Keiko Aiba

This essay will discuss the benefits and challenges women pro wrestlers believe they receive in their daily life. Why is this kind of research needed? Because previous studies in Anglophone countries have suggested that women acquire various benefits by engaging in physical activities such as sports and that such benefits have influenced women's lives outside these particular physical activities. However, the discussion about the ways in which physical activity and sports affect the daily lives of women still has much room for expansion, even among the studies in Anglophone countries.

Meanwhile, no studies in Japan have considered the benefits of sport to women athletes or how it has influenced their daily lives.[2] It is possible that women who do not participate in physical activities are denied the possible benefits of such activities, because women in Japan are generally discouraged to participate in sports. Thus, research needs to be conducted about women athletes. Hence, I will examine women pro wrestlers, engaging in physical activities similar to competitive sports, focusing on what they attained from physical activity and its impact on their daily lives.

In Japan some women have participated in combative sports such as amateur wrestling and judo and done well in international competitions. I define combative sports as competitions or physical activities where attacking opponents is allowed within a team or one-on-one context.[3] For example, amateur wrestling and *judo* fit the second category of combative sports. This essay focuses not on women who participate in combative sports but on women pro wrestlers, who participate in activities similar to combative sports.

The reason is that the skills women pro wrestlers attain from their "fights" in pro wrestling are more impactful than the skills attained from many other combative sports. Pro wrestling has a variety of offensive techniques that include throwing, choking, submission, kicking, and striking techniques. These techniques are basically permitted for use as long as they are not a threat to the life of wrestlers. In contrast, in amateur wrestling, which shares some affinities with pro wrestling, striking, choking, and submission techniques are not allowed (Japan Wrestling Federation).[4]

Moreover, pro wrestlers have to learn to be on the receiving end of various moves as part of their training. While boxers and judoka focus on avoiding attacks from opponents and winning each match as soon as possible, in pro wrestling, wrestlers must cooperate in exchanging moves. Thus, women pro wrestlers have to master taking "bumps," learning to fall correctly to absorb the impact of various moves. In contrast, if you simply fall backwards in judo, you will lose by an *ippon*.[5] Therefore, wrestlers execute and receive a variety of techniques that have greater cumulative impact on the body, deliberately absorbing the impact of various moves on a regular basis, than other combative sports such as amateur wrestling and *judo*. Considering this, I assume that the benefits women pro wrestlers attained from physical activity and its impact on their daily lives are relatively unique, although future studies in experiences of women athletes in amateur wrestling and judo may find some similarities.

Women Pro Wrestlers in Japan

Since the late 1980s, aggressive, hard-hitting pro wrestling with complex techniques has been the mainstream in women's pro wrestling in Japan. Thus, those women who aim to become pro wrestlers must train with their particular wrestling organizations from six months to a year. After obtaining basic physical fitness, they have to master taking bumps (to absorb the shocks when they take moves from their opponents or when they perform them), rope work (running into and moves from the ropes), and individual signature moves. Many, though not all, women pro wrestlers try to enlarge their bodies through increased training and higher food intake after they join a pro wrestling organization. They do so because among women's pro wrestling promoters and women pro wrestlers themselves in Japan, it is assumed that women wrestlers with big bodies, featuring various combinations of muscles and fat, enchant the audience much more than do those with slim and small bodies.

I conducted research to investigate the process of physical formation of women pro wrestlers and the ways in which they perceived their own bodies by conducting interviews with 25 women pro wrestlers (including three retirees) and observing their performances from 2004 to 2005. This essay represents part of that research. All the names of the wrestlers in the text are pseudonyms. The details of the research methods are explained in Aiba.[6]

The Impact of Physical Activities on Women in Previous Studies

Benefits

Two kinds of previous research will be examined here. First, there are studies about what women believe they gained by engaging not only in competitive sports, but also in a wide range of physical activities, including bodybuilding. The second type includes studies on the effects and benefits of athletic activities in women's everyday lives.

Previous studies demonstrate that physical activity led women to regard their bodies as strong and capable, boosted their confidence, and developed a greater sense of unity between mind and body.[7] Furthermore, it has been suggested that women who participate in physical activities developed positive attitudes toward their lives,[8] overcame the division of mind and body,[9] or attained a sense of attunement between their bodies and the outside world.[10]

When women benefit from their physical activities, what impact does it have on their daily lives? The positive impact on their daily lives can be practical or psychological. Practical benefits would include the ability to lift heavy loads without assistance.[11]

The psychological benefit varies. Blinde et al.[12] recognized that, along with their perception that they had strong and competent bodies, female athletes paid more attention to their own health and bettered their understanding about how to care for their bodies. Women athletes studied by Scott-Dixon[13] claimed that, by engaging in physical activities, they could tackle new challenges. Moreover, some women attained confidence that they could escape from potential street assaults.[14] Some women also developed, more generally, a positive attitude toward their lives and prospects.[15] For example, they could muster the confidence in "getting divorced, starting their own businesses, going back to school, confronting an abuser, and getting over an eating disorder."[16]

Challenges[17]

In addition to their benefits to women, physical activities have also led to societal challenges. Women who play sports that require strength and physical power,[18] with bigger, heavier, and taller than normative bodies, have endured negative comments about their body size, physical competence, or the very fact that they engage in those kinds of sports.[19] For example, some women endured negative comments about the fact that they played sports that historically embodied masculinity, such as American or Australian football.[20]

Women's Physical Activities and Physical Empowerment

According to some studies, empowerment is a primary benefit for female athletes.[21] What is "empowerment"? The concept of empowerment is still developing and its definition varies by discipline.[22] However, Kubota[23] points out that previous studies have suggested at least three characteristics of empowerment as a concept. First, those who are empowered are in a status in which they "lack power."[24] Thus, "empowerment" means the process in which "strength is provided"[25] to those who could not fully realize their potential power for some reason. Second, what is gained by empowerment is "what people have internally and something drawn out through reciprocal relationships with others"[26] and means "the power to realize their own abilities, including self-confidence."[27] Finally, the process of empowerment includes not only psychological elements, but also social, political, and economic ones. Thus, empowerment is the process by which individuals realize their own power, or develop abilities that impact or cooperate with others to change the social system at the individual, group, and systemic levels.[28]

According to Wright and Dewar,[29] women who engaged in various sports and physical activities saw themselves as physically strong, the opposite of vulnerability. Here, physical strength implies neither remarkable ability nor muscularity. Instead, it enables them to tackle physical challenges or to pursue individual goals, which in turn become the source of their self-confidence. McDermott[30] showed that women who participated in a long-distance canoe trip learned their real physical capabilities, especially their physical strength. Their experiences provided them confidence in their physical abilities. In a study by Yarnel et al.,[31] women who participated in Camp Blaze, to learn firefighting techniques, experienced an increased consciousness about the control of their bodies and a growing sense of overall competence. This consciousness broadened their understanding about their bodies' potential. By accomplishing what seemed impossible or what they had been scared of, these women re-discovered their bodies' potential, and this discovery empowered them. Hollander[32] studied women who had participated in self-defense training and found that those women viewed their bodies as strong and competent, which strengthened their confidence about their ability to protect their bodies. Wedgewood[33] showed that many girls who played Australian football viewed themselves as strong, defensive, agile, and assertive. Blinde et al.[34] pointed out that individual empowerment is to gain physical competence, to recognize self-efficacy, and to act assertively. Furthermore, women begin to view their bodies as strong and capable by playing sports. These studies suggest that women and girls attain various kinds of physical strength by engaging in sports or physical activities. When strong physical capabilities are gained, the strength suggested here includes not only physical ability, but a sense of invulnerability. The self-recognition in women and girls of physical strength leads them to view their bodies as having tremendous potential. In other words, they begin to view their own bodies not through the lens of others' eyes and expectations, but rather as having the potential to accomplish their own goals.[35] As discussed later, many women and girls in modern Japan cannot fully use their potential physical strength, preventing them from fully realizing their potential. Therefore, physical empowerment refers the process by which women in modern Japanese society attain physical strength and recognize the potential of their bodies.

What Women Pro Wrestlers Attained

The interviews with women pro wrestlers suggested that they attained benefits through pro wrestling and that they were challenged by gender norms. First, I will discuss the benefits that those women attained through pro wrestling. These women pro wrestlers pointed out that the benefits included politeness, kindness, and strength (for more discussion of politeness and kindness, see Aiba).[36] One of the benefits, strength, is divided into three categories; physical strength; mental strength; and a combination of both. Although most women pro wrestlers' accounts concerned only one of those three categories, only the story of Sawako included all three.

Physical Strength: "I can deal with any heavy stuff"

Women pro wrestlers noted that they recognized their physical strength when they carried their own or others' heavy luggage. One wrestler, Rei, as a rookie, carried a lot of her seniors' baggage on her shoulders. That experience provided her confidence that she could carry any heavy load on her shoulders. "Like I can put anything here [on my shoulders]. Hey, I can walk with it, it's a piece of cake," she described. When Sawako had practical training in a hospital to obtain the Level 2 license of a home-caregiver, she had to take care of an elderly person by herself. While one of her friends received support from another nurse during training, Sawako worked alone because she did not need physical assistance on the job. She thought that she "feels rewarded when relied on like that. The elderly, too, may feel comfortable with my big body." She thought it was worthwhile training her body as a wrestler.

The fact that these women pro wrestlers carried heavy luggage with ease, as Rei mentioned, is a benefit of their rookie training. Rookies attained their basic physical fitness through long hours of weight training. In addition, when their pro wrestling organizations were touring, they carried their seniors' luggage, loading and unloading it to or from the tour bus. They also carried heavy iron poles and wooden slates, used to assemble and disassemble the ring, night after night. These experiences built the wrestlers' confidence in their ability to carry heavy loads.

Mental Toughness

Several wrestlers claimed that they became mentally stronger. Sayaka thought she got better at getting along with people after becoming a wrestler. Due to the hierarchical relationship in her wrestling organization, she learned, through the relationship with the seniors, to put her seniors ahead of her own concerns. As a result of these experiences, she became more patient and "can now put up with things she couldn't bear before," which she thought "was good" for her. Masumi, too, explained that, along with the tough training as a rookie, the bitter experiences with her seniors made her strong mentally, so that even when she faced hardship, she could reflect on memories of past difficulties and think, "This is going to be okay because I went through the tough old days."

Physical Strength and Mental Strength

Some wrestlers made a distinction between physical and mental strength. Mika explained that she felt stronger both physically and mentally. Before she became a wrestler, she said she may not have been able to get up again after being thrown out of the ring. After she became a wrestler, she learned to unleash her power skillfully, even when taking others' moves. Because she mastered taking bumps, even when she fell off the stairs, she "did not hit [her] head or break any bones." She also said that, in addition to this physical strength, her mental strength helped her bear physical pain. She believed that her mental strength developed while she endured the miscellaneous tasks and hierarchical relationship as a rookie, and she did not give up easily. Mika claimed that both mental and physical strength combined to make her strong.

Yumiko discussed the two strengths, too. She viewed herself as mentally tougher, which meant she "follows through with what she wants to do." This phrase may indicate that she went through various twists and turns to achieve her dream of becoming a pro wrestler. She also thought that she had better physical strength than others. As she explained, "I choose stairs ... rather than an escalator ... and go up like this, leaping up. As I see myself like that.... I think maybe I'm still OK." In this way, women recognized that they gained politeness, kindness to others, physical and/or mental strength through their involvement in pro wrestling.

Challenges from the Gender Norms

Women wrestlers challenge gender norms in several ways. For example, they often cannot wear "*kawaii* clothes," and they are sometimes mistaken for men.

Giving Up "*Kawaii*" Clothes

"*Kawaii*" clothes are clothes that embody qualities of *kawaii*. For women, being *kawaii* is "friendly, simple, easily picked up, with psychological closeness."[37] Specifically, something little, childish, and nostalgic is recognized as "*kawaii*."[38] Thus, the "*kawaii*" clothes described here are specified as small-size clothes with childish and nostalgic elements. The smallness in size is especially important.

In Japan, the societal category of "young women" tends to be represented with fashionable clothes in small size.[39] As the standard size of fashionable clothes is size 9 (in case of 9AR, the measurements are 83 cm in bust, 64 cm in waist, 91 cm in hip),[40] and many Japanese women try to fit this size by diet and other means.[41] As most "*kawaii*" clothes are manufactured for women, if bodies cannot fit into the size many women prefer, it indicates that the women cannot wear "*kawaii*" clothes. Women wrestlers develop bodies of muscle and fat, rather than the conventional "slim" bodies that represent the gender norm. Consequently, many wrestlers who could no longer wear "*kawaii*" clothes had to alter their clothing.

Appearance

Rie said that as a wrestler, her body was bigger than before. Even when store-bought women's clothes did not fit, she searched for larger sizes and tried to continue wearing feminine attire. In addition, because her character as a wrestler in the organization was meant to possess "adult sexual charms," she tried to maintain that image with feminine clothes in her daily life, trying not turn off fans by wearing "masculine clothing in her private life."

However, even though other wrestlers wanted to dress like Rie, if they could not fit into larger-size women's clothes, they sometimes had to limit or give up on wearing feminine clothes.[42] Maki, another wrestler, dealt with this issue differently. She used to dress in "poor frumpy style" with a sweatsuit, but she changed her mind after performing in the U.S. She realized that she had to dress up in public, as fans might see her anytime. She also began wearing clothes with "a simple form, but good fabric." Maki explained that pro wrestling was widely recognized in the U.S. as a performance, and fans viewed the wrestlers as entertainers. Maki noted that pro wrestlers were admired by people and required to maintain their style outside the ring so as not to hurt their fans' image of them. Also, while she could not find fashionable clothes in Japan when she got larger, in the U.S. there was plenty of larger-size feminine clothing, so she had more choice for her out-of-ring attire.

Men's Clothes or Sweatsuits

Some women wrestlers, who were not able to wear female clothes, chose to wear men's clothes or sweatsuits. Before entering the organization, Sayaka used to wear women's clothes, even though she was big, because she "hated" to wear men's clothes. However as she became a wrestler, she often received hand-me-downs of "men's" clothes from her seniors. While wearing these clothes, her style became more boyish. Eventually she came to like such boyish clothing. She stopped searching for women's clothes, in favor of men's clothes. She explained that women's clothes are too small, but men's clothes have the best size for her, with lots of choices. She told that she "came to like big and cool [men's] clothes" better than women's clothes.

Other wrestlers spent most of their day in sweatsuits. Yoshie explained that she had been living with sweatsuits since she became a wrestler. In fact, partly because her interview took place just after practice at the training hall, she was in her two-piece sweatsuit. "A sweatsuit is kind of formal, but it's casual, too. I wear the sweatsuit anytime. At home I wear the little old one [laugh], when I go out, I change to the better one, then, at practice, I change again to the one for training. I might just wear sweatsuit all day."

Why did she spend all day with the sweatsuit? She explained that it's "easy to move." She wanted to wear clothes that let her move easily because she spent most of her day either training or performing pro wrestling, and had little free time to wear her private clothes. What is interesting here is that, as she mentioned, even if she always wore the same style of sweatsuit, she wore new ones when she went out or entered the pro wrestling arena. She used the old ones at practice or at home. However, she also mentioned that she wore jeans instead of sweatsuits when she would meet someone. She was not completely indifferent to how others perceive her.

Being Mistaken for Men

Features Recognized as Masculine

Several women wrestlers recalled experiences in which they were mistaken for men. They mentioned that they were mistaken as men because of certain features. For example, Aya said that she was often called, "brother," on the street. She mentioned that it happened not because she had a masculine and muscular body, but because her clothes were a T-shirt and jeans, with her hair short. Furthermore, she also explained that her boyish face with no make-up might encourage the mistake. This implied that when a person whose sex is female expresses herself through a style involving short hair and casual style (T-shirt and jeans), some people perceive the person's gender as masculine.

Big bodies, one of the characteristics that lead to women wrestlers being mistaken for men, include broad shoulders, tallness, and wide frames. Sayaka explained that she was mistaken for a man because of her appearance and physical characteristics. She mentioned that her hair was short and her body was big, and that "there is no woman with this wide back," leading others to mistake her for a man.

Reactions

Once Sawako was walking in a beautiful dress at Roppongi with another woman wrestler, her tag-team partner.[43] When a bystander yelled out, calling her a "beautiful queer," she immediately turned and responded, "I'm a woman." The man was shocked and shouted, "Wow, you guys are **** [the name of their tag-team]!" The use of "queer" here seems to indicate a man who dresses as a woman. In other words, he perceived Sawako as a man who dressed as a woman.

Those women wrestlers especially felt discomfort with being mistaken for men in women's public bathrooms. Even if they tried not to care, it made them stressed that others were confounded, staring or pointing out to them that they were in the wrong bathroom. When Yumiko entered a women's bathroom, she felt "disgusted as someone told her, 'Oh, the men's bathroom is over there.'" On other occasions, when other women saw her in the bathroom, they believed that they had accidentally entered the men's bathroom. They would silently go out, check the bathroom signs, and return. They kept watching Yumiko, wondering whether she was a woman or man. She mentioned, however, that this kind of thing happened so often that she became accustomed to it, trying not to care.

Those women wrestlers mistaken for men took it for granted that others misunderstood their sex category based on their appearance, and they mainly explained how they dealt with it. Only Midori expressed her frustration toward those who mistook her sex category. She noted that she did not care if she was mistaken for a man when she was with other women wrestlers, but when she was alone and "some middle-aged woman called out, like, 'You're in the wrong place,' I'm so embarrassed." She felt angry toward that woman and disgusted as other women stared at her. But she did not give up; she said, "I'm a woman," and used the bathroom.

Results

Women wrestlers mistaken for men did not choose consciously to develop a "masculine" appearance. They unwittingly obtained their muscular bodies as a result of their wrestling training.[44] Thus, few women wrestlers believed they had gained any benefits from the fact that they were mistaken for men. However, one wrestler, Sachi, noted that she did not have to worry about getting assaulted on the street at night because she was seen as a man. In this case, too, she implied that the situation was as an unintended by-product of becoming a wrestler. As most wrestlers seldom recognized the benefit of being mistaken for men, they regarded it as bothersome and negative.

Comparison Between the Previous Studies and the Recognition of Women Pro Wrestlers

I will compare the benefits and challenges women wrestlers received and faced through their involvement in pro wrestling with findings in previous studies. First, those wrestlers, too, mentioned practical benefits suggested by previous studies, such as being able to carry heavy luggage without others' help. Moreover, as several studies suggest,[45] those wrestlers recognized that they had gained tremendous physical strength. Other wrestlers claimed that they obtained mental strength through wrestling, while others said they gained both physical and mental strength.

The wrestlers interviewed in this study claimed a benefit from wrestling not mentioned in the previous studies: politeness and kindness to others. This is not because these women were pro wrestlers, but because of the particular social structure in pro wrestling organizations. Some wrestlers learned to extend politeness and kindness to others through their hierarchical relationships with their senior wrestlers, and some wrestlers attained mental strength by enduring their subordinate relationship to their seniors.

Physical Strength as Empowerment

The women wrestlers attained physical strength through pro wrestling, which provided them with confidence. In other words, they attained physical strength and realized that their bodies had potential; as a result, they gained self-confidence in their bodies. In contrast to these wrestlers, many women in modern Japan do not possess such confidence in their physical abilities. The basis of this statement will be explained below, noting the distinction between girls under 19 years old and adult women over 20 years old. The major reason is that most Japanese girls under 19 tend to exercise or participate in sports, which can provide them with physical strength or confidence, but to a much lesser extent than boys of the same age.

The proportion of elementary school girls[46] who spend at least 60 minutes per week performing physical activities was 21 percent in 2013, almost twice that of boys (about 9 percent).[47] On the other hand, the proportion of girls who spend at 420 minutes per week on physical activities was 27 percent in 2013 while that of boys was around 55 percent, indicating a wide disparity between the two groups.[48]

In junior high schools, the proportion of girls who take up to 60 minutes per week for all physical activities was around 30 percent in 2013, three times as many as that of the boys (10 percent).[49] On the other hand, the proportion of junior high school girls who spend up to 420 minutes per week for all physical activities was around 56 percent in 2012, showing a large disparity with junior high school boys (81 percent).[50] In high schools, the proportion of girls who engaged in no physical activities except physical education in school was around 25 percent.[51] With much less participation in athletics compared to boys, fewer girls have access to the possible benefits of sports and exercise, such as increased physical strength or self-confidence.

Meanwhile, how do adult women perceive their bodies? There has been no previous study about this issue in Japan. Some information can be found in "Public Opinion Survey on Physical Strength and Sports,"[52] conducted with over 1,900 men and women age 20 and older. This survey simply shows that more men "have confidence in their physical strength" than women, while more women are "concerned with their physical strength" than men.[53] Do adult women, like girls under 19, not engage with physical activities or sports that enable them to develop physical strength and competence? The situation of adult women's practice of physical activities and sports, in fact, shows a different picture from that of girls under 19. A 2012 study provides data analyzing the practice of physical activities and sports among people from their 20s to their 70s in 2012, categorized into five levels.[54]

This data suggests that the proportion of men who play sports or physical activities of "Level 2" or higher, indicating regular physical activity, averages around 47 percent across all age groups, while that of women is about 51 percent, implying that more women engage in physical activities than men.[55] However, the proportion of men at Level 0 (no regular exercise) is about 23 percent while that of women is about 28 percent. Adult women seem to be polarized in their level of physical activities and sports.[56] Furthermore, analyzed by types of physical activities, the proportion of women engaged in walking and calisthenics is significantly higher than that of men. Still, the types of sport that indicate significantly higher proportion of women than men are interpersonal ball sports (e.g., tennis, table tennis) and exercises (e.g., aerobics dance, yoga).[57] Among four types of physical activities and four types of sports, especially, the proportion of practitioners of the exercise group type tended to list the maintenance or slim-down of their physiques as their purpose of practice more than those in other groups. Thus, many adult women engage in physical activities so as to establish or maintain ideal female bodies, not to acquire physical strength or to realize their bodies' full potential.

In contrast, women wrestlers mentioned that they attained physical strength, regarded their bodies as strong, and gained confidence in their bodies through pro wrestling. Those women wrestlers were also subjected to dominant physical socialization, like other women in modern Japanese society. It is a process by which girls or adult women are strongly encouraged to make ideal female bodies while neither their participation in sports[58] nor development of their physical strength or capabilities[59] is encouraged. Bear in mind here that even before women wrestlers entered their various pro wrestling organizations, most of them had already gained physical confidence through their participation in a wide range of sports. All the women wrestlers in this essay who suggested that they gained physical strength from pro wrestling had engaged in other sports or physical activities before entering their organizations. In other words, many women wrestlers had experienced a process different from the dominant socialization of female bodies, and they experience pro wrestling as yet another physical activity after joining pro wrestling organizations.

As defined above, physical empowerment means the process by which women in modern Japanese society, who do not fully realize their innate physical strength, can attain physical strength and recognize the potential of their bodies. Although women wrestlers, like other girls or adult women, live under the influence of the dominant socialization of bodies in modern Japanese society, they undergo physical empowerment through their involvement in sports and pro wrestling.

Challenges from the Ideal Female Bodies

Many wrestlers were not able to wear *kawaii* clothes because of how they developed their bodies as wrestlers. This essay analyzes the circumstances or feelings of wrestlers who could not wear *kawaii* clothes, and elucidates that "*kawaii* clothes," which signify "young women," control female bodies by establishing a particular size (size 9) as "ideal." The fact that many women wrestlers' bodies do not fit into *kawaii* clothes implies that their bodies are not seen as those of "young women." Moreover, as *kawaii* clothes are mostly produced in size 9, which requires bodies to be slim, these wrestlers are viewed as deviant from the Japanese female body ideal. However, many wrestlers did not attempt to conform to the idea of wearing *kawaii* clothes; they solved this issue by wearing men's clothes or sweatsuits. Although the wrestlers did not challenge the widely-accepted category of "young women" embodied in *kawaii* clothes or the ideal female body, they themselves did not try to fit into the category or the ideal female body. They found new ways by which they could dress and express their bodies, now built for pro wrestling.

Bodies That Are Mistaken for Men

Some wrestlers were mistaken for men because people used the premise in the sex/gender system—it is a system whereby each of the ideological connections of sex category, gender category, and sexual orientation has a dichotomous structure[60]—in the process when they attribute others with gender category. That women wrestlers felt annoyed when they were mistaken for men implies that their bodies were challenged by the sex/gender system, but it also illuminated that they challenged that system.

In the process of gender attribution, first, every person infers whether the sex category is male or female, whether the gender category is a man or a woman, and whether the person is masculine or feminine. Second, "the person's physical characteristics, attitude, and personality propensity"[61] construct the cues to gender and are interpreted either as masculine or feminine. "Observed gender cues are instantaneously and unconsciously weighed, and a gender is attributed, i.e., feminine people are seen as women, masculine people are seen as men."[62] If uncertainty is identified in gender attribution to a particular individual, people have a strong tendency to recognize masculinity in that individual.[63] Specifically, when there is a cue that demonstrates something seen as male, masculinity is recognized assertively. Yet, only when there is a persuasive cue for femininity and when there is no cue for masculinity, is femininity recognized.[64]

The wrestlers who felt discomfort with being mistaken for men continued to identify as women. Thus, they wanted to be recognized as women no matter how they looked. Nevertheless, these wrestlers were unintentionally mistaken for men because they did not show the cues to their gender, which led others to view them as men. Therefore, though it is not *intentional*, they *eventually* challenge the sex/gender system that suggests women should offer clues of gender to show that their gender category is a woman.

Women Pro Wrestlers' Physical Resistance to the Gender Norm

The women wrestlers attained physical strength that many other women did not possess, and they underwent physical empowerment through their sports experience and their engagement in pro wrestling. This implies that women who do not engage in physical activities could experience physical empowerment through physical activities and sport. This essay tried to examine, for the first time, the ways in which physical activities, including sports, impact the daily lives of Japanese women who engage in those activities. The discussion has just begun, and needs to be developed further. Moreover, since the benefits or challenges the women receive or face might change depending on the types of physical activities in which they engage, similar studies across a wide range of physical activities and sports are necessary.

The women wrestlers found that they could not wear *kawaii* clothes because of the bodies they obtained by engaging in pro wrestling. They did not consciously resist the established social category of "young women" or ideal feminine bodies that *kawaii* clothes exemplify. However, some wrestlers did not try to conform to the ideal female body; in their daily lives, they clothed their muscular wrestlers' bodies in alternative styles, in contrast to the *kawaii* ideal. Many of these wrestlers were unintentionally mistaken for men. This is an informal sanction to such women, displaying masculinity in the sex/gender system. Despite these physical sanctions, women wrestlers who were mistaken for men challenge the sex/gender system by not changing their appearance, however unintentionally. This point offers a new perspective for future gender studies as it indicates the possibility that even men and women who seemingly adapt to gender norms may also take actions that threaten those norms, as did the women wrestlers in this essay.

Notes

1. Published originally in Keiko Aiba, *Joshi puroresu no shintai to jenda: kihanteki onnarashisa wo koete* (*Bodies of Women Professional Wrestlers and Gender: Beyond Normative Femininity*) (Tokyo: Akashi Shoten, 2013). Translated by Koko Yutaka.

2. The exception is Robin Kietlinski, *Japanese Women and Sport: Beyond Baseball and Sumo* (New York: Bloomsbury Academic, 2011), but her main focus does not analyze what women athletes believe they attained from physical activity. Although she refers to some materials that show narratives of a few women athletes participating in various sports with self-identifaction, my work is based on original interviews of women pro wrestlers. Therefore, my study is more likely to capture genuine voices of women pro wrestlers than Kietlinski's work.

3. Keiko Aiba, *Transformed Bodies and Gender: Experiences of Women Pro Wrestlers in Japan* (Osaka: Union Press, 2017), 137.

134   Part II. Gender

4. Japan Wrestling Federation, "Resuringu no rūru o shirou (kihon hen)" [Let's Learn the Rules of Wrestling (Basic)], http://www.japan-wrestling.org/special/nyumonn/rule01.html (accessed December 2, 2007).

5. Shinobu Kandori, *Kanwa* [Story of Kandori] (Tokyo: Magajin hausu, 1997), 96.

6. Aiba, *Transformed Bodies and Gender*, 11–12.

7. Elaine M. Blinde, Daine E. Taub, and Linglin Han, "Sport Participation and Women's Personal Empowerment: Experiences of the College Athlete," *Journal of Sport & Social Issues* 17 (1993), 47–60; Jane Granskog, "Just 'Tri' and 'Du' It: The Variable Impact of Female Involvement in the Triathlon/Duathlon Sport Culture," in Anne Bolin and Jane Granskog, eds., *Athletic Intruders: Ethnographic Research on Women, Culture, and Exercise* (Albany: State University of New York Press, 2003), 27–52; Lisa McDermott, "A Qualitative Assessment of the Significance of Body Perception to Women's Physical Activity Experiences: Revisiting Discussions of Physicalities," *Sociology of Sport Journal* 17 (2000), 331–63; Krista Scott-Dixon, "Big Girls Don't Cry: Fitness, Fatness, and the Production of Feminist Knowledge," *Sociology of Sport Journal* 25 (2008), 22–47; Nancy Theberge, "Sport and Women's Empowerment," *Women's Studies International Forum* 10 (1987), 387–93; Nikki Wedgewood, "Kicking Like a Boy: Schoolgirl Australian Rules Football and Bi-Gendered Female Embodiment," *Sociology of Sport Journal* 21 (2004), 140–62; Jan Wright and Alison Dewar, "On Pleasure and Pain: Women Speak Out About Physical Activity," in Gill Clarke and Barbara Humberstone, eds., *Researching Women and Sport* (London: Macmillan, 1997); Careen Mackay Yarnal, Susan Hutchinson, and Hsueh-Wen Chow, "'I Could Probably Run a Marathon Right Now': Embodiment, Space, and Young Women's Leisure Experience," *Leisure Sciences* 28 (2006), 133–61.

8. Blinde et al., "Sport Participation and Women's Personal Empowerment," 54.

9. Satu Liimakka, "I Am My Body: Objectification, Empowering Embodiment, and Physical Activity in Women's Studies Students' Accounts," *Sociology of Sport Journal* 28 (2012), 450–452.

10. Liimakka, "I Am My Body," 452.

11. Scott-Dixon, "Big Girls Don't Cry," 39; Shari L. Doworkin, "A Woman's Place in the … Cardiovascular Room? Gender Relations, the Body, and the Gym," in *Athletic Intruders: Ethnographic Research on Women, Culture, and Exercise*, ed. Anne Bolin and Jane Granskog (Albany: State University of New York Press, 2003), 41.

12. Blinde et al., "Sport Participation and Women's Personal Empowerment," 51.

13. Scott-Dixon, "Big Girls Don't Cry," 43.

14. Doworkin, "A Woman's Place in the … Cardiovascular Room?" 141.

15. Martha McCaughey, *Real Knockouts: The Physical Feminism of Women's Self-Defense* (New York: New York University Press, 1997), 122.

16. McCaughey, *Real Knockouts*, 122.

17. At first I recognized the negative impact that the women pro wrestlers receive from society by engaging in pro wrestling as a "disadvantage." However, because the word "disadvantage" sounded quite derogatory, I looked for a different word. Then, Naoko Ikeda suggested the word "challenge" instead.

18. In sports science, strength means muscles, and power is the product of muscles and speed.

19. Scott-Dixon, "Big Girls Don't Cry," 34–36.

20. Todd A. Migliaccio and Ellen C. Berg, "Women's Participation in Tackle Football," in *International Review for the Sociology of Sport* (2007), 282; Wedgwood, "Kicking Like a Boy," 156.

21. Liimakka, "I Am My Body"; McDermott, "A Qualitative Assessment of the Significance of Body Perception to Women's Physical Activity Experiences," 450–52; Yarnal et al., "'I Could Probably Run a Marathon Right Now,'" 154–55.

22. Jun Kukita, "Enpawāmento towa nanika" [What Is Empowerment?], *Gendai no esupuri* 11 (1998), 21; Hiroshi Sato, "Enjo ni okeru enpawāmento gainen no gani" [Connotation of the Concept of Empowerment in Aid], in Hiroshi Sato, ed., *Enjo to enpawāmento— nouryoku kaihatsu to shakai kankyou henka no kumiawase* [Aid and Empowerment—Combination of Ability-Development and Changes in the Social Environment] (Tokyo: Institute

of Developing Economies, 2005), 5; Lorraine M. Gutierrez, "Working Within Women of Color: An Empowerment Perspective," *Social Work* 35 (1990), 149.

23. Mayumi Kubota, "Enpawāmento ni miru jienda byoudou to kousei-tauwa no jitsugen ni mukete" [Gender Equality for Empowerment: To Facilitate a Dialogue Between Women and Men], *Journal of the National Women's Education Center of Japan* 9 (2005), 30.
24. Kubota, "Enpawāmento," 30.
25. Kubota, "Enpawāmento," 27.
26. Kubota, "Enpawāmento," 29.
27. Kubota, "Enpawāmento," 27.
28. Gutierrez, "Working Within Women of Color," 150.
29. Wright and Dewar, "On Pleasure and Pain," 91.
30. McDermott, "A Qualitative Assessment of the Significance of Body Perception to Women's Physical Activity Experiences," 352.
31. Yarnal et al., "'I Could Probably Run a Marathon Right Now.'"
32. Jocelyn A. Hollander, "I Can Take Care of Myself: The Impact of Self-Defense Training on Women's Lives," *Violence Against Women* 10 (2004), 222.
33. Wedgwood, "Kicking Like a Boy,"159.
34. Blinde et al., "Sport Participation and Women's Personal Empowerment," 51.
35. McDermott, "A Qualitative Assessment of the Significance of Body Perception to Women's Physical Activity Experiences," 357.
36. Keiko Aiba, *Joshi puroresura no shintai to jienda—kihanteki onnarashisa o koete* [Body and Gender of Women Pro-Wrestlers in Japan: Beyond "Normative" Femininity] (Tokyo: Akashi Shoten, 2013), 178–82.
37. Inuhiko Yomota, *"Kawaii" ron* [A Theory of "Cuteness"] (Tokyo: Chikumashobo, 2006), 76.
38. Yomota, *"Kawaii" ron*, 92–132.
39. Chie Asano, *Onna wa naze yaseyouto surunoka—Sesshokushougai to jiendā* [Why Do Women Want to Be Skinny? Eating Disorder and Gender] (Tokyo: Keisou Shobo, 1996), 97.
40. The classification of physiques for clothes of adult women consists of four physiques, and "physique A" is considered the standard. Physique A is defined as follows: "When Japanese adult women's height is classified into 142 cm, 150 cm, 158 cm and 166 cm, and the range of 74–92 cm of the bust size is segmented by 3 cm interval, and the range of 92–104 cm of the bust size is segmented by 4 cm interval, a woman's physique determined with the hip size with the most frequency in all the combinations of each height and the bust size is the physique A" (Kaken Test Center). The 9AR indicates the size nine of the physique A with the height of 158 cm.
41. Teurko Inoue, *Shin joseigaku eno shoutai: Kawaru kawaranai onna no isshou* [New Version of Invitation for Women's Studies: Changes and Stabilities of Women's Lives] (Tokyo: Yuhikaku, 2011), 118.
42. Of course there is a way to make the custom-made clothes that fit to their own physiques, but wrestlers rarely mentioned this strategy.
43. A team consists of two wrestlers or more.
44. Some wrestlers were enthralled by bodies with muscles. For example, Kiriko told that once she got muscles in the process of exercise before the professional test, she tried to get more muscle, "finding myself getting narcissistic." However, what she admired was the body with only muscles, with little or no fat, like that of a bodybuilder, which is different from the body of wrestler, typically with muscles and fat. Moreover, there was no wrestler who mentioned that the motivation to become wrestlers was that they had wanted to acquire the bodies like wrestlers.
45. Blinde et al., "Sport Participation and Women's Personal Empowerment"; Granskog, "Just 'Tri' and 'Du' It"; Scott-Dixon, "Big Girls Don't Cry."
46. The survey by the Ministry of Education, Culture, Sports, Science and Technology (2013) was conducted on the fifth grade as representing the girls of elementary schools, and the eighth grade as the girls of junior high schools.
47. Ministry of Education, Culture, Sports, Science and Technology, *Heisei nijuuyon*

136   Part II. Gender

nendo zenkoku tairyoku/undou nouryoku, undou shuukan tou chousa kekka gaiyou [2012 Summary of Survey Findings on Physical Capacity, Athletic Ability, Fitness Habits and So on in the Entire Country], 2013, retrieved from www.mext.go.jp/component/a_menu/sports/detail/__icsFiles/afieldfile/2013/04/15/1332456_1.pdf4 (accessed December 1, 2013).

48. Ministry of Education, Culture, Sports, Science, and Technology, *Heisei nijuuyon*, 2013.

49. Ministry of Education, Culture, Sports, Science, and Technology, *Heisei nijuuyon*, 2013.

50. Ministry of Education, Culture, Sports, Science, and Technology, *Heisei nijuuyon*, 2013.

51. Sasakawa Sports Foundation, *Seishounen no supōtsu raifu data 2013: 10 dai no supōtsu raifu ni kansuru chousa houkokusho* [The 2013 SSF National Sports-Life Survey of Young People] (Tokyo: Sasakawa Sports Foundation, 2013), 48.

52. Ministry of Education, Culture, Sports, Science and Technology, *Tairyoku supōtsu ni kansuru seron shousa (heisei nijuugo nen ichigatsu chousa)* [Public Opinion Survey on Physical Strength and Sports (January 2013)], retrieved from http://www.mext.go.jp/b_menu/toukei/chousa04/sports/1338692.htm (accessed December 1, 2013).

53. Ministry of Education, Culture, Sports, Science and Technology, *Tairyoku supōtsu*, 2013.

54. With the five levels, Level 0 shows the extent to which a person has no physical activities or sports for the last one year; Level 1 shows the extent to which a person engaged in physical activities or sports at least once for a year, but fewer than twice a week; Level 2 shows the extent to which a person engaged in physical activities or sports more than twice a week; Level 3 shows the extent to which a person engaged in physical activities more than twice a week and taking over 30 minutes for one activity; Level 4 shows the extent to which a person engaged in physical activities or sports more than twice a week, taking over 30 minutes for one activity, with the intensity of activity as "semi-hard or more."

55. Sasakawa Sports Foundation, *Supōtsu raifu dēta 2012* [The 2012 SSF Sports Life Survey 2012] (Tokyo: Sasakawa Foundation, 2012), 70.

56. Sasakawa Sports Foundation, *Supōtsu raifu dēta 2012*, 70.

57. Osamu Takamine, *Undou/supōtsu o okonau mokuteki* [Purposes of Physical Activities and Sports] in *Supōtsu raifu dēta 2012* [The 2012 SSF National Sports-Life Survey] (Tokyo: Sasakawa Sports Foundation, 2012), 29.

58. Keiko Itani, *"Josei no supōtsu girai to supōtsu banare"* [Women's Disliking and Shifting Away from Sports], in Takao Iida and Keiko Itani, eds., *Supōtsu, jiendā gaku heno shoutai* [Invitation for Sport and Gender Studies] (Tokyo: Akashi Shoten, 2004), 199.

59. Shirley Castelnuovo and Sharon R. Guthrie, *Feminism and the Female Body: Liberating the Amazon Within* (Boulder: Lynne Rienner, 1998), 13; Colette Dowling, *The Frailty Myth: Redefining the Physical Potential of Women and Girls* (New York: Random House Trade Paperbacks, 2000).

60. Judith Butler, *Gender Trouble: Feminism and the Subversion of Identity*, 10th anniversary edition (New York: Routledge, 1999), 30; Gayle Rubin, "The Traffic in Women: Notes on the 'Political Economy,'" in Rayna R. Reiter, ed., *Toward an Anthropology of Women* (New York: Monthly Review Press, 1975), 159.

61. Holly Devor, *Gender Blending: Confronting the Limits of Duality* (Bloomington: Indiana University Press, 1989), 147.

62. Devor, *Gender Blending*, 147–48.

63. Suzanne J. Kessler and Wendy McKenna, *Gender: An Ethnomethodological Approach* (Chicago: University of Chicago Press, 1978), 150.

64. Kessler and Wendy McKenna, *Gender*, 150–52; Devor, *Gender Blending*, 49.

"A secret fascination"
Professional Wrestling, Gender Non-Conformity and Masculinity

ELIZABETH CATTE and JOSH HOWARD

On August 14, 2013, a reporter for celebrity news website TMZ caught up with World Wrestling Entertainment (WWE) superstar Darren Young at the LAX baggage claim. The reporter asked Young, "Do you think that a gay wrestler could be successful within the WWE?" Young responded with a smile and a laugh before answering, "Absolutely. Look at me. I'm a WWE superstar and to be honest with you, I'll tell you right now, I'm gay. And I'm happy."[1] And with that, Darren Young became the first openly gay professional wrestler in the WWE and the first active wrestler to "come out" while signed with a major promotion.

As the WWE celebrated Young's decision to speak openly about his sexuality, a fresh wave of journalists and wrestling fans began to pore through the history of American professional wrestling, looking for other moments the sport "grappled" with issues of sexuality. A few ambitious authors connected their initial observations to studies by Sharon Mazer, Danielle Soulliere, or Nicholas Sammond, and noted, as Mazer once did, a range of masculinities "between the flamboyantly feminine to the lumpen macho."[2] While these popular discussions of the importance of Darren Young's "coming out" disengaged from more theorized frameworks, what they shared with the authors above was a tendency to view all of wrestling's non-heteronormative masculinities as part of an evolving genealogy that begins with Gorgeous George in the 1950s and ends with Dustin Runnels' sexually ambiguous Goldust persona from the 1990s.

The implied place of Darren Young's authentic and unperformed sexuality as part of this genealogy is problematic. Specifically, the artificial spectrum from Gorgeous George to Goldust obscures an important shift in professional wrestling from a loosely-connected and -managed enterprise to the singular entity of the Vince McMahon's WWE. Placing WWE performers with limited artistic agency on the same spectrum as self-made performers like Gorgeous George obscures the fact that, for several decades, the WWE suppressed rather than celebrated alternative expressions of male sexuality and masculinity. To begin to understand the complexities of wrestlers who presented alternative male sexualities, we must first take stock of the pre–WWE world of wrestling masculinity.

Pre–World Wrestling Federation/ Entertainment (WWF/E)

Since the 1930s, professional wrestling has followed a simple script. Good guys, commonly referred to as faces, fought bad guys, referred to as heels. Most fans knew these were staged fights and were expected to participate by cheering faces and booing the heels. Beginning in the 1940s, wrestling "gimmicks" emerged that exaggerated character traits to more clearly delineate just who was the face and who was the heel in a match. Before this, wrestlers would occasionally create personas, such as those who based their character on foreign nationalities, but the characters that emerged in the 1940s and 1950s were much more outrageous, flamboyant, and theatrical. Further, adopting a gimmick was a method of survival for wrestlers. Wrestlers with quality gimmicks—whether face or heel—often attracted more people to matches, which then resulted in more pay and higher likelihood of appearing again in future events. Until the 1980s, the wrestling landscape of America was divided up into dozens of wrestling promotions, generally referred to as "territories," owned and controlled, usually, by a single promoter. It was common for wrestlers to compete and earn pay from several promotions a year either through talent swaps organized by promoters or through the enterprise of the wrestlers themselves. Promoters retained final control over their in-ring product. Wrestlers understood this and would often clear their gimmick, matches, and promos with the promoter beforehand—whatever it took to get paid. Sometimes getting paid meant dropping a gimmick or as the legendary Pat Patterson put it, "Back then you needed to survive—and moving on to the next territory was the only way to do that." Wrestling in the territories was a bit hectic, but stability often came with the ability to draw crowds and make promoters money.[3]

Gorgeous George, the wrestler most frequently cited in discussions of professional wrestling and gender, pioneered a distinct style of effeminate character, and through engaging in anti-masculine performance is largely credited with creating the entire concept of a gimmick. Before Gorgeous George, wrestlers easily fit within one of two categories: those who portrayed themselves as legitimate athletes who could become either a face or heel, and performers whose race or ethnicity usually forced them to assume the role of heel. Beginning in the 1940s, Gorgeous George turned gender transgression into an art form and business model by dressing as a "Human Orchid" in pastel colors, lace, and chiffon selected and styled by his adoring wife Betty, who often served as his ring valet. Gorgeous George would enter the ring to "Pomp and Circumstance," becoming one of the first wrestlers to use entrance music, while Betty and occasionally other valets sprayed perfume around the ring to further irritate the crowd. In a war-time and post-war culture that valorized bravery, strength, and moral conviction, George's gender-bending and questionable principles made him an anti-hero that wrestling fans loved to hate.[4]

Despite Gorgeous George's heel status, he became the secret inspiration for some gay men, coming of age in the 1940s and 1950s with few role models. During a time when homosexuality was considered a psychiatric disorder and even Homophile societies performed heteronormative respectability, figures like Gorgeous George provided individuals a window into a world liberated and free regardless of performed identity.[5] Filmmaker John Waters recalled watching George on television: "It was probably the very first thing I ever saw that I thought is this, maybe it was gay, even though he wasn't gay, right? And I didn't know what gay meant yet. I just knew that this was something very, very different and something that could very much interest me. He became a kind of secret fascination."[6] Speaking with the WWE for the 2010 WWE Hall of Fame induction, Waters went on to comment that "Gorgeous George was the first male that made it cool to be feminine even though he wasn't."[7] Waters' recollections suggest the role Gorgeous George served for many gay men in the mid–20th century. George was a role model, perhaps even someone worth idolizing or emulating, despite the fact that he himself was not gay.

Ricki Starr was another early wrestler who leveraged an anti-masculine persona into a successful career. The British-born Starr became a professional wrestler in 1953 after a stint as a Broadway ballet dancer. He incorporated the aesthetics of ballet—including his hallmark ballet slippers—into his style of wrestling. Starr pirouetted and pranced in the ring, but often defeated opponents with expertly delivered drop-kicks. If his fondness for ballet wasn't enough of an indication of gender non-conformity, later in his career Starr began to brag that he was taught to wrestle by a male burlesque dancer named "Toots." Despite his apparent femininity, Starr was a popular wrestler. As one commentator observed, "Starr's a good wrestler when he wants to be, when he cuts out the clowning … but who wants him to cut out the clowning?"[8]

Adrian Street—the son of a Welsh coal miner and genuine tough guy—debuted in 1957 and for a decade wore the persona of a young, clean-cut bodybuilder. In the late 1960s, Street abandoned this gimmick to become "Exotic." Street slowly added effeminate aspects to his character, including glitter make-up, mini-pigtail hairdos, and applying makeup to defeated opponents. Street further escalated this gimmick after leaving the UK for the United States in the early 1980s, exemplified by the release of his 1986 album that included a somewhat suggestive song and music video entitled "Imagine What I Could Do to You." The album also included a self-descriptive song entitled "A Sweet Transvestite with a Broken Nose" with lyrics describing himself as both a king and queen of the ring, comparing his physical characteristics to both boxer Rocky Marciano and Hollywood actress Mae West.[9] Wrestling throughout America's fading regional territories, especially in the South, Street's unconventional persona spoke to and against constructions of manhood associated with his upbringing in a blue-collar mining community in which industry, not entertainment, was the stuff of life. Although the popularity of glam rock and performers like David Bowie buffered Street's commercial success, he displayed a constant anxiety about being mistaken for gay, often bringing his valet and real-life spouse "Miss Linda" to the ring with him. To this day, Street consistently denies in interviews that the "Exotic" persona was gay. He did worry about consequences his persona may have on his career on occasion, but generally dismissed these worries by insisting he used the gimmick to get into the heads of his competitors and their fans. Few expected such a strange character to be a competent, tough, and sometimes brutally aggressive wrestler.[10]

Collectively, these wrestlers—Gorgeous George, Ricky Starr, and Adrian Street—challenged an idea often accepted in competitive sports that to be the "best," one must be physically aggressive, emotionally restrained, successful, competitive, tough, courageous, and, of course, heterosexual. While these personas seem unconventional by today's standards, it is important to remember that these performers existed in a world in which the boundaries between what was considered normal or abnormal had not solidified into our modern categories of "gay" or "straight." As George Chauncey demonstrated in his monograph *Gay New York*, these categories did not fully appear until after the 1940s, and even then constructions of gender remained more fluid outside metropolitan environments.[11] Only Adrian Street, who first achieved celebrity in the 1960s and 1970s before moving into America during the 1980s, worried that his professional persona might have personal consequences.

The Era of Vince McMahon and the WWF/E

The structure of professional wrestling changed in the 1980s, leading to the disintegration of the "territorial" system, in which regional promotions dominated and promoters largely respected territorial boundaries. In the span of about five years, Vincent K. McMahon purchased his father's regional wrestling company, poached top wrestling talents from around the nation, and drove many competitors out of business, partly by taking advantage of the relatively new mediums of cable television and pay-per-view. The company, originally the World Wide Wrestling Federation (WWWF), was renamed the World Wrestling Federation (WWF) in 1979 and, later, World Wrestling Entertainment (WWE) in 2002. Thanks to cable television, McMahon's WWF was one of just a handful of wrestling companies capable of reaching a national audience. Given this exposure, the WWF became the most visible professional wrestling company nationally and, to many Americans, McMahon's style of wrestling and storytelling became synonymous with the entire industry.

With Vince McMahon's consolidation of power, gender non-conformity within professional wrestling became more limited. Before McMahon, an expansive network of territories ensured any drawing wrestler could find work, no matter how "unorthodox" their gimmick. But in the 1980s, once McMahon held control over the majority of these areas, opportunities became severely limited. If a wrestler wanted to earn a paycheck, their persona had to conform to Vince McMahon's worldview, and Vince McMahon's worldview was (and is) one that idolizes traditional hegemonic masculinity and aggressive heterosexuality. This transition between the previous generation's good-natured gender subversion and the more sinister implications of McMahon's worldview were evident in the career of Adrian Adonis.

Adrian Adonis was a popular wrestler in the late 1970s and early 1980s as one half of the East-West Connection with Jesse Ventura. Adonis represented himself as a hyper-masculine, arrogant playboy from New York whose northern toughness was the antithesis of Ventura's slick west coast vibe. But by 1985, the tough guy character had grown stale. Rumors also suggested that McMahon felt the need to punish Adonis for gaining weight and being out of shape. McMahon thus dubbed Adrian as "Adorable." Adonis bleached his hair blonde, donned pink tights, and began to apply far too much eye shadow and rouge to compliment his new attire and persona. On the surface, Adonis seems to be in line with anti-masculine characters such as Gorgeous George and Adrian Street, but Adonis represented a divergence in presentation. Adonis was the worst type of gay stereotype—and he was a gay stereotype, using the term "coming out of the closet" during his "Adorable" debut and appearing during the early days of the AIDS crisis, a time when public perceptions of the gay community were largely homophobic and misunderstood. Adonis would prance about the ring, only to be mocked by commentators, and his extreme weight gain at the time led to even more belittlement from announcers and opponents alike. To McMahon, Adonis' actions demanded he be punished, and the gay stereotype gimmick was that punishment. Adonis' predecessors presented alternative forms of masculinity, but Adonis clearly and falsely represented a social group that in Vince McMahon's organization was only worthy of comedic mockery.

After Adonis, Goldust, performed by Dustin Runnels, became the next WWE performer to adopt an anti-masculine persona and the first to appear regularly on weekly, national cable television on the WWE's highly popular weekly show Monday Night RAW. He debuted in 1995 dressed in golden, feathered robes, a blonde wig, and a full golden mask of face paint. To create the persona, Goldust relied on sexual ambiguity with occasional implications of gay sexual attraction despite the presence of his female valet and real-life wife Marlena. Goldust's sexuality was often questioned by both fellow wrestlers and fans, and Goldust embraced every instance. The only moments where the WWE "scaled back" Goldust's sexuality was when WWE commentator Jerry Lawler referred to him as a "flaming fag" and fans began chanting "faggot" while he wrestled. Goldust began his career as a heel, but in the late-1990s era of crash television and anti-heroes, some fans took to cheering him as a character who defied social norms with his "deviant" persona and dishonorable signature move (which was simply a kick to the opponent's testicles). Like Street, Goldust's persona also spoke to concepts of blue-collar masculinity, but where Street's father was an unnamed Welsh coal miner, Goldust's was wrestling legend "The American Dream" Dusty Rhodes, a Southern, blue-collar grappler well-known to most fans of the era.

Despite some fan support and positive portrayals, Goldust's gender ambiguity often became sinister and menacing. At various times, Goldust participated in homophobic mockery as well. At least once, Goldust performed "mouth-to-mouth" on an unconscious wrestler, Ahmed Johnson, and "felt up" other unwilling men. Through Goldust, Vince McMahon's WWE capitalized on the stereotype that all gay men are deviant sexual predators just waiting for the opportunity to assault straight men. As Brett Grubisic points out, so unnatural was Goldust that he stood out in a world populated by men who portrayed imagined serial killers, maniacs, and the risen dead.[12] Beginning in the early 2000s, Goldust transitioned away from his homoerotic in-ring persona and behavior, though his appearance remained largely the same. Within the recent "PG" world of the WWE, (former) Tag Team Champion Goldust is just a "weirdo" and not a sexual deviant.

McMahon delivered a final damaging blow to queer possibilities with the saga of Billy and Chuck, a tag team who made their television debut for the WWE in 2001. Initially, two stagnant wrestlers, Billy Gunn and Chuck Palumbo, were paired together and adopted a comedy gimmick reminiscent of *Saturday Night Live* sketch "The Ambiguously Gay Duo." Their initial antics were not terribly different from those of Goldust or Adrian Adonis, and usually involved playing up their implied sexual attraction for one another and feminine characteristics for comedic effect. One major difference, however, was that Billy and Chuck's manager, Rico, was not a busty blonde like Goldust's but rather a campy male hair and "personality" stylist. After several months of growing popularity, the WWE took the Billy and Chuck gimmick a step further: Chuck officially "came out" on television and asked Billy to marry him in a "commitment" ceremony. Billy said yes. The WWE heavily promoted the upcoming ceremony, and numerous LGBT groups—most notably the Gay & Lesbian Alliance Against Defamation (GLAAD)—praised the WWE for its progressive programming even though the wedding was obviously not "real." For those familiar with Vince McMahon and the WWE, it was no surprise when Billy and Chuck revealed their wedding was a publicity stunt that had gone too far and they were both actually heterosexual. To make matters worse, the WWE actually recorded the episode several days before it aired, and, in the interim, continued to lead GLAAD and wrestling fans into believing the wedding was on the up-and-up. From that point forward, all references to Billy and Chuck's gay or implied gay past were suddenly forgotten.

Beyond the notable centerpieces of Adrian Adonis, Goldust, and Billy and Chuck, the WWE has also featured repetitive and often crude cross-dressing gimmicks throughout the past few decades. Crossdressing has a long history in wrestling, usually as a form of comedic punishment for male performers. Occasionally, a popular wrestler will be forced to "wrestle in a dress" as a form of humiliation only to embrace the punishment and flaunt their new attire for one night only. Crossdressing has also been used by male wrestlers as a way to "get ahead" in long-term storylines. Such was the case with Santino Marella, a man who failed to win any titles, so he donned a dress, wig, and makeup as his "sister," Santina, to compete against women and win the title of Miss WrestleMania in 2009. In another instance from a Monday Night RAW a decade earlier, wrestler Mark Henry was introduced to a woman backstage. A camera followed the two to a secluded area, where they began to undress. Suddenly, the audience heard Mark Henry express in a panicked tone: "Sweet Jesus! You got a penis!" Laughter could be heard from the crowd watching in the arena. The scene's humor was meant to derive from the fact that Henry, as a heterosexual man, could be "tricked" into sexual action with a person with male genitals, further emphasized by Henry's resulting "trans panic" anger and vomiting.

It is important to note that Vince McMahon embodied an exaggerated but not uncommon worldview that meshed with broader conservative backlash and cultural homophobia. For example, World Championship Wrestling (WCW), owned and operated by Ted Turner and Time Warner from 1988 to 2001, debuted a new tag team in 1999, the West Hollywood Blondes, Lenny and Lodi. These two preceded Billy and Chuck, and their personas could be described in much the same way except their attire was pink, emblazoned with triangles, and Lenny sported pigtails and glitter makeup. Within but a few weeks of their debut, Lenny won the Cruiserweight Championship with Lodi's help only for the two to suddenly disappear from television. Turner Broadcasting Standards and Practices pulled the duo from productions after public protest and numerous complaints, most notably from GLAAD. According to an unnamed Turner executive: "Nobody here is out to do any gay-bashing," after fans were encouraged for weeks to chant gay slurs at the two.[13] This moment aside, without the totalizing force of Vince McMahon one wonders if professional wrestling might have achieved a different trajectory and perhaps witnessed more dynamic representations of gender and sexuality embodied in, for example, the *exóticos* of lucha libre in Mexico or, more recently, Dalton Castle, a "flamboyant" wrestler who primarily performs for American independent wrestling companies such as Ring of Honor.[14]

Gay Wrestlers

Apart from the aforementioned Darren Young, several gay men also wrestled with the WWE, although their sexuality was concealed at the time they were performers. Chris Kanyon (actual name Chris Klucsarits) was a somewhat successful wrestler in the late 1990s and early 2000s who came out as gay after his official retirement from professional wrestling in 2004. At several points after his retirement, Kanyon accused the WWE of discrimination, to the point that he claimed the WWE released him because of his homosexuality. Kanyon recanted these statements and never brought suit against the WWE, but he spoke openly about how his sexuality caused him to fear for his job both in WWE and previous employer WCW. Speaking in 2006, Kanyon stated, "Everyone is looking for a significant other, be it a man or a woman, in their life. There were times I thought I'd never find one, especially with the profession I was in. I always thought if [my sexuality] got out, I'd get in trouble or get fired.... I hope someday being gay is thought of in the same sense as being left-handed ... no big deal."[15] Kanyon suffered from depression and bipolar disorder and, tragically, took his own life in 2010.

About a year after Darren Young came out, so did retired, 73-year-old wrestling legend Pat Patterson. On the June 13, 2014, episode of *Legend's House* on the WWE Network, Patterson spoke of his private life for the first time publicly, most notably telling stories of relationships he kept secret and the mental anguish he went through to hide this life. Patterson's decision to speak openly was met with applause and praise from his fellow pro wrestlers, co-workers, fans, and the company itself. Beyond Patterson's coming out, the past few years have been exemplary for the WWE in terms of gay rights and acceptance. The WWE emphasizes the positive qualities of the Young and Patterson stories in the hopes they will be considered alongside other recently out male athletes like Robbie Rogers, Jason Collins, and Michael Sam. Also in recent years, the WWE has publicly displayed greater support for broader LGBT rights; along with the company's Be A Star anti-bullying campaign, it has openly campaigned against North Carolina's HB2 bathroom law and is presently coordinating with GLAAD to "integrate LGBT storylines" into television programming.[16] However, some of Patterson's recent comments, which likely reflect the WWE's official position, as he is one of its longest-tenured employees, suggest that an individual's sexual orientation is irrelevant to one's WWE career: "If you're a performer, you're a performer ... gay or straight, it doesn't matter."[17]

Further complicating the WWE is McMahon's close business relationships with a number of openly gay men over the years. Pat Patterson has worked for the WWE for nearly 40 years as of this writing, often as on-air talent, and claims often to have never experienced any homophobia in his WWE career, going so far to state "the word 'gay' or 'queer' was never brought up."[18] This is difficult to believe, given Patterson's emotion when coming out publicly and the fact that he is still employed by the WWE, though his remarks are supported by similar claims by former WWE employees.[19] Despite Patterson's claims, his sexuality was often made a joke on-air through tongue-in-cheek or implied jokes.[20] The most recent of these jokes occurred on May 27, 2013, when WWE legend Bret Hart quipped, "When Pat starts getting on his knees, I start getting scared" after Patterson, in an obvious sign of respect, bowed to one knee to shake Hart's hand. Hart later apologized via Twitter.[21] Behind the scenes, McMahon relied heavily on Jim Barnett, an openly gay wrestling promoter, during the company's critical emergence as a national television product in the mid–1980s.[22] Many of Barnett's peers within the wrestling industry had long shunned him for his sexuality, but McMahon hired Barnett regardless. Other gay performers have also been employed by McMahon over the years, including Rosa Mendes, Orlando Jordan, and "The Grand Wizard of Wrestling" Ernie Roth. While McMahon's portrayal of gay individuals and characters is troubling and occasionally outright hateful, his behind-the-scenes business relations seem to indicate that McMahon is willing to work with anyone as long as they could make money for the company.

Conclusion

Despite these recent strides, WWE's regressive presentations of male gender non-conformity and sexuality left a lasting impression on the way we think of professional wrestling. When recent scholars discuss wrestling and masculinity, they are doing so in terms of modern post–McMahon wrestling and usually in terms of Adrian Adonis and the early years of Goldust's career. In 2013, David Shoemaker, a former writer for Grantland and podcast host, released a popular history of professional wrestling, *The Squared Circle*, in which he asserted: "Gorgeous George invented the pompous heel. Within that archetype many subsets flourish: the scaredy-cat heel, the self-obsessed heel, and, of course, the faggot heel."[23] With this simple and arguably callous statement, Shoemaker gathered all presentations of homosexuality and gender non-conformity under one umbrella, represented by "faggot heels" who are to be booed by the fans. In his book, he used the word faggot when describing these men in order to "convey the offensiveness that they were employing with the character at the time."[24] With this, one may assume that wrestlers who adopted anti-masculine personas would thus always be bad guys or "faggot heels" as Shoemaker would put it.

As we have shown, however, wrestlers who adopted anti-masculine personas were not always the bad guys. It is clear that David Shoemaker is speaking to professional wrestling's most recent past in which the WWE provided both a script and blueprint for what masculinity should, or should not, look like. For now, the WWE is content to make amends in deeds, rather than words, but it must be noted that its ability to do so takes advantage of the assumption that the stigmatization of gender non-conformity and gay people is a regretful but inevitable relic of the past. In other words, many organizations and individuals have diluted the force of past transgressions with the belief that homophobia was a natural product of the visibility of gay or non-conforming individuals. But this is not the case, and the long history of professional wrestling offers us a glimpse into a world where diversity was celebrated rather than abused. The interpretation offered here may suggest that a more meaningful reading of professional wrestling can be achieved through interdisciplinary project of queer history and theory, which attempts to restore rather than cleanse cherished cultural products of their gender ambiguity.

Notes

1. "WWE Superstar … I'm Gay," *TMZ Sports*, August 13, 2013, http://www.tmz.com/2013/08/15/darren-young-wwe-superstar-gay/.

2. Sharon Mazer, *Professional Wrestling: Sport and Spectacle* (Jackson: University Press of Mississippi, 1998), 104. Danielle Soulliere, "Wrestling with Masculinity: Messages about Manhood in the WWE," *Sex Roles* 55 (2006), 1–11. Nicholas Sammond, "Introduction: A Brief and Unnecessary Defense of Professional Wrestling," in *Steel Chair to the Head: The Pleasure and Pain of Professional Wrestling*, ed. Nicholas Sammond (Durham: Duke University Press, 2005), 13–15.

3. Mazer, *Professional Wrestling*, 4. Heath McCoy, *Pain and Passion: The History of Stampede Wrestling* (Toronto: ECW Press, 2007), 5. Pat Patterson, *Accepted: How the First Gay Superstar Changed the WWE* (Toronto: ECW Press, 2016), 60–61.

4. Shaun Assael and Mike Mooneyham, *Sex, Lies, and Headlocks: The Real Story of Vince McMahon and World Wrestling Entertainment* (New York: Random House, 2002), 11.
 5. Martin Meeker, "Behind the Mask of Respectability: Reconsidering the Mattachine Society and Male Homophile Practice, 1950s and 1960s," *Journal of the History of Sexuality* 10, no. 1 (2001), 99–105. Marc Stein, *City of Sisterly and Brotherly Loves: Lesbian and Gay Philadelphia, 1945–1972* (Philadelphia: Temple University Press, 2004), 221.
 6. John Capouya, *Gorgeous George: The Outrageous Bad-Boy Wrestler Who Created American Pop Culture* (New York: HarperCollins, 2008), 270–71.
 7. WWE, "2010 WWE Hall of Fame Inductee: Gorgeous George," May 13, 2010, YouTube video, 3:31, https://www.youtube.com/watch?v=iPser68hiT0.
 8. Mazer, *Professional Wrestling*, 95.
 9. Exotic Adrian Street and the Pile Drivers, "Shake, Wrestle, and Roll," Exotic Records, ER-SWR-86, 1986, vinyl.
 10. Adrian Street, *Merchant of Menace* (Gulf Breeze, FL: Adrian Street, 2015), 3–6.
 11. George Chauncey, *Gay New York* (New York: Basic Books, 1994).
 12. Brett Josef Grubisic, "Testing Mettle: Goldust and the Spectacle of Masculinity in the World of Wrestling," *Popular Culture Review* 10, no. 1 (1999), 145.
 13. Lisa de Moraes, "TNT Finally Tosses Its Staged Gay-Bashing Spectacle Out of the Ring," *The Washington Post*, October 12, 1999, http://www.washingtonpost.com/wp-srv/WPcap/1999–10/12/049r-101299-idx.html.
 14. For more on *exóticos*, see Heather Levi, *The World of Lucha Libre: Secrets, Revelations, and Mexican National Identity* (Durham: Duke University Press, 2008). For more on Dalton Castle, see his profile in Kenny Herzon, "At Home with Dalton Castle, Wrestling's Most Flamboyant Star," *Rolling Stone*, December 3, 2015, http://www.rollingstone.com/sports/features/at-home-with-dalton-castle-wrestlings-most-flamboyant-star-20151203.
 15. Cyd Zeigler, "Chris Kanyon Is Gay in the Wrestling Ring," *SB Nation Out Sports*, March 31, 2006, http://www.outsports.com/2013/2/20/4012180/chris-kanyon-is-gay-in-the-wrestling-ring.
 16. Glenn Garner, "WWE Just Made a Serious Move Toward LGBT Inclusivity," *Out Magazine*, August 11, 2016, http://www.out.com/popnography/2016/8/11/wwe-making-move-toward-lgbt-inclusivity. Jodi Savitz, "WWE Sees Opportunity to 'Integrate LGBT Storylines' in Programming," *NBC News*, August 10, 2016, http://www.nbcnews.com/feature/nbc-out/wwe-plans-integrate-lgbt-characters-programming-n627411. Zeke Stokes, "WWE Speaks Out Against #HB2 at North Carolina WWE LIVE Event," *GLAAD Blog*, May 13, 2016, http://www.glaad.org/blog/wwe-speaks-out-against-hb2-north-carolina-wwe-live-event.
 17. Tufayel Ahmed, "Pat Patterson: Being WWE's First Gay Wrestler, Vince McMahon Retiring, and Mentoring The Rock," *Newsweek*, August 9, 2016, http://www.newsweek.com/pat-patterson-being-wwes-first-gay-wrestler-vince-mcmahon-retiring-and-487721.
 18. Ahmed, "Pat Patterson."
 19. Keith Harris, "Being Gay in the WWE? No Sweat Says ESPN's Jonathan Coachman" *SB Nation Cageside Seats*, March 3, 2013, http://www.cagesideseats.com/wwe/2013/3/3/4055874/being-gay-in-wwe-no-sweat-says-espns-jonathan-coachman.
 20. Ahmed, "Pat Patterson."
 21. James Caldwell, "WWE News: Bret Hart Issues Apology for Inappropriate Joke During Bret Hart Appreciation Night," *Pro Wrestling Torch*, May 31, 2013, @BretHart, Twitter, May 31, 2013.
 22. R.D. Reynolds and Bryan Alvarez, *The Death of WCW: 10th Anniversary Edition of the Bestselling Classic* (Toronto: ECW Press, 2014 [2004]), xii–xiii.
 23. David Shoemaker, *The Squared Circle* (New York: Gotham Books, 2013), 50–51.
 24. @AKATheMaskedMan, Twitter, February 20, 2014.

Sasha Banks, the Boss of NXT
Media, Gender and the Evolution of Women's Wrestling in WWE

CHRISTIANA MOLLDREM HARKULICH

When Mercedes Kaestner-Varnado, better known as WWE Superstar Sasha Banks, was ten years old, she wrote in her notebook that she wanted to be the "greatest women's wrestler ever."[1] Ten years later, after a brief career in independent wrestling, Banks signed a contract with World Wrestling Entertainment's (WWE's) NXT developmental promotion. Banks is small for a professional wrestler (5'5", 114 pounds), but carries herself with considerable swagger, wearing shutter shades, studded black leather costumes, and a large gold necklace that spells "Boss" when she enters the squared circle. At *NXT Takeover: Respect* on October 7, 2015, Banks and Bayley wrestled in the first female iron-man match (in which the wrestler who scores the most falls within a set time period, usually 30 minutes, is declared the winner), the longest women's match in WWE history, and the first time a women's match headlined a major WWE event in over 30 years.[2] This match, along with Banks' persona and physique, represents an unprecedented shift in opportunities for female wrestlers in sports entertainment, from their placement on cards to the particulars of their matches.

For most of WWE's nationally-televised history, women have functioned primarily as objects and sex symbols in the storylines of male wrestlers. WWE women wrestlers have typically fit the physical molds of models or Playboy bunnies rather than those of athletes or wrestlers. This is perhaps best exemplified by Sable, a tall, sexy, blonde white woman with long hair, an athletic body, and enhanced breasts. While Sable wasn't the first member of the women's division to match this description, her popularity during the WWE's Attitude era in the late 1990s represented a shift in focus toward women wrestlers whose looks were more important than their wrestling ability.[3]

Banks is, however, part of a new generation of women wrestlers that represent the change to the women's division: The Divas Revolution, which started in NXT and is continuing to evolve as of this writing.[4] Not only has the focus of women's wrestling shifted to high quality in-ring performances, but also to characters and narratives that are not dependent on romantic attachments to male wrestlers. This revolution has transformed the way women wrestlers are viewed and represented; they are now portrayed primarily as serious competitors rather than sex objects and sideshow attractions.

Pro wrestling relies on stereotypes, from physical archetypes and costumes to patterns of behavior and speech. Before wrestling was televised, this iconography of character became a short-hand in storytelling that was part of the mode of performance. Regarding the visual storytelling aspects of wrestling, Roland Barthes wrote: "thus the wrestlers' physique establishes a basic sign containing in germ the whole fight. But this germ proliferates, for at each moment of the combat, in each new situation, the wrestler's body affords the public the marvelous diversion of a humor that finds its natural function in gesture."[5] What Barthes points to is the physicalization of stereotypes and the visual nature of storytelling in the wrestling ring. The body type is tied to gestures; we know the difference between the villain and the hero by the way they stand. We are able to accurately judge the books by their covers, which leaves more time in the narrative for the fight itself and not the exposition of its stakes. Aristotle wrote in *The Poetics* that action makes character; in wrestling, the action begins with posturing and physical presentation.

Each storyline must raise the stakes of the story to the point of violence. Often the plot is simple: a quest for each wrestler to be the best. What makes storytelling in professional wrestling particularly compelling is that the audience understands the obvious heroes (or babyfaces in wrestling parlance) to root for, and villains (or heels) to boo. Within the realm of men's wrestling, we know them immediately: the giant strong-man villain, the good-looking cheater, the do-gooder muscle man. These stereotypes rely on the actions of the men themselves as well their physical appearances. Only very large men can hope to play the giant stereotype, as suggested by Barthes. The exterior stereotype of masculinity is connected to body type, and this body type is both performed and mediated. These are the shells of masculinity, or hypermasculinity—that heightened definition of manliness.[6]

As Patrice Oppliger writes, masculinity in wrestling is tied to acts of violence and aggression. Action makes character, and action is what drives the storytelling of professional wrestling. As previously mentioned, wrestlers in WWE generally fall into either babyface or heel categories, and they can switch (or turn in wrestling parlance) from one to the other based on the narrative. Oppliger, in her 2004 study, outlined the following types of heel characters: "The Violent," "The Psychotic," "The Sexualized Male," "The Feminine Male," "The Homosexual."[7] With the exception of the homosexual, which has fallen out of favor, all of these types are currently present among male wrestlers. There are also aspects of race, class, and nationality that will stereotype a character. Current Superstar Rusev has revived classic Cold War storylines as the bad guy "Russian" (or rather, a Bulgarian Russian sympathizer) who fights Americans. Damien Sandow's heel work relied on anti-intellectual working-class sentiments that sometimes define heels. The face is always the good guy, the do-gooder who always chooses honorable fighting over cheating. In the modern era (2002-present), this is best embodied by John Cena.

In pro wrestling, masculinity defines femininity, and defines itself in relationship to femininity. The instant recognition that Barthes writes about is a short-hand, and those short-hands of visual understanding are often stereotypes. To instantly know something is manly is to inherently know that it is also is not feminine. Stereotypes reinforce the binary relationship between masculinity and femininity, performed through acts of aggressive violence in the ring. It shouldn't be that surprising that women's wrestling, which asks women to act violently and thus inherently undermine gender binary stereotypes that male wrestling characters rely on to build their stories, has taken a long time to be taken seriously within WWE.

What kind of women are violent? Not nice ones, certainly. It's often implied that men are quick to fight, but women are supposed to be the fairer sex and less likely to resort to violence. Women, and the different types of stereotypical female characters, are often portrayed as non-violent. What does a babyface women's champion look like? Where does her urge to fight come from? Stereotypes of violent tendencies in femininity are often described as "mad" or "bad" in American culture.[8] This is not to say that there aren't violent or competitive women who are neither mad nor bad, but that the stereotypes of women in American culture primarily associate violence among women with "bad girl" types or as an aspect of insanity. This, combined with the larger dichotomous categorization of women into either the category of Virgin or Whore leaves very little maneuverability for women wrestlers in WWE to create interesting characters that do not rely on limited common stereotypes.[9] The majority of women have been portrayed as sexually available heel characters who are manipulative or morally loose. Famously, WWE wrestler Lita was forced to turn heel in 2005 when her real-life affair with heel wrestler and "Rated-R Superstar" Edge became public knowledge on the internet. Lita, a talented wrestler, had been in a long-term real-life and in-ring relationship with babyface Matt Hardy. Her real-life betrayal bled into her character's narrative, and the WWE exploited this story angle with an in-ring "live sex" celebration on the January 9, 2006, episode of *Monday Night Raw*.[10] In prior narratives, Lita feuded with rival Trish Stratus over the women's championship, but when Lita exercised autonomy in her sexuality and violated a perceived moral code, Lita became a villain. Until recently, femininity in WWE has been defined largely by the sexual desirability of the character for a perceived male audience, and WWE has used that appeal to boost ratings.

While men's matches have dominated WWE's televised wrestling, it was a woman's wrestling match that helped launch nationally televised wrestling. The match was the main event of the *Brawl to End It All* at Madison Square Garden on July 23, 1984, and featured Wendi Richter challenging 27-year reigning champion The Fabulous Moolah for the then-WWF Women's Championship. Of the ten matches that made up the live event, only the Women's Championship was broadcast live on MTV. What made this match special and relevant to MTV was singer Cyndi Lauper's involvement in the feud. Lauper's song "Girls Just Want to Have Fun" peaked at number two on the Billboard Top 100 charts for two weeks in March, and her music video, featuring WWF manager Captain Lou Albano, was in rotation on MTV. The WWF manufactured a feud between Albano and Lauper, citing Lauper's anger at Albano's sexist comments, in which he attempted to take credit for her success.[11]

Lauper managed Richter in the match against Moolah. A fresh-faced newcomer, Richter had a tall athletic build and wore her long brown hair in a curly rock-star cut. She wore a hot-pink leotard, sunglasses, a modern Kimono-style robe, and matching bright pink hoop earrings into the ring, embodying the spunk and empowerment of Lauper's "Girls Just Want to Have Fun," used as her entrance music. This girl-power anthem embodied a stereotype of rebellion that made babyface Richter's competitive acts of aggression understandable. She could behave violently in service to the competition, and the acts did not color her as crazy or "bad." Albano managed The Fabulous Moolah, a long-time trainer and promoter of women's wrestling. She had recently sold the rights to her women's championship to WWF owner Vince McMahon. Moolah had just turned 61 when the *Brawl to End It All* was filmed. A seasoned wrestler and trainer, Moolah dressed in a well-tailored, short white robe adorned with her championship belt to enter the ring. In her promotional interview with announcer "Mean" Gene Okerland before the match, she and Albano established her character as a classic heel whose only motivation was to retain her title at any cost, including cheating. Although Albano plays into the narrative to establish the feud, the match rests on professionalism and a competitive desire to be the best, free of any romantic entanglements.[12] While Richter can be seen as an object of sexual desire, Moolah's older body is inherently undesirable. Her dirty tricks, skill, and aging body make her a monster. She was a talented wrestler, but was she good for television? McMahon retained exclusive rights to Moolah's wrestling engagements when he purchased the Women's Championship. After McMahon began broadcasting his events nationally via cable television and pay-per-view, Moolah mainly appeared in long, matronly gowns. Richter won the match on MTV, ending Moolah's reign, and launching the "Rock N' Wrestling" connection that would in turn begin the rise of Hulkamania, with popular, flashy wrestler Hulk Hogan as the public face of the WWF. The broadcast of the Richter/Moolah match earned MTV its highest ratings to that point in its existence.[13]

At the first *Wrestlemania* on March 31, 1985, headlined by matches featuring Hulk Hogan and Andre the Giant, Wendi Richter, accompanied again by Lauper, defeated Moolah's younger and more attractive protégé Leilani Kai. Richter's relationship with the WWF quickly soured after *Wrestlemania*; her relationship with Vince McMahon was fraught with tension, purportedly over her contract (she believed she should earn more money due to her prominent role in the company's rapid national expansion). McMahon decided that she would lose the title on November 25, 1985, at Madison Square Garden. Sometimes referred to as the "Original Screw Job," Richter was not informed prior to the match that she would lose the title. Moolah, in disguise as "The Spider Lady," an anonymous masked villain billed from "parts unknown," entered the ring and, within a few minutes, pinned Richter against her will.[14] Although Richter kicked out before the referee's fast three-count, she still lost the title.[15] Moolah didn't just betray her opponent; she betrayed her former student, and this betrayal ended their friendship.

Between *Wrestlemania* (1985) and *Wrestlemania X* (1994), women in the WWF primarily played the roles of valets or managers. There were occasional matches between women wrestlers, but they were usually not featured on larger televised events. As valets and managers, women became beautiful accessories that proved the masculinity of the men they escorted. Perhaps the most iconic woman in this role, who would set the tone for how women were used in storylines for many years to come, was "Macho Man" Randy Savage's manager and real-life wife, Miss Elizabeth. Although Miss Elizabeth was a manager, she hardly ever spoke. She silently supported and doted on Savage. In one of her first major storylines, George "The Animal" Steele developed an unreciprocated crush on Miss Elizabeth, and would pick her up and carry her away from ringside during Savage's matches. Savage then feuded with Steele to protect Miss Elizabeth's honor and his ownership of her. Watching these matches today, it is clear Miss Elizabeth, billed as the "First Lady of Wrestling" because of her beauty-queen ball gown outfits, was used primarily as an object of desire for male fans, who could imagine themselves "rescuing" her from the villainous Macho Man.[16]

The underdeveloped, sexy, and attractive female character is an all-too-familiar trope in television and film. Barrie Gunter's study of gender roles on television shows that through 1995, women were grossly underrepresented on television.[17] Across all television programming, Gunter notes that through 1981 "women were generally outnumbered by men by about three to one."[18] In scripted dramas, the stereotyping of femininity through traits such as a fondness for domesticity, parenthood, and marriage, was deeply woven into television narratives.[19] WWE has also relied heavily on audience familiarity with gender stereotypes in their character development, stereotypes which have been established and reinforced on other television formats. Miss Elizabeth is defined not by her own personality, but by her attractiveness and relationship to a male character. Who is Miss Elizabeth, if she is not also Randy Savage's manager and lover? Miss Elizabeth is familiar to audiences; she is the doting spouse and lover, more concerned with her husband's success than her own interests. Her beauty and costume tells the audience very little about her but a great deal about Randy Savage, whose virility and masculinity are reaffirmed by the support of a beautiful woman.

The series of grudge matches between Steele and Savage were very popular in the mid–1980s, which arguably led to WWE's repeated use of woman-as-sexual-object feuds that persisted through 2015. Ultimately, this type of feud affirms the idea that women in the wrestling ring only exist to support the male wrestlers (as managers, valets, and love interests) and that their wrestling ability and humanity is ultimately unnecessary or secondary to the storyline. Three of the typifying gender-role portrayals in drama that Gunter points to are persistently evident in WWE's narrative structures:

1. Female characters are fewer in number and less central to the plot.
2. Employed women are shown in traditionally female occupations, as subordinates to men—with little status or power.
3. TV-women are more personally- and less professionally-oriented than TV-men.[20]

Wrestling narratives for men are often driven by professional power imbalances (i.e., anti-authority vs. authority) and a competitive desire to be the best wrestler, usually indicated by possession of various championship belts. Until the Divas' Revolution, women's' storylines tended to revolve around male desire.

Betty Jo Barrett and Dana S. Levin did a qualitative analysis of romance narratives in WWE in 2011, more than 15 years after Gunter's study. Barrett and Levin identified six romance narratives that were consistently present in WWE, all heteronormative in nature. They are: "(1) Prince Charming (2) Dark Romance (3) Femme Fatale (4) Gold Digger (5) Cougar (6) Woman Scorned."[21] With the exception of the Prince Charming and Dark Romance narratives that require a woman to be both passive and in danger, all other narratives rely on a sexually aggressive female character who is motivated by wealth, revenge, and/or status. The Woman Scorned narrative has the potential to motivate two women to feud (the goal of every wrestling narrative), but that fight will always be about their personal feelings and not their professional motivations, leaving the feud confined within Gunter's female gender stereotypes. While there is room for subversion, these narratives leave women either in the stereotype of the passive victim, a role that is neither strong nor powerful, but does allow the character to maintain babyface "virgin" status, or as a sexually aggressive and manipulative woman, a stereotype that is vilified and shunned as a whore. There has been little room in these "romance narratives" for a woman wrestler to be a powerful hero that transcends domestic stereotypes.

In 1993, the WWF began broadcasting live wrestling weekly on its *Monday Night Raw* program, and reached its height of popularity during the Attitude Era (roughly between 1998 and 2002), which relied heavily on "edgier" content that amplified the levels of violence and sexuality in wrestling to unprecedented heights. Women's wrestling during this period often featured "matches" that did not occur in the ring but rather in pudding, gravy, and other wet substances or, alternatively, bikini, lingerie, and evening gown competitions. On rare occasions, Women's breasts were "accidently" exposed. Rather infamously, wrestler Jacqueline competed against Sable in a bikini contest on the July 26, 1998, *Fully Loaded: In Your House Pay-Per-View*.[22] Judged by a leering Jerry "The King" Lawler, Jacqueline wore a red thong with straps that extended over her shoulders and barely covered her nipples, with red vinyl thigh-high heeled boots. She danced and gyrated like a stripper. At one point during this dance, the strap fell revealing her nipple. This has since been censored by WWE, but it was originally broadcast live without censorship. Sable revealed her bikini top to be nothing more than adhesive attached handprints, and she was disqualified from the match for not wearing an actual bikini. The women who competed in these matches were often models, valets, and managers with little or no wrestling ability. Beginning with Sable, these women nearly all fit in the same physical type, usually with large breast enhancements. Their long hair, revealing outfits, and overwhelming décolletage are sexually desirable physical attributes one might expect to see in the pages of *Playboy* or on the popular 1990s television show *Baywatch*. When we apply Barthes' idea of a wrestler's physical features telling us a story to women's physiques in the WWF/E from the late 1990s through the early 2010s, we see sexualized objects enhanced to attract and please male audiences. What these women did and said mattered much less than how they looked and what they wore. Character was largely disregarded in favor of sex appeal.

Through the bevy of beautiful women that have performed for the WWE, three in particular stand out for their in-ring ability and their influence on women's wrestling: Chyna, Trish Stratus, and Lita. Chyna (Joanie Laurer) debuted in 1997, in an era of bikini contests and bra and panties matches, with a physique that initially did not fit the mold. Chyna was six feet tall, had spent the last few years training as a bodybuilder, and was eventually billed as the "9th Wonder of the World."[23] Her then-boyfriend, wrestler Hunter Hurst Helmsley, who would go on to be known as Triple H, helped bring Laurer into the WWF. Chyna debuted on the February 24, 1997, *In Your House: Final Four* pay-per-view as Helmsley's bodyguard during a feud with Goldust and his manager Marlena. Chyna entered from the stands, then picked up and shook the diminutive Marlena.[24] Over the next month of RAW episodes, Helmsley (his persona at this point was a well-to-do wealthy man from Connecticut) was constantly accompanied by the leering and silent Chyna. Chyna's body, already taller than the rest of the women in the division, was extremely athletic. With long black hair in a ponytail, a strong chin, and an outfit consisting of running pants and modest tank tops, Chyna's aesthetic did not match the femininity of other women featured on the show. The commentators at the announce table pointed out this difference during Chyna's earliest appearances. At *Wrestlemania 13*, Jerry "The King" Lawler referred to her as a "monstrous Amazon that he [Triple H] calls Chyna" and claimed that she was "so ugly" because "she was breastfed by her father."[25] Chyna's strength and stature was the opposite of the Sable aesthetic, and the potential of being beat up by a girl whose physical power and unconventional appearance threatened their masculinity.[26]

Chyna's initial look is reminiscent of Sporty Spice from the Spice Girls, whose popularity reached its zenith in 1997 with the release of their *Spice World* movie. However, the "Girl Power" aesthetic of athletic pants and halter sports tops is not Chyna's most iconic look. Soon after Chyna joined the WWF, the promotion's Monday night show's name was altered to *RAW IS WAR* during a period of intensifying competition for ratings with WCW's *Monday Nitro*, which aired directly opposite the WWF's flagship show on Monday nights. The program took a turn towards more crude and rude humor and actions attempting to appeal in particular to teenage males as well as the coveted 18–35 male demographic. Triple H and Chyna joined "Heartbreak Kid" Shawn Michaels to form D-Generation X. Chyna began wearing revealing studded leather outfits with her black wavy hair worn down with a straight bang. This look is reminiscent of another strong female warrior on television in the late 1990s: *Xena: Warrior Princess*. By 1999, when Chyna's look had fully evolved, *Xena* aired both during prime time network television and in syndication on USA, the same network on which *RAW* aired. Like *Xena*, Chyna primarily feuded with men. She is the only woman to ever hold the Intercontinental Championship, in addition to a run with the Women's Championship. She is also the first woman, and one of only three, to have ever entered the Royal Rumble.[27] Her height and strength opened up opportunities that no other woman wrestler has since achieved. Like the character Xena, she was allowed to be violent, flawed, and to change her position from heel to face without losing her strength. Until 2000, shortly before her departure from the WWF, Chyna's narratives rarely involved romance. Like Lawler stated, she was a monstrous Amazon, and like the Amazons of myth and television she didn't need a man to fight her battles.

Chyna, unfortunately, did not fundamentally change the way women were treated and used in the WWF/WWE. She began her career as a distinctly unique performer, in contrast to the other women in the promotion, but eventually she transformed, through breast enhancements and a facial reconstruction surgery, to match the Sable aesthetic. She also followed Sable's example and was the second woman from the WWF to pose for *Playboy*. One of her final storylines involved a romantic entanglement with and marriage proposal from wrestler Eddie Guerrero. Stephanie McMahon, Vince McMahon's daughter, also debuted during this period. While Stephanie is now the Chief Brand Officer of the WWE as well as the on-screen Commissioner of *RAW*, she initially appeared on *RAW* in 1999 as Vince McMahon's innocent daughter, a pawn in Vince's feud with The Undertaker. In late 1999, the WWF Creative team, led by writer Vince Russo, wrote Stephanie into an in-ring marriage with Test that was foiled by Triple H's kidnapping of Stephanie during her bachelorette party. This on-screen drama included Triple H's drugging, kidnapping, and non-consensual wedding to Stephanie in Las Vegas. It was strongly implied that Triple H raped Stephanie. Eventually, Stephanie revealed this as a ploy to turn heel against her father by siding with Triple H. Marriage (especially non-consensual marriage) was often an end goal in the narratives around women in the WWE throughout the 2000s. For the writers, weddings were goals and punishments for the women wrestlers that were more important than championships. Once wedded, the narratives focus on the woman's faithfulness and the potential for her honor to be protected or for her to be villainized for cheating.

The rivalry between Trish Stratus and Lita lasted from 2000 through Lita's retirement in 2006. Trish Stratus began her career with the WWF as the manager of tag-team T&A (Test and Prince Albert), a thinly-veiled allusion to "Tits and Ass." The 5'4" blonde former fitness model wore tight pleather outfits that showed off her body and enhanced cleavage. She began wrestling in June of 2000, not long after her debut, as the female member of T&A in a tag team match against the Hardy Boyz and Lita. Lita trained in the Mexican lucha libre style, and competed on the independent circuit before joining the WWF. Lita developed an alternative aesthetic with baggy, wide-leg pants, with her thong rising out of the waist. Beginning with that initial match Lita and Trish Stratus managed to maintain their rivalry through the wide range of romantic narratives they were both involved in. Trish Stratus played Vince McMahon's mistress during a 2001 storyline that involved Vince's real-life wife Linda pretending to be in a coma after Vince demanded a divorce. The wrestler Kane kidnapped, raped, impregnated, and tried to marry Lita against her will during a several-month period in mid-2004. As mentioned earlier, Lita's real-life affair with Edge also became fodder for storylines. Through all of this, Lita and Trish Stratus continued to improve their wrestling techniques and in-ring performances. In current material promoting women's wrestling, the WWE often showcases the in-ring rivalry between the two, while overlooking or minimizing the "soap-opera" elements of their storylines.[28]

In the decade between Trish and Lita's retirements and the Divas' Revolution, women's matches received continually less screen time. New in-ring talent was recruited from WWE reality television show *Tough Enough*, and the semi-regular *Diva Search*. Through these avenues WWE recruited models-turned-wrestlers like Michelle McCool, Layla, and the Bella Twins. Starting in 2013, in partnership with E! Entertainment Television, the WWE launched their first reality television show, *Total Divas*, documenting the Divas' lives outside the ring. This change in recruiting coincided with the dawn of the PG era. Characters were no longer involved in matches with lots of blood, nor were women wrestlers hit by male wrestlers.[29] A majority of the women characters continued to be more focused on looking attractive than working on their character or in-ring ability. The Bella Twins, Nikki and Brie, made their mark as attractive identical twins who used their physical similarity to cheat by swapping out during singles matches. In 2010, WWE retired the Women's championship in favor of the Divas Championship (a title created during a Raw/Smackdown brand split). The Divas Championship belt featured a large pink butterfly that looks more like a Barbie accessory than a professional wrestling title, and it mirrored the trivial way that the Divas matches were treated on television.

On the February 23, 2015, episode of *RAW* the already-limited time reserved for women's matches reached a new low. The only Divas match scheduled for the 3-hour program was a tag-team contest pitting Emma and Paige against The Bella Twins. The match lasted less than 35 seconds from opening bell to the final three-count.[30] The WWE embrace of social media sees their hashtags trend every week. On February 23 the hashtag #GiveDivasAChance trended worldwide and ignited a conversation that has eventually led to the Divas' Revolution. For WWE fans, this hashtag was not a sudden moment of consciousness about the consistent under-use of and short-time allotted for women's matches, but rather a growing discontent brought on in contrast to the higher quality of women's wrestling on *NXT*. At *NXT Takeover: Rivals*, only two weeks before #GiveDivasAChance, Bayley,

Sasha Banks, Becky Lynch, and Charlotte competed in a fatal-four-way match for the NXT Women's Championship. The match lasted approximately 13 minutes, and began Sasha Banks' first run as NXT Women's Champion.[31] The commentators focused on the match's action and the wrestlers' competitive desires to be champion. NXT treated its women wrestlers as legitimate competitors, while the main roster treated them as accessories or a "bathroom break" sideshow. For fans watching both promotions, the difference was obvious, and no longer acceptable.[32] Stephanie McMahon responded to fans' increasing calls for women's wrestling to be portrayed more seriously by calling up Sasha Banks, Charlotte, and Becky Lynch to the main roster on July 13, 2015, episode of *Raw*, and branding this new moment "The Divas Revolution."[33]

The NXT promotion is not just a training ground for wrestling techniques but also for character development. Formerly known as Florida Championship Wrestling (FCW), NXT was the brainchild of Paul "Triple H" Levesque, and operates out of Full Sail University in Orlando, FL. Levesque takes credit both as the creator and executive producer of NXT, and the work that happens there is because of his guidance. Levesque, who married Stephanie McMahon in 2003, is WWE Executive Vice President of Live Events, Talent, and Creative.[34] NXT has shown consistent support for the development of distinctive female characters. Part of that is the behind-the-scenes training that is supported at the NXT training center. Within the training center, women wrestlers are trained and supported by Sarah Amato and Sarah Stock, two experienced wrestlers who worked previously for various independent wrestling promotions. Thus, aspiring women wrestlers are supported and trained not only by retired WWE legends like Dusty Rhodes (who died in 2015), but also by experienced female role models who understand the particular challenges and opportunities women encounter as pro wrestlers.

Developmental wrestlers don't enter the ring until they themselves have developed a suitable in-ring persona. This is a change from the top-down nature of character gimmicks on WWE's main roster, where gimmicks were typically handed to performers by the creative team or Vince McMahon himself. For the women wrestlers, this allows them to find their own inspirations and incorporate them into viable characters. Sasha Banks, for example, has stated that her "Boss" persona came first from her first cousin, rapper Snoop Dogg, who calls himself "the boss," and the look of Nikki Minaj.[35] The hip-hop and rap aesthetic is easily recognizable, one no previous WWE women's wrestler had utilized. Sasha Banks' use of the "Boss" nickname evokes ideas of a "boss bitch," more than a CEO character. Banks wears bright and unnatural hair colors, a staple of Nikki Minaj's look in 2013. Banks is a petite woman, but the character she created is larger than life. Her narratives, on NXT and on the main roster of the WWE, have centered around her wrestling ability and rivalry with Charlotte, the daughter of wrestling legend "Nature Boy" Ric Flair.

Banks' use of these elements make her character instantly recognizable, and draws from a wider range of modern media portrayals of women. Banks grew up watching Chyna, Lita, and Trish Stratus on television, which showed her that her dream was possible. Banks' professional debut occurred in a heavily mediated and branded moment of American culture. The WWE isn't only on USA and pay-per-view; they have their own online streaming network and have a formidable presence on Twitter and other forms of social media. The wrestling audience is often watching and engaging with the WWE across multiple platforms, and has become too savvy for the simple stereotypes of earlier eras; this allows wrestlers to develop more complex characters pulling iconography from a wider range of sources that are still easily recognizable to the audience. For the audience that also watches Ultimate Fighter Championship (UFC) mixed martial arts fighting, it should be no surprise that women are taken more seriously, especially due to the immense success of Ronda Rousey. Rousey signed with the UFC in 2012, one year after UFC President Dana White declared that women would "never" compete in UFC.[36] Rousey's fight with Holly Holm at *UFC 193* drew 50,000 spectators in Australia and garnered the highest ratings for UFC to that point.[37] Women fighting competitively draws a crowd.

Sasha Banks embodies a revolution that involved a clear departure from earlier, often one-dimensional portrayals of women in pro wrestling. The final break with the past came at *Wrestlemania 32*, when Lita announced, in front of a crowd of nearly 100,000 people and the gathered members of the Divas division, that the WWE was retiring the Divas Championship title and replacing it with the Women's Championship title. She also announced that all women wrestlers would no longer be known as Divas but as Superstars, matching their male co-workers' nomenclature. The triple-threat match between Charlotte, Becky Lynch, and Sasha Banks at *Wrestlemania 32* would now decide the first Superstar to hold the new Women's Championship title. The three newly-branded Superstars were featured prominently on giant posters hanging outside the stadium. Their match lasted for over 16 minutes as part of the main card of the program, ending with Charlotte pinning Becky Lynch to win the title. As women's wrestling continues to feature more prominently on the main roster, the Divas Revolution, launched in 2015, ironically resulted in the end of the "Divas," a term loaded with potentially negative gendered connotations, and a descriptor of the WWE's conventional treatment of women as a mere sideshow distraction. The change to Superstars marks the start of an era of more serious and positive portrayals of WWE's women grapplers, deserving of the same respect and admiration as their male counterparts.

Part II. Gender

NOTES

1. "Q&A: WWE Superstar Sasha Banks Talks Battle Ground Event, Cousin Snoop Dogg and Living Her Dream," BET.com, July 22, 2016, http://www.bet.com/news/sports/2016/070/22/q-a-wwe-superstar-sasha-banks-talks-battle-ground-event-cousin.html (accessed August 4, 2016).

2. On July 23, 1984, Wendi Richter defeated the Fabulous Moolah for the WWF women's championship in the main event of the Brawl to End It All, a WWF event at Madison Square Garden that aired on MTV. Only the women's match was aired, scoring a record 9.1 Nielsen rating. "Misc. WWF TV Specials," http://www.prowrestlinghistory.com/supercards/usa/wwf/misctv.html#brawl (accessed March 29, 2017).

3. Michael A. Messner, Margaret Carlisle Duncan, and Cheryl Cooky, "Silence, Sports Bras, and Wrestling Porn Women in Televised Sports News and Highlights Shows," *Journal of Sport & Social Issues* 27, no. 1 (February 1, 2003), 38–51.

4. The term "Diva" was used by the WWF/WWE since April 1999 to refer to all female talent including managers, valets, back-stage interviewers, and wrestlers. As of April 2016, WWE retired the term in favor of referring to all talent as Superstars, regardless of gender.

5. Roland Barthes, "In the Ring," in *Mythologies: The Complete Edition, in a New Translation*, trans. Richard Howard (New York: Hill and Wang, 2012), 6.

6. Patrice A. Oppliger, *Wrestling and Hypermasculinity* (Jefferson, NC: McFarland, 2004), Chapter 6.

7. Oppliger, *Wrestling and Hypermasculinity*, Chapter 6.

8. Paula Ruth Gilbert, "Discourses of Female Violence and Societal Gender Stereotypes," *Violence Against Women* 8, no. 11 (November 1, 2002), 1271–1300.

9. The Madonna-Whore breakdown of female relationships begins with Freudian psychology, but has evolved as a representative model of framing women's existence in relationship to their sexuality in western culture. This has been widely critiqued as a misogynist structure by feminist scholars like Naomi Wolf in *Promiscuities: The Secret Struggle for Womanhood* (New York: Ballantine Books, 1998) and Leora Tanenbaum in *Slut! Growing Up Female with a Bad Reputation* (New York: Harper Perennial, 2000).

10. Vince McMahon, *Monday Night Raw*, January 9, 2006.

11. The WWF changed their name to the WWE in 2002 after losing a copyright case to the World Wildlife Federation; for the sake of clarity I will continually refer to them as the WWE throughout this essay.

12. *The Brawl to End It All*, MTV/WWF, July 23, 1984.

13. Scott Beekman, *Ringside: A History of Professional Wrestling in America* (Westport, CT: Greenwood, 2006) 125.

14. The most well-known screw-job is the Montreal Screw Job that occurred between Shawn "The Heartbreak Kid" Michaels and Bret "The Hitman" Hart on November 9, 1997, during the *Survivor Series* pay-per-view, filmed in Hart's hometown of Montreal. Hart was scheduled to leave the WWF for WCW in December 1997 and was scheduled to defend his WWF championship during the *Survivor Series*. Hart refused to lose the title to Michaels and expected it to end in a disqualification. Fearing Hart would take the belt with him to WCW, Vince McMahon instead decided that Michaels would win without informing Hart. This and other such betrayals are referred to as screw-jobs.

15. David Shoemaker, "Wrestling's Greatest Shoots, Volume 4: Wendi Richter vs. The Spider, a.k.a. The Fabulous Moolah," *Grantland*, July 29, 2013, http://grantland.com/the-triangle/wrestlings-greatest-shoots-wendy-richter-vs-the-spider-a-k-a-the-fabulous-moolah/ (accessed August 26, 2016).

16. "Miss Elizabeth," WWE.com, http://www.wwe.com/superstars/misselizabeth (accessed August 23, 2016).

17. Barrie Gunter, *Television and Gender Representation* (London: Acamedia Research Monograph 14, J. Libbey, 1995), 10.

18. Gunter, *Television and Gender Representation*, 10.

19. Gunter, *Television and Gender Representation*, 12. This information is drawn from

the 1970s and early 1980s, but is relevant to the iconography that makes wrestling types instantly recognizable.

20. Gunter, *Television and Gender Representation*, 12. These are three of seven points, and those most relevant to WWE.

21. Betty Jo Barrett and Dana S. Levin, "What's Love Got to Do with It? A Qualitative Grounded Theory Content Analysis of Romance Narratives in the PG Era of World Wrestling Entertainment (WWE) Programming," *Sexuality & Culture* 18, no. 3 (November 30, 2013), 560–91.

22. Vince McMahon, *Fully Loaded: In Your House Pay-Per-View*, directed by Kevin Dunn, written by Vince Russo and Ed Ferrera, WWF, July 26, 1998. Jaqueline, unlike Sable, was a body-builder and an in-ring talent, and was recently inducted into the WWE Hall of Fame. She is also black, and her portrayal of a sexy and powerful black woman is hindered by the power dynamics of stereotypes of black femininity that are rooted in racism.

23. Aaron Oster, "Remembering Chyna, the WWE Star Who Redefined the Rules," *Rolling Stone*, April 21, 2016, http://www.rollingstone.com/sports/features/remembering-chyna-the-wwe-star-who-redefined-the-rules-20160421 (accessed August 19, 2016).

24. Vince McMahon, *WWF in Your House: Final Four*, directed by Kevin Dunn, WWF, February 24, 1997.

25. Vince McMahon, *Wrestlemania 13*, directed by Kevin Dunn, written by Vince Russo, March 23, 1997. WWF.

26. Eventually, Laurer had several plastic surgeries (breast implants and a surgery to reduce her chin) to achieve a more feminine aesthetic. Triple H and Shawn Michaels made explicit references to Chyna's new breasts in one of their Degeneration X promos, with Triple H saying they should change their name to "Double-D-Generation X."

27. Vince McMahon, *WWF Royal Rumble: No Chance in Hell*, directed by Kevin Dunn, written by Vince Russo and Ed Ferrara, WWF, January 24, 1999. Chyna participated in two Royal Rumbles, 1999 and 2000; Beth Phoenix entered the Royal Rumble in 2010; and Kharma (better known as Awesome Kong in TNA wrestling) entered the Royal Rumble in 2012.

28. *WWE 24*, "Women's Evolution," WWE Network, August 19, 2016. http://network.wwe.com/video/v1057675983?contextType=wwe-show&contextId=wwe_24&contentId=195897548.

29. Lita, Chyna, and Trish Stratus were often in inter-gender matches, and as mentioned Chyna wrestled primarily with men.

30. *WWE Raw*, "Episode #25.23," written by Michael Notarile, USA Network, February 23, 2015.

31. *NXT Takeover: Rivals*, directed by Kevin Dunn, WWE, February 11, 2015.

32. See coverage from Aaron Oster, "NXT, Where the Women Work," *Rolling Stone*, February 26, 2015, http://www.rollingstone.com/culture/news/nxt-where-the-women-work-20150226, and Nick Wray, "WWE Fans Take to Twitter to Protest the Treatment of Women Wrestlers," *BuzzFeed*, February 24, 2016, https://www.buzzfeed.com/nicholaswray/give-divas-a-chance?utm_term=.tr48PMEG3#.tc0kRa67x.

33. Stephanie McMahon, "A Redefining Moment," *The Players' Tribune*, http://www.theplayerstribune.com/stephanie-mcmahon-wwe-divas-announcement/ (accessed August 5, 2016).

34. WWE, "Leadership," WWE.com, http://corporate.wwe.com/who-we-are/leadership (accessed August 30, 2016).

35. William Windsor, "Sasha Banks Talks Cousin Snoop Dogg's Influence on Her Character, Snoop Taking Her to WrestleMania," WrestlingInc.com. August 13, 2015, http://www.WrestlingInc.com/wi/news/2015/0813/599390/sasha-banks-talks-cousin-snoop-dogg-influence-on-her-character/ (accessed August 30, 2016).

36. Michael David Smith, "Dana White Will Change His Mind About Women 'Never' in the UFC," *MMA Fighting*, January 20, 2011, http://www.mmafighting.com/2011/01/20/dana-white-will-change-his-mind-about-women-never-in-the-ufc (accessed September 29, 2016).

37. "Holly Holm's UFC 193 KO of Ronda Rousey Leads FOX Sports to Record Ratings," November 17, 2015, http://sports.yahoo.com/news/holly-holms-ufc-193-ko-ronda-rousey-leads-235417303-mma.html (accessed September 29, 2016).

PART III. CULTURE AND MODERNITY

The Beginnings of Wrestling in Brazil
Theatricality, Marketing and a Colorful Character

RIQUELDI STRAUB LISE,
ANDRÉ MENDES CAPRARO,
NATASHA SANTOS and AARON D. HORTON

Wrestling was part of the first modern Olympics held in Athens, 1896, but did not appear in the programs of the Olympic Games of 1900 and 1904, held, respectively, in Paris and St. Louis. The sport was reinstated to the Olympic program in 1908, in London. Wrestling became relatively popular and, during the 19th century, was systematized and regulated in European countries, especially in France, England, and the United States.[1] Olympic wrestling already had a set of well-defined rules.[2] During the first decades of the 20th century, the first regulatory Greco-Roman institutions emerged. In 1905, the *Fédération Internationale pour le développement de la lutte et de l'haltérophilie*[3] was founded in the city of Duisburg, Germany. In 1912, the *Fédération Internationale de Lutte Amateur* (FILA) was founded in Paris with the intent of standardizing the rules of modern wrestling.[4] A few months before the 1912 Olympic Games in Stockholm, the Swedish Athletics Federation organized the *Union Internationale des Lutteurs*, whose primary objective was to regulate wrestling in the Olympics.[5]

During this period in Brazil, the first professional wrestling events were promoted. By the second decade of the 20th century, the sport had become quite popular in Brazil. This essay examines the origins of and responses to professional wrestling in Brazil, especially in the city of Rio de Janeiro, then-capital of the Republic.

Newspaper and magazine articles[6] on wrestling were the primary sources for this study. Reliance on these sources was necessary because of a lack of official documentation, given that there were no formal regulatory institutions for pro wrestling during this period. Furthermore, newspapers were the dominant form of mass media and therefore the primary venue for public discourse on pro wrestling in Brazil.[7] In the specific case of the establishment and popularization of wrestling in Brazil, newspapers went beyond the dissemination and popularization of the sport, having fostered an intense debate about wrestling in Brazil's emerging social dynamics. We do not intend here to detail the entire history of the introduction and spread of pro wrestling in Brazil, but rather to understand newspapers' (and journalists') perspectives on this new phenomenon.

Brazilian Sociopolitical Context and the Arrival of New Sports Practices

In the 1880s, campaigns for the abolition of slavery and for the end of imperial rule, ensconced for over 70 years in Brazil, intensified. 1888 brought the abolition of slavery, one of the last pillars of political support for the imperial system. With the weakening of the imperial regime and the consequent strengthening of a republican ideal, a military coup proclaimed the Brazilian Republic in the year 1889.[8] President Marshal Deodoro da Fonseca and Vice President Marshal Floriano Peixoto assumed leadership of the transitional government. The government of Marshal Deodoro was brief: he was deposed in 1891. Marshal Floriano Peixoto, also known as the "Iron Marshal," utilized authoritarianism and violence to assume the presidency of the Republic. However, Peixoto remained popular among the people of Brazil for having enacted a series of measures favorable to the country's emerging middle classes. In 1894, Marshal Peixoto supported free elections, resulting in the election of the first civilian president of Brazil, Prudente de Morais.[9]

One of the primary goals of this new Republican government was to transform Brazil into a modern nation. In order to accomplish this, the government invested in basic infrastructure (sanitation, healthcare, and urban development) and new technologies (industrial machinery and electricity).[10] However, such structural changes were not enough for complete modernization; many believed it also necessary to transform popular culture by eliminating customs considered backward:

> To ensure such a construction, economy and culture should work in coordination. It was about promoting interventions in urban space in order to facilitate trade and industry (such as the reformulation of the port and the improvement of roads, such

as highways and railroads), but also to build a new imaginary for the city.... It was about trying to submit the population to [new] physical cultural dimensions.[11]

Modernizing efforts focused primarily on the city of Rio de Janeiro. The federal capital was the most important port in Brazil[12] and the most populous urban center, with roughly 700,000 people.[13] According to Melo,[14] Rio de Janeiro was to embody the modernity and economic growth of the new Republic.

The city increasingly featured wide avenues, public lighting, and modern sanitation. Urban development offered greater mobility with the improvement of roads, squares, and other public spaces. The increasing availability of electricity enabled the construction of new commercial and industrial enterprises, leading to the emergence of a new urban elite, an industrial working class, and the growth of small business.[15] Rio de Janeiro was becoming modern, inspired by great European metropolises such as Paris and London.

Therefore, the first decade of the 20th century in Brazil was characterized by elite efforts to acquire "civilized" customs and behavior: first, by developing a modern, urban social hierarchy and, second, by breaking with the recent past, embodied by slavery and imperial rule, in hopes of approaching an ideal of modernity inspired by Europe. New customs became part of everyday life for Rio's elite, and sports were among the new routines of modern, urban life. The rise and spread of modern sports also went hand-in-hand with urbanization and modernization in Europe and the United States.[16]

In imperial Brazil, there was little appreciation for physical culture. Elites preferred passive leisure over physical activity, because manual labor and exercise traditionally characterized the lives of slaves or laborers. In other words, leisure activities were indicative of one's social class. In addition, there was a widespread belief that sports caused bodily deformities:

However, an influx of new ideas from Europe began to change Brazilian perceptions of athletics. Drawing from contemporary European medical hygienist discourse, physical exercises were increasingly considered essential to disease prevention and the promotion of good health[17]: "in much of the nineteenth century, people lived almost indifferent to sport, as it was believed that physical effort was always harmful to health."[18] Therefore, it is possible to verify a change in the patterns of health and aesthetic of individuals. Through these changes in medical discourse and the adoption of new habits and behaviors, strong and muscular bodies became the standard of health and beauty.[19] The athletic bodies of young upper-class athletes signified not only their social status but also psychological characteristics linked to adventure, boldness, and daring, adjectives typically used to describe "sportsmen."[20] The urbanization of Rio de Janeiro, driven by new technologies, the development of industry, and the growth of the working classes, offered the masses new possibilities for leisure, which included cinema, theater, and sports.

Body deformations caused by sports activities. In "Consequencias Sportivas,"
***O Malho*, December 26, 1903, 10.**

It was also during this period that some combat sports gained prominence in the Brazilian press, such as boxing and jiu-jitsu. Although widely reported on Rio de Janeiro's newspapers, boxing events were considered a barbaric, bestial, and savage practice because of the high levels of violence allowed in their bouts. Jiu-jitsu, although not of European origin, was considered by the newspapers as a modern, civilized sport that combined maximum efficiency with minimal energy expenditure. These characteristics motivated Brazilian authorities to adopt jiu-jitsu as a form of training for the navy and also for the police forces of the city of Rio de Janeiro.[21]

Capoeira, also a popular combat practice, was highly controversial. It was considered by most newspapers as a violent and uncivilized practice, considering that many clashes between capoeira *malta* ended with serious injuries and even deaths, especially given the frequent use of weapons such as razors. The *malta* were organized groups that gathered hundreds of capoeira players and were responsible, according to the police authorities, for causing social disorder. Thus, in the year 1890, a decree included capoeira in the Brazilian penal code. From that year on, the practice of capoeira in public places would result in a sentence from two months to three years in prison.[22]

From Circus to Theater: The Early Years of Wrestling in Brazil

The first mentions of wrestling in Brazil appeared during the last decade of the 19th century. However, these early mentions were not detailed accounts of sporting events but rather part of sensational circus ads: "In addition to other spectacles worthy of interest and applause, there will be a wrestling showcase featuring Hercules from Jorge Henke's troupe versus Angelo Senra Farina, a baker."[23] This description came from an ad for the Great Lusitano Circus, which organized a tour in Rio de Janeiro in 1892. Newspaper ads from the era demonstrate that wrestling was most often featured as part of traveling circuses, sharing the stage with other attractions, such as races between ducks and turkeys, dwarf fights, fighting bulls, acrobats, elephants, and so on.

In 1900, a series of ads announced an upcoming series of short films of wrestling matches, presented in popular theaters in Rio de Janeiro[24] via cinematograph.[25] "Today, the Paris Salon in Rio will feature the following cinematographs: *Felix Faure's Funeral, Wrestling, Transformations, Caught in the Act, Santo Antonio Temptations,* and *Parisian Gang*."[26] Such films were produced in Europe, where wrestling was already quite popular.

By the early 20th century, wrestling featured regularly in Brazil at local circus shows and as a foreign curiosity via new cinematic technologies, but still struggled to achieve widespread popularity in the early years of the 1900s. In 1904, the newspaper *A Noticia* published a story about the arrival of a troupe of foreign fighters[27] who would compete in Brazil's first Greco-Roman wrestling championship. This troupe had recently completed a tour in Buenos Aires, and their event in Rio would be sponsored by several business entrepreneurs: "Paul Pons[28] will be here next week. Nine famous and powerful European and Argentine fighters accompany him to challenge for the universal championship held by this invincible French fighter."[29] The event was held at the Parque Fluminense Theatre in July 1904. Newspapers frequently reported on the matches, indicating a growing interest in wrestling among the Brazilian public. "Yesterday's matches were extremely entertaining. As with other recent wrestling events, the crowd was large and enthusiastic."[30] And still,

> the event at Parque Fluminense indicates that wrestling's popularity is increasing monumentally. Yesterday at the event, the crowd [was so dense] that we couldn't walk among them, and the audience's enthusiasm was extraordinary. [The event's success] is accentuated by the champions' efforts to have their hands raised in victory.[31]

Both stories illustrate the wrestling troupe's spectacular success. The championship tournament lasted nearly a month and in the end, French grappler Paul Pons, leader of the troupe, was crowned the winner. Several Rio newspapers praised Greco-Roman wrestling as a serious and civilized sport,[32] unlike boxing, considered by most Brazilian newspapers to be a wild and bestial practice.

The troupe's success led to a subsequent event in Brazil in 1905. Dubbed by the press as the "second international Greco-Roman championship," the matches were contested by a group of 16 wrestlers of different nationalities.[33] As in the 1904 event, Paul Pons was the troupe's top star. The tournament, held once again in the Parque Fluminense, was wildly successful and received widespread coverage in the Brazilian press. This time, the event lasted roughly 40 days. Pons won the tournament for the second consecutive year, receiving a purse of 20,000 francs. Runner-up Raoul Le Boucher received 5,000 francs and third place finisher Aimable La cally received a thousand francs.[34]

Likely inspired by the success of the first two major wrestling tournaments in Brazil, entrepreneur Paschoal Segreto,[35] organized another Greco-Roman wrestling tournament, held in 1906. The tournament field was composed of 11 foreign wrestlers, none of whom had competed in the previous two tournaments. This tournament was held at the Moulin Rouge Theater, owned by Segreto. Unlike the previous tournaments, Segreto's event was the target of severe criticism by the Brazilian press due to its poor organization and the dubious technical skills of the featured grapplers.

Segreto, also known as "the minister of amusements of Rio de Janeiro," was an entertainment entrepreneur who owned numerous theaters: Carlos Gomes, Maison Moderne, Moulin Rouge, and the Avenida Theatre in Rio de Janeiro, and the Varieties Theatre in São Paulo. Segreto established a new philosophy for popular entertainment, marketed specifically to the working classes according to his motto "fun for everyone, for all classes, for all ages."[36] Previously, these and other theaters mostly featured classical plays and operas, but Segreto sought to appeal more broadly to the masses through a wider variety of events and lower prices.[37]

Even with the failure of Brazil's third (his first) wrestling tour, Segreto persisted with the idea in 1907, staging the fourth edition of the international Greco-Roman wrestling championship at the Moulin Rouge Theater. This time, Segreto hired nine grapplers,[38] including former tournament winner Paul Pons. With more elaborate and efficient marketing (daily ads in the city's major newspapers), the event was well-received by press and public alike. More importantly, Segreto helped further popularize sport in Rio de Janeiro: "Last night was the most sensational championship ever held at the Moulin Rouge. In the vast theater, there was not an empty seat from top to bottom. Those without seats spilled out into the garden."[39]

Given the success of the 1907 tournament, Segreto decided to hold the fifth international championship in 1909. This time, the event was held at the newly-opened Concerto Avenida theater,[40] also owned by Paschoal Segreto's company. By 1909, most newspapers appear to have considered wrestling a civilized activity. Greco-Roman wrestling featured intense physical contact between grapplers, but striking was prohibited, reducing the likelihood of serious injury, in contrast to boxing, for example. Various publications encouraged Greco-Roman wrestling as a means of improving health and preventing disease: "Of all the exercises, the one that most strengthens the heart is wrestling."[41] This article, published in the monthly magazine *Eu Sei Tudo*,[42] also alerted readers to the benefits of a daily intake of lemon juice and tea and specific physical practices as ways of preventing heart problems.

In 1910, the newspaper *O Paiz* published an article about the 1909 wrestling tournament:

> Concerto Avenida recently held the International Championship of Greco-Roman wrestling. Needless to say, this exciting sport attracted innumerable fans and interest. The excellent "troupe"[43] was composed of 16 figures: Paul Pons, Raul de Rouen, Constantinowich, Petersen, Furny, Massetti, Re Carlo D'Anvers, Constant Le Marin, Grenna Raffaele Schakmann, Schneider, Gazau, Dierry, Aimable of La Calmette, wrestlers, and Millo, referee, at a total cost of 40,000 francs per month, not including tickets back to the Old World. The event lasted from August 3 to October 12, 71 days of wrestling, more than two months' worth.[44]

This excerpt offers some valuable information about the fifth international Greco-Roman wrestling championship in Rio. The Paschoal Segreto Company had guaranteed the troupe a specific wage contract and a prime location

Paul Pons (seated at far left) and the troupe of Greco-Roman wrestlers. "Grande Campeonato de Luta Romana," *Fon-Fon*, August 7, 1909, 6.

for the tournament. The troupe was to receive 40,000 francs per month. If the amount was evenly distributed, each group member would receive 2,500 francs per month, for a total of 5,000 francs over the course of the two-month event.[45] The sources do not, however, specify how money was divided among members of the tour, though it is likely that the bigger stars, such as Paul Pons, received a much larger share than other, less-well known wrestlers did.

The 1909 tournament was a critical and financial success,[46] convincing Segreto to stage further Greco-Roman pro wrestling events at his theaters in 1911, 1913, and 1915. By the late 1910s, seven wrestling tournaments had been held in Rio de Janeiro, all of them with different troupes and, for the most part, financially successful, contributing to the popularization of the sport in the federal capital.

Emboldened by his recent successful promotions of wrestling, Segreto brought a troupe of ten female wrestlers to Brazil in 1910. This risky move created certain expectations about the unusual event:

> Theatro São Pedro—On Saturdays and Sundays, it features various films, and in May it is going to open its doors to a great Greco-Roman wrestling tournament—it sounds amazing!—contested by a group of ten representatives of the fairer sex, coming from St. Petersburg, in particular. Therefore, we can no longer call the fairer sex the weaker sex. We always wanted to see a cheap Don Juan seduce these beardless Herculeses. It is going to be quite the spectacle.[47]

The article exhibits a degree of perplexity and sarcasm. In 1910, combat sports in Brazil and elsewhere were still widely considered exclusively masculine endeavors. Female participation in sports occurred passively (as spectators), or was restricted to some boat races,[48] or involvement in commemorative competitions at social clubs. The few women who attended or participated in sporting events were usually from the upper class. Therefore, the concept of women's wrestling whetted the curiosity of the local population.

The figure above was the official presentation of the female Greco Roman troupe in season in Brazil, in 1910. Several wrestlers wear sashes and medals, indicative of past accomplishments. The referee sits at the center while at the far left sat the tour's top star, the Russian Schuwanoff, nicknamed "the golden girl" and considered the most beautiful wrestler.

This event, according to *Revista da Semana*, attracted large audiences to the São Pedro Theater:

> Theatro São Pedro—Full capacity, the theater crowded. Two feature attractions: the musical female troupe *Mirales* performing tasteful musical excerpts, and Greco-Roman strongwomen who compete, to the audience's delight. These two attractions fill the theater every night.[49]

On the one hand, such events began attracting large audiences; on the other, they faced intense opposition. One of the main critics of these events was Mr. Sadinoel, columnist from *Revista da Semana*. In his articles, the writer frequently criticized wrestling for its violent nature and the fact that these practices were at odds with widely held views of the ideal feminine aesthetic:

> Imagine our graceful patricians engaging in of punching, slams, and the brutality of rough acrobatics.... Detestable, simply detestable.... Act immediately to dissuade locals from supporting the ungainly and irreverent cultivation of this violent sport that masks and depresses the aesthetic charm of feminine grace....[50]

Or even

> Greco Roman wrestling! I never thought that these people were so enamored of the violence of this furious sport as performed by the amazing agility of female bodies.... However, the public doesn't want fair, calm contests. No. What people want there in São Pedro is bullfighting, with ferocious slams. If the fighters slow down the action and the fight goes quiet, the public yawns and demands furious action.[51]

Perhaps the author was trying to exaggerate the violent nature of the matches. In both passages, he notes actions prohibited by the rules of traditional Greco Roman wrestling, such as punches, slams, and slaps, highlighting their alleged brutality, which he viewed as incompatible with the female nature. Greco-Roman style did indeed forbid striking and all holds below the waist, so apparently these ladies were engaging in something resembling catch-as-catch-can wrestling, which had fewer restrictions and was the most popular style in the United States and England. In order to emphasize his aversion for women's matches and wrestling in general, the author exaggerated the wrestlers' use of violent tactics. In the second excerpt, Sadinoel expresses his dissatisfaction with fans' seeming preference for combat sports over highbrow entertainment, such as classical theater, emphasizing that wrestling fans were uncivilized and bloodthirsty. Sadinoel wanted to convince others that wrestling was a sport unsuitable for women.

Jose Floriano Peixoto: Homegrown Star

The success of international wrestling troupes attracted large audiences to theaters, but still something was missing: the presence of Brazilians. Early wrestling events featured wrestlers from the United States, Belgium, England, France, and other countries, but no Brazilians. However, Brazilian grappler José Floriano Peixoto would become a top draw in the country in 1911.[52] Floriano's matches usually attracted large audiences: "Shortly before midnight the Brazilian amateur José Floriano Peixoto, in a great victory, defeated the Austrian champion Goldback. The crowd that filled the wide theater of Tiradentes Square cheered Floriano."[53] Peixoto competed in numerous matches, including victories against Frenchman Noel Bordelais,[54] Italians Giovanoni[55] and Legatto,[56] and the São Paulo champion José Baldi.[57]

Matches between José Floriano and foreigners were covered regularly by several Rio newspapers. Frequent coverage of these matches drew increasing public attention, leading to greater attendance at the events. Newspapers began to feature extensive reports of matches involving Brazilian wrestlers. Widespread coverage of José Floriano Peixoto's matches may have been due to his great potential as a national icon,[58] especially because he was the son of ex-president Marshal Floriano Peixoto. Furthermore, the increasing coverage and popularity of Floriano's matches took on a nationalistic character, as he represented Brazil in a series of matches against foreign wrestlers. This is a recurring theme throughout the modern history of professional wrestling; promoters and wrestlers feature events that play upon nationalist sentiments, often by pitting a "national hero" against foreigners, stirring up fans in the process and, most importantly, convincing them to spend their time and money to watch their hero (hopefully) vanquish the foreign foe.

Floriano's victories against foreign wrestlers helped popularize wrestling in Rio de Janeiro, but he was also concerned with the physical and moral development of the city's youth. Committed to promoting opportunities for young people, Floriano founded Sport Club José Floriano, part of the Escola Athletica José Floriano (José Floriano School of Athletics), where he served both as director and teacher. The school taught various athletic skills, including gymnastics, shooting, and wrestling. His promotion of physical and moral education had involved efforts to implement "general courses of physical education" in the Escola Nocturna Gratuita do Centro Cívico Sete de Setembro, reported by the newspaper *A Epoca* in 1913:

> Today, Brazilian champion José Floriano Peixoto begins offering physical education classes at Centro, in order to contribute to Brazilian youth—a mission inherited from his glorified father: the precious legacy of raising the moral level of Brazilians—with free instruction for people. Centro will contribute to the triumph of the hopeful youth of our beloved country.[59]

José Floriano Peixoto was also a supporter of Greco-Roman tournaments and amateur boxing. Such competitions were held with increasing frequency and featured regularly in various newspapers, allowing these sports a relatively short period of popularity. Floriano's involvement, both as a wrestler and promoter, particularly of combat sports, played a crucial role in the popularization of wrestling and boxing in Brazil.

The popularity of wrestling in Rio de Janeiro was boosted by the relative success of a series of tours by international troupes, as well as José Floriano Peixoto's status as a homegrown star. Wrestling's rising popularity led to the establishment of several amateur championships in which the majority of athletes were Brazilian. These championships depended heavily on Floriano's support, especially through his training of wrestlers at the Escola Athletica José Floriano.

On the one hand, Peixoto represented an attractive hero to the audience, as a Brazilian grappler with tremendous charisma and excellent wrestling ability, and, of course, as son of the ex-president. On the other hand, there were lingering suspicions regarding the legitimacy of some of his matches. A long article written by a certain "E. S." in 1913, attempted to dispel claims that Floriano had participated in "fakes":

> Useless enemies have tried to mar his brilliant reputation, claiming that his victories were setups. This is a base insinuation that the invincible Brazilian champion has dispelled, not only by virtues of his actions, but also by his popular support, available only to those who are truly noble and worthy.[60]

The article was a response to the accusation that Floriano's victories were "bought fights." The original sources of such accusations are uncertain, but the fact that a major newspaper such as *A Epoca* published a vehement defense of Floriano is an indication that such rumors were widespread and deserving of response. "E.S.'s" article made an impassioned defense of the wrestling hero's legitimacy by highlighting Floriano's personal virtues: "Gentle and kind, Zeca is a true friend of our sports world, where he is admired not only for his merits as a sportsman, but also for the beautiful qualities of his refined character."[61] Many journalists and fans likely already suspected that wrestling featured "performance" elements, but "E.S." argued that Floriano's matches were completely legitimate, suggesting that this newspaper had an interest in preserving the reputation of the Peixoto family. Therefore, political issues probably motivated the defense of Floriano, especially given that *A Epoca* subscribed to the republican ideals advocated by his father, the Marshal and former President.

Criticism: Greco-Roman and Transgressions

Despite support in several circles, including popular medical discourse and the various periodicals that portrayed wrestling as a civilized endeavor in line with efforts to modernize Rio society,[62] the sport faced severe criticism over ongoing violations of rules in various matches that violated the accepted boundaries of good sportsmanship. Various papers noted that rule-breaking was common and, in some cases, there was even a need for police intervention. In 1911, *A Noite* and *O Seculo* reported on a series of incidents during a match between Clement La Boucher and Rishbacher. According to *A Noite*:

> The match began at 10:30 PM and lasted until midnight without any result ... slaps, punches, and the other many blows ... were common throughout the match, infuriating police who were presiding over the spectacle.... Several times, the Civil Guard wanted to intervene, but everything turned out well despite the fact that Clement did not cease for a moment with his brutalities.[63]

O Seculo reproduced, in full, the police report from the match:

> In violation of all the rules that govern this sport, fighters gave themselves up to the capoeira game, slaps, and all manner of follies, angering the audience, who demanded police intervention.... I entered the ring and declared to the judge that if those brutalities keep happening, I would suspend the show on his behalf. The barbarities committed by fighters were undermining presiding officials' authority and offended the audience, who aimed to enjoy a sport of established rules, not a vicious bloodsport.[64]

These sources illustrate the frequency of rule-breaking in the contest. According to the police report, such rough tactics went beyond the sporting arena and entered the criminal sphere. In this particular case, state action by way of police intervention becomes justifiable, because the levels of violence in the match were not in line with accepted social norms, as emphasized by the negative fan reaction.

Because of frequent rule-breaking and excessive violence, some newspapers began to question wrestling's value as a sport. In 1913, the newspaper *A Noite* highlighted police efforts to limit violence in wrestling matches:

> Because of the prohibited blows of fighters, there have been protests from all the spectators ... throwing chairs and other objects on the stage. This excess is justified by the rudeness of fighters who obey neither the referee nor the police. After the abuses in last Saturday night's match, if the police invited them to come to the station to explain this event that is called Greco-Roman wrestling but seems more like dogs fighting over a bone, wrestlers would refuse to go to the police station for questioning.[65]

Given the constant rule-breaking in pro wrestling, public discourse in some newspapers began to turn against the sport. Criticism was amplified by the wrestlers' seeming impunity and ongoing violent tactics. The papers were critical of referees who were, theoretically, supposed to enforce the rules, and especially of Paschoal Segreto, the most prominent pro wrestling promoter.

On March 12, 1915, a wrestler called Kormandy responded to a referee's warning by attacking him and tearing his shirt. This episode triggered a series of violent actions by fans in the theater.[66] Some newspapers began demanding that Segreto stop condoning the excessive violence. However, in March 1915, a small column in *A Noite* suggests that some violent acts by certain wrestlers were premeditated to draw fans:

174 Part III. Culture and Modernity

> In wrestling, there are two perfectly different aspects: sportsmanship in the interest of the public, and the commercial, related to the interests of the company. When one and the other can be combined, that is, when the company employs methods to increase their income without violating the boundaries of good sportsmanship, everything is fine. However, when it capitalizes on the violent tactics of a rough wrestler as a means of promoting future matches, we cannot support it.[67]

This source implies that some journalists viewed the frequent rule violations among wrestlers as a shady promotional tactic by Paschoal Segreto, who hoped to use the controversy and scandal to promote future events. Such suspicion called pro wrestling's credibility as a legitimate sport into question. Fans furious at a particular wrestler's cheating would be very likely to spend money to see him get his comeuppance in a future rematch. This sort of promotional tactic has been a fundamental component of pro wrestling since the late 19th century. While civil authorities and journalists frequently condemned rule-breaking and violence in wrestling, paying fans kept coming back for more, encouraging promoters to continue using such methods to generate interest and revenue. However, these so-called "frauds" that aimed to draw more fans through increasing violence, seem to have had the opposite effect, as spectators often reacted negatively to rough play and rule-breaking. For example, in a May 17, 1915, match between two foreign wrestlers, Youssouf and Gallant, the former cheated to win the match, which "angered the audience so much that for half an hour the theater stage was the target of all sorts of projectiles: hats, canes, chairs funds, pieces of wood."[68]

Issues related to violence and rule-breaking continued to receive frequent coverage in Rio's major papers, and *A Epoca* began to suggest police intervention if matches went beyond the acceptable boundaries of "sport":

> It is certain that the decisions about the matches are up to the Segreto Company, but police cannot remain indifferent to scenes of violence and disrespect to the audience. What if one of the wrestlers uses a prohibited move ... [or] if using many unfair punches and kicks, produces injuries that our criminal code deems assault? In this case, shouldn't the Company fine or suspend the offender? Nobody will affirm the boundaries. Everything has a limit ... when the wrestlers cross the line of acceptable behavior ... the police should intervene.[69]

This excerpt argues that the Paschoal Segreto Company should be responsible for enforcing the rules in the matches it promoted. Given the constant rule violations and the company's apparent indifference, the newspaper questions whether in the event of an accident, brought about by prohibited actions, the jurisdiction would fall under sporting or criminal enforcement. According to the theoretical precepts recommended by Elias and Dunning, sports regulations should serve to minimize possible serious injury to participants.[70] On the other hand, Segreto and countless other promoters were intentionally relying on showmanship and controversy in their matches in order to provoke intense fan reactions, with the ultimate intent of building interest and revenue for future matches. If a villainous wrestler won a match by cheating, then fans would likely pay good money to see him defeated in a future rematch. During this era, such pro-wrestling controversies were also common in the United States, as local authorities would often attempt to stop matches or ban certain moves (such as Ed "Strangler" Lewis' headlock), failing to realize that wrestling had become more show than sport. For their part, promoters and wrestlers were extremely careful to maintain the illusion of reality ("kayfabe" in insider wrestling terminology), only recently (Vince McMahon in the 1980s, for example) admitting that pro wrestling was more entertainment than sport.

Final Considerations

The sources discussed in this essay offer a better understanding of the history of pro wrestling in Brazil. At the end of the 19th century, the term "Greco-Roman [wrestling]" typically referred to circus sideshow attractions, but by the beginning of the 20th century, thanks to visits from a series of international wrestling troupes, the sport achieved greater visibility and respectability as a modern, civilized sport, at least according to the newspapers. The popularization of pro wrestling in Brazil was aided greatly by José Floriano's popularity, due partly to his high-profile matches against foreigners that capitalized on an emerging sense of nationalism in the country. Floriano also worked to incorporate sports into school curriculums in order to promote the physical and moral education of Brazilian youth. During this period, the first Greco Roman amateur championships took place, exclusively featuring Brazilian athletes, further evidence of the sport's growing popularity. By 1920,[71] however, pro wrestling had become highly controversial due to its increasingly excessive violence and rule-breaking, as well as fans' unruly behavior at the matches. Criticism from various circles, including newspapers and police, as well as increasing (well-founded) suspicions that wrestling was more performance than sport, ultimately limited the sport's popularity in Brazil after a brief period of success.

Notes

1. Silvia Vieira and Armando Freitas, *O que é boxe* (Rio de Janeiro: Casa da Palavra, 2007).
2. In Brazil, a summary of the rules that would guide such disputes was published in the newspaper *A Noite*: "Blows should be delivered with open hands between the head and waist; opponents may cross legs as long as they are not standing; prohibited techniques: a) twisting fingers; b) *zancadilla*; c) legs crossing while standing; d) twine necklace; e) American arm," "Voltam aos 'rinks' do Rio os homens do muque," *A Noite*, February 22, 1913, 4.
3. "Naissance de la FILA," United World Wrestling, last modified 2016, https://unitedworldwrestling.org/fr/organization/united-world-wrestling (accessed June 22, 2016).

4. Orlando Duarte Figueredo, *A história dos esportes* (São Paulo: Editora Senac, 2003); Eduardo Colli, *Universo olímpico: uma enciclopédia das Olimpíadas* (São Paulo: Códex, 2004).
5. "Naissance de la FILA," accessed June 22, 2016.
6. The survey was made possible by the National Library Foundation, which provides access to the Brazilian Digital Hemeroteca, which is a site of national newspapers that provides consultation to its digital collection ("Hemeroteca Digital," Biblioteca Nacional Digital), last modified 2016, http://bndigital.bn.br/hemeroteca-digital (accessed June 22, 2016).
7. Tania Regina de Luca, "História dos, nos e por meio dos periódicos," in Carla Bassanezi Pinsky, ed., *Fontes Históricas* (São Paulo: Contexto, 2008), 111–53.
8. Luís César Amad Costa and Leonel Itaussu A. Mello, *História do Brasil* (São Paulo: Scipione, 1999).
9. Francisco de Assis Silva and Pedro Ivo de Assis Bastos, *História do Brasil* (São Paulo: Editora Moderna, 1983).
10. Nicolau Sevcenko, ed., *História da vida privada no Brasil—República: da Belle Époque à Era do Rádio* (São Paulo: Companhia das Letras, 1998).
11. Victor Andrade de Melo, *Cidade Sportiva: primórdios do esporte no Rio de Janeiro* (Rio de Janeiro: Relume Dumará/Faperj, 2001), 71.
12. Sevcenko, *História da vida privada no Brasil*.
13. Leopoldo Costa, "O Brasil entre 1900 e 1910," *Blog Stravaganza*, 2011, http://stravaganzastravaganza.blogspot.com.br/2011/08/como-era-o-brasil-entre-1900-e-1910.html (accessed September 2, 2013).
14. Melo, *Cidade Sportiva*.
15. Melo, *Cidade Sportiva*.
16. Ricardo de Figueiredo Lucena, *O esporte na cidade: aspectos do esforço civilizador brasileiro* (Campinas: Autores Associados, 2001).
17. Maria Cecília de Paula Silva, "A Educação Física Escolar/ Saúde: o discurso médico no século XIX," *Revista Brasileira de Ciências do Esporte* 2 (January 2004), 97–112.
18. Lucena, *O esporte na cidade*, 28.
19. Victor Andrade de Melo, "Das touradas às corridas de cavalo e regatas: primeiros momentos da configuração do campo esportivo no Brasil," in Mary del Priore and Victor Andrade de Melo, eds., *História do Esporte no Brasil: do império aos dias atuais* (São Paulo: Editora da UNESP, 2009).
20. "The term 'sportsman,' in that period, referred not only to practitioners of physical activity, but also represented a lifestyle guided by an ideal of chivalry; a competitive ethic, but respectful towards the opponent (whether in sports or in activities related to daily life—searching for a job, for example); but mainly a life of activism and action, always justified by health hygienically." André Mendes Capraro, *Histórias de matches e de intrigas da sociedade: a crônica literária e o esporte futebol* (São Paulo: Annablume, 2013), 86–87.
21. Riqueldi Lise, *Entre diretos, ceintures avant, chaves de braço e rabos de arraia: os primórdios dos combates intermodalidades na cidade do rio de janeiro (1909–1929)*, Dissertation, Curitiba, Universidade Federal do Paraná, 2014, 151f.
22. Lise, *Entre diretos*, 151f.
23. "Grande Circo Lusitano," *O Pharol*, March 17, 1892, 3.
24. In the late 19th century, the expansion of the power grid, the increase of the working class and the concentration of population in large urban centers favored the development of popular theaters in Rio de Janeiro. These theaters were a recreational alternative for the less-privileged classes.
25. The Lumière brothers invented the cinematograph, which was a predecessor of cinema.
26. "Palcos e Salas," *A Noticia*, January 29, 1900, 3.
27. Although some sources announced that the troupe had nine fighters, only eight names were identified: Pons (French), Anglio (Martinican), Riztmer (German), Le Boucher (French), Wanders (Belgian), Romanof (Russian), Dumond (French), and Deriaz (Swiss).
28. Paul Pons was the team leader: "In 1888, the French Paul Pons, also called 'the Colossus,' became the first World Professional [Wrestling] Champion [by defeating] the Pole, Ladislau Pytlasinski." United World Wrestling, "Naissance de la FILA."

29. "Telegramma de Buenos Ayres," *A Noticia*, July 16, 1904, 2.
30. "Campeonato de Lucta Romana," *A Noticia*, August 2, 1904, 3.
31. "Campeonato de Lucta Romana," *A Noticia*, August 9, 1904, 3.
32. Norbert Elias and Eric Dunning, *A Busca da Excitação* (Rio de Janeiro: Difel, 1992), 45.
33. Giovanoni (Italian), Le Meunier (French), Youssouff (Turkish), Amalhou (Martinican), Steurs (North-American), Poireé (French), Schakmann (German), Sudakoff (Russian), Le Boucher (French), Decronzas (Swiss), Pons (French), Furny (English), Milo (Italian), Webers (German), Carpini (Italian), and La Calmette (French).
34. "Lucta Romana," *O Paiz*, September 22, 1905, 2.
35. Born March 22, 1868, in San Martin di Cileno, Italy. He arrived in Brazil in 1883 and became the premier entertainment promoter in Rio de Janeiro in the early 20th century.
36. William de Souza Nunes Martins, "Paschoal Segreto: 'Ministro Das Diversões' do Rio de Janeiro (1883–1920)," Master thesis, Universidade Federal do Rio de Janeiro, 2004.
37. The cheapest tickets for the shows of varieties, which included Greco-Roman, cost $2.50, seats $4.50 and cabins $15.50 ("Moulin Rouge," *O Paiz*, August 15, 1907, 8). By comparison, in this period, a kilogram of roasted and ground coffee cost $1 ("900 réis o kilo," *Correio da Manhã*, January 6, 1915, 6). Currently one kilogram of roast and ground coffee in Brazil costs about U.S. $2.
38. Amalhou (Martinican), Calvet (French), Caseaux (French), D'Anvers (Belgian), Le Boucher (French), Omer (French), Ottinguer (German), Limousin (French), Pons (French) ("Moulin Rouge," *O Paiz*, August 26, 1907, 8).
39. "Lucta Romana," *O Paiz*, August 26, 1907, 3.
40. The Theater Concerto Avenida opened on November 12, 1908, and became the largest and most modern popular theater in Rio de Janeiro ("Theatros," *O Seculo*, November 13, 1908, 2).
41. "O perigo do coração," *Eu Sei Tudo*, January, 1918, 21.
42. *Eu Sei Tudo* was a monthly, illustrated magazine, averaging around 140 pages per issue, that circulated throughout Brazil from 1917 to 1957. A variety magazine, it published a range of materials from recipes to political debates, but usually did not cover sports. The magazine used high-quality printing and was richly illustrated with photographs and cartoons. Despite occasionally dealing with political matters, the magazine did not usually take strong political stances.
43. While the picture published in *Fon-Fon* (Figure 2) presents a troupe composed of 14 fighters, the newspaper *O Paiz* presents the group with fifteen fighters and the referee.
44. "A Empreza Paschoal Segreto," *O Paiz*, March 17, 1910, 7.
45. In an approximate conversion values, 5,000 francs today amounts to approximately U.S. $20,000. Luiz Otávio Laydner and Fábio Quio Takao, "Exclusivo: Maeda ensinava jiu-jitsu no Rio 10 anos antes dos Gracies," last modified September 2, 2013, http://www.ishindo.org.br/conde-koma-rio-de-janeiro-antes-dos-gracie (accessed November 14, 2013).
46. "Luta Romana," *Jornal do Brasil*, August 4, 1909, 12; "Luta Romana," *Jornal do Brasil*, October 8, 1909, 12.
47. "Ribaltas," *Revista da Semana*, May 1, 1910, 13.
48. Melo, *Cidade Sportiva*.
49. Revista da Semana, "Ribaltas," *Revista da Semana*, May 22, 1910, 25.
50. Sadinoe, "Reflexões," *Revista da Semana*, May 8, 1910, 17.
51. Sadinoel, "Reflexões," *Revista da Semana*, May 22, 1910, 28.
52. Son of Marshal Floriano Peixoto and a boxing practitioner, Jose was an accomplished Greco-Roman wrestler, and was experienced in capoeira, shooting, and acrobatics. See Figure 4.
53. "Lucta Romana," *O Seculo*, April 2, 1915, 3.
54. "Lucta Romana," *O Paiz*, September 14, 1911, 6.
55. "Lucta Romana," *O Paiz*, May 29, 1913, 9.
56. "Lucta Romana," *O Paiz*, January 28, 1914, 7.
57. "Sports," *A Noite*, December 27, 1914, 5.
58. Pierre Bourdieu, *Coisas ditas* (São Paulo: Brasiliense, 2004), 163.

59. "Ecos Sociaes," *A Epoca*, December 25, 1913, 5.
60. E.S., "Sport," *A Epoca*, April 3, 1913, 3.
61. E.S., "Sport," 3.
62. Edivaldo Góis, Jr., and Hugo Rodolfo Lovisolo, "Descontinuidades e continuidades do movimento higienista no Brasil do século XX," *Revista Brasileira de Ciências do Esporte* 1 (September 2013), 41–54.
63. "Lutca Romana," *A Noite*, August 22, 1911, 3.
64. "Lucta Romana," *O Seculo*, August 22, 1911, 2.
65. "O pugilato como espectáculo," *A Noite*, April 28, 1913, 2.
66. "Sports," *A Noite*, March 12, 1915, 5.
67. "Sports," *A Noite*, March 21, 1915, 5.
68. "Sports," *A Noite*, May 17, 1915, 5.
69. "Sports," *A Noite*, March 14, 1915, 6.
70. Elias and Dunning, *A Busca da Excitação*.
71. By which date almost all pro wrestling matches in the United States, and therefore probably Brazil as well, were predetermined, their primary objective having transitioned from presenting legitimate athletic competition to matches intended to maximize fan excitement (or outrage) in order to continue drawing paying audiences to future events.

The Transmission of Cultural Values Through Professional Wrestling
A Cross-Cultural Comparison

Tyson L. Platt

Professional wrestling is a form of entertainment in which two or more parties cooperatively perform a routine consisting of strikes, holds, and counter-holds that build toward a predetermined finish. As a form of entertainment, professional wrestling matches are designed to tell a story based around combat. In order for the story to be engaging and interesting to the audience, it must be culturally relevant. That is, the story being told must align with some values or beliefs of the audience in order to convey a narrative. By aligning with cultural values, professional wrestling allows the viewer to interpret professional wrestling as a series of image depicting morality plays.

Semiotician and critic Roland Barthes has argued that professional wrestling is consumed as a set of related but largely independent carnivalesque images, exaggerated for clarity, that are executed as a demonstration of "the great spectacle of Suffering, Defeat, and Justice."[1] While recognizing the considered nature of the morality play underlying matches, he suggests that each moment represents an image that can be consumed and understood independent of the whole match. In contrast, the present essay argues for a *gestalt* interpretation of wrestling matches. That is, each match must be understood as a whole phenomenon rather than as a series of emotionally-tinged sensations.[2] Barthes ultimately views professional wrestling through a very narrow lens: an obvious protagonist battles a villainous antagonist and through a series of exaggerated and fantastic images, the audience is entertained. While this may describe some matches, it does not adequately capture the variety and subtlety that defines many matches. This author attributes Barthes' failure to a critical distinction: that of spectator and fan.[3] Barthes writes from the view of a spectator, largely naïve and even dismissive of historical antecedents of the match and not invested in the motivations of the performers. The interpretation of the fan, one who watches wrestling regularly and is invested in characters and stories, would likely be substantially different than that of Barthes.

While independent elements such as holds and facial expressions can be analyzed, professional wrestling is best understood as a ritualized display of battle containing a clear beginning, middle, and end between archetypal rivals. In this sense, the structure of professional wrestling matches bears a resemblance to both ancient and modern theater.[4] Unsurprisingly, early professional wrestling matches, including those of professional wrestling's first superstars William Muldoon and John L. Sullivan, were performed by travelling troupes in a manner similar to travelling theatre troupes.[5] Similarly, pioneer wrestling promoter Toots Mondt worked in vaudeville entertainment prior to promoting wrestling.[6]

Many previous academic texts concerning wrestling have focused on the characterizations of performers and execution of matches. However, professional wrestling must first and foremost be understood for what it is: a business. As such, the goal of promoters is to present one or more pseudo-competitive bouts to audiences who are willing to pay money to view them. This is relevant because it suggests that the desires of the paying fan supersede any aesthetic role that wrestling may play (for an in-depth look at how business concerns override aesthetic concerns, see Hornbaker[7]). In this sense, professional wrestling differs from traditional theater. It is not intended to be a timeless aesthetic expression by performers. Instead, it is a routine devised to generate revenue. For this reason, the presentation of professional wrestling can be seen as reflecting the values and attitudes of the spectators more so than those of the performers.

The cooperation between opponents in professional wrestling is referred to as *working*. Worked matches are defined by mutually agreed-upon finishes, in which one party usually wins and the other party loses. Working often involves more elaborate staging in which certain moves or sequences of moves are planned in advance and performed in cooperation. In many cases, professional wrestling moves can only be safely performed in cooperation. For instance, a *huricanrana* (a move in which a standing opponent is flipped by the legs of their opponent) or head-scissor takeover can only be accomplished if the recipient of the move flips their body forward.[8] Working also involves a reduction in the force of strikes accompanied by exaggerated gestures in order to suggest to the audience that a strike was delivered at full velocity. The extent to which wrestling matches are worked varies substantially between wrestling styles (e.g., lucha libre relies more heavily on cooperative aerial maneuvers than does heavyweight American wrestling), cultures (e.g., Japanese wrestling is less reliant on a reduction in the intensity of strikes than lucha libre), and individuals (e.g., some wrestlers work *stiff*; that is, they strike with greater intensity than other wrestlers).

The reliance on cooperation rather than competition reflects a need to entertain audiences. As late as the early 20th century, some professional wrestling was performed competitively. The competitive aspect of wrestling often produced exceedingly long matches that were perceived as boring to audiences and frequently ended without a clear victor. For instance, William Muldoon and Clarence Whistler wrestled to a nine-hour draw in January 1881.[9] A desire to maintain or boost attendance at events created one of several incentives for presenting professional wrestling as a worked form of entertainment. As professional wrestling transitioned away from competition between parties, various non-wrestlers were able to exert an influence on the structure and outcomes of matches. Key among those influences were wrestling promoters (individuals financially invested in the presentation of professional wrestling) and wrestling bookers (individuals employed by wrestling promoters to plan the outcomes of matches and plan multi-match programs between wrestlers). As promoters and bookers were primarily concerned with presenting a form of entertainment that spectators would pay to see, they arranged matches and programs that could appeal to particular audiences. Since audiences could vary widely in different regions and even within the same region, promotional tactics and match presentation varied widely. For instance, the World Wide Wrestling Federation (WWWF) in New York routinely drew large audiences of minorities by featuring ethnic champions such as Bruno Sammartino (Italian) and Pedro Morales (Puerto Rican). Personas in wrestling were often crafted to reflect the values of the audience. For instance, the Junkyard Dog (African American) was presented to largely black audiences in New Orleans as the quintessential hero of the Mid-South Wrestling: an honest individual, sensitive to injustice and perseverant in the face of extreme adversity. Conversely, the villains of professional wrestling were portrayed as the antithesis of a given audience's values.

A particular culture's values can be examined through the lens of professional wrestling. While professional wrestling occurs in some form in most parts of the world, the United States and Japan have been among the most popular regions for presenting professional wrestling. Both regions have supported multiple major professional wrestling promotions (largely through reliance on television) for many decades. As such, professional wrestling in each region reflects the values of its audience. This statement is supported by the ability of top promotions in each country to regularly promote wrestling events on a weekly or monthly basis, occasionally drawing crowds exceeding 50,000.

American and Japanese Professional Wrestling

The modern era of professional wrestling began with the rise in popularity of television. Between 1948 and 1955, professional wrestling was broadcast on all three major American broadcasting networks largely due to its low cost of production and high level of consumer interest.[10] Television was such an important promotional tool that wrestling has been featured continuously on major television stations since the late 1940s. While American professional wrestling was well-established prior to television, professional wrestling and television were introduced in Japan at approximately the same time. The convergence of wrestling and television in Japan created a symbiotic relationship that was even stronger than in America. In 1957, professional wrestling was the highest-rated television programming of any genre in Japan and it remained popular programming throughout the 20th century.[11] Due to wrestling's immense popularity, television was used as the primary vehicle for promoting live wrestling events in Japan throughout the 20th century.

Professional wrestling (as an explicitly worked presentation) was first promoted in Japan by American Bobby Bruns in 1951. Bruns wrestled recently retired sumo Rikidozan to a draw, and while the show was considered successful, Bruns did not promote further wrestling shows in Japan.[12] In 1953, Rikidozan established the Nihon Puroresu Kyōkai (Japanese Wrestling Association or JWA) in order to regularly promote wrestling in Japan. As professional wrestling was an American import, it bears a great resemblance to American professional wrestling in terms of rules and general appearance. However, Japanese wrestling was also strongly influenced by sumo and judo. This is apparent from the makeup of early Japanese wrestling cards, which featured a mixture of American pro wrestlers (Dick Beyer), ex-sumo (Rikidozan) and ex-judoka (Masahiko Kimura). While pro wrestling was already viewed by many American audiences as a form of non-competitive entertainment when it first appeared on television, it was presented as a serious, legitimate form of competition in Japan. Gimmicks, colorful personalities, and elaborately-staged (and unrealistic) move sequences were eschewed in favor of presenting wrestling as a legitimate fight between the most credible of performers.

Wrestling Heroes

In wrestling parlance, the protagonists, heroes or goo guys of a wrestling match are referred to as *babyfaces*. As heroes to an audience, babyfaces must embody values that are venerated by a particular culture. By analyzing the characteristics of the most successful babyfaces, one can better understand those values which are held in highest esteem by a culture.

In American professional wrestling, babyfaces are first and foremost good people. That is, they behave in a manner that is consistent with the moral and ethical standards of the audience. Key among those behaviors is good sportsmanship and a refusal to cheat. However, these ethical characteristics are often exaggerated in American babyfaces to a cartoonish degree. For instance, American babyface phenomenon Hulk Hogan often urged his fans to "say your prayers and take your vitamins," as if to suggest that his chiseled physique and penchant for victory was a function of wholesome American values rather than hard physical work and performance-enhancing substances. In modern American pro wrestling, the success of a babyface is driven more by following a moral code than by in-ring competence. A survey of the history of American babyfaces reveals that the most successful ones are rarely as technically competent as their villainous opponent. For instance, in Johnson & Oliver's[13] review of the most successful babyfaces of all time, four of their top five wrestlers could be considered technically limited. That is, the wrestlers had a fairly small move set, limited understanding of amateur wrestling techniques, and were not perceived by their peers to be exceptionally athletic or agile. However, all of those wrestlers were enormously popular and financially successful. The limitations in technical expertise seem to be an important condition, rather than constraint, for successful American babyfaces. In limiting their technical expertise, the American babyface must rely on their superior morality in order to overcome obstacles. This trope has historically been used to build empathy towards the protagonist. In some cases, additional disadvantages to the babyface are used to further build empathy. For instance, in a 1980 match in Mid-South Wrestling, a previously-blinded Junkyard Dog wrestled top heel Michael Hayes while his vision was still supposedly impaired.[14] This situation was exacerbated by the antagonists' willingness to rely on illegal tactics for victory. Thus, the babyface enters a contest with multiple disadvantages. By creating near-insurmountable odds for the "hero," the audience is allowed to invest in characteristics of the babyface that reflect their own values. Such a representation of American babyfaces can currently be observed in WWE's top star, John Cena. Cena has a fairly small move set and is overtly presented to audiences as being technically limited. However, Cena's reliance on his moral code (commercialized through slogans such as "Never Give Up" and "Hustle, Loyalty, Respect") allows him to defeat his dishonorable opponents.

In addition to being moral actors, American babyfaces are generally attractive and overtly charismatic. Given the apparent physical demands of wrestling and the grizzled appearance of successful amateur wrestlers, one may expect that successful babyfaces should look haggard and injured from their journey to the top of the card. However, this is almost never the case. American babyfaces are usually larger than average, in very good physical condition, and show few if any signs of injury. That is, they are symbols of health and vitality presented in a manner consistent with ancient Greek ideals of masculinity, especially those associated with the Spartan martial model of masculinity.[15] For instance, WWE's top three babyfaces of the last 30 years (Hulk Hogan, The Rock, and John Cena) were identifiable by their bulging muscles and movie-star good-looks. All three also pursued acting careers during and after their wrestling careers to varying degrees of success. Additionally, American babyfaces tend to engage in acts intentionally aimed at forming a connection with the audience such as shaking hands, miming to the crowd during matches, and smiling widely for cameras. Although American babyfaces tend to be more attractive and charismatic than average persons, they are usually humble and, at times, self-deprecating. This combination of above-average physical and moral characteristics with humility is an important feature of successful American babyfaces.

In contrast, Japanese babyfaces are primarily competent. That is, they are highly skilled at one or more styles of combat due to their intense dedication to the craft. Unlike American babyfaces, successful Japanese babyfaces are presented to and perceived by audiences as the most technically-skilled competitors in the world. Ultimate Japanese babyface Antonio Inoki presented himself to audiences as a skilled martial artist even though he had little martial arts training. He established his competence as a *shooter* (wrestler capable of legitimately hurting opponents with wrestling holds) by wrestling world-renowned shooter Karl Gotch in 1972.[16] Compared to American babyfaces, whose portrayal of masculinity can be traced to Spartan martial ideals, Japanese masculinity in professional wrestling can be traced to the Bushido code which emphasizes justice and courage but also accentuates courtesy and self-control.[17] As a result, Japanese babyfaces are often stoic and respectful even when faced with unethical tactics by opponents. Because pro wrestling has traditionally been presented as a legitimate sport in Japan, audiences assume that the most skilled competitor will win; this assumption is rarely present in American pro wrestling. This supposition by Japanese audiences is consistent with Bushido principles of honesty and sincerity. Thus, Japanese babyfaces are presented as highly dedicated and hard-working. As a result of their dedication to their craft, Japanese babyfaces are often physically disfigured (i.e., cauliflower ears) and less overtly attractive than their American counterparts.

Japanese babyfaces rarely interact directly with the crowd before or during a match, because to do so would indicate a lack of attention being paid to one's technique and one's opponent. For similar reasons, Japanese babyfaces are generally stoic and serious. After a match is finished, the demeanor of the babyface often changes and he may become emotional in victory or defeat. The shift in presentation appears to reflect the *honne/tatamae* distinction that is an important component of Japanese society. Whereas many cultures recognize a difference between one's private and public image, the Japanese honne/tatamae distinction is more formal and suggests a social obligation to one's tatamae (public face) at the expense of one's honne (private face).[18] In this context, the shift in emotional expression makes substantially more sense. In preparation for a match, one's tatamae demands total devotion to the craft. Directly acknowledging and interacting with the crowd could be perceived as a deliberate rejection of one's tatame, and doing so could undermine a characterization that aligns with the values of the crowd. The expression of the honme/tatame dichotomy may also be viewed as an expression of the Bushido principles of courtesy[19] and self-control.[20] Once a match has reached its conclusion, the work of the wrestler has been completed and the demands of the tatamae are no longer present so the wrestler can express their "true" self. For instance, the normally stoic and reserved Kazuchika Okada began weeping following his January 2015 loss to longtime rival Hiroshi Tanahashi.[21] In doing so, Japanese wrestlers give their audience insight into both sides of their reality while subtly promoting the importance of the honne/tatamae distinction. The distinction between public and private is deliberately suppressed among American babyfaces. That is, American babyfaces often explicitly indicate that their public and private personas are identical. In the absence of a strong social public/private distinction, American babyfaces present the equivalence of their public and private personas as evidence of trustworthiness. For instance, after winning a match through hard work and perseverance, top American babyface John Cena often celebrates through energetic and cheerful engagement with the audience. The vigor and joy of the post-match celebration is in accordance with the tone of the match itself.

Both American and Japanese babyfaces are presented as perseverant, but the characteristic is more exaggerated in Japanese babyfaces. Relative to their opponents, Japanese babyfaces tend to be smaller and physically weaker. In a competitive context, the size difference represents a severe disadvantage. This disadvantage is used as a means to establish the toughness and *fighting spirit* (*toukon*) of the babyface. Fighting spirit is a key concept in Japanese pro wrestling and an important component of successful babyfaces. Fighting spirit refers to a wrestler's ability and willingness to overcome extreme adversity and is a physical manifestation of the Bushido principle of courage.[22] It can be viewed as the motivating factor for continuing to fight when victory is unlikely. Given the time of wrestling's import to Japan (shortly after World War II), fighting spirit is an important mechanism for the elevation of perseverance as a venerable trait. Immediately following World War II, the

Japanese public was demoralized and humiliated in defeat. By presenting babyfaces, such as Rikidozan, with fighting spirit, wrestling was able to encapsulate the most important value of that time: an unwillingness to surrender in the face of severe adversity. Although Japan was severely devastated by the war, the nation's deliberate willingness to start anew led to a rapid and successful economic revival. Japanese pro wrestling's reliance on fighting spirit reinforced the notion that successful people may not always win, but their willingness to persevere will lead to ultimate victory.

Wrestling Villains

In wrestling parlance, villains are known as *heels*. As with babyfaces, an analysis of heels can reveal the latent values held by a culture. As with many antagonists, heels reveal these values by engaging in behaviors that are considered outside of the limits of morality and, in many cases, justice.

American heels are the antithesis of their babyface counterparts. Whereas American babyfaces are ethical in their actions, American heels are principally unethical. As prominent wrestling announcer Jim Ross has noted, the most defining feature of a heel is their willingness to cheat.[23] They are willing to use unfair tactics to gain victory and are often dishonest in defeat, suggesting that the babyface opponent used unfair tactics to win or outright denying that they lost. Additionally, American heels tend to be less attractive and less eloquent in their speech. They exhibit behaviors that suggest savagery and a lack of forethought but often antagonize audiences for their lack of civility and intelligence.

Although American heels are often more technically competent than their babyface counterparts, they rarely win due to their technical expertise. Instead, the babyface generally places the heel in a position in which the heel would have to work very hard to gain a competitive advantage. Instead of working toward a competitive advantage, the heel takes shortcuts that could be perceived as unethical by the audience and that would not occur in the babyface. In doing so, the heel deliberately defines the parameters of morality within the context of a wrestling match; by explicitly antagonizing the crowd with their antics, the heel indicates to the audience the limits of fairness and often tempts the babyface into following suit. The babyface's refusal to engage in similar antics further helps to establish the babyface's dedication to their moral code, and further allows the audience to invest in the babyface due to their certainty that he is the "good guy."

In Japan, the role of the heel is often understated relative to that in American wrestling. As opposed to being presented as an immoral and unethical person, Japanese heels are often presented as seemingly insurmountable challenges to the babyface. This is consistent with the Japanese presentation of professional wrestling as a competitive sport; in competitive sports, rivalries need not be based on personal animosity but instead on the likelihood that the opponent will present a significant challenge. Thus, the fundamental role of the Japanese heel is to provide the ultimate challenge to the babyface. By presenting a significant challenge, heels allow babyfaces to express aspects of the Bushido code that would not otherwise be possible. For instance, after repeated bullying tactics by the heel toward the babyface, the babyface may allow the heel a short recovery period following an intense attack. The respite is inconsistent with opportunities offered by the heel, but it allows the babyface to express the Bushido principle of mercy.[24] This is not to say that personal characteristics are not exploited by Japanese heels; in many cases, transparently Western devices (such as Stan Hansen's cowboy hat) are used to signify that the heel is an outsider and thus not aligned with the values of the audience. Traditionally, many heels in Japanese pro wrestling have been *gaijin* (foreigners). Gaijin are usually American, significantly larger than their babyface counterparts, less stoic and more active before matches. While Japanese heels rarely cheat during matches, they engage in a variety of shortcuts and bullying tactics that can be perceived as lacking in sportsmanship.[25] The lack of reliance on deliberate rule-breaking helps to establish the credibility of both heel and babyface; a heel who cheats may have cheated in the past and thus may not be a legitimate threat to the babyface. As the success of a babyface hinges on credibility, their opponents must also be credible.

The babyface/heel dynamic is even more suppressed in matches in which both opponents are Japanese. Often, the heel/babyface distinction is completely eliminated in favor of a purely competitive match structure. That is, both sides struggle valiantly for victory. These matches often reflect the *senpai/kohai* distinction in Japanese culture. This formalized distinction encourages deference and respect by junior members (kohai) toward senior members (senpai) and an expectation of guidance by senior members of junior members.[26] In the context of wrestling, this distinction can be emphasized by a hard-fought match between a veteran and a relative novice. The veteran almost always gains victory in these matches, but the novice gains valuable experience that can be used to improve one's craft. In these situations, neither performer is inherently cast in the role of the heel. However, either party can become a heel in the context of the match by flagrantly disregarding the expectations inherent in the senpai/kohai system. For instance, a veteran who bullies a novice may be seen as failing to meet his obligation to teach through his actions. Conversely, a novice who fails to be sufficiently respectful toward a veteran may be viewed as villainous for refusing to adhere to the social system.

Match Structure

The cross-cultural differences in the assumptions made by audiences about the nature of wrestling, the presentation of wrestling as competitive sport, and the roles played by wrestlers combine to determine how matches must be structured in order to generate the most substantial investment from audiences. Match length, move sequencing, and the roles in which wrestlers are cast figure prominently into the structure of matches. The match corresponds to the plot of the central narrative in wrestling, with babyfaces serving the role of protagonist and heels serving the role of antagonist. However, as social structures and values differ considerably between Japan and the United States, the general structure of matches differs considerably across cultures.

American pro wrestling commonly involves four stages. In the first stage, the competitors face off and trade holds and counter-holds. This usually leads to the babyface gaining a competitive advantage. For instance, in a 1998 World Championship Wrestling (WCW) match between top babyface Bill Goldberg and top heel Kevin Nash, the competitors begin by struggling in a series of collar-and-elbow tie-ups in which Goldberg gains an advantage through sheer strength (Starrcade, 1998). The function of the first stage is to establish the credibility of the babyface as a person willing to fight injustice (in the form of the heel). In the second stage, the heel relies on some nefarious tactic (e.g., illegal holds, weapons, interference by other parties) to gain an advantage. In the Goldberg/Nash match described above, Nash leaves the ring for a moment after being overpowered by Goldberg. By leaving the ring, Nash establishes (a) his lack of courage and (b) his willingness to exploit the rules of the match to his advantage.[27] By relying on illegal of morally-questionable tactics, the heel is allowed to establish his moral inferiority to the babyface and establish the motivation for the babyface to continue to fight. This advantage is generally maintained for an extended period. During this time, the babyface repeatedly tries to overcome the heel's advantage by attempting to apply legal holds and strikes. However, since the heel is both more technically-accomplished and willing to break rules, the babyface's attempt to rely on technical expertise fails and he must instead call upon his resolve and superior morality. This period, during which the babyface is unfairly dominated by the heel, is known as a *heat sequence* and is intended to build sympathy for the babyface. The heat sequence generally involves one or more *hope spots*, in which the babyface attempts to reacquire a competitive advantage through hard work but is unfairly prevented from doing so by the heel. An example of an extended heat sequence can be observed in a 1986 match between Ric Flair and Ricky Morton. During this stage, Morton relies on his determination to narrowly avoid defeat. In doing so, he motivates the fans to invest in his struggle to overcome the overwhelming obstacles created by his opponent.[28]

In the third stage, the babyface gains a competitive advantage due to their hard work, persistence, and reliance on sound technique. The third stage is the most important stage for the transmission of moral values because it communicates to the audience that perseverance and dedication to one's moral code (in this case, an adherence to the rules agreed upon by all parties) is rewarded with dominance over less moral actors. In some situations, the transition from the second to the third stage is absolute (e.g., The Undertaker often quickly sits up after enduring a prolonged attack indicating an immediate shift in competitive advantage in the match[29]) whereas in other situations it is gradual (e.g., Bryan Danielson gradually mounted comebacks after brutal attacks by Takeshi Morishima[30]). This stage is usually shorter than the heat sequence and leads to the final stage in which the finish occurs. The finish can take one of three forms: (1) the babyface overcomes the heel's nefarious tactics to gain victory, (2) the heel relies on some unfair advantage such as cheating to gain victory, or (3) the match ends in a non-finish (e.g., time-limit draw, double disqualification, count-out).

Often a series of matches between two or more wrestlers, known as a *program*, is planned by a promoter. In the case of wrestling programs, a clean finish may be saved for the final match of the program. Thus, many matches end in non-finishes. The non-finishes are used to generate more interest in the final match, which often involves some type of special stipulation (e.g., cage match, Texas death match). For instance, ECW babyface Tommy Dreamer lost every match to archrival Raven until finally winning in Raven's last match in the company.[31] While babyfaces generally win the final match in a program, there are some cases in which the heel wins the final match. Most major American wrestling promotions (e.g., WWE) are built around one or more top babyfaces who audiences will pay to see wrestle. However, some wrestling promoters (e.g., Jim Crockett Promotions) have found that they generate more revenue by having babyface challengers who chase a heel champion.

Japanese matches, especially those between a Japanese babyface and a gaijin heel, are structured in a different manner. In the first stage, the competitors face off and trade holds and counterholds. Instead of one party gaining a clear advantage, both sides struggle for an advantage and are worn down in the process. A clear modern example of this stage can be observed in a 2017 match between Katsuyori Shibata and Tomohiro Ishii. At the beginning of the match, Shibata and Ishii exchange powerful strikes with neither party overtly acknowledging the damage amassed. While only subtly acknowledged by either participant, the impairment in performance created by the strike exchange represents the first test of the courage and character of each participant.[32] The weakening of opponents that occurs in the first stage has two functions. First, it establishes the credibility of both heel and babyface. In

Structure of typical American heavyweight singles professional wrestling match.

doing so, the audience is provided with two pieces of information that are essential to an investment in wrestling as a contest: (1) the babyface is a skilled competitor who the audience can invest in with some faith in his victory and (2) the heel represents a legitimate threat to the babyface. The second function of this stalemate is to establish the means by which the babyface can demonstrate his fighting spirit. In the first stage, both opponents become tired and injured but must continue on.

In the second stage, the properties of heels and babyfaces are revealed by their reactions to pain and exhaustion. The babyface continues to rely on practiced techniques to gain an advantage, but the heel relies on bullying and unfair (though rarely illegal) tactics such as stomping a grounded opponent. The heel may repeatedly attempt to place the babyface in an indefensible position so that he can deliver strikes or holds with little concern of retaliation. For instance, gaijin Stan Hansen often stomped a downed opponent while the opponent was entangled in the ring ropes. As touching the ring ropes is grounds for breaking a hold, stomping a downed opponent is evidence of both deceit (breaking of agreed-upon rules) and cowardice. Conversely, the injured babyface may intentionally stand face-to-face with the heel and exchange strikes. The function of the face-to-face confrontation is to further establish that the babyface is willing to test his skills on equal

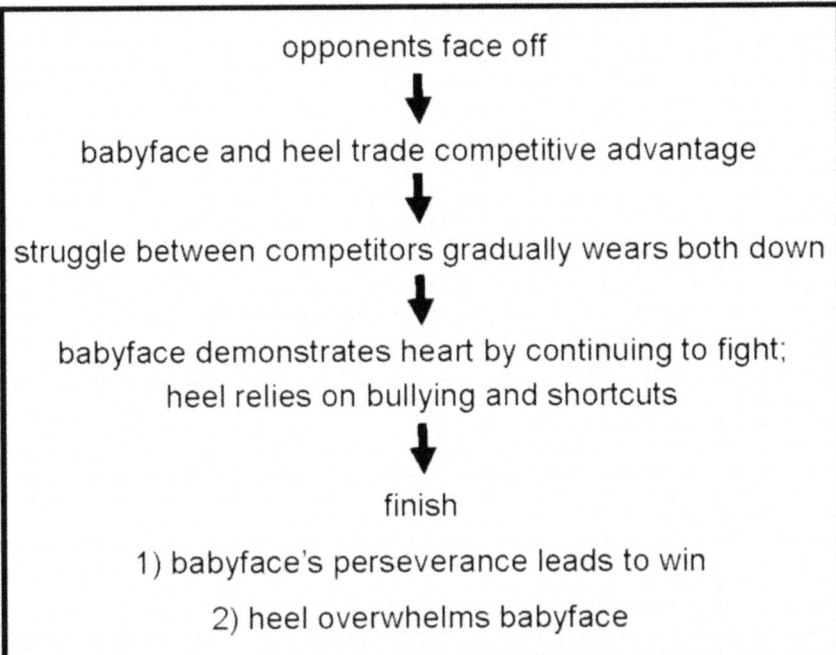

Structure of typical Japanese heavyweight singles professional wrestling match.

footing with the heel, even though the babyface is at a great disadvantage due to the size, strength and previous tactics of the heel. This is the essence of fighting spirit and is the single most important quality that a Japanese babyface must convey. By fighting with a clear disadvantage, the babyface may demonstrate the qualities of courage, honor and justice that are key to the Bushido code.[33] The finish of the match occurs in the third stage. During this stage, one of three outcomes will be observed: (1) the babyface overcomes the larger heel through perseverance, (2) the heel overwhelms the babyface and gains victory, or (3) the match ends in a non-finish. Relative to American pro wrestling, Japanese pro wrestling is less reliant on non-finishes.

Paradoxically, although wrestling is presented as legitimate competition in Japan, victory is less essential for success in Japan than in the United States. Whereas in the U.S. a loss by a babyface ultimately means that evil triumphed over good, in Japan a loss can be viewed as an opportunity. As the central characteristics of Japanese babyfaces are their competence, dedication, and fighting spirit, a loss represents a significant challenge to these qualities and offers the babyface an opportunity to demonstrate those qualities to the audience. For instance, in post-match press conferences, Japanese babyfaces often acknowledge and accept their defeat but indicate that they will work harder and challenge their competitor again when they have refined their skills. This sentiment was expressed directly by Kota Ibushi in 2015 when commenting on his loss to Shinsuke Nakamura.[34]

Cultural Values Conveyed in Professional Wrestling

Professional wrestling is a highly-stylized form of combat-based entertainment. As the primary social role of professional wrestling is to entertain spectators rather than establish competitive superiority, the ability of professional wrestling to attract and maintain audiences hinges on its ability to convey a narrative that is relevant to its audience. Because of the participatory nature of viewing wrestling (e.g., the jeers of a crowd may encourage a heel to continue a treacherous line of attack of their opponents), the cultural values conveyed by professional wrestling can be seen as emerging as an interaction between performers and their audiences. For instance, "Stone Cold" Steve Austin rose to main-event status by engaging in tactics previously reserved for heels (e.g., attacking an unsuspecting opponent, using illegal objects, bullying referees). However, the audience embraced the tactics as necessary for fighting a corrupt organization (WWF). According to social learning theorist Albert Bandura, humans often learn about cultural values and modify their behavior accordingly through observation rather than direct experience.[35] Professional wrestling represents a type of reciprocal observational learning in which both performer and audience express values through their behavior, and those behaviors are used by the other party to modify their own behaviors. It may also be viewed as a form of cathartic release in which the audience is able to release anxieties about unfairness and injustice in a socially-acceptable setting.[36]

The continued popularity of professional wrestling, for over a century in the United States and six decades in Japan, attests to the efficacy with which professional wrestling serves as a vehicle for the transmission of cultural values. While the popularity of professional wrestling has waxed and waned throughout its history, sometimes piquing the interest of large swaths of the population and other times marginalized by as a form of fringe entertainment, it has been continuously promoted throughout the United States and Japan since its introduction.

In order to appreciate its longevity, one must understand the evolving narrative that is conveyed in professional wrestling matches. Narratives evolve because they reflect the cultural values that are most prized at the particular time a match is presented to its audience. Some values are deeply ingrained in a particular culture and are thus less variable over time (e.g., the senpai/

kohai system sometimes expressed in Japanese pro wrestling can be observed in business, organized sports, and other social interaction) whereas others are more transient (e.g., American pro wrestling often featured Russian heels during the Cold War).

Across cultures, professional wrestling represents a hypermasculinized drama in which performers simulate struggle, pain, and triumph for the enjoyment of the audience. Wrestling emphasized, to an exaggerated degree, the key indicator of masculinity: physical prowess. For instance, one of the biggest wrestling stars of the 1980s and 1990s, Randy Poffo, adopted the last name Savage and the nickname "Macho Man." The terms *savage* and *macho* both connote physical prowess. The emphasis on masculinity can still be observed today; Ring of Honor wrestler Silas Young refers to himself as the "Last Real Man in Wrestling" and chastises his opponents and audience for their lack of "manliness." Oppliger has argued that one way that wrestling promotes hypermasculine attitudes is by converting all emotions into anger, which is then used as a mechanism to defeat opponents.[37] This is especially true for behaviors associated with vulnerability, such as fear, which are allowed to be expressed in more masculine ways.[38] Oppliger further contends that the ultimate goal of a professional wrestling match is to shame one's opponent more so that to achieve victory.[39] However, while this contention may be reflective of World Wrestling Entertainment (WWE, previously the World Wrestling Federation [WWF]), it is not representative of all professional wrestling. Both within and across cultures, winning is often the primary motivation for engaging in a match. American promotions Ring of Honor and Evolve were founded on the concept of sportsmanship, in which wins and losses determine one's position on a card. These ideas have been formally codified in Ring of Honor's "Code of Honor."[40] This is even truer in Japan where wins and losses are often the sole determinants of a wrestler's position in an organization. Japanese organizations including New Japan Pro Wrestling and Pro Wrestling NOAH often formally recognize one or more *aces* (the top performer in an organization). The designation of an ace is determined by the wrestler's performance in key matches rather than the flashiness of their appearance or their humiliation of opponents. New Japan Pro Wrestling's current ace, Kazuchika Okada, ascended to the position by defeating previous ace Hiroshi Tanahashi for the IWGP Heavyweight Title at their biggest event of the year.[41]

Although seemingly limited as a medium, professional wrestling has served as an effective and efficient means of reinforcing cultural values. While presentation of a hypermasculinized drama lends itself to conveyance of masculine values, the abundance of female performers (e.g., all-female wrestling promotions Shimmer Women Athletes in the U.S. and Stardom in Japan) and female viewers[42] suggests that the values being conveyed are more universal that a cursory glance may suggest. While an emphasis on physical and mental strength may traditionally align with masculine values, such characteristics are increasingly valued by females. This can be observed in a variety of facets including increases in female representation in the military[43] and competitive sports.[44] Ultimately, hypermasculinity appears to be a means rather than an end; by exaggerating internal and external features of performers, moral boundaries are more clearly delimited and allow for clearer transmission of cultural values. Because performers are cast in archetypal roles, there is less subtly in the transmission of those values and they can be conveyed to a wider audience.

The central message conveyed by American professional wrestling is related to the good-versus-evil dichotomy. Specifically, American wrestling promotes and reinforces the notion that success in various areas is a function of being a moral and ethical person. By demonstrating to audiences that a hero is one who stays true to his moral code even in the face of extreme adversity, American pro wrestling overtly communicates to its audience that the path to success in life is through following one's moral code. In expressing this sentiment, the nature of the heel is predefined as lacking in similar moral virtues and a willingness to engage in behavior outside of what is acceptable for a babyface. Thus, in order to succeed one must first be morally equipped to sustain the challenges of less scrupulous and more physically dominant challengers. This is perhaps most apparent in one of the most famous American wrestling matches: Hulk Hogan versus Andre the Giant at Wrestlemania III. In the build-up to the match, Hogan was presented as an honest, hard-working, morally-bound superhero, while Andre the Giant was presented as a lying, cheating, unstoppable force.[45] In this context, success cannot be attained merely through dedication and practice of one's craft but through thoughtful and considered application of one's morality to all adverse conditions in life. Similarly, American wrestling transmits the value of humility by presenting humble and self-deprecating babyfaces; a wrestling persona can have similar characteristics to that of a babyface (good looks, charisma, etc.), but if lacking humility, he is likely to be positioned by promoters and perceived by audiences as a heel.

More subtly, American professional wrestling embraces a law-and-order paradigm that presents a breaking of often arbitrary rules as evidence of immorality. From its early history, pro wrestling has been embraced by law enforcement to varying degrees. For instance, the first publication to regularly feature pro wrestling articles and results was the *National Police Gazette* (1845–1977). Some of the language used within the wrestling business betrays the law-and-order aspect of pro wrestling: wrestlers who were employed by promoters to protect against double-crosses were referred to as *policemen*, organizations that were operated outside of the purview of the National

Wrestling Alliance were referred to as *outlaw promotions*, and wrestlers who use various means to curry favor with promoters are known as "politicians." Additionally, individuals assumed to have engaged in criminal behavior have often been cast as heels, even when the guilt is implied by association (e.g., Russians, Cubans, and Japanese have, at various times, been cast as heels due to their nationality). Both American and Japanese professional wrestling have appealed to nationalistic sentiments, frequently casting individuals in stereotyped roles in order to further delineate hero from villain.

The primary narrative of Japanese pro wrestling is centered upon hard work, competence and perseverance. Specifically, Japanese pro wrestling overtly communicates that success is a product of intense dedication and resolution. Unlike American pro wrestling, the relationship between being "good" and successful is reversed in Japanese pro wrestling. Whereas American pro wrestling presents victory as an invariable *outcome* of being a "good" person, Japanese professional wrestling presents victory (or lack thereof) as a *means* of becoming a better person. This is often reflected in post-match interviews in which a wrestler will indicate that the loss was a learning experience that would help them to improve their technique and, once improved, the wrestler will request a rematch.

The emphasis on fighting spirit, engendered in most main-event performances, can be viewed as a mechanism for promoting and reinforcing a strong work ethic in viewers. Fighting spirit sequences in matches explicitly establish that, in the face of hardship, persistence and dedication to a task will lead to success. However, there is a subtle implication that success will not be immediate and that early failures are a critical element of long-term success. For instance, Katsuyori Shibata's hard-fought loss to Kazuchika Okada established that Shibata had the grit and determination to be a main-event attraction.[46] In loss, Shibata was elevated in the promotion.

Japanese professional wrestling also reinforces an acceptance of a strong hierarchical system in which one's position in the system predetermines the outcomes of conflicts within the system. Specifically, since those higher in the social order acquired their position due to dedication and persistence, those lower in the social order are not equipped with the necessary tools for victory over those higher in the social order. This belief is codified in the kohei/senpai system which assumes the senior member's superiority regardless of actual performance. That is, the technical superiority of a senior member is established by their placement in the social hierarchy rather than being established through direct competition with junior members. For this reason, Japanese wrestlers often maintain main event status for a much longer period than their American counterparts.

Irrespective of culture, professional wrestling represents a relatively stable mechanism for reflecting and promoting values held by audiences. In that sense, it is similar to other forms of popular media such as fictional television shows, movies and novels. However, the reliance on fixed character types (babyfaces and heels) allows for a more transparent and easily-understood conveyance of information. By casting characters in clearly-defined roles, professional wrestling allows viewers to invest in matches with relatively little prior knowledge of wrestling. For this reason, professional wrestling (especially American professional wrestling) bears a striking resemblance to superhero comic books. Unlike other forms of popular entertainment, professional wrestling attempts to straddle a line between reality and fiction. As such, professional wrestling may be viewed as a precursor to the reality television boom of the early 2000s that is still popular today. By blurring lines between reality and fantasy, audiences are better able to relate to wrestlers as real people and therefore internalize the content conveyed by performers. The simplicity of form, reliance on archetypes, and creation of a false reality combine to make professional wrestling an effective and efficient means for transmitting culturally relevant information.

Notes

1. Roland Barthes, "The World of Wrestling," in *Mythologies* (New York: The Noonday Press, 1991), 15–25.
2. Edward P. Kardas, "Gestalt Psychology," in *History of Psychology: The Making of a Science* (Belmont, CA: Wadsworth Cengage Learning), 337–46.
3. Matthew J. Robinson et al., "Fans vs. Spectators: An Analysis of Those Who Attend Intercollegiate Football Games," *Sports Marketing Quarterly* 14 (2005), 43–53.
4. Gerald W. Morton and George M. O'Brien, "Professional Wrestling's Roots in Theatrical Traditions," in *Wrestling to Rasslin': Ancient Sport to American Spectacle* (Bowling Green, OH: Bowling Green State University Popular Press, 1985), 103–25.
5. Scott M. Beekman, *Ringside: A History of Professional Wrestling in America* (Westport, CT: Praeger, 2006), 25.
6. Jimmy Wheeler, "Joe 'Toots' Mondt Biography," *Professional Wrestling Historical Society*, http://www.prowrestlinghistoricalsociety.com/mondt-joe-toots.html (accessed April 10, 2017).
7. Tim Hornbaker, *The National Wrestling Alliance: The Untold Story of the Monopoly that Strangled Professional Wrestling* (Toronto: ECW Press, 2007).
8. WrestlingGWA's Channel, "GWA How to: Hurricanrana + Kontermöglichkeit," YouTube video, 01:30, posted April 11, 2011, https://www.youtube.com/watch?v=ZmGgSJsvBSM.
9. Karl Sterne, *Pioneers of Wrestling* (Haleyville, AL: DragonKing Pro Wrestling Press, 2002), 7.
10. Shaun Assael and Mike Mooneyham, *Sex, Lies, and Headlocks: The Real Story of Vince McMahon and the World Wrestling Entertainment* (New York: Three Rivers Press, 2004), 13.
11. Allen Guttmann and Lee Thompson, *Japanese Sports: A History* (Honolulu: University of Hawai'i Press, 2001), 168.
12. John F. Molinaro, *Wrestling Observer's Top 100 Wrestlers of All Time* (Toronto: Winding Stair Press, 2002), 14–17.
13. Steven Johnson and Greg Oliver, *The Pro Wrestling Hall of Fame: Heroes and Icons* (Toronto: ECW Press, 2012), 1–72.
14. Greg Klein, *The King of New Orleans: How Junkyard Dog Became Professional Wrestling's First Black Superhero* (Toronto: ECW Press, 2012), Loc 927–1003, Kindle.
15. Scott Rubarth, "Competing Constructions of Masculinity in Ancient Greece," *Athens Journal of Humanities and Arts* 1, no. 1 (January 2014), 21–32.

16. Molinaro, *Wrestling Observer's Top 100 Wrestlers of All Time*, 20–23.
17. Inazo Nitobé. *Bushido: The Soul of Japan*, 13th edition (Urbana: Project Guttenberg), Kindle edition, 15–42.
18. Takashi Naito and Uwe P. Gielen, "Tatemae and Honne: A Study of Moral Relativism in Japanese Culture," in Uwe P. Gielen, Leonore L. Adler and Noach Milgram, eds., *Psychology in International Perspectives* (Amsterdam: Swets and Zeitlinger, 1992), 161–72.
19. Nitobe, *Bushido*, 28–33.
20. Nitobe, *Bushido*, 52–56.
21. New Japan Pro Wrestling, "10th Match Tanahashi Hirozu vs Okada Kazutika," NJPW World Video, 01:04:09, http://njpwworld.com/p/s_series_00248_1_14.
22. Nitobe, *Bushido*, 17–21.
23. Jim Ross, "@JRsBBQ," *Twitter*, April 14, 2014, https://twitter.com/JRsBBQ (accessed June 2, 2015).
24. Nitobe, *Bushido*, 21–27.
25. Stan Hansen and Scott Teal, *The Last Outlaw* (Gallatin, TN: Crowbar Press, 2011), 194–219.
26. Naito and Gielen, "Tatemae and Honne," 161–72.
27. World Wrestling Entertainment, "WCW Starrcade 1998," WWE Network video, 02:44:51, http://network.wwe.com/video/v31359919?contextType=wwe-show&contextId=starrcade&contentId=68029522&watchlistAltButtonContext=series.
28. World Wrestling Entertainment, "Ric Flair vs. Ricky Morton, Steel Cage Match for the NWA Championship, The Great American Bash, July 5, 1986," *Ric Flair and the Four Horsemen* DVD (World Wrestling Entertainment, 2012).
29. World Wrestling Entertainment, *Tombstone: The History of the Undertaker* DVD (World Wrestling Entertainment, 2012).
30. Ring of Honor, "Bryan Danielson vs. Takeshi Morishima," *Manhattan Mayhem II* DVD (Ring of Honor, 2007).
31. World Wrestling Entertainment, "ECW Hardcore TV 216, June 10, 1997," WWE Network video, 46:32, http://network.wwe.com/video/v500791883/?contentId=&contextType=wwe-show&contextId=ecw_hardcore_tv.
32. New Japan Pro Wrestling, "Seventh Game, NEW JAPAN CUP 2017 Semifinal Katsuyori VS Tomohiro Ishii Shibata," NJPW World video, 32:40, http://njpwworld.com/p/s_series_00430_3_07.
33. Nitobe, *Bushido*, 15–41.
34. *New Japan Pro Wrestling*, AXS, originally aired October 30, 2015.
35. Albert Bandura, *Social Learning and Personality Development* (New York: Holt, Rinehart and Winston, 1963).
36. Seymour Feshbach, "The Drive-Reducing Function of Fantasy Behavior," *The Journal of Abnormal and Social Psychology* 50, no. 1 (January 1955), 3–11.
37. Patrice A. Oppliger, *Wrestling and Hypermasculinity* (Jefferson, NC: McFarland, 2004), 64.
38. William S. Pollack and Ronald F. Levant, "Toward the Reconstruction of Masculinity," in Ronald F. Levant and William S., eds., *A New Psychology of Men* (New York: Basic Books, 1995), 229–51.
39. Oppliger, *Wrestling and Hypermasculinity*, 65–66.
40. "Time Limit—Code of Honor—Rules," Ring of Honor, http://www.rohwrestling.com/content/time-limit-code-of-honor-rules (accessed April 22, 2017).
41. New Japan Pro Wrestling, "Ninth Game Kazuchika Okada VS Hiroshi Tanahashi," NJPW World video, 1:00:42, http://njpwworld.com/p/s_series_00361_2_09.
42. Dave Meltzer, *Wrestling Observer Newsletter*, November 17, 2014.
43. Eileen Patten and Kim Parker, "Social & Demographic Trends," *Pew Research Center*, last modified December 22, 2011, http://www.pewsocialtrends.org/2011/12/22/women-in-the-u-s-military-growing-share-distinctive-profile/ (accessed March 12, 2015).
44. Women's Sports Foundation, last modified 2016, https://www.womenssportsfoundation.org/ (accessed October 18, 2016).
45. World Wrestling Entertainment, "Prime Time Wrestling 101, February 13, 1987,"

WWE Network video, 1:29:15, http://network.wwe.com/video/v166577683/?contentId=&contextType=wwe-show&contextId=prime_time_wrestling.

46. New Japan Pro Wrestling, "First Nine Games IWGP Heavyweight Championship Bout Kazuchika Okada VS Katsuyori Shibata," NJPW World video, 1:03:48, http://njpwworld.com/p/s_series_00432_1_09.

The "Sportification" of Wrestling in France
Strength, Performance and Regulation (1852–1913)

FRÉDÉRIC LOYER and
JEAN-FRANÇOIS LOUDCHER

While the French wrestling federation may have been created quite late (1913) wrestling has a long history in the country. In antiquity, sources attest to a "free" style that allowed all holds and strikes.[1] The Greco-Roman style, which prohibited holds below the waist, first developed in the mid–19th century by Jean Broyasse ("Exbroyat"), former soldier of the French Empire. Pinfall is achieved by forcing an opponent's shoulders to the floor. Wrestling was called "open-handed" to distinguish it from boxing, and eventually coming to be known (inaccurately) as "Greco-Roman."[2] Modern wrestling was thus shaped by freestyle (aka "catch-as-catch-can") and Greco-Roman techniques.[3] Why, as soon as it became a regulated "sports" did both the public and aspiring grapplers lose interest in wrestling? Is it because the quality of their presentation practice was eroded during this period (1852–1913)?

Throughout the 19th century, wrestling was one of many circus sideshows, often found at fairgrounds or music halls. It was also, however, a popular middle-class activity, both as a means of physical improvement and a skillset for self-defense. Wrestling was also among the first sports in France to feature an amateur championship, held partly in response to professional wrestling matches intended to promote performance rather than genuine competition.

In short the story of wrestling is that of strength and skill. But it is also and above all that of its regulation, whether technical or institutional, through a process of tighter legal, judicial, and political constraints. This study will draw on various documentary sources, such as rare books written about wrestling at the end of the 19th and beginning of the 20th centuries, reviews and newspapers (*La Vie au Grand Air, Le Vélo, L'Illustration, Les Sports*) between 1880 and 1913,[4] and image archives and postcards of the period to arrive at a better understanding of wrestling's status in France at the turn of the century.

The Rise and Fall of "Flat Hand" Fighting (1852–1880): Between Brute Force and Controlled Strength

The Spectacle of Brute Force

Wrestling's rapid growth in popularity in the 19th century it was due to the Greco-Roman style, first used by circus showmen.[5] Wrestling's growing popularity was also due to the widespread popularity of gymnastics as a strength-building exercise. Therefore, from 1852, boxing and wrestling matches were staged for several months in famous arenas in Rue Montesquieu à Paris. Mathieu de la Loire, Blanchard de Lyon, Quintin de Lyon, Loubet de Nîmes, Creste de Provence, Quiquine d'Avignon, and Rabasson du Midi,[6] wrestled in tournaments that captured the public's imagination. Greco-Roman wrestling emphasis on physical strength and individual competition did little to promote a more unified national "French" identity.[7] While stirring up regionalism, these shows were part of a broader emphasis on health and fitness throughout Europe.[8] The development of a centralized state under the July monarchy (1830–1848) and the Second Empire (1852–1870), helped exacerbate local resistance[9] but laid the foundation for a republican democracy based on healthy, patriotic, and moral values.

However, the Second Empire was a politically difficult time. Formidable physical strength could be seen as a unifying element, but was also frightening. Therefore, promoters of athletic events had to ensure that gymnastic, boxing, and wrestling events were apolitical,[10] as public displays of physical strength could become a means of challenging the regime. State security closely monitored athletics, as evinced by numerous police reports that note, in minute detail, various "assaults on proper morals" at popular events.

State surveillance hardly hindered wrestling. On April 8, 1853, the Salle Montesquieu theater banned wrestling,[11] but the Salle Valentino began hosting wrestling in 1856.[12] Wrestling's early success was due to promoter Rossignol-Rollin, a charismatic former lawyer from Lyon. Rossignol-Rollin gave wrestlers sensational nicknames: "M. Edouard, 'Steel Biter,' Gustave d'Avignon, 'Backbreaker,' Emile les esgourdes, Albert, Fortress of Béziers, Mina, Hercules of

Midi, Alfred the Paris Pretty Boy, etc."[13] Rossignol-Rollin drew inspiration from the mythical games of antiquity, promising fans that his matches would take place "on the same stage as the ancient Olympics and the Greco-Roman games,"[14] Rossignol-Rollin's identification of his wrestlers with the Greek Olympic competitions of antiquity may have led to French open-hand wrestling being increasingly known, misleadingly, as "Greco-Roman."

In any case, the exercise of strength invaded the capital in 1858, according to Jules Vallès:

> The music halls are closed for Lent but we do not complain too much, never has there been so much outdoors in the streets, the squares, and the crossings. It's a triumph for the acrobats, the strongmen, the jugglers, and the albinos among the cobbles. For a month or two we are not going to be able to walk in Paris without hearing the sick rattle and the trombones playing top C on the boards of the hut; never have these poor devils ... taken so many blows, whacks, and punches.[15]

Although public displays of strength in wrestling (and other events), evoking images of the ancient games, were popular among fans, it provoked a different response from the authorities. By 1859, wrestlers had become a source of concern for the Paris chief of police, who wrote:

> Gentlemen, I have noticed that, every year, in the festivals around Paris wrestlers are allowed to set up their booths beside the market stalls and entertainers, on sites allocated for public entertainment and allow the spectators to wrestle them. This type of display has, in general, an undesirable influence on the minds of a certain class of people which is naturally inclined to respect no other authority than brute force.[16]

Why such a reaction, and why so late?

Strength Mastered

It was the public display of physical strength that posed a problem for the Prefect. If unregulated, wrestling could upset the middle class order. To this end, authorities began imposing tighter regulations on athletics.[17] France's many gymnastic clubs were allowed to continue under close government supervision. Already restricted by a raft of legislation introduced between 1849 and 1850, the government chose to closely monitor events rather than prohibit them outright. The ministerial decree of March 19, 1859, tightened regulation by specifying that "authorization for extraordinary shows should be requested two days in advance and contain a detailed description of the spectacle."[18]

Surveillance proved a more effective means of regulating wrestling than outright prohibition. M. Guénépin repeatedly sought permission for a fairground show throughout 1850, only to be refused on the grounds of "competition." Permission was finally granted on February 5, 1851. The Prefect's letter stated:

> For these reasons I would add a far greater consideration. It seems much more preferable to see the population confined to the Champs Elysées for entertainment of all kinds than to discover they have gone outside the gates during the evening to spread into the hostelries and other suburban meeting places, where the false political doctrines are propagated more freely than anywhere else.[19]

The letter was not a one-off.[20] Others also indicated the government's desire to divert the public from possible protest rallies. To this end, athletic events were severely restricted. A notice from May 31, 1852, provided a restrictive framework for future athletic events:

> Only gymnastic and training activities where strength is not used in a manner which may cause accident, excessive fatigue, or injury of any sort [are permissible, so] that the public may not in any way be indisposed and suffer affront to its feelings of humanity and convenience.[21]

Consequently, fight promoters would have to comply with these regulations. Hubert Lecour, the first to launch a public gymnasium, suggested his venue should focus on the study, in theory and practice, of athletics.[22] Performances were closely regulated. Boxing and wrestling were permitted, but their nature was redefined in accordance with the new rules. Now, their goals were to train athletes to control their bodies and achieve social and political conformity:

> The worst of the people were responsible for the worst times of the Revolution because they relied on force of arms and fear of the upper classes: these bad times will never return as long as the enlightened classes have faith in the power of mind over body.[23]

Under the new restrictions, Antoine-Hippolyte Triat was the most successful athletic promoter, opening his own gym in 1855. It is unsurprising that wrestling and boxing were not included in his gym's offerings. Did he anticipate the growing perception in France that gymnastics were a positive, healthy activity, in contrast to increasingly negative views of wrestling?

The Decline of Wrestling

Political and judicial challenges to wrestling would have a permanent effect on its success in France. Wrestling would soon experience a decline, particularly in middle-class interest in these kinds of events. *Le Sport*, created by Eugène Chapus in 1854, regularly reported on wrestling and other acrobatic spectacles until 1858, when it ceased doing so[24] in favor of covering horse racing and other mundane events. After 1865, the journal ceased coverage of "Assauts" Vigneron, the most famous human cannonball. Touring circuses in the provinces resumed while combat sports seemingly declined. Many former wrestling stars ended up working for circuses as public interest and official support for wrestling declined. Even circus strong men drew fewer and fewer spectators; the famous Louis Vigneron, Batta the "gentleman athlete" who "lifted a horse at arm's length," and "l'athlète Bonnes" who once thrilled fans at the Pere Noël arena by lifting 200 pounds[25] finished their careers in poverty.[26]

Some, however, sought to bring wrestling back to theatres. In 1865, Eugène Paz opened a private "Grand gymnase" in Paris, and wrestling was initially part of training and warm-up exercises. Soon after, he began organizing matches between professionals. While he featured quality athletes, the gymnasium boss closely monitored and regulated the matches; he eliminated the elements of conventional wrestling and separated spectators and performers with a panel of judges who determined the winners. The events were popular, as "more than 3,000 people attended each session and the highest circles of Paris society were found there."[27] The promotion was, however, short-lived. In the light of public interest, Eugène Paz would have feared seeing the 'medical' nature of his gymnasium distorted.[28] Whatever it may be, the enclosure of wrestling matches seemed to be opposed to the greater seriousness now associated with gymnastics.

Public sports changed considerably during this difficult period, which saw an escalation in military preparations because of rising concerns over Prussia, who had easily defeated Austria in 1866. Partly to promote health and physical preparedness, gymnastic exercise was incorporated into educational curriculums (the Victor Duruy laws of 1869) and cycling became increasingly popular. In the early years of the Third Republic, founded after Napoleon III's defeat during the Franco-Prussian War, Greco-Roman wrestling continued to struggle to find an audience, due likely to artificial constraints imposed by the authorities. While boxing had been adopted and regulated by the Joinville military academy in the early 1870s,[29] wrestling was largely an informal recreational activity, an occasional break for soldiers from repetitive and unexciting exercise, as evidenced by numerous postcards from the period.[30] Wrestling did not generally feature as an official component of school and military athletic programs.[31] English influence soon manifested in France via the increasing popularity of football and rugby, but wrestling still struggled to find an audience.

Renewal (1885–1905)

Technical Wrestling

At the end of the 19th century, wrestling again enjoyed considerable success in the fairground booths, then on stage in Paris casinos. The owners of touring fight rings presented their teams and fired up the crowd by offering 500 Francs to anyone who could topple one of their wrestlers.[32] Bouts were held between professional and amateur fighters, which the latter would sometimes win. It could also happen that the star of a rival fight stable would wade in to challenge the champion for the honor of the house, offering spectators high-caliber wrestling. Several of these wrestlers came from the back rooms of bars, using their physical abilities as a way of making money.[33] However, their techniques were only useful in honest matches.

Some of the best wrestlers of the turn of the century, notably those from the Bordeaux region, where wrestling was widespread, were not all full-time professionals. Sundays and several evenings a week, the amateurs trained in small gyms. Wrestlers usually met informally in the backrooms of bars, turned into informal "athletic arenas." The front of the establishments were open to all, but the back rooms were used as an arena for physical exercise enthusiasts, with weights and a square, sawdust-covered canvas ring.[34] In these places, hidden from the public, famous wrestlers such as Faouët, Félix Bernard, and Pietro Dalmasso learned their trade. For the simple pleasure of physical confrontation, they knocked the stuffing out of each other. "We fought for glory there. The meets ... were organized honestly. Everyone tried to win to the best of their ability."[35] These legitimate matches were the foundation for major developments in wrestling.

The parade at a carnival, 1908 (postcard, personal collection).

Greco-Roman wrestling became less static, and more specialty moves were invented and associated with particular individuals. Some holds were named after the wrestlers who used them: for example, the Arpin head lock, the Paul Pons hip hold, the Dumont "bottom of the bag" pinning maneuver, and the François Le Bordelais "necktie." These mirrored an increasingly innovative individual know-how that arose at the end of the 19th century. Greco-Roman wrestling then displayed a major technical evolution through the use of a multiplicity of holds. New techniques appeared: "the front belt," "the reverse belt," "the head lock," "the hip hold," "the arm lock," "the arm bend," etc. Léon Ville (in 1891)[36] and Paul Pons (in 1903)[37] popularized such techniques, which became fundamental in wrestling. But beyond the question of technique and more difficult to envisage, was the educational use of wrestling.

Wrestling, a New Educational Interest

It was in the 1880s that we find the first didactic writings on the discipline, revealing a new educational interest. Serpeille, journalist for the daily *Petit Journal* and author of the preface to Léon Ville's work *French Wrestling Organized for Communal Exercise*,[38] recognized the ensemble of qualities offered by the discipline: "This exercise develops the muscles, gives grace and suppleness and, for its practice, there is no need to loosen the purse strings." He observed, however, that the activity was not present in the army, schools, or gymnastic clubs. The delay in codifying and formalizing the activity explains in part the absence of wrestling in physical education curricula.

Léon Ville, a former army officer, after visiting the athletic and wrestling arenas with their numerous professionals, attempted to present wrestling in an organized and coherent format.[39] He tried to codify "open-hand" wrestling by producing the first specific rules, which became the basis for the "Greco-Roman" style.[40] His aim was primarily to promote wrestling for the physical development of the youth and the regeneration of the "race."[41] Each basic technique was demonstrated in several steps, then repeated by students on command, according to a series of timings.[42] But it was a failure! Wrestling was poorly suited to an analytical approach and collective performance in front of an instructor.

In general, wrestling, still associated with feats of strength, was not incorporated into military and educational programs. It was poorly adapted to healthy gymnastic methods, built around reasoned and analytical movement (i.e., Swedish gymnastics). Like weightlifting, wrestling was linked with money, cheating, and brute force. It appeared to be a spectacle without dignity or discipline. While boxing quickly gave rise to instructors, wrestling created professional entertainers.

The "backwards belt." L. Ville, *Wrestling and Wrestlers*, preface by Baron of Vaux (Paris: Rothschild, 1891) (photograph by Nadar).

Professional Championships

At the turn of the century, public interest in wrestling focused heavily on the results of competitions between individuals. More than that, it became a matter of promoting the health of the French race (and thus the nation) through the celebration of strength and competition, as evidenced by an increasing number of international competitions (Olympic Games in 1896, cycling, football, athletics, etc.). Turkish wrestlers, who first appeared in France in 1895,[43] participated in these events, ushering in a new period of prosperity for professional wrestling. Promoter Joseph Doublier of Lyon, on tour in the Middle East, was staggered by the strength of three Turkish wrestlers, who he quickly signed to contracts. Taking on their French counterparts, Turkish grapplers quickly adapted to the rules of Greco-Roman wrestling, proving to be physically and technically superior. In Turkey, the traditional oiled wrestling was an integral part of male life and no festival was complete without it. Victory was gained by taking three steps with the adversary in hand or by throwing him to the ground on his back. In Turkey, wrestling has always enjoyed favorable treatment by the government, and is practiced by children from a young age. Turkish wrestling demands great speed, agility, and resistance, and these qualities would bring variety to the extremely static form of wrestling practiced in France at the time.

In addition to the Turkish wrestlers, the arrival of a few Swiss grapplers and the Russian Ladislas Pytlasinski inspired Alexandre de Lucenski, editor of the *Journal des Sports*, to organize a professional world championship in1898. He did not hesitate to publicize it heavily in his society pages in hopes of overtaking his direct rival, *Le Vélo*. The world wrestling championship, held at the Casino de Paris, was a complete success. The public packed in to witness the victory of the Frenchman Paul Pons, nicknamed the "Colossus." While the fights did not start until 11 p.m., spectators were already being turned away by 9:30 p.m.: "No similar event in France or abroad had such success as this one, which brought a cash bonanza for the Casino de Paris."[44] In 1899, the title was won by Kara Ahmed, a Turkish wrestler whose picture in the papers in traditional costume added to the myth and legends of the "strongman."[45] These foreigners aroused curiosity. People came to see the Russian George Hackenschmidt, the Dane Ingeman Petersen, the Cossack Ivan Poddubney, and many others. The craze for these first encounters was perhaps due to the public interest in seeing legitimate, honest competition. However, the cost of organizing these events and the desire to increase revenue rapidly transformed the presentations into sporting parodies, solely aimed at entertainment.

Thanks to these popular events, wrestlers were able to earn cash rewards and receive tremendous public attention. The professional championships began in November, with the finals held during the Christmas holidays, and were supported by sponsors, among which sports journals were at the forefront. Sponsors sought to promote their brands by linking them with the high-profile matches, hoping to attract an ever-increasing range of consumers.[46] The journals helped promote various sponsors as well: "W. Allen sports agency—all the news on wrestling, boxing swimming, etc.," "Super-vieille—the wrestling specialist," and so on.[47]

The success of wrestling in Paris as other European cities (Saint Petersburg, Berlin, and London, for example), grew year after year. Beyond the world championships, several professional tournaments were held in music halls. From 1899, the "Grand Prix de la Ville de Paris" was launched by the journal *Le Vélo*, and held on the stage of the Folies Bergère.[48] Ladislas Pytlasinski took the victory and a purse of 3,000 francs against Constant le Boucher. The most important such tournament was the "Golden Belt." Billed as the annual challenge of the "kings of the ring," it was sponsored by the journal *L'Auto* and staged at the Folies Bergères beginning in 1902.[49] Paul Pons won the title three years in a row.

In most Paris cabarets, wrestling shows resembled an exhibition or a staged show, with a great variety of typical techniques performed in front of the audience. The athletes often practiced rigged fights, which was necessary to attract and impress spectators. From then on, wrestling could no longer be genuine because it was necessary to manage the "human capital" to keep fans coming back for more.⁵⁰ The transition from sport to spectacle, which allowed new techniques and movements, fueled a change in the way strength was perceived. Spectacle therefore provided new challenges to traditional representations of the "strong man,"⁵¹ to which women notably seemed to adapt more quickly.

Women's Wrestling

At the end of the 19th century, female wrestling experienced rapid growth. Women's wrestling was very popular in Rouen and Paris. Albert de St. Albain, journalist for the daily *Les Sports à Paris*, wrote about Pietro Dalmasso's Compagnie des Folies Bergères, which featured a dozen female members who wrestled each other with relentless enthusiasm: "The chest of the most battered [wrestler] turned black and Pietro said to me: it is nothing, it happens. A rub down with alcohol will make the skin yellow."⁵² In 1904, the Bal Tabarin amusement hall opened on Montmartre, and, like the Moulin Rouge, featured exotic dancing. It won over the public, however, by hosting women's wrestling bouts. By taking center stage and performing with great skill and technique, female wrestlers asserted their physical potential and challenged popular, gendered notions of physicality. Through this "neutralization"⁵³ of gender, a woman could challenge a man as "an equal" and experience a certain leeway in the exhibition of her body, almost to the point of eroticism.

For others, the technical presentation was the reason for this feminine practice. In 1899, *Le Vélo* sent Frantz Reichel to the Nouveau Concert hall in Montmartre, where women's wrestling was held. These were promoted by Ajax, a male wrestler who had toured the fairgrounds for two months with his wrestling shows. The journalist confessed that while "having arrived very skeptical," he had not "been able to stop myself from admiring the grace of

Paul Pons, winner of the "golden belt," 1902. *La Vie au Grand Air* 222, December 13, 1902, 844.

their movements."[54] He even acknowledged something truly attractive about the girls: "Supple and cat-like, the female wrestlers have, amidst the brutality of the contest, a beauty in their attacking moves and for the parade which is pleasing and captivating!"[55] In the end, women wrestlers' expression of a particular strength, drawing on movement and technique, became accepted socially and culturally. This display overcame some of the gender barriers in a time when a female athlete was still an object of curiosity.

Professional wrestling was not part of the greater multi-discipline federation of the regulatory body, the Union des Sociétés Françaises de Sports Athlétiques (USFSA). Nevertheless, the demand for purely amateur wrestling was much lower than that for the more-spectacular pro variety. This posed a problem for the governing body, as physical exercise took on an increasing importance with the rise of federations and international competitions.

The Emergence of Competition Wrestling (1895–1913)

Wrestling in the Gymnasium: Between Fitness and Self-Defense

At the beginning of the 20th century, physical exercise was growing rapidly in popularity. There were 20 private gymnasia in Paris in 1860,[56] 156 in 1900, and 187 in 1905.[57] A wealthy clientele attended the biggest gymnasia of the period, multi-purpose halls offering a variety of activities: hydrotherapy, massage, chiropractic treatment, fencing, boxing, and wrestling. Works by Léon Ville on French wrestling[58] and Joseph Charlemont on French boxing[59] showed a common concern for healthy exercise. Dietary regimes, to be followed for healthy living, and sport-specific apparel added an aesthetic and utilitarian dimension.

Wrestling was, however, absent for a long time from the activities identified by the outdoor magazine *La Vie au Grand Air* in its page dedicated to "sporting snippets": cycling, motoring, gliding, athletics, horse racing ... were for the middle classes, even if the working class was beginning to take up some of them. After 1900, wrestling featured more frequently in exercise regimens and periodicals; in 1904, *le journal* reported that: "the number of young people taking up the sport of wrestling is growing day by day."[60] In 1905, it dedicated several pages to the "True Sportsman," Etienne Giraud, who was featured as an example of a practitioner of both boxing and wrestling: "He learned wrestling with Constant le Boucher and boxing under Castérès, three times a week he could be seen in the ring at Bayle, or on the boards at the ring in the Rue Volney."[61]

Yet, this evolution was also possible because wrestling offered displays which were now in tune with the mood of the time. Strength and movement had taken hold, responding to new concepts of health and beauty. Fifty years earlier, "beauty was strength. Strength was reckoned to be Herculean; they had huge shoulders, a prominent belly and bulging calf muscles."[62] At the turn of the century, health was increasingly understood as internal, as evidenced by the importance given by doctors and scientists to the value of a physiology based mainly on cardio-vascular capacity.[63] The spirometer replaced the dynamometer, while athletes went from the gymnasium to the stage.[64] In higher-class halls, strength took on a more "internal" form, marked by more discreet signs of a new energy and stamina, revealing a certain healthiness and a different image of the powerful male. Elsewhere, the ostentatious expression of strength, appealing to a working class audience, offered an alternate image of the strong man. Edmond Desbonnet understood this divergence when he invented a means to satisfy the demands of the different body cultures and their followers.[65]

The need for a new culture of strength and self-defense was a reaction to personal and collective concerns about safety. It was a time of revived nationalist movements, largely inspired by media sources such as *Le Matin* or *La Patrie*. Viewed as a means of self-defense and used in conjunction with French boxing, so-called "Parisian" wrestling was performed in various ways. Charlemont, for example, combined punches and kicks, with the "body holds of wrestling."[66] Emile André, Emile Maitrot, André Buvat, Ernest Régnier, Georges Dubois, and others showcased self-defense moves of varying originality.[67]

In this context of domestic and international fears (the Japanese defeat of Russia in 1905, tensions with Germany), the introduction of ju-jitsu provided an alternative to wrestling. Mainly due to the victory of Ernest Régnier over Georges Dubois in 1905, the Japanese martial art challenged the popularity of wrestling and French boxing, both widely portrayed as defensive techniques.[68] On December 8, 1905, a month after the Regnier v Dubois contest, *La Vie au Grand Air*[69] featured a comparison between wrestling and ju-jitsu. The analysis showed that while similarities existed between the two disciplines, French wrestling techniques permitted the immobilization of the opponent but did not put the shoulder or elbow at risk, unlike Japanese arm holds that could dislocate an opponent's elbow or break his shoulder:

> The ju-jitsu fighter takes hold of the arm in such a way that, if he presses his attack to the limit, the arm or shoulder will give way. It is up to the man caught in the hold to submit when he fears the worst will happen. French wrestling strictly prohibits holds of this nature.[70]

Ju-jitsu made an impression through the diversity of its holds and blows causing falls, dislocations, and unconsciousness (via chokes). Régnier's legendary status was built around his switch to the Japanese style, changing his name to Ré-Nié, and the "key" hold he applied to his opponent's arm, forcing an immediate submission and end to the fight. This arm lock technique seemed like magic. Articles abounded in the specialist press and the major daily papers: "Everything has gone ju-jitsu! The streets, the newspapers, the theatres, the music halls echo with this magic word, which sounds like a clarion call to victory."[71] Edmond Desbonnet soon opened a hall in Paris at 55 rue de Ponthieu, near the Champs-Élysées, where Régnier himself taught the secrets of the Japanese method, attracting the upper echelons of Paris society: "I opened a ju-jitsu school, the public poured in, I saw the Duke of Broglia, Prince Caraman, Chimay, Prince Murat etc…, the most eminent men of letters, arts, industry."[72] The physical culture teacher was part of a commercial framework in which demonstrations and music hall spectacles were enjoying rapid expansion and rising profitability.[73]

Professional wrestlers, however, viewed ju-jitsu as an intrusion that would negatively affect their popularity and income. They protested against the Japanese sport, which they viewed as an Asian affront to the hitherto respected Greco-Latin tradition. Ignoring the counsel of Edmond Desbonnet, Ernest Régnier held exhibition fights and accepted challenges: "Ré-nié listened to his friends, the flatterers. He wanted to crush all the fighters and, despite my advice, he agreed to fight in public on stage at the Folies Bergère, where he took on the challengers. That was his loss."[74] Wrestlers organized a "trap" to humiliate Régnier at the Folies Bergère. In a challenge match against the ju-jitsu practitioner, Jean Witzler, an unscrupulous wrestler, egged on by Raoul Le Boucher and Paul Pons, head butted Ré-Nié in the face; taken by surprise, he fell to the floor. After such humiliation, the public largely turned away from ju-jitsu.[75] Régnier's efforts to revive interest were met by failure. In 1908, he challenged Ivan Poddubney, a multiple-time world professional wrestling champion.[76] The wrestler, 1m 83 tall and weighing 112 kg, easily overwhelmed Ernest Régnier, 1m 65 and 63 kg. The arrival of two Japanese experts failed to revive the general public's interest, despite exhibitions and demonstrations given in cabarets and music halls. Matches pitting judokas against wrestlers, respecting neither rules nor conventions, became a farce; for example, on December 31, 1908, British boxer Sam MacVea defeated Japanese judoka Tano Matsuda in 14 seconds.[77] Training, competition, and self-improvement, all cardinal virtues of modern sport, appeared, however, to take great strides during ju-jitsu's brief popularity in France.

Freestyle Wrestling and "Catch": An Imaginary Narrative Foreign to Sport?

Finally, the presentation of physical strength in wrestling was greatly altered thanks to its shift towards technique and agility, as well as new patriotic and international dimensions. They influenced body cultures promoting rival fighting styles and emphasizing both individual and collective health and physique. Wrestling seemed to bring together different ways of showing off strength, but ambiguities emerged between sporting and performative forms of the practice.

Without argument, acrobatic wrestling and catch are activities that offer different images than those engendered in pure sport. In the music hall championships, results were increasingly decided in advance: "such a man, before taking the stage, knows who he will throw, or be thrown by, and when."[78] Edouard Nytram, French amateur champion in 1908 and 1909, later turned professional, exposed some of the performance-based, cooperative holds used on the music hall stages: "The execution of a 'bridge,' allowing the wrestler to keep his shoulders off the floor, showed that, unless supported, it was easy to overturn."[79] With a minimum of effort and maximum of sham, wrestlers aimed to arouse enthusiasm: "Wrestlers pulled faces, let out violent groans, huffed and puffed, but in reality they were as relaxed as you who were watching them."[80] The fights did not last long, and troupe managers would often designate which moves would end matches. Conversely, genuine wrestling bouts went on for hours, and the public grew tired of interminable grappling in which each combatant tried to execute a standing hold. The bouts were decided by strength, with limited appeal to casual spectators.[81] To casual fans, mat wrestling was particularly boring. Fénélon de Bordeaux, referee for amateur and professional championships, stated that "there is no limit for the duration of a fight on the ground which is sometimes abused."[82] Interest turned increasingly to a more spectacular style, emanating from Great Britain and the United States: "catch as catch can." Wrestlers could use their legs to push, lift, grasp, or perform different scissor holds,[83] and both upper- and lower-body holds were allowed, including ankle twists and arm locks.[84] Leg holds, banned in Greco-Roman wrestling, made it possible to perform extravagant moves such as the "crotch lift,"[85] which allowed an opponent to be lifted and thrown to the ground. A new sporting practice had arrived with this "freestyle" wrestling.

"Catch as catch can" was featured at the 1904 Olympic Games in St Louis, where only Americans participated in wrestling. The style was also used at the London games in 1908. It was not, however, on the bill for Sweden in 1912 (no boxing either), because officials from different countries failed to agree on which moves were allowed or prohibited,[86] unlike in Greco-Roman wrestling. The first generation of catch wrestlers could easily perform their spectacular moves in cooperation. With catch, the line between professional showmanship and pure amateur sport was blurred. Predetermined matches, performed at fairs and on casino stages, drew professional wrestlers attracted by the promise of easy money.

In November 1913, a catch-as-catch-can tournament billed as the "championship of champions" was staged at the Nouveau Cirque de Paris. The Pole Stanislaus Zbyszko, introduced as "the iron man with 52cm biceps,"[87] appeared as one of the main contenders to win the tournament. But the fights were fixed. The journal *La Vie au Grand Air*[88] published a letter by Maurice Deriaz reporting on the tournament, which took place at Bordeaux, while some of those very same wrestlers were in action in Brussels. He described in minute detail how the bouts unfolded, as well as the small print of the contracts the wrestlers had to sign. These encounters held the public interest, because they put on stage two emblematic figures: the straight-up good guy against the devious and dodgy baddie. The outcome was an exercise in imaginary justice, because this type of fight always pitted the "complete bastard" against the hero,[89] and it was the latter who usually won despite his opponent's dirty tricks. Breaking the rules was desirable, because it enraged spectators who appeared to believe in the pantomime. A myth, that is to say a story, in the sense of Roland Barthes, recounted an imagined order to which everyone relates according to their expectations and socio-cultural background. If, in the middle of the 19th century, the stage shows of Rossignol-Rollin presented a depiction of the classical heroes, did not the catch model showcase the world of doubt, or even disorder? A new image seemed to develop based on a challenge to the standards of the hero: his supremacy is not acquired, even if the outcome is a foregone conclusion, and the way in which it is achieved is as important as the result. Catch subscribed to this path, which modern sport has not yet really followed, in creating a largely imaginary champion overcoming adversity but not yet social injustice.

The Institutionalization of Competition Wrestling: A Stake in the Domination of the Sporting Field

It was in the trendy gyms of the capital that, during the *Belle Epoque*, a form of amateur wrestling sprang up which would influence its development as a sport. In 1902, the 500 members of Stade Français (created in 1883) obtained from Paris authorities the use of the magnificent gymnasium in Rue Huyghens every Thursday: "on an immense red carpet laid on a bed of sawdust the wrestlers learned their craft under the enlightened direction of François le Bordelais."[90] In fact, a split was occurring between Greco-Roman wrestling, which espoused the values of amateur sport, and the freestyle catch wrestling practiced by the professionals. Paschal Grousset who prefaced the work of Léon Ville, *La Lutte Française*, under the pseudonym of Philippe Daryl, warned against professional wrestling and its excesses: "it is necessary for wrestling to stop being a vulgar game at funfairs to become again a real sport, clean, elegant and polite."[91]

Even while the professional Greco-Roman style was still predominant, Pierre de Coubertin was promoting an amateur version.[92] For the first Olympic Games of the modern era in 1896, he introduced "Roman and Greek wrestling." This definition upheld the wish to return to the myth of Olympia, but the inversion of Roman and Greek no doubt reflected Coubertin's desire not to confuse the Olympic activity with the fairground exhibitions taking place at that time. Only five entrants, none of whom were French, took part in the competition. A single tournament was held with one weight category. The winner was not a trained wrestler, but the German gymnast Schumann, who also won the pommel horse and parallel bars events. Wrestling was not included in the second Olympics in Paris in 1900, because it was difficult to arrange an amateur event in the capital of professional wrestling.

Nevertheless, in 1905, the first French amateur Greco-Roman wrestling championships were held under the aegis of the *La Vie au Grand Air*[93] newspaper. Organized in three weight categories, it streamlined the process of making wrestling a sport by breaking with the "all in" ethos which reigned among professionals. In this tournament, wrestlers were grouped according to their professions (casual laborers, porters, butchers, mechanics, factory workers, grocers). In 1909, the amateur Greco-Roman championships were still being organized by *La Vie au Grand Air* and, for the first time, the magazine *La Culture Physique*, thereby illustrating Edmond Desbonnet's influence.[94] The professor of body culture denounced the flabby bodies of the professionals, contrasting them with those of the amateurs, who posed on the pages of the newspaper, displaying bulging and sharply-defined muscular physiques.[95] The amateur practice developed a body aesthetic based on health and moral values, rather than performance and spectacle.

However, contrary to Anglo-Saxon sporting practices (including football/soccer) which were arriving in France at this period and were characterized *inter alia* by increasingly precise regulations, wrestling matches still occurred under vague rules. Allowed or prohibited holds, the method of achieving victory and the awarding of points, and duration of fights, were frequently subject to variation (and negotiation). Therefore, in the 1909 tournament, matches had no time limits, and the heavyweight final went on for two and a half hours.[96] This illustrated the need for a governing body to oversee the sport.

On February 14, 1912, USFSA sanctioned the French Boxing Federation (FFSB), founded in 1903 by Albert Bourdariat, Frantz Reichel, Van Roose, and Paul Rousseau, to regulate wrestling. A commission was tasked with appointing an organizing committee, with Frantz Reichel, secretary general of USFSA, at its head. The launch of a professional boxing federation at the same time, under the direction of Léon Sée, editor of the *La Boxe et les Boxeurs* journal, partially explained this situation. This organization was in competition with the FFSB. The creation of a wrestling commission, as with the National Sports Committee in 1908 and the Olympic and Sporting Committee in 1911, were part of the problematic return to the sports movement by a Parisian and media middle class.[97] To this end, they were quick to organize the French championships for Greco-Roman wrestling with professionals at Wagram Hall in April 1912, while purporting to be staunch defenders of amateur sport.

Wrestling, particularly active in the north of France, was part of a working-class heritage that preferred the freestyle form. At the end of the 19th century, there was limited recreation for miners and other laborers after work. These men looked to exercise their physical talents for leisure. Wrestling took place standing up and involved a direct and manly attack on the opponent to knock him off balance. Wrestling's success in northern France was equally due to its proximity to Belgium and Germany, countries with a strong tradition of valuing the practice of wrestling.[98] As in France, wrestling expanded in the second half of the 19th century in the colliery centers, and matches were organized along the Rhine basin.[99]

Rougher, working-class wrestling (including catch) found itself in opposition to the Greco-Roman style, with its more strict code of rules, backed by Parisian promoters. However, at the beginning of 1913, two regional leagues (Nord-Pas-de-Calais and Pyrénées) and that of Paris were amalgamated, leading to the constitution of an official autonomous federation on April 25. Frantz Reichel remained honorary president. The number of weight categories was increased and the rules were continually refined in collaboration with the international federation.[100] Freestyle wrestling, which banned dangerous catch moves (such as ankle twists and arm bends), was predominant because it appeared more open and more varied than the Greco-Roman style. It thus became a popular spectacle, and the number of professionals increased rapidly. Frantz Reichel resigned the following year due to match-fixing.[101] Other amateur championships were attempted on the initiative of the French Weightlifting Club with the support of the newspapers *La Vie au Grand Air, La Santé par les Sports and la Culture physique*.[102] But wrestling (particularly catch) would continue to be confused with the professionalism and showmanship.[103] The practice of wrestling, from then on, was fairly low key in that it was not supported by elite social classes, who wanted to maintain wrestling as an amateur discipline.

In the end, this ambivalent situation revealed the benefits of power, of course, but also the relationship between the different physiques on display in wrestling's various forms. The body culture that developed in purely competitive wrestling was in some ways a hybrid. It introduced, in the freestyle form, techniques that were no more difficult to perform in their combination of movements than those performed in show fights and catch. On the other hand, wrestling emphasized a certain body aesthetic based on the more limited techniques of Greco-Roman wrestling, placing the emphasis on physical effort and amateurism. But the pure displays of strength in Greco-Roman contests, which appealed to the growing Parisian middle class, did not capture the imagination like catch/performance wrestling, which attracted a larger (and much more working-class) audience due to its dramatic elements and showmanship.

Conclusion

Wrestling in France experienced many ups and downs before achieving recognition as a sport. First practiced by fairground entertainers in the Greco-Roman style as street theatre and sideshows, it gained ground in France during the second empire to the point that it could be featured in increasingly larger venues. Following the appearance of new physical cultures promoting the organized sports (gymnastics, cycling, etc.), wrestling suffered something of a decline. Between 1885 and 1890, it experienced a revival. Physical bulk and static grappling were discarded in favor of a spectacle of strength and movement, attracting different social classes. During the Belle Epoque, wrestling became a sport due to this professionalization of the spectacle and also through its commercial promotion as a healthy practice. The Greco-Roman style, still practiced in the more exclusive gymnasiums, promoted the use of controlled strength and more modest, though no less powerful, bodies. Elsewhere, wrestling briefly shed its image as a means of self-defense in favor of the (short lived) ju-jitsu craze, which promised victory through the mastery of seemingly mystical techniques rather than sheer physical strength. The image of the strong man evolved. If the expansion of freestyle wrestling was propagated by certain sections of the working class, which valued unbridled strength as something that threatened the establishment, the Greco-Roman form had the support of middle-class individuals, business, and media, who were captivated by the evenly-matched, competitive contests. Legitimate, competitive wrestling, rooted in these tensions, became a pawn in the struggle to control and regulate the sporting domain. The creation of the freestyle wrestling federation in 1913 provided an opportunity to regulate and limit the practice. However, neither Greco-Roman or freestyle wrestling attracted the attention of the public at large, who continued to favor catch pro wrestling, with its more spectacular performative elements.

The story of competitive wrestling is thus the result of this plurality of practices and performances that did not conform to the image of a single style, emanating only from the lowest social classes.[104] It demonstrated at the same time not only an evolution in the expression of strength, but also a particular situation which France had cultivated. Its evolution illustrated the evolution of "controlled" and "uncontrolled" strength propounded by Norbert Elias in relation to sport. Catch pro wrestling offered a synthesis of the various styles of wrestling popular in the late 19th century. Strength, whether static or in motion could be put on display in catch matches. But more importantly, mythological imagery became a key characteristic of catch. Certainly, from the ancient Greek myths to those of the masked man and villain losing against the good guy, an evolution has taken place. However, fundamentally, are these narratives not designed to inspire dreams and transcend reality by evoking the timeless story of man respecting or defying the gods? But the latter, transformed and disguised, have come down from Olympus and now do their work in the sporting arena.

NOTES

1. Jean-Jules Jusserand, *Les sports et les jeux d'exercices dans l'ancienne France* (Paris: Plon, 1901).
2. The ancient form allowed attacks on the legs.
3. Jean-François Loudcher et Jean-Nicolas Renaud, *Education, sports de combat et arts martiaux* (Grenoble: PUG, 2011).
4. References in 54 issues of the journal *La Vie au Grand Air* (1898 to 1913) covering wrestling in a total of 117 pages. Thirteen revues carried a cover illustration relating to wrestling and 24 carried a wrestling-related headline.
5. "Marseille won 500 francs for winning against Arpin," *L'Illustration*, March 20, 1852, 192.
6. Jean-François Loudcher, *Histoire de la savate, du chausson et de la boxe française: d'une pratique de rue à un sport de compétition (1797–1978)* (Paris: L'Harmattan, 2000).
7. Jean-François Loudcher, "Identité de l'EPS et identité nationale : une réflexion historico-épistémologique autour de la notion de culture corporelle comme enjeu de mondialisation," in Jean-François Loudcher, ed., *Education physique et sport dans le monde contemporain* (Besançon : A.F.R.A.P.S., 2011), 15–46.
8. Pierre Arnaud, *Le corps en movement* (Paris: Privat, 1981).
9. Aurélie Epron, *Histoire du gouren (XIXe-XXIe siècles): l'invention de la lutte bretonne*, thèse de doctorat en STAPS, Université Rennes 2, 2008.
10. "Propriétaires de cafés, estaminets et autres établissements publics, situés dans le ressort de la Préfecture de Police," in "1.D'interdire tout chant politique ou immoral," Police Ordinance, November 17, 1849. Archives de la Préfecture de Police de Paris (A.P.P.P), DB101.
11. *L'Illustration*, April 8, 1853.
12. *Le Sport*, Wednesday, May 7, 1856.
13. Fioravanti, "L'Histoire de la Lutte," *La Vie au Grand Air* 166 (November 17, 1901), 678.
14. Fioravanti, "L'Histoire de la Lutte," 678.
15. Jules Vallès, "Portrait de Carcassone dit le Barbare," *La Chronique parisienne*, n. 2 (1858).
16. "Wrestling-Prohibition of This Type of Spectacle in the Seine Department," Circular of May 31, 1859, A.P.P.P., *Recueil Officiel des circulaires émanées de la Préfecture de Police*.
17. Jean-François Loudcher, Christian Vivier, and Michel Herr, "Michel Foucault et la recherche en histoire de l'éducation physique et du sport," *STAPS* 38 (October 1995), 7–17.
18. Arrêté Ministériel, March 19, 1851, A.P.P.P., DB104.
19. Letter from the prefect to the minister of the interior, Paris, February 5, Archives Nationales (A.N.), F21–1160.

20. Letters from March 22, April 2, and April 19 1851, A.N. F21-1160.
21. "Gymnastique, Saltimbanques, Luttes de Gymnastique," Circular, May 31, 1852, A.P.P.P., DB105.
22. Jean-François Loudcher, "Le gymnase du sport Lecour (1853–1854)," in Jean-François Loudcher and Christian Vivier, eds., *Le sport dans la ville* (Paris: L'Harmattan, 1998), 273–284.
23. Loudcher, "Le gymnase du sport Lecour (1853–1854)."
24. Loudcher, *Histoire de la savate*.
25. Léon Ville, *Lutteurs et gladiateurs* (Paris: Tolra, 1895), 174–75.
26. From the eyewitness account of H. Renault, during the session of August 22, 1872 at Boulogne-sur-mer, Louis Vigneron died in the performance of what made him famous, the "cannon": "Alas the poor promoter had been largely ignored: there were barely 20 of us. He desperately needed it to be a success because the facilities were quite modest, poor even. A few planks laid on the sand, a tatty canvas to keep the sun off and a few rickety metal benches." *L'escrime*, April 16, 1882, 200–1.
27. Léon Ville, *Lutteurs et Gladiateurs* (Paris: Tolra, 1895), 148.
28. Andrieu, *L'homme et la force; des marchands de la force au culte de la forme*, 200–8.
29. Loudcher, *Histoire de la savate*.
30. Frédéric Loyer, *Histoire de la Lutte et du Catch en France* (Caen: Les Presses Universitaires de Caen, 2010).
31. *Manuel de gymnastique*, approved by the War Ministry, July 26, 1877 (Paris: Imprimerie Nationale, 1877). Jean-François Loudcher and Christian Vivier, "Les manuels de gymnastique et d'éducation physique officiels et officialisés (1869–1931)," in Jean-Paul Clément and Michel Herr, eds., *L'identité de l'éducation physique scolaire au XXème siècle* (Clermont-Ferrand: A.F.R.A.P.S., October 1993), 311–27.
32. A workman's daily wage was two francs in the mid–19th century and around ten francs by the beginning of the 20th.
33. Paul Pons, first world champion in 1898, winner of the "golden belt" several times and the Paris tournament, was the perfect example of a worker who climbed the social ladder through wrestling. This young blacksmith learned "open-hand" wrestling at Bordeaux in a bar frequented by dockers. He lived in poverty and performed in the fairground booths to augment his income. He then left Bordeaux for Marseille and then Paris, where he appeared at the Neuilly and Nation festivals as well as the Foire du Trône, before managing a small gym in the Avenue des Tilleuls. Fioravanti, *La Vie au Grand Air* 218 (November 15, 1902), 777.
34. *La Vie au Grand Air* 17 (December 1, 1898), 196–98.
35. Paul Pons, *La Lutte et les lutteurs* (Paris: Lafitte et Cie, 1903), 25.
36. Léon Ville, *La lutte et les lutteurs* (Paris: Rotshschild, 1891).
37. Pons, *La lutte et les lutteurs*.
38. Léon Ville, *La lutte française arrangée pour exercices d'ensemble* (Paris: Société des Athlètes Français, 1885), 3.
39. Ville, *La lutte française*, 17.
40. Ville, *La lutte française*, 15–16.
41. Ville, *La lutte française*, 11.
42. Ville, *La lutte et les lutteurs*.
43. *Le Petit Journal Illustré*, March 31, 1895.
44. *La Vie au Grand Air* 498 (April 4, 1908), 223.
45. *La Vie au Grand Air* 66 (December 17, 1899), 160.
46. Philippe Tétart, *Les Voix du Sport. La Presse Sportive à la Belle Epoque* (Biarritz: Atlantica, 2010).
47. *La Vie au Grand Air*, May 1, 1899, 428.
48. *L'Illustration* 2921 (February 18, 1899), 106–10.
49. "La Lutte à Paris—La 'Ceinture d'Or,'" *La Vie au Grand Air* 218 (November 15, 1902), 776–77.
50. Andrieu, *L'homme et la force*.

51. The link between the superhuman and the Nietzschian philosophy of quest for power developed at that time is obvious.
52. *Les Sports à Paris*, December 13, 1897.
53. Christian Vivier and Jean-François Loudcher, "L'Image de la femme sportive existe-t-elle?" in Guido Laurent and Gianni Haver, eds., *Images de la Femme Sportive* (Geneva: Georg Editeur, 2003), 239–54.
54. *Le Vélo*, December 13, 1899.
55. *Le Vélo*, December 13, 1899.
56. From 1847 to 1869, the number of establishments increased nearly four-fold while the population of Paris did not even double. Andrieu, *L'homme et la force*, 115.
57. Gilbert Andrieu, *L'homme et la force, une histoire de la force à travers des pratiques corporelles commercialisées au XIX*^{ème} *siècle*, Doctoral thesis, Université de Paris, 1987, 627–36.
58. Léon Ville, *La lutte française arrangée pour exercices d'ensemble* (Paris: Société des Athlètes Français, 1885), *La lutte et les lutteurs* (Paris: Rotschild, 1891), *La lutte française* (Paris: L. Breton et C*^{ie}*, 1891), *Lutteurs et gladiateurs* (Paris: Tolra, 1895).
59. Joseph Charlemont, *L'Art de la Boxe Française et de la Canne* (Paris: Chez l'auteur, 1899).
60. *La Vie au Grand Air* 326 (December 8, 1904), 998.
61. *La Vie au Grand Air* 337 (February 23, 1905), 146–148.
62. Louis Veron, *Mémoires d'un bourgeois de Paris* (Paris: C. de Gonet, 1853), 34.
63. On this subject one can refer to the very clear description given by Christian Pociello on the change of the paradigm towards the science of movement. *Etienne-Jules Marey, Georges Demeny, La Science en mouvement (1870–1920)* (Paris: PUF, 1999).
64. Gilbert Andrieu, "Du gymnase au stade ou de l'hygiène esthétique à la compétition sportive," *Science et motricité* 12 (1991), 3–15.
65. Edmond Desbonnet, *Les rois de la force* (Paris: Librairie Athlétique, 1910).
66. Joseph Charlemont, *L'art de la boxe française et de la canne*, 121–33.
67. Aaron Freundschuh, "New Sport in the Street: Self-Defence, Security and Space in Belle Epoque Paris," *French History* 20 (2006), 424–41.
68. Michel Brousse, *Les Racines du Judo* (Bordeaux: Presses Universitaires de Bordeaux, 2005), 81–133.
69. Fioravanti, "Comment on travaille un bras au Japon," *La Vie au Grand Air* 378 (December 8, 1905), 1029.
70. Fioravanti, "Comment on Travaille un Bras au Japon," *La Vie au Grand Air* 378 (December 8, 1905), 1029.
71. *Le Sport Universel Illustré*, January 14, 1906.
72. Edmond Desbonnet, "Comment je fis découvrir le Jiu-Jitsu à Paris. Comment après une vogue extraordinaire il fut délaissé" *La Culture Physique* 584 (December 1938), 357–61.
73. Julia Csergo, "Extension et Mutation du Loisir Citadin, Paris XIXe Siècle et Début XXe Siècle," in Alain Corbin, ed., *L'avènement des loisirs* (Paris: Seuil, 1995), 149.
74. Desbonnet, "Comment je fis connaître le ju jitsu à Paris. Comment après une vogue extraordinaire il fut délaissé," 357–61.
75. *La Vie au Grand Air* 375 (December 8, 1905).
76. *La Vie au Grand Air* 535 (December 12, 1908), 454.
77. *La Vie au Grand Air* 538 (January 9, 1909).
78. Jacques Mortane, "Les Truquages dans le Sport—La Lutte," *La Vie au Grand Air* 591 (January 15, 1910), 40.
79. Mortane, "Les Truquages dans le Sport—La Lutte."
80. Mortane, "Les Truquages dans le Sport—La Lutte."
81. Frédéric Loyer, *Histoire de la Lutte et du Catch en France* (Caen: Les Presses Universitaires de Caen), 2010.
82. Fénélon De Bordeaux, *La Lutte* (Paris: coll. Sport pour tous, 1903), 12.
83. Employing the legs in the execution of different "scissors" moves in possible: "head hold with the legs, squeezing the face between the legs and a body scissors."
84. *La Vie au Grand Air* 544 (February 20, 1909), central page.

220   Part III. Culture and Modernity

85. *La Vie au Grand Air* 544 (February 20, 1909), 117.
86. Raïko Petrov, *100 ans de Lutte Olympique* (Budapest: FILA,1997).
87. *La Culture Physique* 212 (November 1, 1913).
88. *La Vie au Grand Air* 822 (June 20, 1914).
89. Rolland Barthes, "Le Monde où l'on Catche," in Roland Barthes, *Mythologies* (Paris: Seuil, 1957), 19.
90. *La Vie au Grand Air* 181 (March 2, 1902), 141.
91. Léon Ville, *La Lutte Française*, 16.
92. Raïko Petrov, *La lutte olympique à travers les millénaires* (Budapest: FILA, 1993).
93. Pierre Lafitte, founder of *La Vie au Grand Air* in 1896, also founded *L'Auto-Vélo* (Frantz Reichel, chief editor). Lablaine Jacques, *L'Auto-Vélo* (Paris: L'Harmattan, 2010).
94. Through the association of these two publications, a single vision of body culture and modern sport, conceived by Edmond Desbonnet, Pierre Lafitte, and Frantz Reichel, emerged.
95. *La Vie au Grand Air* 533 (December 5, 1908), 539 (January 16, 1909), 542 (February 6, 1909).
96. The regulations evolved in 1912, to a period of one hour, then two periods of 20 minutes alternating between standing moves and floor moves. The duration of the fight is now three two-minute rounds with a thirty-second interval between rounds.
97. Jean-François Loudcher and Eric Monnin, "Aux Origines de l'Institutionnalisation du Comité National et Sportif," in Michaël Attali and Natalia Bazoge, eds., *Diriger le sport* (Paris: CNRS, 2012), 21–36.
98. Wrestling remained a important activity in Germany and Switzerland since the second half of the 19th century. Allen Birmann, *Manuel de lutte libre* (Vevey, Suisse: Loertscher et fils, 1876). The original edition in German was published by librairie H-R Sauerloender at Aarau in 1870.
99. *Cinquante ans de lutte gréco-romaine et de lutte libre dans la FILA* (Lausanne: FILA, undated), 30.
100. It transitioned from an instant fall (shoulder blades touching the floor) to a controlled fall (first one, then three seconds). The increase in the number of values would allow the development of standing moves.
101. Jacques Mortane, "Our Colleague Frantz Reichel Quickly Took Pains to Distance Himself from This Shambles," *La Vie au Grand Air* 820 (May 6, 1914), 512.
102. *La Culture Physique* 215 (December 13, 1913), 21.
103. Loyer, *Histoire de la Lutte*. In 1951, the affiliation between professional and amateur wrestling was banned and the French Wrestling Federation became truly amateur.
104. Jean-Paul Clément, *Etude Comparée de Trois Arts Martiaux: Lutte, Judo et Aïkido* (Mémoire pour le diplôme de l'Institut national du Sport et de l'Education Physique, 1980).

Part IV. Wrestling and Media

"I couldn't carry a tune in a bucket"
Music in the Memphis and Mid-South/UWF Professional Wrestling Territories and the Transformation of Southern Political Culture, 1958–1987

Christopher L. Stacey

In 1983, WWF owner Vincent K. McMahon found a perfect opportunity to link professional wrestling with the national music and celebrity culture. "Captain" Lou Albano, a heel manager in the WWF, teamed up with Cyndi Lauper, an enormously popular pop singer who made regular appearances on the cable television station Music Television (MTV). Linking Albano and Lauper was just one of many strategies McMahon utilized to transform the World Wrestling Federation (now World Wrestling Entertainment) into the most dominant wrestling promotion in the country. Before Vincent K. McMahon introduced what would become the "rock and wrestling" promotion to meld professional wrestling, television, music, and entertainment, the Memphis (encompassing large portions of Tennessee and Kentucky and officially referred to as Continental Wrestling) and Universal Wrestling Federation (UWF, formerly Mid-South Wrestling, encompassing Arkansas, Louisiana, Mississippi, and Oklahoma) wrestling territories allowed their wrestlers to produce music to promote their characters, gimmicks, and promotions.[1] Although both Memphis and UWF did much to preserve kayfabe, the illusion of "realism" within the business, the incorporation of music served as a precursor for what the wrestling business would become in the modern era.[2]

The Memphis and UWF territories served as perfect models for McMahon to emulate in incorporating music and entertainment in building his sports entertainment empire. The changing role of music in the Memphis and UWF territories reflect the changes in politics and culture in the South from the 1950s through the 1980s. In the 1950s and 1960s in Memphis, an undercurrent of anti-authoritarian youth culture simmered in a cultural milieu that served as the impetus of the Civil Rights movement. The emergence of rock and roll in the city of Memphis helped spur a preexisting interest in professional wrestling, allowing for the growth of a symbiotic relationship between musical artists, record companies, and the wrestling business.

By the early 1980s, most professional wrestling promotions had incorporated music into their shows. However, the UWF and Memphis regions no longer had the synergetic relationships with the music industry that they possessed in the '50s, '60s, and '70s. Instead, both promotions emulated what was hip, popular, and relevant to their respective territories. The nation, particularly the South, began embracing a form of political and cultural conservatism that formed the basis of the Reagan revolution in the 1980s. The use of music in UWF territory was regional and insular in nature. The Fabulous Freebirds tag team reflected this apparent subtle shift in the history of professional wrestling in the South. Their gimmick and ring entrance was based on the musical group Lynyrd Skynyrd and represented the populist, working-class angst of Southern whites who eventually became integral to the Reagan revolution. By the early 1980s, Vincent K. McMahon's New York–like World Wrestling Federation had begun its process of buying out its territorial competition. Besides taking advantage of cable television, McMahon forged a partnership with several popular rock and roll figures successfully integrating music, cable television and professional wrestling. The Memphis and UWF territories were torn asunder as a result.

In the 1950s and 1960s, Memphis emerged as one of the premier musical entertainment cities in the United States. Some of the biggest names in music cut records and performed in Memphis, including Elvis Presley, B.B. King, Jerry Lee Lewis, and Johnny Cash. Professional wrestling in Memphis was inundated by counter-cultural elements in rock and rhythm and blues in the South, contributing to what would become a large-scale Civil Rights Movement. The connections between music and wrestling in Memphis linked producers and musicians, and wrestlers seeking to break into the wrestling business through music, or attempting to become musicians to enhance their wrestling careers.[3]

Sputnik Monroe (born Roscoe "Rocky" M. Brumbaugh) personified the future of wrestling and sports entertainment and the undercurrent of restless youth culture in the South in the 1950s and 1960s associated with the music scene in and around Memphis. Jim Cornette, a well-known manager and booker who got his start in the Memphis territory recalls: "It was only natural that a man with this much notoriety against the establishment would be wrestling's version of Elvis Presley with the blacks and the high school boys—look through a lot of Memphis high school yearbooks from 1959, '60, or '61 and you'll see teenage guys with white streaks in their hair—and that kind of appeal sold records." Monroe also became involved in the integration of the city of Memphis after local officials arrested him socializing with his African American friends (fans) in a local Memphis "Negro" café. After his arrest, he enlisted the help of a local African American attorney, Russel Sugarmon, to defend him and call attention to the oppression of segregation. Monroe thus became a central figure in the history of the integration of Memphis and became one of many sports figures in the 20th century important to the African American struggle for civil rights.[4]

Like many others who wrestled in the Memphis territory in the '50s, '60s and '70s, Monroe understood the entertainment aspect of the business and took full advantage of it. Monroe knew the founder of Sun Records, Sam Phillips. Phillips was responsible for signing some of the most popular and nationally-renowned names in music, including Elvis Presley. Presley even dated a female wrestler in the territory, Penny Banner, and performed multiple times at the Ellis Auditorium, then a hub of numerous events in the territory. Through Monroe, Phillips, and, of course, Elvis, the Memphis Territory became known for its "rock and wrestling" well before Cyndi Lauper, Music Television, and Vincent K. McMahon. The Memphis territory became identified with wrestling and wrestlers' use of music to the extent of producing it themselves because of the proximity and connection with the burgeoning record industry in Memphis.[5]

The relationship between Sam Phillips and Monroe typified the outrageousness of the business of professional wrestling and music. As a heel (bad guy character) wrestler, Monroe wanted to "draw heat" (garnering anger and ire from wrestling fans) any way he could. Thus, he and Phillips hatched a plan for Monroe to draw heat using a gimmick involving Phillips' freakishly-muscular 12-year-old son, Jerry. Monroe had Jerry Phillips train a bit with the midget wrestlers in the territory and then took him to bars, restaurants and other public places in the Memphis area, with a cigar in his mouth, claiming he was a midget wrestler. The angle worked so well for three years that an angry, deranged fan in Bentonville, Arkansas pulled a knife on Monroe and the younger Phillips, so Phillips' parents logically ended the charade.[6]

Like many other stars who wrestled in the Memphis Territory from the 1950s through the 1970s, Monroe cut a record. His lack of a singing voice did not matter. "Getting over" (spurring interest of the fans to attend matches or watch wrestling on television) with fans mattered most for Monroe. In an interview before he died, Monroe confirmed that he took up singing to further his wrestling career: "I was always inspired by music, but I couldn't carry a tune in a bucket." He recorded several songs in November 1959 with Peak

Records, located conveniently on the corner of 2nd and Beale streets, down the street from Ellis Auditorium, the same venue where Elvis performed regularly, even singing occasionally at wrestling cards. Monroe's wife asked him quite bluntly who would purchase any record he made; he responded "nobody," but told her it might further his wrestling career.[7]

Monroe was so lacking in musical talent that he "spoke" in one of the tracks. Like most wrestlers who made music in the Memphis Territory, he tried to draw heat (getting over as a bad guy, or heel) via music. The logic made sense through the lens of the wrestling business: getting over, wrestling, and creating a heel gimmick was much easier to accomplish, thus most songs that came out of the Memphis Territory were to push heel wrestlers or draw heat. The concept for the song "Sputnik Monroe Hires a Band" was Monroe as leader of a band hired to play rock and roll, but he ends up berating them for being too "country and western." One by one, Monroe "runs off" the band members. This song likely was created to elicit ire from the more "traditional" fans who liked country music and thought rock music was too edgy or was corrupting the youth of America. Several other wrestlers in the Memphis Territory cut records to advance their careers in the ring, including Jackie Fargo, Jerry Lawler, Jimmy Hart, Jimmy Valiant, Len Rossi, and Ploughboy Frazier. Underscoring the importance of the relationship between wrestlers and the recording industry, Jackie Fargo parlayed his friendship with Eddie Bond into several records. Bond had toured with Elvis, Johnny Cash, Roy Orbison, and Carl Perkins, and was eventually inducted into the Rockabilly Hall of Fame.[8]

One notable star from the Memphis territory broke into the wrestling business after a successful career in music. Before he became a heel manager in the mid–1960s, Jimmy "The Mouth of the South" Hart was a member of The Gentrys, best known for their 1965 hit "Keep on Dancing." Hart attended high school with the other "King" of Memphis, Jerry Lawler, who broke into the business because of his artwork. Like Lawler, Hart entered the business doing something other than wrestling or managing. In 1979, Hart was asked to write a promotional song for Jimmy Valiant, one of the biggest stars in the Memphis Territory. His first significant role in wrestling was as a manager for Jerry Lawler; both men bonded over the fact that neither man drank or did drugs. Hart remained involved in music during his wrestling career in Memphis. As late as 1979, he was still doing cameo appearances with his old band, The Gentrys.[9]

Like Jerry Lawler, Jimmy Hart also cut a record while he was involved in the wrestling business. Intentionally or not, he drew some legitimate heat and criticism in 1982 for his song "We Hate School," a campy song about disliking the schoolteacher and loving rock music. The song garnered some unwanted *real* criticism for promoting an anti-educational message—so much so that Hart felt obliged to do a bit of damage control in an interview: "We don't want anybody to drop out. Everybody needs an education. It's just that it gets so boring. That's all we're saying." The criticism and Hart's response reflect the concern to preserve kayfabe, the illusion of realism in the business that endured in Memphis in the early 1980s while Vince McMahon was actively reconceptualizing wrestling as "sports entertainment." The backlash from the song also reflects changes in Southern culture between the 1960s and 1980s. In an already parochial region re-embracing political and cultural conservatism, pushing the envelope to appeal to young people was not as accepted as it had been in the 1960s or 1970s. To make amends with his critics, the ever-prescient Hart seemed to recognize this transformation in Southern culture in the same interview: "What's funny ... is that we're about as straight as a bunch you'd find anywhere. If a guy were to light a joint in our car, we'd stop and make him get out. We can't afford it. It wouldn't just effect [sic] us, but a lot of people who have spent time and money on us, and to whom we owe some appreciation...."[10]

While Jimmy Hart's first love was music, Jerry Lawler, the undisputed "King" of Memphis Wrestling, broke into the business because of his love of art. As a teenager, he got a job working in a local grocery store. He started drawing pictures on posters to help the store promote its specials (and to get away from bagging, as Lawler explains in his autobiography). Eventually, Lawler began drawing caricatures of wrestlers and brought them to wrestling events at the Ellis Auditorium. Someone at the auditorium convinced him to send a few to Lance Russell, host of the Channel 13 Memphis wrestling show.[11]

Lawler got his chance to make an impact in the business through a television appearance. Beginning in the 1950s, like many other territories (but especially Memphis) nationwide, the wrestling business benefited from wider exposure through television. In fact, commentators Lance Russell and Dave Brown became legends in their own right as hosts of the local wrestling show in Memphis.[12]

Russell and Brown showed a few of Lawler's drawings on the air; eventually Russell called Lawler and asked him to send the station more drawings of wrestlers. Lawler kept sending in drawings of various wrestlers for several weeks until Russell invited him to come in the studio to talk about them. At age seventeen, Lawler appeared on Channel 13 to discuss his artwork. Lawler credits his high school art instructor, Helen Stahl, for potentially launching his art career by getting him a full-scholarship at Memphis State University (now University of Memphis). Despite getting a full scholarship and being drafted for military service at the height of the Vietnam War, Lawler already had his foot in the door by supplying the promotion with his artwork and running errands for Jackie Fargo, one of the Memphis territory's biggest stars.

Eventually, in 1970, Lawler got his shot as an in-ring performer and launched his wrestling career.[13]

Like Monroe, Hart, and other mentors and peers, Lawler cut a record in 1977 to garner more attention and in this case, more heat. Lawler described the impetus for producing the song "Bad News": At the time I was doing a lot of trash talk on TV, talking like Elvis and insulting everyone around Memphis. I was pretty well hated." Lawler then recounted that he sold 20,000 45 rpm records of "Bad News" at matches; fans would buy them just to break them. Jim Blake, who helped produce and promote Lawler's records, encouraged such behavior by suggesting fans to buy two copies: one for listening, one to break. Lawler was well aware of Jimmy Hart's success with The Gentrys, so he also performed in a few Beale Street nightclubs and the Memphis Music Festival to promote the song and, by extension, himself.[14]

Jim Cornette confirms Lawler's success at drawing heat through his song: "Lawler was 27 at the time and already one of the top box office attractions in the sport for almost five years due to his dominance of the Memphis market, which was due to just what he does here: bragging. He did the best and most believable smart-ass, school bully promos ever in wrestling, and here he sets his bragging to music." Lawler's producer, Jim Blake, had hoped to begin a rivalry with Elvis to draw even more heat, but Elvis died soon thereafter. Through his death and musical martyrdom, Elvis cemented himself as the real King of Memphis before a potential rivalry with Lawler could begin.[15]

In 1977, "Handsome" Jimmy Valiant, one of the most popular professional wrestlers in the Memphis Territory, produced a hit song, "Son of a Gypsy." Valiant became one of the hottest babyfaces (or wrestling good guy) in Memphis, and his path from heel to babyface had much to do with the catchy rock song he cut as his introduction to the territory. The original plan for Valiant was to portray himself as a flashy, arrogant, self-confident, self-deluded heel from New York City who would feud with Lawler for the Southern Heavyweight Championship. Considering the prevalence of regional pride which still existed in the South, along with a healthy hatred of "Yankee" outsiders, the gimmick should have worked.[16]

Instead, Memphis wrestling and its fans embraced the song and, by proxy, Jimmy Valiant. With the help of Jimmy Hart, Valiant promoted the tune to disc jockeys in Memphis, particularly those at WMC-FM 100, one of the largest rock stations in Memphis. The song became so popular that the fans failed to respond negatively to Jimmy Valiant as a heel, even after several matches with the popular Lawler. Sensing the fans' love for both Valiant and his catchy song, already playing regularly on several local radio stations, bookers in the Memphis territory dropped initial plans for the feud and made Valiant a babyface. Until Valiant, no wrestler had produced anything resembling a local or national hit record, so "Son of a Gypsy" therefore represented the first time a song really helped a wrestler "get over" (become popular) in the Memphis Territory. The song combined catchy guitar riffs with lyrics that helped the offbeat and flashy Valiant connect with fans. After several wrestlers produced musical duds that largely failed to advance their wrestling careers in any meaningful way, Valiant found some funky magic in "Son of a Gypsy"; it spoiled a planned wrestling angle, but help him become a babyface star who rivaled Jerry Lawler's popularity in Memphis.[17]

"Exotic" Adrian Street typified both where professional wrestling had been and where it was going. Debuting after Gorgeous George and before Goldust, Street was neither the first nor last professional wrestler to create a gimmick challenging traditional gender and sexual stereotypes. His persona relied on the stylistic outrageousness of many fashion, music and cultural trends in the 1980s. Born in Brynmawr, Wales, Street ran away from home and a possible lifetime as a mineworker when he was just 16 years old. Wearing women's attire, make-up and a kaleidoscope of colors, including plenty boas and feathers, Adonis drew heat by prancing, preening, and skipping around the ring blowing kisses to fans and his opponents alike. Adonis wrestled in several territories, including the AWA, Southwest Championship Wrestling, the WWF, and Mid-South. Despite his effeminate gimmick, Street was known as one of the toughest—and best—workers in the business. In an age that saw the resurgence of conservatism and the moral majority, Adonis created the perfect blend of cultural, social and sexual elements of his gimmick which was simultaneously hip and infuriating—a perfect recipe to get much-needed heat and attention of fans who could not ignore him.[18]

Street had a transcendent cultural appeal in wrestling in the 1980s. In 1986, he released an album, *Exotic Adrian Street and the Pile Drivers—Shake, Wrestle N' Roll* (Burger Records), featuring such heat-seeking tunes as "A Sweet Transvestite with a Broken Nose" and "Sadist in Sequins." Although the "glam sham" look and sound, made famous by David Bowie and his "Ziggy Stardust" persona, informed Street's cultural influences, one of his earliest recollections of music and rock and roll came from Elvis Presley and the Memphis music scene: "I loved Little Richard, Chuck Berry, Jerry Lee Lewis, Buddy Holly, Fats Domino, The Platters, The Everly Brothers and all the rest, but even then as far as I'm concerned, ELVIS WAS THE KING." Lastly, Street's persona, including overtones of homoeroticism, homosexuality, and transgender identity allowed him to acquire more heat, especially in the South. Like many other professional wrestlers and angles in the 1980s, it tapped into contemporary political controversies—in this case, how the Reagan administration was handling the AIDS epidemic and conflicting perceptions about homosexuality and the gay rights movement in general.[19]

The Fabulous Freebirds, recognized now by many in the business to be one of the best three-man tag teams in wrestling history, also utilized music in building their gimmick. The Freebirds, formed in 1979, consisted of Michael "PS" (Purely Sexy or Prissy Sissy) Hayes, Terry Gordy, and Buddy Roberts (Jimmy Garvin later replaced Roberts). They debuted in Dallas-based World Class Championship Wrestling (WCCW), but also appeared in the WWF, Mid-South, and World Championship Wrestling (WCW), among others. According to Jay Ambler, the Freebirds also were the first tag team to enter and depart the ring to music.[20]

From the outset, the Freebirds recognized the connection between music, wrestling, and popular culture. The team chose its moniker from a song of the same name by Lynyrd Skynyrd, a group that represented Southern, working-class angst. Their wild-eyed Southern boys gimmick paralleled the emergence of the band Lynyrd Skynyrd; before making their own rock song and video, they came to the ring to the Skynyrd tune "Freebird." Because of changes in the nation's political culture, their gimmick was more emulative than ground-breaking. With rock and roll well-established and widely accepted nationally in by the late 1970s, the Freebirds' appeal was confined to the largely-conservative South. In the 1960s and 70s, using rock and roll in wrestling often challenged long-held traditions and represented counter-cultural elements of American society.[21]

In 1984, Michael P.S. Hayes wanted the Freebirds to make a music video. Perhaps attempting to copy Vince McMahon's recent effort to mix rock and roll and wrestling in promoting the WWF, Hayes, then wrestling mostly for the UWF, did the same. Mixing music and wrestling was not new, but creating a song and music video for cable television was novel. Like past wrestlers who made music (Valiant, Blassie, etc.), the Freebirds hoped their video would advance their wrestling careers. Hayes recalls that it was "quite an ordeal" to convince Terry "Bam Bam" Gordy to participate and that "we did it for us." To convince the hesitant Gordy, Hayes told Gordy that making music was "natural" for the Freebirds: "Terry, we ride up and down the road, okay, we listen to the same Lynyrd Skynyrd tape, we throw down some beer and a couple other things...." Hayes clearly recognized the connection between the music and wrestling businesses.[22]

In 1983, the Fabulous Freebirds released their song, "Badstreet USA" with the help of Jimmy Papa at Grand Theft Records. The song was a gritty, soulful rock tune that claimed the Freebirds were tough guys from the "mean streets of Atlanta." Four years later, Michael Hayes produced a full album that failed to make any impact beyond wrestling fans. Furthermore, "Badstreet USA" failed to embrace the obvious regionally-based "redneck" gimmick that defined the Freebirds. By the 1970s, the definition of "redneck" had changed to the extent that many Southerners embraced the term to express post-civil rights frustrations with the growth and influence of the federal government.[23]

The gimmick translated well enough for the Freebirds to remain popular in the South; the song was tailor-made for their most famous feud, with the Von Erichs in WCCW. The Von Erichs were part of a wrestling family whose identity revolved around the real-life triumph and tragedy of a family-run wrestling organization. The handsome, athletic Von Erich brothers wrestled in WCCW, an organization run by their father, Fritz Von Erich (Jack Adkisson), and were perfect rivals for the Freebirds; although *also Southerners,* Hayes, Roberts, and Gordy were viewed by Dallas fans as outsiders from Atlanta. Like so many of their predecessors, the Fabulous Freebirds enjoyed most of their success not as musicians, but as wrestlers; their involvement in music stemmed from a desire to reach more fans. Unlike their predecessors in the Memphis territory, however, the Freebirds' involvement in the music industry was neither counter-cultural nor novel. Furthermore, the emergence of the Freebirds occurred concomitantly with Vincent K. McMahon's successful efforts to take his promotion national through cable television and pay-per-view events, imitating a pattern already utilized in the Memphis territory by linking wrestlers with national celebrities and musicians.[24]

In 1986, the Freebirds found another three-man tag team as a perfect foil in the UWF, and the incorporation of music was again integral to selling the feud. "Cowboy" Bill Watts, owner of the UWF, involved himself in several six-man tag team matches with various partners, including Terry Taylor, "Hacksaw" Jim Duggan, Ted DiBiase, against Eddie Gilbert, various Russian wrestlers, and the Freebirds. The various six-man tag team matches were hyped through Watts' hyper-nationalistic promos, further emphasized by use of the Bruce Springsteen hit "Born in the USA" as entrance music. Watts obviously understood the changes in American politics and culture in the 1980s; he hoped to take the UWF national and challenge Vincent K. McMahon's rapidly growing WWF juggernaut, but his effort ultimately failed, partly because it was ill-prepared to transition a regional (and Southern) promotion to a national audience.[25]

The incorporation of popular forms of entertainment occasionally raised the ire of both wrestlers and fans preferring a more "traditional" presentation of wrestling. In late 1970s Memphis, fans and one wrestler in particular raised the time-honored question surrounding wrestling: the possible declension of kayfabe. The conflict over kayfabe and the health of the business, particularly regarding the quality of wrestling versus its entertainment aspects, resonates with fans, wrestlers, and promoters alike.

In January 1978, the *Memphis Press Scimitar* ran several articles about the frustrations of a fan whose views represented some who were displeased with the direction of Memphis wrestling. David Jones, a 28-year-old truck driver, expressed his frustrations with the "put-up stuff" and "sham" in wrestling, participating in an impromptu fan protest at an event that caused $1,200 worth of damage to several glass doors at the Mid-South Coliseum. At first glance, Jones seems caught up in the show and oblivious to the pre-planned, choreographed nature of the business: "The referees must be dumb and blind if they can't see and hear all the junky stuff. If they can't hear or see, they need to get new referees." Jones even brought his ire to Memphis city officials by staging a more formal protest by frustrated fans, calling for the Mayor to launch an investigation of the incident.[26]

Underscoring the vague line between perception and reality in wrestling, Jones reveals his awareness of the choreographed or worked nature of professional wrestling: "There's a lot of sham and put-up stuff in wrestling, I guess we know it ... but we become followers and we like the entertainment. But we want it to be on the level. When we are promised something, we want that to happen." Jones went on to explain his awareness of the entertainment aspect of the show, but claimed: "If you see a man beat in the face with (a) chain wrapped around the other wrestler's fist and another guy smashes a wrestler senseless with a crutch—and both victims show up the very next Monday night without a bruise or a cut—you figure they're a couple of fakes or they are just $6 million dollar men using bionic parts." He further claimed that while serving in Vietnam, "I put on wrestling matches in camp for entertainment. We'd draw straws to see who's [sic] arm would be stuck to draw blood. We put blood in capsules that we hid in our hands. During a match we'd smash them on each other. It looked bloody and brutal but it was just for entertainment." For a professional wrestling fan, Jones' sentiment is timeless—cognizant of the worked nature of pro wrestling, his displeasure stemmed from the lack of believability that some attributed to the entertainment aspect of the business, claiming that he wanted to see "some good wrestling again." Jones understood the choreographed nature of the show, but was concerned about the declension of kayfabe.[27]

Jones was not alone in his frustrations with the seemingly-inevitable transition from wrestling to sports entertainment; bookers, announcers, and even wrestlers themselves noticed the changes entertainment brought to the business. Lance Russell, the voice of Channel 5 and Memphis Wrestling, remarked bluntly in 1978 that "there are too many guys in the business today who can't wrestle." Such concerns led the Memphis promotion to begin a camp to train young, aspiring professional wrestlers.[28]

A year earlier, Mario Galento, aka Bonnie Lee "Butcher" Boyette, an aging professional wrestler, had been training young wrestlers in the territory. Galento wrestled in several territories, including Memphis, in the 1950s, 1960s, and 1970s. In 1977, the *Memphis Press Scimitar* ran an article in which Galento lamented the lost "art" of professional wrestling. Sixty-six at the time, Galento was a living reminder of the physical demands of the business. A veteran of more than 7,000 matches, Galento boasted that his nose was broken seven times and his ears resembled cauliflowers, a time-honored physical feature among both boxers and wrestlers.[29]

Like David Jones, Lance Russell, and other fans critical of the growing importance of entertainment in the wrestling business, Galento criticized the decline of the quality of the wrestlers and the wrestling. On one occasion, he told his students "who were watching some TV wrestling, that I'd give them $1 for every real submission hold they saw. I had 12 guys there, and I had a stack of 50 one-dollar bills.... I'd had them for about four months. And they sat there and watched for a whole hour, and at the end of it I still had my $50 in hand." He also became annoyed when a handful of students praised the work of Jerry Lawler and Jackie Fargo. To Galento, Fargo and Lawler represented the direction of professional wrestling in the late 1970s, increasingly featuring more entertainment than wrestling. The piece further highlighted Galento's dedication to a seemingly dying craft, noting his dabbling in karate, judo, and sumo as a means of improving his performance.[30]

Galento, like others involved in a business in transition, recognized the growing influence of entertainment in professional wrestling, but was concerned about its effect on kayfabe. He noted that "I'm not knocking wrestling ... it's not wrestling they do now. I *am* praising the show that they're doing." According to Galento, by the 1970s, the transition from wrestling to sports entertainment was already well underway. The aging, traditional grappler, though recognizing the powerful draw and influence of popular forms of entertainment in pro wrestling, concluded that it was degrading the in-ring ability of wrestlers. Like his contemporaries who used music in hopes of advancing their wrestling careers, Galento appeared in two movies at the peak of his career, *Frontier Woman* (1956) and *Natchez Trace* (1960). Both movies failed to attract any significant attention from critics, and it is unclear whether Galento's appearances in these films had any impact on his wrestling career. The fact remains that even one of the more "traditional" wrestlers, who criticized the decline of quality wrestling and kayfabe, recognized the growing importance of incorporating elements of popular entertainment into the wrestling business.[31]

By the 1970s, new forms of entertainment and technology changed the business of professional wrestling. Although always incorporating elements of drama and choreography from the outset, the advent of rock and roll, with its rebellious elements, offered wrestlers, especially heels, new ways of generating interest in their characters. The incorporation of new forms of music allowed some wrestlers to tap into changing attitudes regarding civil rights in the 1960s and 70s, and working-class populist angst of Southern whites by the 1980s. The Memphis and Mid-South territories were the epicenters of utilizing these popular forms of entertainment to advance their promotions. Ironically, the same forces that propelled the popularity of both promotions were also seeds of their demise. When Vincent K. McMahon utilized cable television, pay-per-view special events, and an aggressive business model of buying out the territories, he also pushed professional wrestling further into the realm of sports entertainment.

NOTES

1. See Scott M. Beekman, *Ringside: A History of Professional Wrestling* (Westport, CT: Praeger, 2006), 125, for a discussion of Music Television's (MTV) involvement in the World Wrestling Federation's promotion of its wrestlers and events. See https://upload.wikimedia.org/wikipedia/commons/a/af/NWA_Professional_Wrestling_Territories.png (accessed September 13, 2016) for a good geographic depiction of the major territories during the mid to late 20th century.

2. David Shoemaker, *The Squared Circle: Life, Death and Professional Wrestling* (New York: Gotham Books, 2013) organizes the history of professional wrestling into four eras: the Golden Era, Territorial Era, Wrestlemania Era, and Modern Era.

3. See Pete Daniel, *Lost Revolutions: The South in the 1950s* (Chapel Hill: University of North Carolina Chapel Hill, 2000), chapter seven, for an analysis of the counter-cultural elements of the music scene in Memphis and other parts of the South and its connection to the Civil Rights Movement.

4. Jim Cornette and Mark James, *Rags, Paper and Pins: The Merchandising of Memphis Wrestling* (self-published, 2013), 308.

5. Hall, *Sputnik, Masked Men, and Midgets*, 25; Cornette, *Rags, Paper and Pins*, 308.

6. Cornette, *Rags, Paper and Pins*, 311; Peter Guralnick, foreword in Robert Gordon, *It Came from Memphis* (London: Faber and Faber, 1995), 36–37.

7. Sara Hoover, "Sputnik Monroe: Wrestler … and Troubadour," May 23, 2013, http://wknofm.org/post/sputnik-monroe-wrestler-and-troubadour-0 (accessed September 14, 2016).

8. Hall, *Sputnik, Masked Men, and Midgets*, 97–104, http://www.rockabillyhall.com/EddieBond1.html (accessed September 14, 2016).

9. Jimmy Hart, *The Mouth of the South: The Jimmy Hart Story* (Toronto: ECW Press, 2004) chapters three and four; Jerry Lawler with Doug Ashville, *It's Good to Be the King … Sometimes* (New York: Pocket Books and the World Wrestling Entertainment, 2002), 165–67; *Memphis Press Scimitar*, June 15, 1979, Vertical File #582, University of Memphis Special Collections.

10. "Hart Wrestles with Music but Not His Ego," *Memphis Press Scimitar*, April 4, 1982, Vertical File #582, University of Memphis Special Collections.

11. Lawler, *It's Good to Be the King … Sometimes*, 48–49.

12. Beekman, *Ringside*, 81–83; http://m.bleacherreport.com/articles/1326770-wwe-wcw-etc-why-lance-russell-belongs-in-any-top-5-commentators-list (accessed September 14, 2016).

13. Lawler, *It's Good to Be the King … Sometimes*, 48–57.

14. Lawler, *It's Good to Be the King … Sometimes*, 165–66.

15. Cornette, *Rags, Paper, and Pins*, 314.

16. Scott Bowden, "Anatomy of an Angle: Mercy, Daddy! Handsome Jimmy Valiant Cuts Record, Turns Heel," http://kentuckyfriedwrestling.com/theword2/handsome-jimmy-valiant-turns-heel-feuds-with-jerry-lawler-bill-dundee-in-memphis (accessed September 15, 2016).

17. Cornette, *Rags, Paper, and Pins*, 316–17.

18. Steven Green, "Exotic Adrian Street and the Picture That Won't Shut Its Gob," *BBC News*, October 29, 2014, http://www.bbc.com/news/uk-wales-27889890.

19. Quoted in "Exotic" Adrian Street, *My Pink Gas Mask* (self-published, 2012), 202; http://burgerrecords.11spot.com/vinyl/color-vinyl/exotic-adrian-street-and-the-pile-drivers-shake-wrestle-n-roll.html (accessed April 21, 2017); Charles Kaiser, "The Real Record of the Reagans on Gays," *Slate*, March 11, 2016, http://www.slate.com/blogs/outward/2016/03/11/the_reagans_surrounded_by_discreet_gays_still_did_little_to_help_with_aids.html (accessed April 21, 2017).

20. David Shoemaker, aka "The Masked Man," *The Squared Circle: Life, Death, and Professional Wrestling* (New York: Gotham Books, 2013), 83–88, http://www.obsessedwithwrestling.com/profiles/f/freebirds.php (accessed September 14, 2016).

21. Louis M. Kyriakoudes and Peter A. Coclanis, "The 'Tennessee Test of Manhood': Professional Wrestling and Southern Cultural Stereotypes," in Harry L. Watson, ed., *Southern Cultures: The Fifteenth Anniversary Reader* (Chapel Hill: University of North Carolina Press, 2008), 356.

22. Michael Hayes, *The Stone Cold Steve Austin Show Unleashed!*, Podcast One, EP106, April 10, 2014.

23. Patrick Huber, "A Short History of Redneck: The Fashioning of a Southern White Masculine Identity," in Harry L. Watson, ed., *Southern Cultures: The Fifteenth Anniversary Reader* (Chapel Hill: University of North Carolina Press, 2008), 317.

24. Shoemaker, *The Squared Circle*, 65–81.

25. http://www.kayfabememories.com, UWF #11, 2 (accessed September 15, 2016). For example, see https://youtu.be/mbPXyoLn-uM (accessed September 15, 2016); https://youtu.be/0etdnvBmyQw (accessed September 16, 2016); https://youtu.be/nyfRl75FY7c (accessed September 15, 2016).

26. *Memphis Press Scimitar*, January 28, 1978, Vertical File #1068, University of Memphis Special Collections.

27. "Too Much 'Drama,' Too Little Wrestling, Some Say," *Memphis Press Scimitar*, January 31, 1978, Vertical File #1068, University of Memphis Special Collections.

28. "Too Much 'Drama,' Too Little Wrestling, Some Say."

29. Dan Henderson, "Relic of a Manly Art," *Memphis Press Scimitar*, September 11, 1977, Vertical File #5381, University of Memphis Special Collections.

30. Henderson, "Relic of a Manly Art."

31. Henderson, "Relic of a Manly Art," http://www.imdb.com/title/tt0048097/fullcredits?ref_=tt_ov_st_sm (accessed September 15, 2016; http://www.imdb.com/title/tt0054112/ (accessed September 15, 2016).

Pile Driving the Past
WWE '13 *and Mediating the History of WWE Through Video Games*

Andrew Baerg

"The Attitude Era" represents one of the most beloved periods in professional wrestling history. For a brief window of time, intense competition with rival wrestling company World Championship Wrestling (WCW) moved WWE to take more risks with its wrestlers, promos, and storylines. This essay focuses on the professional wrestling video game, *WWE '13*,[1] and its mediation of the so-called "Attitude Era." The paper is grounded in theory devoted to the relationship between digital games and history. It then utilizes this theory as a backdrop in analyzing how *WWE 13's* mediates this period of wrestling history. The essay then argues for some of the implications of this mediation by exploring how the game positions players to identify with the interests of the WWE as they engage the game's version of history.

Digital Games and History

Historical narratives have provided much inspiration for digital game developers over the course of the past three decades. Most prominently, video games oriented around war have made frequent use of history as a thematic backdrop against which digital battles can be fought. The very first three-dimensional first-person shooter, *Wolfenstein 3D*,[2] allowed players to fight against Nazis in an appropriation of a history-based trope that would be frequently employed in other military games in the years that followed. Additionally, some games, like those in the ever-popular *Civilization*[3] series, have employed the mediation of historical processes as a primary driver of game mechanics.

Despite the use of history as inspiration and/or source material for video games, scholars have only recently begun to consider the role of history in the digital game and its implications for how players understand this history. Some existing contributions have focused on the history game's pedagogical potential.[4] Others have concentrated on the mediation of history in specific games[5] or on the representation of prominent events like World War II.[6] Appropriate to this project, scholars have also theorized the digital game-history relationship more broadly.

One of the first to engage the question of history's relation to the video game is William Uricchio. Uricchio argues that the interactivity digital games afford players enables both medium and player to challenge the question of historical fact. Uricchio sees it as no coincidence that poststructuralist historiography arises in the same context as hypertext and video games. Both challenge older understandings of facticity and authorial control. In addition to challenging facticity and authorial control, digital games also challenge traditional forms of representation via an emphasis on simulation. Simulation allows for a degree of interactivity considerably greater than that offered in representation. This interactivity enables players to experience history as dynamic possibility rather than as ensconced past.[7]

Chapman discusses this notion of interactivity in terms of affordances games offer players as they engage history. Affordances represent the range of actions that might be taken in a situation. Digital games offer a different set of affordances in their mediation of history than more traditional representational media.[8] In many respects, Uricchio's and Chapman's discussion of video games and the affordances offered by simulation resonates with Ferguson's discussion of counterfactuals.[9] Digital games open up space for asking "what if" questions—questions which consider plausibility and probability with respect to historical events.[10]

In noting this shift away from the fixity of history via traditional representation into the possibility space of simulation, Fogu identifies virtualization as an important process that occurs in the move toward rendering history as virtual past. Digital mediation in computer and video games shifts attention away from questions related to conventional representation into an "*experience of the virtual past*,"[11] a virtualization of history. This virtualization continues a process begun by cinema in which the historical epic film provided audiences with a sense of verisimilitude in being situated within the visual space of past events. However, in being combined with the more sophisticated technologies afforded by digital media, this virtualization of the past has not only enabled an experience of what was, but also an experience of various configurations of what might have been.[12]

Where Uricchio, Chapman, and Fogu consider the implications of history and the digital game text, Rejack theorizes about the potential effects of a history-based game on the player. Rejack argues that the digital game's mediation of military history allows for players to experience a more "sympathetic identification with the past."[13] If a video game should bring together traditional primary source material like photographs and documents with gameplay, Rejack suggests that it can generate player emotion regarding a particular event or character, such as a lost soldier, in a way that ultimately legitimates the accuracy of the historical narrative. Hess sees a complimentary effect in the military game, one that potentially becomes a "participatory public memorial."[14] Hess suggests that this memorial privatizes and domesticates the past, while concurrently politicizing the future. Although this history is highly ideologically loaded, Hess sees the history-based military video game affording players historical immediacy by immersing them in a simulation of events from the past.

Elliot and Kapell also address the question of the player by reflecting on the type of engagement history-based video games offer. They suggest three ways in which players engage history. Most germane to this project are the ways in which players engage history in digital games via gameplay choices. In this respect, following from a possibility space/counterfactual perspective, players can make decisions that alter the ensuing narrative of the game. Players not only learn about historical events and people, but also about contingency and consequences. Because video games are interactive, choices inherently have effects and these effects can serve as a highly useful way for players to learn about historical processes beyond the more pedestrian details of people, dates, and events. The more agency a game affords its players, the greater the potential for understanding history as contingent. Elliot and Kapell see this form of player engagement as the most powerful way in which digital games might teach history. For them, it moves players to see history as more than a static set of facts in which one thing inevitably leads to another. Subsequently, video games allow players to participate in "constructing meanings and understanding history as a process rather than a master narrative."[15]

This essay builds on the theoretical work above by exploring how the wrestling video game *WWE '13* mediates the history of the Attitude Era for its players and then presents some implications that follow from this mediation. Before exploring how the game mediates wrestling history and speaking to the implications of this mediation, it is helpful to delineate how one might approach the video game text.

Methodology

The textual analysis of a digital game both follows from and differs from more conventional textual analyses. Like other types of textual analyses, digital game scholars focus on representational concerns attached to images, sound, and formal structures within the text. However, the digital game necessitates a move beyond representation, given the demands its text places upon the player.[16] Players must be able to recognize and respond to a game's systems in order to play the game.[17] These systems may include anything from rules determining the parameters of player activity to the varying abilities of avatars a player controls or characters the player encounters. Meaning subsequently derives from a player's interactions with these representations and the game's systems. Examining a game via textual analysis allows the researcher to carefully consider the design of a game's systems, how this design influences the meaning players may take from the game, and the kinds of values a game presents its players through representation and engagement with its systems.[18]

These elements of digital game analysis serve as the framework for this project. Following from this approach to the video game text, I have spent more than 40 hours playing *WWE '13*. The interactive nature of a digital game's meaning makes the researcher's experience an important part of the analytic process. To be sure, my experience may not be generalizable across the range of these games' players and their experiences[19] and my interaction with the game cannot make any claim to completely representing precisely what others will have seen and heard. Yet, my extensive interaction with the game is similar enough to that of others that it allows for discussion and comparison.[20] As a consequence, this kind of textual analysis provides a viable approach to understanding the meaning of the digital game and reflecting on this meaning's broader implications in culture and society. With this project, the concerns of digital game textual analysis will be directed toward the question of the game's relationship to history and address some of the implications following from this relationship.

Although a recognition of the various facets of the production and reception process can be important and enhance our understanding of new media texts like digital games,[21] this essay will concentrate on textual analysis rather than a more extended discussion of how the games are produced or how players respond to these games. The textual analysis that follows provides a detailed examination of how *WWE '13* mediates wrestling history to its players.

WWE '13 *and the Attitude Era Mode*

Since 2000, the *WWE* series of games has provided annual versions of professional wrestling simulations. Until *WWE '13*, each of the previous 13 iterations of the game focused on contemporary wrestlers with an attendant emphasis on enabling the series' players to generate matches between their favorite current stars. *WWE '13* was the first title in the series to foreground history and allocate considerable development resources to a new game mode concentrated on a pivotal period and worker(s) in wrestling history. Since the release of *WWE '13*, ensuing editions of the game have emphasized this past-present mix, with recent titles concentrating on Wrestlemania XXX,[22] a Historical Showcase mode featuring the CM Punk-John Cena and Triple H-Shawn Michaels feuds,[23] the career of Stone Cold Steve Austin,[24] and Bill Goldberg.[25] The ongoing inclusion of history-based gameplay modes in these franchise sequels speaks to the success of *WWE '13* and its mediation of history for wrestling fans. The game's initial use of history afforded players the opportunity to return to the Attitude Era of the late 1990s.

The Attitude Era mode in *WWE '13* allows players to experience important matches that occurred between August 11, 1997, and March 28, 1999. This mode traces Attitude Era history through the lens of six mini-series. These series include the ascension of the Hunter Hearst Helmsley-Shawn Michaels tag team, the explosive popularity of Stone Cold Steve Austin, the relationship between the Brothers of Destruction—Kane and the Undertaker, the rise of The Rock, Mankind's obstacle-laden struggle to the top, and select matches leading up to and at Wrestlemania XV. Each of these six mini-series is then subdivided into four to ten individual matches that together relate an overarching historical narrative. The game communicates its historical narrative of the Attitude Era in two ways: (1) textual information; (2) images and sounds either taken directly from or simulated from contemporary television broadcasts of the matches.

Textual Information

First, ahead of each individual match, the player is provided textual information about the combatants, the date of the match, its location and the show on which it appeared. A further paragraph of textual information appears beneath these details to provide context for the match to come. As an example, ahead of the February 2, 1998, match between Steve Austin and Road Dogg, the contextualizing paragraph states, "After winning the Royal Rumble, the rivalry between Stone Cold Steve Austin and current WWE Champion, Shawn Michaels, quickly escalated with this match on Monday Night Raw. In addition, this was the first time that D–Generation X and the New Age Outlaws conspired together … a sign of things to come." These paragraphs typically situate the impending match within the context of its immediate predecessor in the sequence.

More textual information is provided with a television ratings timeline that appears once the player has agreed to participate in the match. This timeline provides a graph comparing the television ratings of the WWE's

Monday Night Raw and its competitor at the time, World Championship Wrestling's (WCW) *Monday Nitro*. The timeline presents ratings for September 4, 1995, through September 4, 2000, a period the WWE has famously dubbed the "Monday Night Wars." As players work through the various matches, they see both promotions' respective ratings immediately preceding the match about to be played. As a consequence, players are not only provided context about the individual wrestlers battling in the ensuing match, but also given the slightly broader context of the wrestling industry at the time. With each victory, players move forward in time and see how the ratings battle between the WWE and WCW unfolded. The timeline provides insight into how specific matches and storylines shaped the television audience's relative interest in both promotions and the WWE's ultimate victory over its competition.

Players are not only provided context for the match they are about to play, but they are also provided with objectives. These objectives serve as the guidelines for what the player must accomplish in the ensuing match to move the game's historical narrative forward. They represent how the player might interact with the game in becoming a virtual part of history. As an example, in the September 20, 1997, match between Shawn Michaels and the British Bulldog, the player is tasked with completing one primary objective and four secondary objectives. To achieve the primary objective, the player must use Shawn Michaels and simply defeat the British Bulldog. To achieve the secondary objectives, the player must have Michaels

1. perform a diving attack off the top rope to the outside of the ring.
2. perform 2 Signature Diving Elbow Drops.
3. hit the Sweet Chin Music.
4. win by submission.

Achieving the primary objective moves the historical narrative along and unlocks the next match in the series.

Without completing the primary objective, the player's journey through the Attitude Era comes to a halt and matches further along in the history remain locked. Achieving the secondary objectives replicates what occurred at critical junctures in the match. The *Monday Night Raw* audience watching the show on September 20, 1997, did witness Shawn Michaels perform a diving attack off to the top rope, execute two of his signature diving elbow drops, hit his trademark Sweet Chin Music kick and win by submission. These secondary objectives effectively function as conventional wrestling "spots," key moments in a match that wrestlers perform to tell their intended story. Completing these secondary objectives triggers extra content that includes bonus playable matches and animated cut scenes that replicate what television viewers would have seen in watching the WWE that night. Reliving more history becomes a reward for reliving history.

Video and Audio

The textual information provides context for each match in the mode, but the second way in which this history is mediated greatly enlivens the experience for the player. *WWE '13* either directly uses video and audio of the original source television broadcasts or renders this video and audio in digitally animated form. The game employs these sounds and images from episodes of *Monday Night Raw* and WWE pay-per-view events that occurred during the period of the Monday Night Wars.

Upon entering the Attitude Era mode and selecting the first match, the player immediately experiences this televisual representation of history. The player sees the same standard definition introduction to the first match as those watching the opening video sequence to any late 90s version of *Monday Night Raw*. Flames and sparks flare in an old, abandoned industrial building as Stone Cold Steve Austin walks through it. Underneath these fiery images, pulse-pounding guitar riffs set the stage for the aggression that is to unfold. Interspersed between the flames and Austin's strutting are quick cuts to clips of other prominent wrestlers featured during the period. The introduction concludes with a crudely rendered "Raw" graphic. After having viewed this initial video sequence, the player cannot help but be positioned to step into a history that is inextricably linked to television. These types of video sequences occur preceding other featured matches throughout the Attitude Era mode.

WWE '13 also renders televised history in digitally animated form to further reinforce the player's journey into the past. *WWE '13* reproduces the most important visual details for each wrestler as accurately as possible. The combatants are represented wearing the same attire they wore for the respective matches being played. From Dude Love's tie-dyed rainbow shirt to Kane's red and black mask, each wrestler's clothing is represented with careful verisimilitude. This accurate visual representation is also carried over into the various choreographed ring entrances as well. Stone Cold Steve Austin's no-nonsense strut, The Rock's 'People's Eyebrow' and Bret Hart's giving away of his trademark sunglasses to a young ringside spectator all speak to the game's commitment to visual fidelity in its representation of ring entrances. Each wrestler's trademark moves are also included as an important element in the simulation. Whether it be Shawn Michaels' Sweet Chin Music, the Undertaker's Tombstone, or Mankind's Mandible Claw, the game allows players to deploy each wrestler's signature move(s). Only basic kicks and punches exist as generic attacks. All other moves appear unique to their respective grapplers.

This commitment to reproducing televisual fidelity is expressed in a variety of different ways. Once the wrestling action begins, players do not experience their opponent in first person perspective. Instead, every angle of vision replicates the conventional television camera angles viewers would see were they watching the match at home. The only breaks from these television camera angles occur when gameplay requires them. Further legitimation of the televisual quality of the mediation comes at the conclusion of each match. Before being taken back to the Attitude Era mode's menus, a copyright graphic appears in the lower right corner of the screen in keeping with the graphic contemporary viewers would have seen to alert them to the end of the broadcast from the late 1990s.

This fidelity to television is not only linked to what players see, but is also tied to what players hear. *WWE' 13* provides the player with audio taken directly from the source broadcasts. This audio includes dialogue from interviews and snippets of commentary from the original television presentation that would precede a given match. It also includes audio taken directly from the broadcast of the original match as well. As they play the match, players hear the same commentary from presenters Jim Ross and Jerry Lawler as they would have were they watching that night's rendition of *Monday Night Raw*. One of the more interesting examples of this audio comes from a match in which Stone Cold Steve Austin serves as ringside commentator. The player never sees Austin doing this commentary, but is alerted to his presence by the other presenters before hearing Austin speak. The virtual Austin converses with the other presenters as the player's match occurs and does so using the same dialogue the real Austin used the night of the original broadcast. Similar types of commentary occur at other points in the various matches as well. To add to the verisimilitude of sound, each wrestler's theme music loudly plays upon his entrance to the ring. These audio touches generate an increased level of immersion in the history the game offers.

The game employs video and audio directly from the WWE archives, but also mixes this material with digitally-animated versions of these broadcasts. In some instances, the televisual dialog transitions directly into an animation that provides a digitally-rendered version of what occurred. The digital version mixes the original source audio with animated renditions of what television viewers would have seen on a particular night's broadcast. Rendering the television source material in animated form blurs the effect of the narrative's unfolding. For example, the player will have been controlling a wrestler like Hunter Hearst Helmsley in a match via the conventions of digital animation. Triple H may then appear in an audiovisual sequence taken directly from an original episode of *Monday Night Raw*. He may then appear a third time in a sequence in which the dialogue and actions have been taken from the actual dialogue and actions that occurred on the broadcast, but with the visuals rendered digitally. The player ends up controlling a virtual Triple H, watching the real Triple H on the original television broadcast, and then watching the virtual Triple H cut his original promo in animated form. These types of mixing and matching of game action, original source video, and digitally-animated versions of source video occur throughout the Attitude Era mode.

Implications

Several implications follow from *WWE '13*'s structured, orderly mediation of history. Among these include the commodification of wrestling history, the way the game positions the player to identify with both the wrestlers and the company, and the significance of this positioning for the player's understanding of wrestling history through the game. Clearly, the mere presence of the Attitude Era mode in *WWE'13* speaks to how history can be and is commodified. The commodification of history has certainly occurred in other media in the past and continues with the likes of the WWE Network, but it is a relatively new phenomenon for the sports video game. This commodification presents clear benefits to the game's developers. Deploying history becomes as much about generating capital as about any earnest and serious engagement with the history of a person or event. Looking to the past becomes an additional way in which developers distinguish one annual title from the next. Adding a historical mode to a game justifies a consumer's purchase of a game that may otherwise be little different from the previous year's version. With the inclusion of historical modes, a game developer's marketing team is also subsequently given a tangible, marketable feature to attract potential buyers. Marketing history is literally written all over the game's DVD case so that potential consumers cannot help but notice its inclusion. The history of wrestling, therefore, becomes a means of creating additional content in hopes of generating greater profits.

History as commodity also connects to the challenges of licensing sport logos, athletes, and spaces. When it comes to history and sport, licensing simultaneously frees and shackles the nature of its digital mediation. *WWE'13* provides an excellent example of this dichotomy. With access to the archive of *WWE* material, the game's developers were allowed to creatively deploy these materials in ways that would not be possible without a license. To be allowed to integrate the *WWE's* source video and audio from original broadcasts into the game more effectively provides the player with a sense of the original context of reception and/or returns players to their original experience of these events. This benefit of providing context is evident throughout the experience. At the same time, licensing is also restrictive, in that it limits the types of voices the developers might draw upon in mediating this history. As stated above, the voice of history in *WWE '13* is the voice of the WWE alone. For the developers to step outside of the WWE's source material and interview other interested parties would be to potentially compromise their access to this material and their relationship with the company.

Beyond the way the game commodifies wrestling history, the way in which this history is mediated has implications for the ways in which players are positioned. At a glance, it seems curious that the developers should not simply continue a pattern of alternating the player-controlled animated match sequences and the passively-presented source material from old *Monday Night Raw* television shows. However, the rendering of televisual sequences in animated form allows the player to experience a more seamless mediation of history in the game. Even though players cannot control the wrestlers in these sequences, the scripted animated phases of the game allow the player to identify more closely with the wrestler being represented and the events happening to him. Without the scripted animated sequences, the player might be less inclined to identify with the primary figure in the sequence, given the visual differences between seeing a wrestler on television and seeing that same wrestler through a computer artist's digital rendering. In spite of game consoles' increasing move toward photorealistic graphics, a clear distinction can still be made between what a player sees on television and on a console. However, the developer's decision to render televisual material through a digital artistic rendering proves to be a successful way to engage players in wrestling history.

Via its representation of all of these details, *WWE '13*'s Attitude Era mode presents itself as part historical source material and part simulation of a historical source. However, key to the player's experience of this history is that the status of this source material never comes into question. This history is presented as the definitive, cohesive history of these events. In fact, the textual description of each match is headed by a title that declares it, "The History." Appearing as potentially innocuous, the title could be read as simple background in being "The History." However, it could also be read as a claim for the objectivity of the historical narrative the player experiences. This history is "*The* History." Apparently, there simply is no other way to relate these events. *WWE '13* claims to present us with exactly what happened in and around each of the featured matches.

Part of the reason for the definitive nature of this history comes from the narrative's point of view. Players relive this history entirely through the lens of the WWE as organization and never through any of the individuals who participated in these events or those they may have affected. The organization becomes the unspoken agent of focalization—the entity ostensibly presenting history to the player. None of the wrestlers who appeared in these matches have their voices heard unless these voices are drawn from the original television broadcasts. The player does not see additional interviews with the wrestlers that might shed light on their experiences in these matches. Additionally, none of those more indirectly shaped by these events (e.g. family members, members of WWE's rival WCW, WWE's writers) appear as part of the narrative either. The history being mediated is an organizational history through and through. The WWE's invisible hand paternalistically coaxes players along the game's timeline without any contributions from outside its company walls.

The existence of the television ratings timeline also affirms this organizational point of view. As players work through the various matches and see how the television ratings unfolded, they become complicit in serving the interests of the WWE. With the realization that the WWE ultimately won the *Monday Night Wars* against its rival, an implied cause-effect relationship is established between the matches that occurred and the WWE's ratings victory. These exciting matches occurred with the resultant effect that a larger percentage of the wrestling audience chose to watch the WWE as opposed to WCW. For the player to step into this history and become the cause that has the effect of giving the WWE this result is to position the player to identify with the company. With each replication of a match and its resulting progression of the historical narrative, players align themselves with the WWE in its ultimate conquest of rival WCW. *WWE '13* ultimately relates history from an organizational perspective.

Given these constraints, players remain very much subject to the developers' authorial control. Even as *WWE '13* offers a way to interact with a historical narrative, the game establishes boundaries around the player's experience. The player cannot proceed to different events along the timeline without completing preceding requirements. One might even go so far as to say that failing to stick to the developers' prescribed history impoverishes the player's understanding by closing off content that could otherwise potentially enrich the understanding of these events. Failing to achieve secondary objectives in a given match can cause the player to miss out on important contextual cues that help explain future events along the timeline. Even worse, failing primary objectives halts the mode altogether until that objective is completed. Failing to win a challenge leaves the player stuck on the timeline to try, try, and try again. With its linear movement through the past, *WWE '13* mediates history in keeping with Booth's category of traditional narrative reconstruction.[26] The game positions player to believe that these events could not have unfolded in any other way but the way in which they are represented here.

As a result, contrary to Uricchio, Fogu, and Elliot and Kapell, *WWE '13* provides an exception to the digital game's potential for challenging notions of historical fact and/or a furthering history as a space of possibility. Any type of poststructuralist historiography that might be conveyed through the digital game is offset by the sheer linearity of the history in the game. *WWE '13* offers timelines players must work through virtual node by virtual node. The game functions as less possibility space and more of a linear movement through a chronology of events that occurred. Any sense of contingency and its consequences is highly limited. There is no space for counterfactuals. For players to attempt to enact counterfactuals by avoiding primary objectives is to close off future matches in the mode and shut down the overarching narrative. For players to try to enact counterfactuals by avoiding secondary objectives is to experience knowledge gaps by losing out on contextually-useful cutscenes that allow for deeper meaning-making.

Consequently, the linear nature of the narrative combined with the way the narrative positions its players yields a bit of a slightly modified version of Thomas Carlyle's "Great Man" theory of history, one in which history is "the History of the Great Men who have worked here. They were the leaders of men, these great ones."[27] History in *WWE '13* is predominantly the history of the great men who led the company to success in the Attitude Era. The Rock, Triple H, Shawn Michaels, Kane, The Undertaker, Mankind, and Stone Cold Steve Austin are celebrated as the primary drivers of WWE's defeat of WCW. Without them and their leadership, the story may have been different. Although this might be expected, of the 65 matches in the Attitude Era mode, only two involve women. Trish Stratus, Lita, and Stephanie McMahon are the only women to appear in the mode. This history is about the Great Man Wrestler through and through. However, due to the way the game positions players, the Great Man concept is extended to the Great Organization. As stated above, the player's journey through the timeline is not only about individual triumphs. It is also about the triumph of the WWE. The narrative illustrates how WWE emerged victorious over arch-rival WCW and won the Monday Night Wars. Great Men contribute to the Great Organization, which itself becomes an industry leader.

Despite of the potential difficulties offered by the challenge of linear history, *WWE '13* still successfully generates Rejack's "sympathetic identification with the past"[28] via the strategies the game employs to virtualize it. The primary source material *WWE '13*'s developers have drawn upon does an excellent job of allowing the game to generate this sympathetic identification. This identification operates on two levels.

On the first level, the game's matches enable identification with wrestlers and with WWE as an organization in keeping with the discussion above. As they progress through Attitude Era matches, gamers achieve the primary objectives by controlling each wrestler with his respective historically accurate attire, theme music, and moveset. As players achieve the secondary objectives, they execute the same spots as the wrestlers who participated in these matches. Players become the Undertaker and throw Mankind off the top of the cage at their infamous Hell in a Cell match. In proceeding through the series of matches, players identify with WWE by fighting off the challenge of WCW in the Monday Night Wars. The television ratings timeline provides players with a genuine sense of their contribution to the defeat of WCW as they win each match and increase WWE's popularity.

However, perhaps more important is a second level of identification, an identification attached to fandom. Because the source material comes from WWE's television broadcasts, the experience of sympathetic identification occurs at a second level with the player's past experiences of fandom. The television footage used to transition into the matches becomes a means for players to travel back in time and experience nostalgic wrestling fandom from the late 1990s. As they work through various matches on the Attitude Era timeline, players will undoubtedly remember where they were, what they were doing, and who they were with for some of wrestling's most iconic moments. Jim Ross' astounded commentary following the Undertaker's tossing of Mankind off the steel cage, "Good God Almighty! Good God Almighty! He killed him! As God is my witness, Mankind is broken in half!" cannot help but trigger a player's memory about the event. As such, this exploration of wrestling history represents as much a journey back to experiences of players as it does the wrestlers who were part of these events. This experience of history would appear to be unique across digital games in any genre. Given that so many digital games concentrate on a more distant and impersonal historical past, few, if any, allow players an opportunity to relive their own experience of the past. *WWE 13*'s Attitude Era mode allows for this uniquely personal, nostalgic experience of history.

Because of the ways in which these two levels of identification work, the game's mediation of the Attitude Era becomes that much more effective. If players are identifying with wrestlers from the past and their actions become the mechanism for advancing the historical narrative, they partner with WWE by perceiving the narrative through the organization's lens. In addition, allowing players to identify with their previous experience of fandom makes this history personal in a way that few other games can.

Conclusion

This essay has drawn on theory addressing the relationship between digital games and history. It has used this theory as a guiding framework for the analysis of the wrestling video game, *WWE' 13,* and its mediation of the Attitude Era. The game's mediation of this period positions the player to identify with the wrestlers and, more importantly, with WWE itself. As a result, players are positioned to understand the overarching narrative of the

Attitude Era strictly through the lens of the WWE as organization, a lens that potentially limits the perspective the player might otherwise develop on the events that occurred. Despite the potential limitations the game places on this player understanding, the game ultimately offers the opportunity to travel back into one's personal past.

Although perhaps not as popular as the WWE Network and the capacity it offers wrestling fans to delve into the history of sports entertainment, wrestling video games have become one of the more popular means by which fans have come to understand and appreciate the industry's past. With *WWE '13*, Yukes, the game's developer, began a successful trend that has persisted into the present. Utilizing wrestling's past has been beneficial to the developer and popular with players. This popularity makes the potential for scholarly interventions into the space vital to the discipline, the games' respective developers, and to the players who experience them.

NOTES

1. Yukes, *WWE '13* (Osaka: 2K Sports, 2012).
2. Id Software, *Wolfenstein 3D* (Richardson, TX: Apogee, 1992).
3. MPS Labs, *Civilization* (Hunt Valley, MD: Microprose, 1991).
4. For some examples, see John Pagnotti and William B. Russell, "Using *Civ IV* to Engage Students in World History Content," *The Social Studies* 103 (2012), 39–48. Shannon Kennedy-Clark and Kate Thompson, "What Do Students Learn When Collaboratively Using a Computer Game in the Study of Historical Disease Epidemics, and Why?" *Games and Culture* 6, no. 6 (2011), 513–37. Kevin Kee, "Computerized History Games: Narrative Options," *Simulation & Gaming* 42, no. 4 (2011), 423–40.
5. See Harrison Gish, "Playing the Second World War: Call of Duty and the Telling of History," *Eludamos. Journal for Computer Game Culture* 4, no. 2 (2010), 167–80. Aaron Hess, "'You Don't Play, You Volunteer': Narrative Public Memory Construction in Medal of Honor: Rising Sun," *Critical Studies in Media Communication* 24, no. 4 (2007), 339–56.
6. For examples see James Campbell, "Just Less Than Total War: Simulating World War II as Ludic Nostalgia," in Zach Whalen and Laurie N. Taylor, eds., *Playing the Past: History and Nostalgia in Video Games* (Nashville: Vanderbilt University Press, 2008), 183–200. Eva Kingsepp, "Fighting Hyperreality with Hyperreality: History and Death in World War II Digital Games," *Games and Culture* 2, no. 4 (2007), 366–75. Eva Kingsepp, "Immersive Historicity in World War II Digital Games," *HUMAN IT* 8, no. 2 (2006), 60–89. Allison Tanine, "The World War II Video Game, Adaptation, and Postmodern History," *Literature/Film Quarterly* 38, no. 3 (2010), 183–93.
7. William Urichhio, "Simulation, History and Computer Games," in Joost Raessens and Jeffrey Goldstein, eds., *Handbook of Computer Game Studies* (Cambridge: MIT Press), 327, 332, 335.
8. Adam Chapman, "Affording History: *Civilization* and the Ecological Approach," in Matthew Kapell and Andrew B.R. Elliott, eds., *Playing with the Past: Digital Games and the Simulation of History* (New York: Bloomsbury Academic, 2013), 62–63.
9. See Niall Ferguson, *Virtual History: Alternatives and Counterfactuals* (New York: Basic Books, 1999).
10. Ferguson, *Virtual History*, 85.
11. Claudio Fogu, "Digitalizating Historical Consciousness," *History and Theory* 47 (2009), 114.
12. Fogu, "Digitalizating Historical Consciousness," 115.
13. Brian Rejack, "Toward a Virtual Reenactment of History: Video Games and the Recreation of the Past," *Rethinking History* 11, no. 3 (2007), 414.

14. Hess, "Public Memory Construction," 340.
15. Andrew B.R. Elliot and Matthew Kapell, "Introduction: To Build a Past That Will 'Stand the Test of Time'—Discovering Historical Facts, Assembling Historical Narratives," in Matthew Kapell and Andrew B.R. Elliott, eds., *Playing with the Past: Digital Games and the Simulation of History* (New York: Bloomsbury Academic, 2013), 14.
16. Tanya Krzywinska, "The Pleasures and Dangers of the Game: Up Close and Personal," *Games and Culture* 1, no. 1 (2006), 121.
17. For an extended discussion of rules and systems, see Gonzalo Frasca, "Simulation Versus Narrative: Introduction to Ludology," in Mark J.P. Wolf and Bernard Perron, eds., *The Video Game Theory Reader*, edited by Mark J.P. Wolf and Bernard Perron (New York: Routledge, 2003), 221–35.
18. Krzywinska, "The Pleasures and Dangers," 121.
19. Markus Montola, "Implications for the Study of Games," *Simulation & Gaming* 43, no. 3 (2012), 307.
20. Montola, "Implications for the Study of Games," 309.
21. Gary Osmond and Murray G. Phillips, "Reading *Salute*: Filmic Representations of Sports History," *The International Journal of the History of Sport* 28, no. 10 (2010), 1464.
22. Yukes, *WWE '14* (Osaka: 2K Sports, 2013).
23. Yukes, *WWE '15* (Osaka: 2K Sports, 2014).
24. Yukes, *WWE '16* (Osaka: 2K Sports, 2015).
25. Yukes, *WWE '17* (Osaka: 2K Sports, 2016).
26. Douglas Booth, "Sport Historians: What Do We Do? How Do We Do It?" in Murray G. Phillips, ed., *Deconstructing Sport History: A Postmodern Analysis*, edited by Murray G. Phillips (New York: State University of New York Press, 2006), 36–38.
27. Thomas Carlyle, *On Heroes, Hero-Worship, & the Heroic in History* (London: James Fraser, 1841), 1.
28. Rejack, "Toward a Virtual Reenactment," 414.

Lowland Gorilla Ballerina Acrobat
Brock Lesnar, Sherdog.com and the Perception of Professional Wrestlers Competing in Combat Sports

EVAN KARL NAGEL

Like it or not, professional wrestling and mixed martial arts (MMA) have a long and storied relationship. While many MMA purists share the sentiment that pro wrestling is a joke, the truth of the matter is that without "sports-entertainment," combat sports as we know them today would not exist. Despite numerous attempts at rewriting history, the renowned Helio Gracie, the Gracie family patriarch and creator of Brazilian jiu-jitsu, learned his craft from his brother Carlos, who was taught by Mitsuyo Maeda, a judoka-turned-professional wrestler.[1] The Ultimate Fighting Championship struggled financially until they began using professional wrestling promotional tactics to hype feuds (such as Tito Ortiz vs. Ken Shamrock).[2] Some may point to the sport of boxing as the source of UFC's promotional strategy. Most notably, their argument highlights the legendary Muhammad Ali, who popularized exaggerated showmanship in boxing in the 1960s and 1970s. Ali admitted, however, that his inspiration for this tactic came from the firsthand advice of famed professional wrestler, "Gorgeous" George Wagner.[3] Three of the first six inductees into the UFC Hall of Fame (Mark Coleman, Dan Severn, and Ken Shamrock) were former pro wrestlers.[4] One of the biggest pay-per-view draws in UFC history, Brock Lesnar, was a successful pro wrestler before his MMA debut.[5] One could even make the argument that it was this past that made him an attraction. Despite the wealth UFC has generated by utilizing pro wrestlers and pro wrestling promotional tactics, many MMA purists and pundits publicly ridicule pro wrestling. While there is a large fan overlap between MMA and wrestling, there is nevertheless a very vocal anti-pro wrestling movement among the MMA fan-base.[6]

Lesnar was often the subject of scorn due to his pro wrestling past, despite holding a 5–3 overall record and a two-year stint as UFC Heavyweight Champion.[7] Some MMA journalists, other fighters, and MMA-only fans raised questions about Lesnar's legitimacy. From his MMA mid–2007 debut to his then-final UFC fight in 2011, debates raged among the three groups about Lesnar's credibility as a fighter.[8] Through the lens of Lesnar's brief but successful UFC career, this study analyzes outsider perceptions of professional wrestling.

By examining journalist, fan, and fighter interactions on Sherdog.com, an internet hub for MMA news and discussion, this article will examine Lesnar's career. The information found on Sherdog, along with several other sources (namely UFC fighter interviews and the writings of MMA historian Jonathan Snowden) show both changing trends and steadfast constants among outsider perceptions of Brock Lesnar and professional wrestling. But before the study proper, we will briefly examine the history of MMA and the UFC prior to Lesnar's 2007 debut.

MMA Background

MMA, or mixed martial arts, was arguably invented by the UFC in 1993. Rorion Gracie, having brought his family's version of Brazilian jiu-jitsu to the United States, hoped to promote his family's product and legacy through the Ultimate Fighting Championship.[9] Initially dubbed "War of the Worlds," Gracie and advertising agent Art Davie pitched the idea of a "big tournament, a battle of styles in which the various martial arts would compete for supremacy," to emerging pay-per-view providers that typically featured professional wrestling, boxing, and pornography. One such channel, Semaphore Entertainment Group, saw a series of one-night tournaments as a potentially profitable spectacle.[10] On November 11, 1993, the first Ultimate Fighting Championship event took place in Denver, Colorado. This inaugural broadcast featured an eight-man tournament in which Rorion's younger brother Royce emerged victorious.[11]

At the time, MMA as a whole was somewhat erroneously marketed as not having rules.[12] Politicians, most notably Arizona senator John McCain, latched onto this description, deriding the sport as "human cockfighting," managing to get it banned in numerous states and dropped from several pay-per-view providers throughout the mid- to late 1990s.[13] It took new ownership (casino operators Lorenzo and Frank Ferritta), along with help from the New

Jersey State Athletic Commission and Nevada's Marc Ratner setting up standardized rules, to put "the UFC ... on the road to nationwide legitimacy," in early 2001.[14]

By this point, the one-night, open-weight tournament setup was long gone in favor of nine weight classes and heavily-hyped individual matchups. The new UFC heavily promoted the light heavyweight (205 pounds) division through fighters such as Chuck Lidell, Tito Ortiz, Vitor Belfort, Randy Couture, and an aging Ken Shamrock, who fought at many early UFC events before working as a pro wrestler for the WWF. For three and a half years, they dominated the company's main event scene, both inside and outside the octagon.[15] Ortiz's feuds with Lidell and Shamrock relied heavily on pro wrestling promotional tactics, including exaggerated, hate-filled derision of one's opponents.[16] Due to his wholesome "All-American" demeanor, Olympic pedigree (as an alternate for the U.S. wrestling team in 1988, 1992, and 1996), and being cast by fans and promoters alike as, "the perpetual underdog," Randy Couture managed to become the face of the newly revitalized company.[17] Thanks to the UFC, MMA began to earn respect and credibility as a mainstream sport. Despite its newfound success and acceptance, the company was still losing money. Its prominent stars and rivalries had not been enough to pull the UFC out of the red. The Ferrittas were now $44 million in debt, and that number was increasing rapidly. According to Snowden, "the promotion could either get on television or get out of the fight business."[18]

Two events helped rebuild the company, increasing their larger fan base. The first was the 2005 debut of *The Ultimate Fighter*. On the show, 16 fighters (eight light heavyweights and eight middleweights), were divided into teams coached either by Couture or Lidell. Two winners, one from each weight class, would be given UFC contracts. With "lose-or go home" fights occurring every episode, a new, slightly younger fan base was drawn to the colorful, polarizing personalities. The live finale featured two bouts, including a spectacular and bloody three-round battle between light-heavyweight finalists Stephan Bonnar and Forest Griffin (seen by 3.3 million viewers) that many MMA observers see as a turning point that saved UFC by introducing millions of new fans to the product. The second milestone in UFC's revival came in late 2007, when the UFC announced the signing of former three-time WWE Champion Brock Lesnar.[19]

Born on 12 July 1977, Brock Lesnar dominated athletics from a young age and was particularly obsessed with winning wrestling titles. In 2000, his final year of NCAA eligibility, he won the Division I Heavyweight championship, having finished second the year prior.[20] Shortly thereafter, Lesnar signed the biggest developmental deal in World Wrestling Federation history.[21] He made his main roster debut in March 2002. Just over a year later, he was already a three-time WWE Champion.[22]

However, his career was over relatively quickly. Simply put, Lesnar did not enjoy the wrestling business, particularly the frequent travel, and left the WWE in early 2004.[23] On April 29, 2006, he signed with K-1, a Korean-owned fledgling MMA promotion. Joining the UFC over a year later, he soon became a lightning rod for MMA fans to vent their hatred of pro wrestling.[24]

Target on His Back

In both forum threads and article archives, there is only a brief mention of Lesnar's single K-1 fight. In the one article found prior to this, his gigantic but clumsy opponent Min-Soo Kim was described as a "wet washcloth," and Lesnar was prophesied to become, at best, a "mediocre mixed martial artist."[25] The earliest forum discussion about Lesnar was from October 20, 2007, when he signed with UFC.[26] From the very start, the majority of Sherdog.com commentators questioned his legitimacy. They focused on Lesnar's chest tattoo, pro wrestling career, or how he had not proven anything with the Kim fight, all in a condescending manner.[27]

While Sherdog journalists acknowledged his 106–5 NCAA Division I record, they focused primarily on his professional wrestling career. One particular article stated, "Well, it finally happened. All you fans out there who jokingly wondered aloud how Hulk Hogan would do against Royce Gracie have been granted your wish in the form of former UFC heavyweight champion Frank Mir taking on collegiate wrestling standout turned WWE ballerina turned mixed martial artist Brock Lesnar."[28] Hulk Hogan had no background in combat sports, whereas Lesnar had been wrestling as an amateur since he was in junior high, so the comparison was far from fair.[29] The writer continued, "Besides, don't tell me you don't want to see the look on Lesnar's face when he realizes that the running lariat isn't viable in MMA." While the author did mention Lesnar's 106–5 collegiate record, he also pointed out, "That was seven long years ago, however. Lesnar has spent most of his time since then wearing uncomfortably tight underoos."[30] An anonymous Sherdog writer dissented: "A win … is something hardcore MMA fans are praying for. For reasons known only to those individuals, this fight has taken on somewhat of an 'us against them' theme, with Mir representing the truest form of real fighting while Lesnar is the personified figure of fallacy."[31]

However, "those individuals" who scoffed at Lesnar's credibility seemed to include most of Sherdog's writers, such as Mike Sloan and Steven Curtis. During a pre-fight debate, Sloan picked Lesnar to win in the second round while still mocking pro wrestling. Curtis stated, "While Lesnar scrambles around the Octagon, looking for a folding chair to hit Mir over the head with in round two, Mir will apply a triangle choke. Lesnar will look to his corner for.... Chief Jay Strongbow or anyone who might help. Roddy Piper will throw in the towel, and Brock will join ... the 'MMA ain't no joke' club."[32]

On February 2, 2008, at UFC 81, Lesnar simultaneously proved his critics right and wrong. He started the fight, "like a caged animal, knock[ing] Mir down with a punch and nearly end[ed] him on the ground." The referee, Steve Mazzagatti, broke them apart, signaling the judges to deduct a point from Lesnar for illegal punches to the back of the head. The break gave Mir time to recover. When the bout restarted, Lesnar charged forward, allowing Mir to apply a knee bar and win by submission. Lesnar admitted after the fight that he had made a "foolish amateur mistake."[33]

His forum critics were surprisingly forgiving after the fight. While many were behind Mir before the bout, one post-fight thread features those same people giving Lesnar credit.[34] Even beforehand, a few posters suggested Brock could win by "ground and pound." Afterwards, many acknowledged Lesnar's potential; for example, one poster noted, "Another 12–24 months of 6 day-a-week training and he puts Frank Mir and most of the UFCs heavyweights in the hospital. But not quite yet." Another said, "rookie mistake made against one of the best sub guys in the business. There's no shame in that."[35] Not everyone was complementary, with someone commenting, "half the wrasslin' fans in the bar didn't understand why he tapped. They just didn't get the fact their hero was moments away from not walking."[36] However, there were very few negative comments about Lesnar's pro wrestling background. Sherdog writers largely displayed newfound respect for him. One article stated, "Lesnar lost his heavily-hyped bout, of course, but the 90 seconds he was active has managed to convince the industry that he has unlimited potential."[37] The majority consensus was that he had all the right tools, but needed more experience. Mir was rewarded with a title fight against UFC interim Heavyweight Champion Antonio Rodrigo Nogiuera.[38] Lesnar moved down the card, with his next fight set for UFC 87, on August 1, 2008, against "Texas Crazy Horse" Heath Herring.[39] This fight represented an anomaly in the MMA community's perceptions of his legitimacy.

Prior to this bout, most Sherdog writers were unsure who would win. One claimed Herring would win because "it won't be long before Lesnar makes a mistake that costs him the fight."[40] Another expected Herring to "pull off the upset."[41] Most, however, refused to make a firm prediction, and few made mention of WWE. Several articles examined his training regimen. For example, Brian Knapp described Lesnar as a "real-life Incredible Hulk," and "part man, part tank," yet focused on how he and head trainer Gregg Nelson prepared for Herring.[42] Lesnar was quickly portrayed as a legitimate contender on Sherdog, despite his past. Like MMA journalists, fighters were divided when predicting the fight. An expert panel of fighters was nearly split, with nine picking Lesnar and seven picking Herring.[43] There are no pre-fight threads discussing the matchup, but a term that appeared frequently in post-fight posts was "gatekeeper": the fans essentially viewed Herring as a protector of MMA, to determine who was or was not worthy of continuing to fight in UFC.[44] The most delegitimizing comments prior to the fight came from Herring.

Lesnar was respectful in his prefight interview, stating he took the Texan seriously, particularly his striking ability and "unorthodox grappl[ing]."[45] Herring, on the other hand, treated Lesnar as a joke, claiming that unlike his opponent, he was actually a serious fighter and that "career-wise, for [Lesnar], this fight doesn't make any sense."[46] He pointed specifically to his fight against former professional wrestler Paul "Giant" Silva (in PRIDE, a Japanese MMA promotion) as proof that Lesnar's size advantage was irrelevant.[47] Silva, a former basketball player, had no prior combat experience, however, and Herring still needed three rounds to win. Snowden commented, "even watching Silva flail around for a minute or two was painful ... because it was embarrassingly unskilled and just plain bad."[48] In comparing him to Silva, Herring refused to acknowledge that Lesnar held any credibility or legitimacy. Finally, Herring declared, "This will be the final nail in the coffin as far as he is concerned."[49] Ironically, the UFC 87 clash resulted in Herring's retirement, as Lesnar broke the Texan's orbital bone seconds into the fight, and dominated en route to a unanimous decision.[50] Commentator Mike Goldberg even said that Lesnar had "shown the difference between a national champion and an actor ... someday he might be the UFC Heavyweight champion."[51] The Sherdog analysis said of Herring, "There he was, a veteran of more than 40 professional fights, battered, beaten, and bloodied by a man ... written off as a sideshow attraction ... to lure in gullible fans."[52]

Sherdog writer Jordan Breen called out fans for criticizing Lesnar's mock bull-roping Herring after the bell while applauding Eddie Alvarez performing post-fight backflips off the cage. He also mentioned Herring's insistence on being introduced second because Lesnar was "just an amateur." Breen suggested that MMA needed "good old-fashioned pro wrestling heel tactics," and that the likes of Ortiz brought the "gimmickry," well before Lesnar. It certainly did not make his victory less legitimate.[53] Forum fans were split over whether Lesnar had proved himself against Herring. One poster said, "Did you expect anything less from Lesnar? He's used to the WWE shit and is going to be an asshole."[54] Others said they could not wait for Lesnar to get "KTFO or cut like a pig"[55] because they viewed his post-fight antics as "classless,"[56] or those of a "douche"[57] and felt that the UFC should "flush this turd so he could end his career in [pro wrestling promotion] TNA."[58] One commenter dissented, "the only people who think Lesnar is a boring fighter are those that hate wrestling.... Those that hate wrestling shouldn't be watching MMA." Another said, "as a fighter, I respect Brock.... Maybe not his mouth though."⁵⁹ Despite ongoing negative reactions, MMA media and a growing number of fans were starting to view Lesnar as a legitimate heavyweight contender. UFC president Dana White decided to capitalize on his growing star power by giving him a fight against fan favorite Randy "Captain America" Couture for the UFC heavyweight championship at UFC 91.⁶⁰

Taking Captain America's Shield

Beforehand, most Sherdog writers, forum participants, and fighters considered Lesnar undeserving of a title bout after only three professional fights. On October 29, an anonymous article argued, "Many have pointed to Lesnar's lack of professional MMA experience in questioning his credentials as a worthy title contender."⁶¹ One fan said, "Nobody that's been a member for 3 or more years and posts regularly actually thinks Lesnar is gonna win."⁶² Another espoused, "even in a wheelchair I pick Randy."⁶³

The experts largely agreed with fan assessments; of 44 fighters and media members surveyed by Sherdog, 28 picked Couture. Mac Danzig said, "I think Randy wins this fight with experience and overall ability. It seems like Lesnar's best chance of winning is if he can hold someone [down] for three rounds like…. Herring. I don't think he can do that to Randy. Plus, he has a giant penis tattooed on his chest, which can't be helpful." Although he expected Lesnar to win, Stephane Vigneault claimed that a former pro wrestler winning the title would delegitimize MMA: "Lesnar [will] beat Randy and become UFC heavyweight champion after four fights; [it's] gonna be ridiculous and very bad for the sport. Pro wrestling fans [are] gonna think all pro wrestlers would beat real MMA fighters, but [the] UFC sees the [money] with Lesnar." Vigneault seemed to believe in the stereotypical image of pro wrestling fans as gullible in his assumption that they would assume untrained pro wrestlers could defeat trained MMA fighters. Overall, most who picked Couture did so because of his greater experience and history of overcoming difficult odds, with little mention of Lesnar's WWE exploits.⁶⁴

Sherdog writers were divided. Jake Rossen gave Couture even odds of emerging victorious. While Rossen praised Lesnar's speed and strength, he also joked about the challenger's legitimacy and wrestling past. Comparing Lesnar to a 700-pound black bear, Rossen argued that "fifty years on and the man vs. beast promotional hook is alive, well and coming to a pay-per-view provider near you on Saturday." He thought Lesnar's inexperience would result in, "a rear-naked choke in Lesnar's immediate future." He said that if Lesnar lost, "Alternately, he could smash a steel chair over Dana White's head."⁶⁵ Brian Knapp said the fight could go either way, and did not mention Lesnar's wrestling past.⁶⁶ Loretta Hunt pointed out that Lesnar was "a novice, with only one-fifth of the fights Frank Mir had." She made no mention of his WWE career, other than quoting Mir, who said, "If Lesnar fought a bum off the street, it'd be a marquee matchup."[67] Journalists debated whether Lesnar deserved a title shot, but pro wrestling featured very little in their analyses. The same was not true after the Couture fight.

Lesnar ultimately dominated Couture, winning by technical knockout in the second round.[68] While Sherdog writers acknowledged Lesnar as a legitimate champion, many continued to mock his pro wrestling background. Rossen said Couture had essentially fought the equivalent of a "lowland gorilla," calling the new titleholder "a former WWE acrobat."[69] In Luke Thomas' "Winners and Losers: UFC 91," column, he listed Lesnar as the biggest winner, arguing that "By capturing the most coveted position in the UFC's heavyweight class, Lesnar has more than secured himself a place as a true competitor in this league and sport."[70] However, he listed MMA fans among the "losers," claiming they would be flooded with, "the Great Unwashed ... dyed-in-the-wool professional wrestling stalwarts," echoing Vigneault's earlier sentiments. While he admitted one could be a fan of both fighting and "the camp of make-believe," his words portrayed wrestling fans as unsophisticated and unwelcome inside MMA.[71] Not all journalists viewed the potential influx of wrestling fans as bad. Jason Probst, for example, stated: "Imagine how much the sport would grow if this guy keeps improving and winning against the top names challenging him.... The biggest thing MMA has lacked has been a long-term champion that is a gravitating force to draw in new fans. The role would fit Lesnar perfectly—the Goliath that everyone wants to see fight, some to see him destroy and others to see if he can be toppled." Probst made sure, however, to classify this as a "devil's bargain," implying a sullying of spirit would result from associating with a professional wrestler.[72]

On Sherdog's forums, the few comments made post-match were rather conciliatory towards Lesnar, apart from poster Shwame's claim that "Cock chest is the worst champion ever."[73] There were not sufficient forum posts to assess fan reaction to this fight.

UFC 100

During the buildup to UFC 100 on July 11, 2009, and its heavyweight unification fight between Lesnar and Mir (who had beaten Noguiera for the interim belt), the latter attempted repeatedly to delegitimize the former. The often-abrasive Lesnar remained relatively subdued. He talked about what he learned since he last fought Mir, and his desire for revenge: "I don't dislike Frank in any way, other than he's got a win over me.... I don't like to lose."[74]

I found only a handful of negative quotes from Lesnar about Mir in the pre-fight promo package, in which Lesnar boasted, "I am the UFC heavyweight champion … the [interim] belt he has isn't even real."[75] He also said, "what a lucky way to win…. I gifted him that knee bar" and concluded by declaring, "I have zero respect for him and I'm going to win this fight."[76]

Mir on the other hand, stated, "If Brock Lesnar was never in the WWE he would never have gotten a title shot. And he knows that…. All I remember from his last time is him whimpering as I was tapping him."[77] In a Spike TV interview, he boasted that "Brock Lesnar, a man, had to ask another man [the ref], to come over to me, another man, and help him because I was about to break his leg. Yeah, and I was the one scared."[78] Mir's hyper-masculine boasts suggest that the idea of losing to Lesnar was an affront to his manhood due to the latter's past as a "fake fighter." Mir's manager filmed a video in his (the manager's) son was "playing Lesnar as a muscle-bound imbecile."[79] Mir compared Lesnar's punches to "having your little sister jump on your back and [pull] your hair."[80] Mir also accused him of being an MMA mercenary: "I fight because I enjoy fighting. I enjoy the preparation and the training and the mindset, everything that goes behind it. I don't know if we can say the same about Lesnar. If Lesnar was making $10,000, would he show up to fight?"[81] Mir added, however, that "if there's any animosity, I think probably … it's that neither one of us feels like maybe we have the same amount of respect we should have and what we want to attain right now in the heavyweight division."[82] Perhaps the Brazilian jiu-jitsu black belt had simply been playing the heel role to boost interest (and therefore pay-per-view buys) for the fight.

Prior to the second Mir fight, one finds widespread acknowledgment of Lesnar's credibility as champion among journalists and fighters. One Sherdog article proclaimed, "Brock Lesnar is everything the UFC has ever hoped for … a man built like a side-by-side refrigerator, arrogant, temperamental and with an existing, powerful brand dragged from another industry. He may be the single biggest box office draw the company has right now. And he can actually fight."[83] In Sherdog's UFC 100 preview, 19 of 27 fighters picked Lesnar to win. Veteran Billy MacDonald admitted, "I want to pick Frank Mir badly in this one, but I am going to have to pick Brock by ground-and-pound…. Lesnar won't get caught that easily this time around."[84]

Some analysts remained unconvinced of Lesnar's fighting ability or value to MMA. Despite earlier praise, Rossen declared that Lesnar "will continue to perform well against plodding heavyweights, but Mir has surprising agility…. Lesnar won't be able to resist the urge to tackle him early. It will be the beginning of his end."[85] Bill Mesi said "I like nothing about him; attitude, skill, just nothing about him makes him good for the sport," but nonetheless picked Lesnar to win the fight.[86] Most coverage ignored or barely mentioned his WWE past. One can assume fans did, however, despite a lack of extant threads in the forum archives. As Snowden explains, "His critics saw a pro wrestler who didn't understand their sport ... and, worse than being lucky, was actually good. Tens of thousands wanted to see him fight and win. Thousands more wanted to see him humbled."[87]

At UFC 100, Lesnar seemingly embraced the heel role, playing upon many purists' ongoing disdain for him. After the pre-fight instructions, Lesnar refused to touch gloves with Mir, resulting in the crowd audibly gasping. This was considered an ultimate sign of disrespect. Lesnar won in dominating fashion, with a second-round victory via referee stoppage (Lesnar was raining down punches on a defenseless Mir). As the crowd booed, Lesnar walked up to the battered, bloodied Mir and continued talking trash, forcing UFC officials to separate them. He then flipped off the crowd. In his in-cage, post-fight interview with commentator Joe Rogan, Lesnar further infuriated fans, saying, "Keep going, I love it! ... Frank Mir had a horseshoe up his ass a year ago. Tonight I yanked it out and beat him over the head with it!" Lesnar added that he was going to "hang with my friends and family ... and hell, I may even get on top of my wife tonight. Thank you, you've been great!"[88]

UFC President Dana White cornered the champion backstage and demanded a public apology. At the post-fight press conference Lesnar stated, "I acted very unprofessionally after the fight, and I'll leave it at that ... you guys ask me all the time if there's anything I can drag over from WWE, and I guess you've seen a little bit of that tonight. I'm used to selling pay-per-view tickets. Dana came back, and we had our whip-the-dog session. I screwed up, and I apologize." The fight made everyone acknowledge Lesnar's fighting legitimacy, but his post-fight actions confirmed negative stereotypes many fans had of professional wrestlers. In an interview with Sherdog, White blamed the WWE for Lesnar's outburst.[89]

"Carwin-Eating Carnivore"

One of the most vocal critics of Lesnar's "unsportsmanlike" antics at UFC 100, was Shane Carwin, a top-tier heavyweight. Days after the Mir-Lesnar bout, Carwin condemned the former WWE's superstar's behavior: "He may be a champion but he has a long way to go before he earns the respect of a champion. The fans are why we do this. Brock, this sport is not about fat paychecks and drama. It is about hard work and sacrifice for a shot to do what you did last night."[90] Rossen countered his criticism, noting that "Carwin will ... face a rather sad irony: If he goes on to face Lesnar for the belt, he will benefit considerably from Lesnar's ability—which is unmatched in the sport ... to sell a fight. And I suspect that he won't turn down a percentage of pay-per-view purchases or a bonus on principle."[91]

Carwin's condemnation of Lesnar led directly to obtaining a title shot at UFC 106.[92] One month after the match was announced, Lesnar suffered a serious case of diverticulitis, an intestinal disease. The fight was postponed indefinitely, and Carwin defeated Mir for the Interim Heavyweight title in the meantime.[93] Once Lesnar returned to full health, and a unification bout with Carwin was set for UFC 116 in July 2010.[94] The match had all the makings of a full-blown WWE rivalry, which both Lesnar and Carwin used to great effect.

Two aspects affected how the MMA world viewed the Carwin-Lesnar fight. The first related to how the combatants promoted the bout. Lesnar realized that playing the role of an arrogant, self-centered, disrespectful 'rassler would increase buyrates, which would in turn lead to a bigger paycheck. Accordingly, he called Carwin's belt "fake."[95] When Carwin replied that winning that belt was the best day of his life, Brock responded, "If that is the greatest day of your life, I feel sorry for you."[96] In the *Las Vegas Sun*, Lesnar stated, "He's a tough guy. He's undefeated, but some of the guys he's beaten aren't worthy of having on your record.... He hasn't fought anybody.... I really think he's 1–0 [as Carwin's actual record was 12–0]."[97]

He also granted several exclusive interviews to his former WWE manager and real-life best friend Paul Heyman, for the latter's website. Heyman helped hype the fight, pro wrestling-style: "The beast is less than 170 hours away from being unleashed. The gladiator will enter the Ultimate proving ground. The hunter gets to come face to face with his ... prey. The meat eater is salivating.... On July 3rd, Brock Lesnar plans on being a Carwin-Eating Carnivore. Someone say Grace before this meal. Brock Lesnar will be too busy licking his chops.... Dinner is about to be served. And all table manners will be left outside the Octagon."[98]

Carwin, a former collegiate Division II champion, prided himself on the differences in how he and Lesnar behaved outside the octagon, most notably the way they "might treat people differently. Those are the instances I spoke of."[99] Lesnar was perfectly fine playing the heel foil for Carwin, the righteous babyface and defender of MMA.

MMA insiders participating in the "Pros Pick" UFC 116 panel were particularly harsh in their assessment of Lesnar. Not only did 38 of 61 pick Carwin, but many made clear their hatred for Lesnar and what they believed professional wrestling represented. Jason von Flue said: "I'm thinking Carwin is going to beat the poop out of Lesnar in this one. Carwin has the size and power to offset Lesnar's raw size and wrestling and his lack of skill in striking. Carwin in round two by KO or TKO. The only thing that could make this better would be Cain Velasquez running in and turning this into a three-way death match. Oh, I shouldn't say that; we might end up seeing that happen on Monday Night Raw. I really could imagine the WWE doing a parody of that."

Doug Marshall said, "I think if Carwin gets him to the ground and slaps on a camel clutch [a pro wrestling submission hold], it's over. On the other hand, if Brock can get to the top and Jimmy "Superflys" him, he might squish Carwin."[100] Mesi said he chose Carwin solely because "I wish ill things to happen to Brock. There, I said it, and I feel better about it." Finally, Kit Cope expressed, "I'm thinking the same thing that most of the people I know are thinking, which is that, finally, here's somebody big enough and strong enough to get that gigantic phallic tattoo out of our faces."[101] Having largely been absent since the Herring fight, Lesnar's critics, journalists and fighters alike, once again mocked his pro wrestling background. However, both groups were largely silenced by the champion's second-round submission victory.[102]

His successful defense against Carwin seemingly brought an end to the pro wrestling-centered attacks on Lesnar's legitimacy. Loretta Hunt wrote, "It was a telling title defense, demonstrating that what the 6-foot-3, 265-pound wrestler currently lacks in striking ability, he can make up for with resilience.... Lesnar also showed a refreshing humility discussing the UFC's decision to back him with so little cage time on his resume."[103] Jake Rossen said, "Is there any question Lesnar is the number one heavyweight? This one's rhetorical: there isn't."[104]

Pro wrestling, however did not benefit from Lesnar's UFC success. Most MMA observers appeared to believe the champion had "moved beyond" his past profession. An anonymous Sherdog contributor proclaimed, "Just about everyone watching this watershed moment in heavyweight MMA history was expecting Lesnar to deliver one of his trademark braggadocio-laced interviews. Instead we got something entirely different: a humble Lesnar thanking his trainers, family and God for helping him.... The former collegiate wrestling champion even thanked his opponent."

After the Carwin fight, pro wrestling was only mentioned briefly and matter-of-factly in reference to or to delegitimize the competing product.[105] Former Olympic gold medalist (Atlanta 1996, in freestyle wrestling) and WWE superstar Kurt Angle had managed to bring an air of legitimacy to pro wrestling.[106] All Lesnar managed to prove to MMA purists was that he could fight. Nothing from his pro wrestling past was considered vital or changed MMA fans' perception of sports-entertainment, other than his ability to promote pay-per-views.[107]

Goodbye to UFC

Lesnar's next challenger was Mexican American amateur wrestling and kickboxing standout Cain Velasquez. Prior to their clash on October 21, 2010, at UFC 121, Sherdog writers treated him as a legitimate champion, as with the Carwin fight. One noticeable difference, however, was an apparently heightened respect for Lesnar among MMA insiders. In "Pros Pick," 28 picked Cain while 25 picked Lesnar, but almost everyone expressed positive sentiments about the titleholder. No WWE references were made, and many complimented his skill and "heart of a fighter," admitting that Brock had defeated top-quality competitors.[108] Such respect remained even after he lost to Velasquez via first-round TKO.[109] Despite Knapp describing the one-sided loss as "an annihilation,"[110] and Tim Leidecker describing it as "an impressive and decisive performance from Velasquez," nobody on Sherdog wanted to see Lesnar run out of the UFC.[111] Indeed, they ranked him number two in the heavyweight division despite the loss.[112] In the build to Lesnar's final UFC fight, against Dutch kickboxer and former Strikeforce heavyweight champion Alistair Overeem, many fans remained unconvinced.

While the forums again offered a lack of evidence, for the first time, readers were allowed to comment on articles. Comments on articles about Lesnar were mostly negative. Returning from a diverticulitis relapse that took him out of a match against Brazilian fighter Junior dos Santos, Lesnar was pitted against Overeem to see who would face dos Santos, who had defeated Velasquez for the heavyweight title.[113] Even before the fight was announced, vitriolic comments appeared frequently beneath Lesnar articles. Responding to an article in which White said rumors of Lesnar retiring due to diverticulitis were ridiculous, poster guestjisdo remarked, "lesnar is a complete joke ... he should have stayed with wrestling or whatever."[114]

In the comments section beneath an article entitled "A Brock and a Hard Place," numerous fans dismissed Lesnar's previous victories. Bigconanman wrote, "Who exactly has Brock ever beaten. 48 yr old ... couture, Frank Mir, who ... is a terrible wrestler. or wait, how about Heath Herring." Anon concurred, "Couture was an aging LHW who outwrestled him. Carwin beat the piss out of him before gassing. Velasquez verified Carwin's point that Lesnar cannot take a punch. Only the win over Mir was impressive." ByeByeLesnar said, "As soon as Brock gets hit one time, you will all see the Bit*h in him resurface." Amok attitude defended Lesnar, noting that "wins over mir, couture and herring mean something and everyone has to reckon [with] that." These divisive sentiments grew after Lesnar lost via TKO minutes into the fight following several stiff kicks to his liver.[115]

After the fight, Lesnar announced that he'd promised his family that he would retire from MMA if he lost. In "Lesnar Made Right Decision," Critchfield praised Lesnar's UFC accomplishments: "As a high-profile crossover from the sports entertainment business, Lesnar proved to be more than a Johnny-come-lately hoping to capitalize on his celebrity to.... Instead of being spoon-fed opponents to help build hype, Lesnar was given Mir in his Octagon debut. His least accomplished foe in the UFC ... was Heath Herring, a Pride Fighting Championships veteran with more than 40 professional bouts. Lesnar became a star, not by way of promotional smoke and mirrors but by virtue of his own talent. And while not a pioneer, he certainly helped grow the UFC brand, giving the company a bankable star that could drive pay-per-view buys."

Of the 172 responses, 58 (38 percent) not only disagreed with Critchfield's sentiments, but attempted to delegitimize Lesnar's MMA career. Shaolindo wrote, "Got a couple of wins over name guys then didn't do anything else. The only difference was he has the ufc hype behind him ... which was a complete joke." Marving_andrei agreed: "thats true, he won the title fairly and defended it many times, wait, we are talking about wwe, right?" Heyyou said, "his wwf antics, have no business in mma, PERIOD! Happy to see him finally go." Sir AC added, "It's unfortunate that despite what Lesnar was able to accomplish in his short and relatively experienced career ... he will be labeled a farce in MMA because of ... professional wrestling." Craig-Beruntz, one of the 28 percent who expressed pro–Lesnar sentiments, countered:

> No heart? The guy never grew up in the sport or had the experience others had and he stepped in against top competition. True, he should have spent a lot more time on his striking defense, but he was never given an easy fight. Despite the hate going around on this site right now, the man almost died with his disease. And does he get a tuneup like most would? No. He steps in against the K-1 World Champion ... he never had the time to learn the skills to be competitive in the long term, but you can't claim he has no heart.[116]

Despite the Sherdog media and MMA insiders giving Lesnar credit for his accomplishments, MMA-exclusive fans on the website were split in how they viewed his UFC career.

Conclusion

After returning to WWE in 2012, Lesnar often expressed his desire to return to the UFC. "I didn't want to leave the UFC on a losing streak. That's just the competitive guy inside of me." In late 2014, he began training to prepare for a potential fight, as his WWE contract was set to expire in March 2015. Instead, Lesnar signed a three-year WWE extension, claiming, "My legacy in the Octagon is over."[117] To everyone's surprise, however, Lesnar, WWE, and UFC announced an agreement on June 6, 2016, that would allow Lesnar to compete at UFC 200 in July against top-ten heavyweight Mark Hunt. Almost immediately, MMA purists on Sherdog claimed that Lesnar's WWE background made him unwelcome inside the Octagon. Criticisms of

Lesnar were by no means unwarranted, as he had not fought since 2011 and would fight the ninth-ranked heavyweight in the world.[118]

However, Hunt himself remarked, "I will send this pretender back so he can play house with the other part-timers.... Don't confuse wrestling with real fighting."[119] Betonline, a sports-gambling website that sponsors Sherdog, proclaimed: "This is easy money and we urge everyone to take full advantage of all those loony Lesnar fans while you can. Just don't go to the kitchen for a fresh beer after the bell on this fight 'cuz it might be finished by the time you get back to your seat." To be fair, many fans criticized the article's uneven reporting,[120] but Sherdog still attracted a vocal, anti–Lesnar readership. On one such thread, many comments favored Lesnar, or expressed some degree of respect for pro wrestling, but there were still plenty of anti–Lesnar MMA purists. One post read, "Lots of brock support over hunt. Also there is a movement that believes the earth is flat." Someone quipped, "Well I for one was confident Hunt would beat Lesnar until I read here that Lesnar beat The Rock in WWE."[121] Such statements represented a small minority of the whole. However, the day after the fight, which Lesnar won via decision, Sherdog writer Eric Stinton complained, "The presence of Brock Lesnar immediately evoked feelings of the age-old kissing cousins relationship between MMA and professional wrestling."[122] Little had changed since Lesnar last fought in UFC; his previous and current involvement with WWE was just as divisive.

Lesnar, due partly to his WWE past, was a polarizing figure throughout his career in UFC. However, most of the vitriol toward said past was limited both in scope and scale, never seriously hindering his MMA acceptance. Sherdog journalists only doubted his legitimacy at the start of his fight career. Prior to fighting Mir and Herring, the site's analysis based their assessments of Lesnar on his WWE background, making him an easy target for snide comments.[123] After demonstrating his potential against Mir[124] and by completely dominating Herring, Sherdog writers rarely doubted his legitimacy, and only infrequently called him a "former WWE superstar." By his late 2011 retirement, most writers applauded him for his many accomplishments despite his short MMA career. To the press, Lesnar was welcome to return to UFC whenever he pleased.[125]

Fighters and other MMA insiders were harder to convince, not just of his legitimacy as a fellow combatant, but also of the positives stemming from Lesnar's pro wrestling fame. Lesnar's first two UFC opponents, Mir and Herring, were dismissive of his chances against them.[126] With each success, more fighters acknowledged Lesnar's raw potential, despite some lamenting a pro wrestler holding the championship.[127] Even after the Carwin fight, many MMA insiders mocked Lesnar's WWE connection, even if no longer doubting his skill.[128] But by the Velasquez and Overeem fights, few joked about his "phallic tattoo" or of him utilizing pro wrestling maneuvers.[129] He had become accepted, if somewhat begrudgingly, by most of his fellow competitors.

Analysis of fan perceptions proved most difficult in this study. Prior to the Mir and Herring fights, forum threads offered ample evidence that most fans agreed with journalists' and fighters' largely dismissive views toward Lesnar. Many joked about his pro wrestling past and generally displayed little respect for Brock's fighting legitimacy.[130] However, after his first three victories, many fans expressed respect for Lesnar's raw talent and rapidly-improving skill. Unfortunately, there are no extant threads about the most pivotal bouts in establishing his legitimacy, the rematch against Mir and his title defense against Carwin. Fan outrage was mentioned in the Sherdog press after the Mir fight, but there were no direct links to or evidence of it beyond the cascade of boos in the arena.[131] The wealth of comments in response to Sherdog articles about Lesnar before and after the Overeem fight partly compensated for the earlier absence of data. These revealed a fan base deeply divided about his MMA contributions. Many were thankful for the fans he brought to MMA and for having entertaining fights. Others chose to mock his UFC accomplishments and WWE career.[132] After four years in MMA, Lesnar was just as polarizing as he was when he started. Despite his many critics, he managed to achieve a level of respect and legitimacy among MMA journalists, fans, and fighters that seemed impossible prior to his arrival.

Notes

1. Jonathan Snowden, *Shooters: The Toughest Men in Professional Wrestling* (Toronto: ECW Press, 2012), 62–63.

2. Jonathan Snowden, *Total MMA: Inside Ultimate Fighting* (Toronto: ECW Press, 2008), 458, 529–31, Kindle edition.

3. Denny Berkholder, "How Muhammad Ali's Fascination with Pro Wrestling Fueled His Career, Inspired MMA," http://www.cbssports.com/general/news/how-muhammad-alis-fascination-with-pro-wrestling-fueled-his-career-inspired-mma (accessed March 25, 2017). He said in a 1969 interview he had met the grappler in Las Vegas in 1961. Seeing that the 13,000 arena was packed to see the wrestler in action, the then-Cassius Clay asked George his promotional secret. Ali told the Associated Press, "I talked with Gorgeous for five minutes after the match and started being a big-mouth and a bragger.... He told me people would come to see me get beat. Others would come to see me win. I'd get 'em coming and going."

4. Jonathan Snowden and Kendall Shields, *The MMA Encyclopeida* (Toronto: ECW Press, 2010), 342–43.

5. Snowden and Shields, *MMA Encyclopedia*, 249.

6. Tristen Critchfield, "Viewpoint: Lesnar Made Right Decision," http://www.sherdog.com/news/articles/Viewpoint-Lesnar-Made-Right-Decision-38691 (accessed August 8, 2016).

7. Snowden, *Shooters*, 269, 274.

8. Tristen Critchfield, "Viewpoint: Lesnar Made Right Decision," http://www.sherdog.com/news/articles/Viewpoint-Lesnar-Made-Right-Decision-38691 (accessed August 8, 2016). He returned on July 9, 2016, to fight Mark Hunt at UFC 203.

9. Snowden, *Total MMA*, 52–53.

10. Snowden, *Total MMA*, 58–61.

11. Snowden, *Total MMA*, 76,82.

12. Snowden, *Total MMA*, 86–87.

13. Snowden, *Total MMA*, 215–17.

14. Snowden, *Total MMA*, 388.
15. Snowden, *The MMA Encyclopedia*, 531–34.
16. Snowden, *Total MMA*, 318–21.
17. Snowden, *Total MMA*, 69–71.
18. Snowden, *Total MMA*, 530.
19. Snowden, *Shooters*, 269.
20. Snowden, *Shooters*, 257.
21. Snowden, *Shooters*, 257.
22. "Smackdown 213," http://network.wwe.com/video/v31370751/milestone/31377099/?contentId=&contextType=wwe-show&contextId (accessed August 9, 2016).
23. Snowden, *Shooters*, 263.
24. Snowden, *Shooters*, 267–69.
25. Jake Rossen, "The MMA Education of Brock Lesnar," http://www.sherdog.com/news/articles/The-MMA-Education-of-Brock-Lesnar-7703 (accessed August 9, 2016).
26. Sherdog.com Staff, "Heavyweight Lesnar Signs with UFC," http://www.sherdog.com/news/news/Heavyweight-Lesnar-Signs-with-UFC-9597 (accessed August 9, 2016).
27. The thread has since been deleted, so I am unable to directly quote what any of the posters said.
28. Anonymous, "Apocalypse Now, as WWE Meets UFC," http://www.sherdog.com/news/articles/1/Apocalypse-Now-as-WWE-Meets-UFC-11086 (accessed August 9, 2016).
29. "Hulk Hogan," http://0362dc8.netsolhost.com/halloffamers/bios/hogan.asp (accessed August 9 2016).
30. Anonymous, "Apocalypse Now, as WWE Meets UFC," http://www.sherdog.com/news/articles/1/Apocalypse-Now-as-WWE-Meets-UFC-11086 (accessed August 9, 2016).
31. Mike Sloan, "Frank Mir's Precarious Predicament," http://www.sherdog.com/news/articles/Frank-Mir146s-Precarious-Predicament-11058 (accessed August 9, 2016).
32. Mike Sloan and Steven Curtis, "Great Sherdog Debate: Mir Vs. Lesnar," http://www.sherdog.com/news/articles/1/Great-Sherdog-Debate-Mir-vs-Lesnar-11114 (accessed August 9, 2016).
33. Snowden, *Shooters*, 270.
34. "Will Frank Mir Submit Lesnar?" http://forums.sherdog.com/threads/will-frank-mir-submit-lesnar.723050/ (accessed August 9, 2016).
35. "Will Frank Mir Submit Lesnar?" http://forums.sherdog.com/threads/will-frank-mir-submit-lesnar.723050/page-2 (accessed August 9, 2016). "Ground and pound" is a tactic, commonly used by wrestlers in MMA, that involves taking down one's opponent and battering them with punches from the top position.
36. "Will Frank Mir Submit Lesnar?" http://forums.sherdog.com/threads/will-frank-mir-submit-lesnar.723050/page-3 (accessed August 9, 2016).
37. Jake Rossen, "Five Questions in the Wake of UFC 81," http://www.sherdog.com/news/articles/Five-Questions-in-the-Wake-of-UFC-81–11158 (accessed August 9, 2016).
38. Snowden, *MMA Encyclopedia*, 292–93.
39. Snowden, *MMA Encyclopedia*, 546.
40. Anonymous, "UFC 87 Breakdown: Herring Vs. Lesnar," http://www.sherdog.com/news/articles/UFC-87-Breakdown-Herring-vs-Lesnar-13952 (accessed August 9, 2016).
41. Tim Leidecker, "Herring a Seasoned Foe for Lesnar," http://www.sherdog.com/news/articles/Herring-a-Seasoned-Foe-for-Lesnar-13973 (accessed August 9, 2016).
42. Brian Knapp, "Lesnar's Learning Curve," http://www.sherdog.com/news/articles/Lesnars-Learning-Curve-13970 (accessed August 9, 2016).
43. Mike Sloan, "Pros Pick: UFC 87," http://www.sherdog.com/news/articles/Pros-Pick-UFC-87–13949 (accessed August 9, 2016).
44. "Herring: Page 2," http://forums.sherdog.com/threads/herring.828728/page-2 (accessed August 9, 2016).
45. Brian Knapp, "Lesnar's Learning Curve," http://www.sherdog.com/news/articles/Lesnars-Learning-Curve-13970 (accessed August 9, 2016).
46. Anonymous, "UFC 87 Breakdown: Herring Vs. Lesnar," http://www.sherdog.com/news/articles/UFC-87-Breakdown-Herring-vs-Lesnar-13952 (accessed August 9, 2016).

47. Loretta Hunt "Lesnar Has Makings for Greatness," http://www.sherdog.com/news/articles/Lesnar-Has-Makings-for-Greatness-13972 (accessed August 9, 2016).
48. Snowden, *The MMA Encyclopedia*, 419. This was not said about the Silva-Herring fight, Silva's ability in general.
49. "UFC-Brock Lesnar Vs Heath Herring," https://www.youtube.com/watch?v=8jV9ZStdEtA (accessed August 9, 2016).
50. Snowden, *The MMA Encyclopedia*, 177.
51. "Brock Lesnar vs Heath Herring Full Fight Night," https://www.youtube.com/watch?v=SQfNLU8znWA (accessed August 9, 2016).
52. Anonymous, "What Waits for Brock Lesnar," http://www.sherdog.com/news/articles/What-Waits-for-Brock-Lesnar-13998 (accessed August 9, 2016).
53. Jordan Breen, "Bull Ropes and BS: 'Respect' and Fan Foolery," http://www.sherdog.com/news/articles/Bull-Ropes-and-BS-Respect-and-Fan-Foolery-13999 (accessed August 9, 2016).
54. Herring," http://forums.sherdog.com/threads/herring.828728/page-2 (accessed August 9, 2016).
55. Herring," http://forums.sherdog.com/threads/herring.828728/ (accessed August 9, 2016).
56. Herring," http://forums.sherdog.com/threads/herring.828728/page-2 (accessed August 9, 2016).
57. Herring," http://forums.sherdog.com/threads/herring.828728/ (accessed August 9, 2016).
58. Herring," http://forums.sherdog.com/threads/herring.828728/page-2 (accessed August 9, 2016).
59. Herring," http://forums.sherdog.com/threads/herring.828728/ (accessed August 9, 2016).
60. Snowden, *Shooters*, 272–73.
61. Sherdog.com Staff, "Ageless Couture Banking on Experience," http://www.sherdog.com/news/articles/Ageless-Couture-Banking-on-Experience-14953 (accessed on August 9, 2016).
62. "Sig Bet on Couture-Lesnar??? Page 1," http://forums.sherdog.com/threads/sig-bet-on-couture-lesnar.875669/ (accessed August 9, 2016).
63. "Sig Bet on Couture-Lesnar??? Page 2," http://forums.sherdog.com/threads/sig-bet-on-couture-lesnar.875669/page-2 (accessed August 9, 2016).
64. Mike Sloan, "Pros Pick: Couture Vs. Lesnar," http://www.sherdog.com/news/articles/Pros-Picks-Couture-vs-Lesnar-15167 (accessed August 9, 2016).
65. Jake Rossen, "A Brock and a Hard Place," http://www.sherdog.com/news/articles/A-Brock-and-a-Hard-Place-15098 (accessed August 9, 2016).
66. Brian Knapp, "Fighting Father Time," http://www.sherdog.com/news/articles/Fighting-Father-Time-15141 (accessed August 9, 2016).
67. Loretta Hunt, "Mir Banking on Couture Victory," http://www.sherdog.com/news/articles/Mir-Banking-on-Couture-Victory-14522 (accessed August 9, 2016).
68. Snowden, *The MMA Encyclopedia*, 547.
69. Jake Rossen, "Size Matters: A UFC 91 Postscript," http://www.sherdog.com/news/articles/Size-Matters-A-UFC-91-Postscript-15191 (accessed August 9, 2016).
70. Luke Thomas, "Winners and Losers: UFC 91 Winners," http://www.sherdog.com/news/articles/1/Winners-and-Losers-UFC-91–15210 (accessed August 9, 2016).
71. Luke Thomas, "Winners and Losers: UFC 91 Losers," http://www.sherdog.com/news/articles/2/Winners-and-Losers-UFC-91–15210 (accessed August 9, 2016).
72. Jason Probst, "The Lesnar Effect: It's Here to Stay," http://www.sherdog.com/news/articles/1/The-Lesnar-Effect-Its-Here-to-Stay-15193 (accessed August 9, 2016).
73. "Sig Bet on Couture-Lesnar??? Page 3," http://forums.sherdog.com/threads/sig-bet-on-couture-lesnar.875669/page-3 (accessed August 9, 2016).
74. Mike Harris, "Lesnar-Mir 2 More Than Strength vs Skill," http://www.sherdog.com/news/articles/LesnarMir-2-More-Than-Strength-vs-Skill-18354 (accessed August 9, 2016).

75. "UFC 100: Lesnar vs Mir II- Extended Preview," https://www.youtube.com/watch?v=3JujiuD9MrA (accessed August 9, 2016). He also referred to it a "make-believe belt."
76. "Brock Lesnar vs Frank Mir FULL FIGHT—UFC Fight Night—UFC 100," https://www.youtube.com/watch?v=Z974XiPixpQ (accessed August 10, 2016).
77. Snowden, *Shooters*, 274.
78. "Frank Mir Trash Talks Brock Lesnar & More (2009)," https://www.youtube.com/watch?v=Tc_Ua8VddNk (accessed August 9, 2016).
79. Snowden, *Shooters*, 275.
80. "Brock Lesnar vs Frank Mir FULL FIGHT—UFC Fight Night—UFC 100," https://www.youtube.com/watch?v=Z974XiPixpQ (accessed August 10, 2016).
81. Joe Hall, "Lesnar-Mir Quick Quotes," http://www.sherdog.com/blog/LesnarMir-Quick-Quotes-18287 (accessed August 9, 2016).
82. Loretta Hunt, "Mir Banking on Couture Victory," http://www.sherdog.com/news/articles/Mir-Banking-on-Couture-Victory-14522 (accessed August 9, 2016).
83. Jake Rossen, "UFC 100 Primer: Lesnar-Mir Red Ink," http://www.sherdog.com/blog/UFC-100-Primer-LesnarMir-Red-Ink-18468 (accessed August 9, 2016).
84. Mike Sloan, "Pros Pick: Lesnar Vs. Mir," http://www.sherdog.com/news/articles/Pros-Pick-Lesnar-vs-Mir-18391 (accessed August 10, 2016).
85. Jake Rossen, "UFC 100 Primer: Lesnar-Mir Red Ink," http://www.sherdog.com/blog/UFC-100-Primer-LesnarMir-Red-Ink-18468 (accessed August 9, 2016).
86. Mike Sloan, "Pros Pick: Lesnar Vs. Mir," http://www.sherdog.com/news/articles/Pros-Pick-Lesnar-vs-Mir-18391 (accessed August 10, 2016).
87. Snowden, *Shooters*, 274.
88. Brock Lesnar vs Frank Mir FULL FIGHT—UFC Fight Night—UFC 100," https://www.youtube.com/watch?v=Z974XiPixpQ (accessed August 10, 2016). He also said he would drink a Coors because (UFC sponsor) Budweiser wasn't paying him anything … while standing on top of a Bud Light logo.
89. Brian Knapp, "Update: Post-Fight Antics Dim Lesnar's Afterglow," http://www.sherdog.com/news/news/Update-PostFight-Antics-Dim-Lesnars-Afterglow-at-UFC-100–18481 (accessed August 10, 2016).
90. Snowden, *Shooters*, 276.
91. Jake Rossen, "Carwin Reacts to Lesnar Victory," http://www.sherdog.com/blog/Carwin-Reacts-to-Lesnar-Victory-18537 (accessed August 10, 2016).
92. Snowden, *Shooters*, 276.
93. Snowden, *MMA Encyclopedia*, 251.
94. Snowden, *MMA Encyclopedia*, 56.
95. "UFC 116: Brock Lesnar Pre-fight Interview." https://www.youtube.com/watch?v=BCNhEP6hD0E (accessed August 10, 2016).
96. "UFC 116: Lesnar vs Carwin—Extended Preview," https://www.youtube.com/watch?v=T9RlEtoX5Ys (accessed August 10, 2016).
97. Jake Rossen, "Lesnar Dismisses Carwin's Chances," http://www.sherdog.com/blog/Lesnar-Dismisses-Carwins-Chances-20020 (accessed August 10, 2016).
98. Paul Heyman, "Brock Lesnar Is Determined to Be a Carwin-Eating Carnivore," https://www.heymanhustle.com/carwin-eating-carnivore/2/ (accessed August 10, 2016).
99. Steve Marrocco, "UFC 116 preview: Is Brock Lesnar's blessing Shane Carwin's curse?" http://mmajunkie.com/2010/07/ufc-116-preview-is-brock-lesnars-blessing-shane-carwins-curse (accessed September 25, 2016).
100. Mike Sloan, "Pros Pick: Lesnar Vs. Carwin," http://www.sherdog.com/news/articles/1/Pros-Pick-Lesnar-vs-Carwin-25450 (accessed August 10, 2016).
101. Mike Sloan, "Pros Pick: Lesnar Vs. Carwin," http://www.sherdog.com/news/articles/3/Pros-Pick-Lesnar-vs-Carwin-25450 (accessed August 10, 2016).
102. Snowden, *MMA Encyclopedia*, 56.
103. Loretta Hunt, "No Quit in Lesnar After Shaky Opening Round, Velasquez Next," http://www.sherdog.com/news/news/No-Quit-in-Lesnar-After-Shaky-Opening-Round-Velasquez-Next-25475 (accessed August 10, 2016).
104. Jake Rossen, "FC 116 Postmortem: Lesnar's Rank Secured, Leben Hits a Double,"

http://www.sherdog.com/blog/UFC-116-Postmortem-Lesnars-Rank-Secured-Leben-Hits-a-Double-25488 (accessed August 10, 2016).

105. Anonymous, "Storylines That Emerged from UFC 116," http://www.sherdog.com/news/articles/The-Storylines-That-Emerged-from-UFC-116-25486 (accessed August 10, 2016).

106. *Survivor Series 1999—Wrestlemania XIX 2003.* network.wwe.com (accessed December 2015–February 2016).

107. Anonymous, "Storylines That Emerged from UFC 116," http://www.sherdog.com/news/articles/The-Storylines-That-Emerged-from-UFC-116-25486 (accessed August 10, 2016).

108. Mike Sloan, "Pros Pick: Lesnar Vs. Velasquez," http://www.sherdog.com/news/articles/1/Pros-Pick-Lesnar-vs-Velasquez-27697 (accessed August 10, 2016).

109. Snowden, *Shooters*, 282.

110. Brian Knapp, "Velasquez Dethrones Lesnar at UFC 121," http://www.sherdog.com/news/news/Velasquez-Dethrones-Lesnar-at-UFC-121-27716 (accessed August 10, 2016).

111. Tim Leidecker, "UFC 121 'Lesnar Vs. Velasquez' Analysis; The Main Card," http://www.sherdog.com/blog/UFC-121-Lesnar-vs-Velasquez-Analysis-The-Main-Card-27738 (accessed August 10, 2016).

112. Anonymous "Sherdog Official Mixed Martial Arts Rankings," http://www.sherdog.com/news/rankings/1/Sherdog-Official-Mixed-Martial-Arts-Rankings-27767 (accessed August 10, 2016).

113. Snowden, *Shooters*, 283–84.

114. Mike Whitman, "WHITE: LESNAR'S RUMORED RETIREMENT 'RIDICULOUS,'" http://www.sherdog.com/news/news/White-Lesnars-Rumored-Retirement-Ridiculous-35254 (accessed August 10, 2016).

115. Brian Knapp, "A Brock and a Hard Place," http://www.sherdog.com/news/articles/A-Brock-and-a-Hard-Place-38585 (accessed August 10, 2016).

116. Tristen Critchfield, "Viewpoint: Lesnar Made Right Decision," http://www.sherdog.com/news/articles/Viewpoint-Lesnar-Made-Right-Decision-38691 (accessed August 10, 2016).

117. Tristen Critchfield, "Brock Lesnar on Potential UFC Return: 'My Legacy in the Octagon Is Over,'" http://www.sherdog.com/news/news/Brock-Lesnar-on-Potential-UFC-Return-My-Legacy-in-the-Octagon-Is-Over-83801 (accessed August 10, 2016).

118. Jordan Breen, "BROCK LESNAR ANNOUNCES RETURN BOUT VERSUS MARK HUNT IN UFC 200 CO-MAIN EVENT," http://www.sherdog.com/news/news/Brock-Lesnar-Announces-Return-Bout-Versus-Mark-Hunt-in-UFC-200-CoMain-Event-106031 (accessed August 10, 2016).

119. Tristen Critchfield, "Mark Hunt to 'Pretender' Brock Lesnar: 'Don't Confuse Wrestling with Real Fighting,'" http://www.sherdog.com/news/news/Mark-Hunt-to-Pretender-Brock-Lesnar-Dont-Confuse-Wrestling-with-Real-Fighting-106093 (accessed August 10, 2016).

120. Anonymous, "Hunt vs. Lesnar: UFC 200's Best Bet," http://www.sherdog.com/news/articles/Hunt-vs-Lesnar-UFC-200s-Best-Bet-107705 (accessed August 10, 2016).

121. "R.I.P. Bork. In-shape Hunt Is Coming for You," http://forums.sherdog.com/threads/r-i-p-bork-in-shape-hunt-is-coming-for-you.3277277/ (accessed August 10, 2016).

122. Eric Stinton, "Opinion: The Time Warp That Was UFC 200," http://www.sherdog.com/news/articles/Opinion-The-Time-Warp-that-Was-UFC-200–107773 (accessed August 10, 2016). Lesnar later failed both his out-of-competition and fight night drug tests. As of this writing, his victory has not been overturned.

123. Anonymous, "Apocalypse Now, as WWE Meets UFC," http://www.sherdog.com/news/articles/1/Apocalypse-Now-as-WWE-Meets-UFC-11086 (accessed August 9, 2016).

124. Jake Rossen, "Five Questions in the Wake of UFC 81," http://www.sherdog.com/news/articles/Five-Questions-in-the-Wake-of-UFC-81-11158 (accessed August 9, 2016).

125. Tristen Critchfield, "Viewpoint: Lesnar Made Right Decision," http://www.sherdog.com/news/articles/Viewpoint-Lesnar-Made-Right-Decision-38691 (accessed August 10, 2016).

126. Mike Sloan, "Frank Mir's Precarious Predicament," http://www.sherdog.com/news/articles/Frank-Mir146s-Precarious-Predicament-11058 (accessed August 9, 2016).
127. Mike Sloan, "Pros Pick: Couture Vs. Lesnar," http://www.sherdog.com/news/articles/Pros-Picks-Couture-vs-Lesnar-15167 (accessed August 9, 2016).
128. Mike Sloan, "Pros Pick: Lesnar Vs. Carwin," http://www.sherdog.com/news/articles/3/Pros-Pick-Lesnar-vs-Carwin-25450 (accessed August 10, 2016).
129. Mike Sloan, "Pros Pick: Lesnar Vs. Velasquez," http://www.sherdog.com/news/articles/1/Pros-Pick-Lesnar-vs-Velasquez-27697 (accessed August 10, 2016).
130. "Sig Bet on Couture-Lesnar??? Page 1," http://forums.sherdog.com/threads/sig-bet-on-couture-lesnar.875669/ (accessed August 9, 2016).
131. Brian Knapp, "Update: Post-Fight Antics Dim Lesnar's Afterglow," http://www.sherdog.com/news/news/Update-PostFight-Antics-Dim-Lesnars-Afterglow-at-UFC-100–18481 (accessed August 10, 2016).
132. Tristen Critchfield, "Viewpoint: Lesnar Made Right Decision," http://www.sherdog.com/news/articles/Viewpoint-Lesnar-Made-Right-Decision-38691 (accessed August 10, 2016).

Macho Madness and the Mania ("Oh Yeaaaah, Dig It!")
Mediatization, Masculinities and Affective Memories of WWF's Halcyon Days (c. 1984–1993)

DAMION STURM

The halcyon days of the then World Wrestling Federation (WWF)[1] remain an important era in the lives of many professional wrestling fans. Between approximately 1984 and 1993, the WWF created and staged an array of successful events, presented a roster of highly acclaimed wrestlers and experienced an unprecedented period of success. Moreover, the WWF began moving away from strict adherence to kayfabe, the illusion that the knowingly hyperbolic wrestling matches could also be viewed as legitimate and unscripted "sporting contests," while maintaining and upholding this basic premise.[2] Despite its overt fabrication, the WWF's events and performers would resonate for mainstream media and large global audiences. As such, a stellar cast of heroes and villains ("faces" and "heels") provided entertainment and diverse talking points for fans enamored with these hyper-muscular men and the characters they portrayed. It is these mediated masculinities, events, and contemporary fan memories that will be examined in this essay.

Hulkamania

The rise of the WWF arguably can largely be attributed to one wrestler: Hulk Hogan. From the mid–1980s through to the early 1990s, Hogan headlined most major WWF events and gained fame in broader popular culture. More often than not, Hogan was the WWF champion, headlining seven of the first eight *Wrestlemania* events (with the exception of *Wrestlemania IV*, though its finale, a WWF championship tournament final between "Macho Man" Randy Savage and "The Million Dollar Man" Ted DiBiase, helped launch Hogan's year-long friendship, then feud with new champion Savage) and most other major events until the early 1990s. Hogan's wrestling character deployed a heroic "All American" persona, symbolizing American power and progress as he often wrestled either much-larger foes or stereotypical foreign heels.[3] Self-referencing his biceps as "24-inch pythons," Hogan literally embodied an imposing blonde, bronzed, and hyper-muscular "hulk" figure. His gimmicks included ripping his 'Hulk Rules' singlet upon entering the ring, body-slamming larger opponents, and following matches with a series of muscular poses for fans.

As crowd favorite, Hogan and "Hulkamania" helped popularize wrestling to a larger audience. Hogan encouraged his "little Hulksters" to "train, say their prayers and to eat their vitamins," while garnering large merchandise sales of "nearly any item that can carry a name, emblem, or 'Hulkster Rules' slogan"[4] across attire, action figures and teddy-bears. Of course, the performative work of other notable (un)popular wrestlers who supported or feuded with Hogan during this time were fundamental to his success and star power. In this regard, a cast of popular "faces," including "Macho Man" Randy Savage, The Ultimate Warrior, Jake "the Snake" Roberts and Brutus "the Barber" Beefcake were pitted against supposedly villainous "heels" such as "The Million Dollar Man" Ted DiBiase, Andre the Giant, Ravishing Rick Rude and the Honky Tonk Man. We will consider some of these lively, if not somewhat cartoonish and gimmick-laden, wrestling characters[5] in due course.

Wrestlemania

The WWF's national and international appeal flourished during the 1980s through its mediated exposure and creation of successful annual events. Vince McMahon had purchased the World Wrestling Federation (WWF; formerly the World Wide Wrestling Federation or WWWF until 1979) from his father in 1982 and embarked on an aggressive strategy of expansion. McMahon encroached upon other wrestling territories and recruited key wrestlers from other organizations,[6] while the media was pivotal to his plans for nationwide promotion.[7] By the mid–1980s, the WWF was getting coverage on larger broadcast networks. *Saturday Night's Main Event* was screened on NBC from 1985, usually featuring top stars such as Hogan, while both *WWF Superstars of Wrestling* and *Wrestling Challenge* were syndicated by the WWF from 1986.[8]

The latter two shows recapped key events, ran wrestler promos (interviews), introduced new talent, and provided the space to develop (kayfabe) rivalries that could feature in later matches.[9]

The creation of four "mega" wrestling events would further ensconce the WWF as synonymous with "wrestling" in the minds of many fans. First staged in 1985 at Madison Square Garden in New York City (and available via closed-circuit telecast in theaters across the United States), *Wrestlemania* drew heavily upon celebrity tie-ins, including Mr. T (of *A-Team* fame) as Hogan's tag-team partner in the main event. By *Wrestlemania III*, this annual card had mushroomed into the WWF's flagship event, largely thanks to the new medium of pay-per-view television. Three other significant, annually-run, events would also be established during the late 1980s. Alongside *Wrestlemania*, *Survivor Series* (established 1987), *Royal Rumble* (1988; pay-per-view event from 1989), and *SummerSlam* (1988) were the original "big four" of the WWF's pay-per-view events. Initially created to counter rival Jim Crockett Promotions/National Wrestling Alliance events, the "big four" solidified the WWF's national expansion and international media exposure, while generating significant revenue streams.[10] The big four events also constituted the prime space for key (kayfabe) rivalries to be resolved or intensified, or for new storylines to gain subsequent traction.[11]

Summarizing the position of the WWF at the end of the 1980s, Mazer observed,

> A stable of 75–80 wrestlers ... perform in over 1,000 live events per year—events which, according to the WWF, drew 8 million spectators in 1987 ... an estimated 20 million viewers tune in weekly to the WWF's syndicated wrestling programs ('Superstars of Wrestling' and 'Wrestling Challenge') broadcast nationwide on more than 300 channels (1989) ... the WWF takes in $200 million per year in merchandising alone. The gate last year was approximately $80 million. 'Wrestlemania V' alone took in $1.7 million.[12]

For context, it should be noted that WWF events began to dovetail after 1990. For example, *Wrestlemania VII* was moved from the Los Angeles Memorial Coliseum (100,000 capacity) to the Los Angeles Memorial Sports Arena in 1991, primarily due to poor ticket sales, resulting in a final attendance figure of 16,158.[13] Additionally, public knowledge of widespread steroid use impacted upon the WWF's popularity in the early 1990s, with McMahon, Hogan and many established stars implicated in the controversy and subsequent trial in 1994.[14]

Method

My research combines textual analysis with secondary wrestling literature to examine how the WWF era has been conceptualized, as well as to better understand how contemporary online fans make sense of and engage with representations of the WWF. The textual analysis is based upon approximately six months of observing (and occasional engaging with) WWF-themed Facebook pages specifically focused on this time period. While other pertinent archival and fan forum sites exist and, indeed, readers are encouraged to browse *Kayfabe Memories* and *Wrestling Classics* forums, the Facebook pages have been chosen given the pervasive usage of social media sites in everyday life. By focusing solely on WWF wrestling fandom, my research acknowledges a risk of reverting back to "common knowledge" stereotypes of fans. That is, such an approach can negatively represent fans as "intense" consumers of media often assumed to be somewhat obsessive, singularly-focused, duped, and overly consumeristic (see critique in my work with Andrew McKinney).[15]

Rather, fan performances can be enacted and enlivened while browsing daily social media spaces such as Facebook without, for example, marking fandom as something exceptional or extraordinary outside of other interests or hobbies.[16] Moreover, using Facebook as a fan source is a strategic attempt to reflect the ordinary and, at times, mundane ways fandom can occur across other everyday functions and tasks. In relation to the Facebook pages, these include *Hasbromaniacs—WWF Hasbro Figures & Wrestling Customs Old School, The Golden Era, WWF Old School, WWF Stars of the 80's & 90's Old School Wrestling/WWE Figures and Games, WWF The Golden Years, WWF Vintage*, as well as three wrestler-specific sites—*Bret Hart, Macho Man Randy Savage*, and *Remembering Randy Savage*. However, replication and duplication is common. Therefore, four particular sites received especial attention: *Chizzad Madness Unofficial 80s-90s WWF, Old School Pro. Wrestling Talk, Old School Wrasslin*, and *80's Mania: Reliving The Good Ole' Days of Rasslin'.* Collectively, these sites elicit and evoke mediated memories by sharing images and clips or provoking debates about specific wrestlers. For example, the sites commonly asked if a specific wrestler could be considered "hall of fame worthy" or "the greatest champion," while many sought feedback on the "greatest heel," "greatest tag-team," or provided more detailed WWF behind the scenes stories for contemplation.

Characteristically, the latter four sites tended to provide more authoritative insights and information. These sites are run by and attract what are commonly referred to as "smart" fans,[17] those who are "smart to the business" and approach wrestling as "would-be insiders."[18] Smart fans seek out insider information, "shoot interviews" (wrestlers breaking kayfabe to talk about the industry), and knowledge about the inner workings or significant "backstage" stories for wrestlers and events.[19] This stands in contrast to fans known as "marks" who, perceivably, are the stereotypically duped and populist respondents. Smart fans tend to disparage "marks" as they often "root unreflexively for the most popular faces."[20] Collectively, the WWF-themed Facebook sites provide fertile terrain to better understand smart (and mark) fan knowledge, interests, and evaluations of various elements of WWF history. By examining their public responses, interactions, and reflections, rich descriptions of personal experience and nostalgic memories surfaced regarding wrestlers and/or events that mattered to them.

Affective Performances of Smart Fandom

It is clear that stereotypical fan practices and behaviors persist for the WWF, particularly as mediated consumption inflicts and remains salient to fan engagements with this historical artefact. Staged in pre-internet times, original WWF audiences were reliant on television and pay-per-view telecasts. In contemporary times, different media forms are enhancing these lived fan memories. In a traditional consumptive framework, pre-packaged WWF box sets are pervasive, with an abundance of major events (e.g., *Wrestlemania*, *Survivor Series*) or career sketches and best matches of prominent wrestlers (e.g., Hulk Hogan, Randy Savage, the Ultimate Warrior) readily available for purchase. Moreover, the made-to-order production and circulation of WWF action figures, epitomized by the *Hasbromaniacs* Facebook page, points to the nostalgic yearning for collecting, trading, and playing with such objects.[21]

Theories of fandom also recognize the performative dimensions that shape fan identity constructions through consumption.[22] The performances of fandom produce an array of social practices and relations,[23] while fandom is conceived as an active and ongoing project of self.[24] The engagements, activities, and encyclopedic knowledge of smart fans preserving, revising, and interrogating the WWF archival record points to their active performances.[25] Such performative variations have arguably accelerated in contemporary times. New media and digital platforms afford the viewing and uploading of wrestling footage, interviews, and other rare archival materials via instantaneous (global) interconnections.[26] Gaming further blurs notions of kayfabe and caters to nostalgic forms of performative play.[27] Finally, social media networks furnish new forms of fan participation, sustain nostalgic manifestations, and provide an impetus to the memories and dialogue surrounding this era of the WWF, while solidifying smart fan hierarchies.[28]

Described as emotional "passion work" by Annette Hill,[29] smart fandom is clearly underpinned by affective attachments, investments, and relationships. I observed, "conceived as a broader attachment to objects, places and things, affect shapes our investment toward and in such things; specifically the levels of invigoration, intensities and energies that are 'felt' and enacted."[30]

In this regard, the WWF operates as a nostalgic object wherein affect materializes for and mobilizes its fans.[31] Smart fans are also engaging in forms of affective labor; the often-voluntary and unpaid "emotional" work done to sustain the archival record and strengthen the community.[32] In many respects, affectively invested smart fans are utilizing digital media to refashion these halcyon days as a durable and also permeable record that takes on its own form. That is, through their tireless, affective labor, this era in WWF history is continually reconstructed and re-energized by fans and administrators across these platforms. Fueled by fan memories, engagements, and investments, the archival record operates as a living, contested, and constantly updated historical artefact.

Unsurprisingly, all the sites are underscored by a nostalgic yearning for the past and a decrying of the current state of professional wrestling. For example *Old School Pro Wrestling Talk* (April 17, 2017) posted an image of the main event from *Wrestlemania VI*, with the caption "What is today's equivalent of Hogan v Warrior? Seriously." One fan responds, "Nothing. There aren't two full-time wrestlers on today's WWE roster that can touch the star power of Hulkamania or Ultimate Warrior." Another fan sums up some of the differences, while signposting his preference for the past:

> The WWE just isn't the same as the WWF. It was about characters you got behind that weren't forced on you. Each guy developed there own style, and you just enjoyed it for what it was. Now it's about story's and trying to make you deliver its real and entertaining. But it's not. It's mass produced wrestles with no background. Your just forced into what you are meant to like [sic].

Both perspectives point to the diminished role and interest in contemporary wrestling for many older fans, the nostalgic allure of the WWF and the appeal of its larger-than-life wrestlers. The second quote also points to how notions of kayfabe and the wrestlers-as-workers were perceived to undergird the WWF.

Significant to many smart fan activities are their evaluations of wrestler performances (gimmicks, "workers" and showmanship), accompanied by considerations of the role of WWF faces and heels. In this regard, smart fans do not unquestioningly support the crowd favorites. For example, "Hacksaw" Jim Duggan is regularly critiqued for his American patriot stereotype (indicated by his perceived stupidity and blind obedience), for not convincingly either working with other wrestlers nor providing good matches, and for relying upon his gimmick (hitting people with a two-by-four plank of wood) rather than any technical flair within the ring. In contrast, Bret "Hitman" Hart often wins praise for his persona, gimmicks, and work. Hart alternated between face and heel, as well as both an individual wrestler and as part of the "Hart Foundation" tag-team (with brother-in-law Jim "The Anvil" Neidhart) during this period. With commentators often referring to his "excellence of execution," Hart's technical and tactical wrestling style, as well as ability to work matches through (kayfabe) injuries and dramatic comebacks against opponents, ensured his popularity with WWF crowds and with contemporary smart fans. While a recognized talent during the halcyon days, it should be noted that Hart's career took on greater significance when he replaced Hogan as the WWF's top star in the post-steroid scandal era.

Constructing Kayfabe and the Appeal of Wrestling

Most contemporary forms of wrestling explicitly break kayfabe through an emphasis on (over)dramatic storylines, more "extreme" representational styles and marketing wrestling as entertainment.[33] Contextually, in relation to the role and performance of kayfabe, the WWF era (circa 1984 to 1993) to some degree mirrored and reproduced an upgraded version of the older, more traditional forms of theatrical wrestling Barthes had witnessed and theorized. For Barthes, wrestling offered a "spectacle of excess" and the moral playground for a physical battle of good and evil.[34] He notes, "what is thus displayed for the public is the great spectacle of Suffering, Defeat, and Justice"[35] with affliction etched upon, carried, and embodied by both the vanquished and victorious wrestlers. Notably, muscular heroes would often battle out-of-shape (or monstrous) villains.[36] Wrestling matches also operated as a spectacle, not a sport, with the knowing audiences intrigued by these physical and theatrical displays of morality.[37]

This simple binary of good and evil arguably persisted during the WWF halcyon days. Muscular physiques would also be a hallmark of wrestling from the 1980s. Most wrestlers possessed bodybuilder-like proportions,[38] notably heels such as Ravishing Rick Rude, Dino Bravo, and the Powers of Pain alongside the popular faces Hulk Hogan, Ultimate Warrior, and "British Bulldog" Davey-Boy Smith. More pertinently, the WWF provided a spectacle predicated on heroes (faces) versus villains (heels). Introducing some of the prominent WWF wrestlers helps contextualize both the fan favorites and perceived heels or villains that smart fans critically evaluate. Wrestlers such as Hillbilly Jim, Koko B Ware, Tito Santana, Rowdy Roddy Piper, Junk Yard Dog, Ricky "the Dragon" Steamboat, "Hacksaw" Jim Duggan, Jimmy "Superfly" Snuka, Jake "the Snake" Roberts, Bret "Hitman" Hart, Brutus "the Barber" Beefcake, and Dusty Rhodes, were notable babyfaces of the late 1980s and early 1990s. These wrestlers tended primarily to be crowd-friendly individuals, all with distinctive gimmicks to maintain their popularity. Similarly, in the tag-team arena, the Killer Bees, the Rockers, the British Bulldogs, and the Bushwhackers remained fan favorites, while Demolition, the Hart Foundation, and the Powers of Pain alternated as popular tag-team faces and heels.

Might Is Right: Hulk Hogan

Henry Jenkins described WWF wrestling as "masculine melodrama" which, akin to Barthes, focused on embodied and personalized displays of social justice in the ring.[39] For Jenkins, "WWF wrestling, as a form which bridges the gap between sport and melodrama, allows for the spectacle of male physical prowess … but also for the exploration of the emotional and moral life of its combatants."[40] Played out by a cast of stereotypical heroes and villains, the violence of the physical combat was ultimately enshrined in the doctrine that "might is right."[41] Arguably, no other wrestler embodied the notion of 'might is right' better than Hulk Hogan. As noted earlier, Hogan was the face of the WWF during its halcyon days, deploying a heroic "All American" persona, wrestling much-larger foes or stereotypical foreign heels while headlining most major WWF events.

Conversely, smart fans tend to be critical of Hogan's star status and in-ring work. Hogan images, news, or debates posted on the WWF Facebook sites have a polarizing effect. On the one hand, Hogan is often lauded for his role, with Hulkamania perceivably changing and elevating the WWF during this era. On the other hand, many point to backstage stories of his insistence on creative control and behind-the-scenes manipulations as a means of safeguarding and solidifying his status as top star. This can result in disparate accounts that celebrate, begrudgingly acknowledge, or seek to discredit his contribution to and significance for the WWF. For example, on *80s Mania* (July 19, 2016), a fan reflects on an image of Hogan: "Even as a young boy, I thought he was full of shit. How he had longevity at the top, I'll never know. He couldn't wrestle worth shit, and never tried to improve."

A debate that ensues between fans on *Old School Wrasslin* is even more telling (September 5, 2016):

> Hogan sucks, knew 3 moves and they all looked awful. Hogan was a backstage politician. He refused to lose to people. If you have seen one Hogan match you have seen them all. He got pushed to the moon because of his promos and connection with the fans. Vince didn't care he couldn't wrestle for shit.

This is supported by another fan, who asserts "Hogan didn't make wrestling. He did help make it mainstream." A subsequent set of rebuttals are then provided from different fans: "Both of you are idiots. Hogan made wrestling," "the man, the myth, and the legend!! God don't make super down to earth Hero's like him anymore," "It was so much better back then Hulkamania still lives!!!!!!!" "F*** you Hulk Hogan made wrestling what it is today" and "I loved Hogan since I was a kid and I always will." We will see further critiques of Hogan resurface in discussions of other wrestlers below.

Arguably, some of these reflective criticisms by one-time Hogan fans mirror Henry Jenkins' own reflexive appraisal of the WWF era. Disillusioned by its campy, childish nature and subsequent explicitly salacious transformation, Jenkins abandoned the WWF during the mid–1990s.[42] For some of these now-mature fans, perhaps they have also recognized the child-like, cringeworthy, and regressive WWF stereotypes surrounding Hogan. For others, it might be the uneasy realization that they were operating as the "marks" that they now detest.[43]

Performing Kayfabe: The Ultimate Warrior

Two other men rivaled Hogan for popularity during the late 1980s. Both "Macho Man" Randy Savage and the Ultimate Warrior garnered significant followings and challenged Hogan's status as the WWF's top babyface. Savage as worker will be discussed shortly. Alternatively, for the Ultimate Warrior, many fan appraisals note his power and presence, but also acknowledge that he was a poor worker. The Warrior emerged as a new talent and increasingly popular face in 1987. With his face-paint, tassels, bodybuilder physique, and high-energy entrances, he quickly became a fan favorite. For example, one fan on *Old School Wrasslin* (July 31, 2016) asserts, "The Warrior had me in awe with the way he manhandled everyone in the ring. 1st match I saw him in was SummerSlam88, vs The Honky Tonk Man." This sub-30-second defeat of Honky, as well as subsequent ongoing feud with Ravishing Rick Rude, tends to get the most fan attention.

Nevertheless, the Warrior remains a polarizing figure. A thread on *Old School Wrasslin* (August 1, 2016) highlights these disparities. Responding to spiteful comments, a fan asks, "Why you bad mouthing Warrior?" before receiving the reply, "Probably because the U.W was a bum who couldn't wrestle." These two fans engage further: "Talk shit about the Warrior and roids and not being able to wrestle. Shit to me that sounds like Hogan also. Where is the shit talk about him?" The second fan responds, "Hogan could wrestle and built WWE dip shit. Warrior couldn't entertain worth a shit. Hogan wasn't juiced to the gill like Warrior's ass was." Other fans provide contributions which emphasis his significance. For example, 'It's your opinion to hate on Warrior but Warrior plays a strong part in the elevation of the Golden era of the WWE. Hate it or love it his character will live on forever." Another adds, "RIP ... was larger than life with his awesome charisma!"

Further fan contributions on the same thread praise Warrior while acknowledging his shortcomings. For example, "You just hate on the fact that Warrior got over so strong by doing less moves and doing shit his way and still having a strong impact on sports entertainment." Another adds that he

> won't discredit or throw him under the bus like a lot of people still do with Warrior over shit that happened decades ago. Warrior made Vince a lot of money for his company and left a hell of an impact despite the bullshit he did in his past. He deserves his place in the HOF.

Finally, another fan asserts that "Warrior sucked at wrestling but still a legend.... He seemed larger than life when I was a kid!" Similar conflicting responses can be found when images from Warrior's encounters with Rude are posted. Indeed, many fans suggest Rude was the better worker. Some examples from *Old School Wrasslin* (August 1, 2016) reflect this. "Rude was twice the show stopper than the Warrior. The Warrior runs in grab the ropes and acts like a fool." Another suggests, "Post should read, 'Rude carrying Warrior,'" which gets the response, "Rude always carried Warrior."

On the same thread, others demonstrate their "shoot" knowledge and awareness of power struggles behind the scenes. Contesting these rumors, a mark's aspersions are corrected: "No. Rude really did beat the fuck out of him backstage." Another adds, "Rude knocked him out backstage when Warrior said his character couldn't lose to a guy like Rick Rude." However, other fans move to recognizing and reconciling assessments of the Warrior. As one fan suggests, "Both were great. Rude was ten times the worker Warrior was but you're a fool if you deny Warrior's charisma and connection to the crowd back in the late 80s and early 90s." We also witness a fan's transitory moment as he reflects upon his own previous viewing and status: "That was a fun match to watch when it first aired. My lil mark self marked out when Warrior beat Rude." Comically, this fan acknowledges his one-time "mark" status of blindly cheering on the popular faces, while implying a later acquired smart fan's appreciation of Rude as worker and the value of heels.

Performing Kayfabe: Heels

A strong cast of heels drew the ire of crowds as foils for Hogan, Warrior, and other babyfaces. A prominent list of wrestlers performed their characters and gimmicks with aplomb during the 1980s and early 1990s, including the Iron Sheik, King Kong Bundy, Andre the Giant, Harley Race, Greg "the Hammer" Valentine, Haku, Bad News Brown, Dino Bravo, The One Man Gang/Akeem, Outlaw Ron Bass, Mr. Perfect, the Undertaker, Sgt. Slaughter, Ric Flair, and Earthquake. Other notable wrestlers transitioned from face to heel (Rick "the Model" Martel) or vice versa (the Big Boss Man, Hercules). As tag-teams, notable heels included the Islanders, the Bolsheviks, the Fabulous Rougeau Brothers, and the Brain Busters, although many of the aforementioned individuals had at one point been paired in "heel" tag-teams during this time. Crucial to heel performances was the work of seeming creditable, embodying the "bad" persona and making the crowd root against them.

In this vein, villains often embodied regressive racial, cultural, and class-based stereotypes. As rule-breakers, they would exploit any advantage to win, particularly if they could not match their rivals' heroic physical powers.[44] Hence, foreign villains were presented as duplicitous (the Bolsheviks, the Iron Sheik), while racially-coded depictions of primitive (the Islanders) and unruly black bodies (Bad News Brown) perpetuated stereotypes of the non-white "other."[45] Additionally, heel managers such as Bobby "the Brain" Hennan, Slick, Mr. Fuji, Frenchy Martin, and Jimmy Hart would frequently distract, interfere, or provide foreign objects to be used as weapons.

Conversely, the heroic counter-posed such threats: protecting America through patriotic displays (Hulk Hogan, Hacksaw Jim Duggan), protecting their "damsels in distress" ("Macho Man" Randy Savage, Jake "the Snake" Roberts) or their animals (the British Bulldogs), retaliating against unprovoked attacks (Brutus "the Barber" Beefcake), and offering either inspirational figures (Tito Santana) or athletic eye candy (the Rockers) for crowds to support. The heroes usually prevailed through the morally-infused assumption that good would ultimately triumph, although kayfabe storylines sometimes permitted heroes to also cheat to achieve social justice.[46]

The WWF "good" versus "evil" storylines are both simplistic and effective in their design. Mazer notes that the wrestling event is "conspicuously constructed around a set idea of what an audience expects to see ... wrestlers are self-conscious performers with their eyes always on the crowd, competing for the spectators' passions and inviting them to play along."[47] To facilitate this playfulness, the event replicates and relies upon a fundamental sporting premise, all the while blurring "real" sporting representations with sports entertainment. The televised coverage, the role of knowledgeable and hyperbolic commentators (exemplified by ex-wrestlers Jesse "the Body" Ventura and Gorilla Monsoon), and the WWF star system of recognizable characters enticing or incensing the crowd underscores its affective components.

Rich Villain: Ted DiBiase

The "Million Dollar Man" Ted DiBiase worked the crowd by portraying a smug, privileged, and elitist character. DiBiase taunted opponents and crowds as being beneath him. Playing on class-based stereotypes, DiBiase tried to exploit the less fortunate and to buy favors with his "everybody has a price" tagline which included targeting other wrestlers or officials. Having been unsuccessful in attempts to buy the WWF championship, he created his own Million Dollar Belt, proclaiming himself the "Million Dollar Champion." His bodyguard Virgil would usually accompany him ringside, often inserting himself within matches to assist DiBiase. As one fan on *Old School Wrasslin* (August 17, 2016) notes, "Ted DiBiase was always a great heel that's why guys like him still get respect. He had charisma and the 'it' factor." Another fan suggests that "Ted DiBiase trying to buy the WWF championship off Andre The Giant is one of the most iconic and controversial moments in the history of pro wrestling" (August 1, 2016). DiBiase remained one of the prominent headlining heels of the late 1980s. In relation to the Mega Powers versus Mega Bucks main event at *SummerSlam88*, a fan on *Old School Wrasslin* (August 17, 2016) notes that "Savage and Dibiase more than carried this match." His portrayal of character, deployment of gimmicks, and work via in-ring performances and promos make him a well-respected heel among smart fans.

Poignantly, Robert Rinehart (1998) suggests that the WWF enacts an avant-garde performance that, collaboratively, the wrestlers, spectators, and its kayfabe mechanisms of production all participate in.[48] In this vein, criticisms of wrestling as mere ruse or pseudo-sport fail to capture the essence of the WWF. Operating between sport and drama, reality and art, and between masculine and feminine spaces (as narrative, as representation and in its contradictory embellishment of the male body), the WWF spectacle provides an array of endearing liminal elements for its spectators.[49] Collectively, the WWF resembles conflict, emotions, and sport, all the while imitating and parodying each of these facets.[50]

Persona and Gimmicks

The WWF was playfully aware of its own kayfabe, infusing theatrical, comical, and exaggerated displays while maintaining the illusion of competition. This extended to the wrestlers and the characters that they portrayed. Mazer surmises,

> The wrestlers present themselves as larger-than-life figures from a comic-booklike world. They wear costumes that range from brief to extravagant, make their entrances to personalized theme music, carry trademark props, and offer signature gestures and shouts.... The wrestlers provoke the crowd with invective and insolence, but also impress them with breathtaking athleticism and prodigious showmanship.[51]

Part of this athletic showmanship involved maintaining a steadfast consistency both inside and out of the ring, notably by never breaking character in front of fans.

Bad Elvis: The Honky Tonk Man

The Honky Tonk Man warrants attention for his ability to incense the crowd, parody popular culture and for his later refashioning by fans. Honky portrayed an Elvis Presley impersonator, with his gimmicks including a rhinestone jumpsuit, slicked hair and sideburns, and bringing a guitar to the ring that he would often use as a weapon against his opponents. He would also shake his hips, offer to sing, and reference Elvis song titles through his promos, wrestling moves, or airbrushed tights. As one fan on *Old School Wrasslin* (August 25, 2016) succinctly suggests when comparing Honky and the Warrior, "HTM was more entertaining on the mic and in the ring." Additionally, on *Old School Pro. Wrestling Talk* (August 23, 2016) one fan notes that Honky "was a gas in interviews with Jimmy Hart ... they cheated so much to win," while another reveals, upon meeting Honky in recent years, he told him "how easy it was to hate him. He thanked me." A similar sentiment is shared on *WWF The Golden Years* (August 19, 2016) where two fans state "[they] loved Honky Tonk Man he is the one heel that is easy to hate," and that he was "one of the best heels of all time." Collectively, many fan posts from the different sites attest to him being the greatest-ever Intercontinental champion given the longevity of his reign and his gimmick of deploying of dirty tactics to retain it.

Wrestler identities have been articulated in different but essentially overlapping ways. For some authors, the term "gimmick" applies to the portrayed character, with Lawrence McBride and Elizabeth Bird noting that "the performers assume alien identities within the tight delimitations of the wrestling show. These identities, called 'gimmicks,' are the morally significant agents in the plots of wrestling shows, which involve cheating villains ('heels') and honest heroes ('babyfaces')."[52] Similarly, Costantino Oliva and Gordon Calleja suggest that gimmicks are "the character that is played by a wrestler, resulting in the sum of fictional elements, attire and wrestling ability."[53] For other authors, "persona" is the preferred term. Nicholas Sammond conceptualizes a blurred line between performer and character, and between performer and persona,[54] while Dalbir Sehmby emphasizes that wrestlers activate persona by "using their real life situations to build fictional narratives."[55] For our present purposes, "persona" is used to describe the portrayal of a character, while "gimmick" refers to the individuated nuances and signatures (such as moves, attire and props) deployed by wrestlers.

Wrestlers as "Workers"

Sehmby's notion of fictional narrative is an important component for the WWF era.[56] As active creators of their own personas, many wrestlers strove to blend characters, gimmicks, and technical virtuosity within their performances.[57] WWF wrestlers were also operating in a time when they still had some creative and agential license for improvising matches and crafting characters.[58] Indeed, by the 2000s, wholesale scripted matches and characters were increasingly becoming the norm, with the now-WWE relying heavily on scripts produced by television writers.[59] Within this context, the terms "work" and "worker" become pertinent. Sehmby notes:

> "Work" refers to the ability of the wrestlers in a match to con a spectator into believing its reality. Hence, every wrestling show is a successful "work" if the audience is caught up in the show and believes the emotion and fighting to be real.... Ultimately successful "work" makes the viewer actually believe or doubt what is real and what is not real.[60]

Wrestlers strived to please audiences by putting on a show that looked convincing and engaged the crowd. However, they also needed to "work" in unison with the other wrestlers. Laurence de Garis emphasizes the duality of this "work," observing that a professional wrestling performance is "more co-operative than contested," while "the performer and spectator coproduce the performance,"[61] particularly as fan reactions have historically directed the flow of matches.

Savage Worker: The "Macho Man"

As noted earlier, "Macho Man" Randy Savage rivaled Hogan for popularity during the late 1980s. However, unlike Hogan, Savage consistently receives positive accolades. Alternating as face and heel throughout his career, Randy Savage was "an excellent technical wrestler"[62] who possessed a mastery of skill, speed, and aerial displays within the ring, as well as a flamboyant wrestling persona. Co-headlining many of the major events in 1988 and 1989, Savage both partnered and feuded with Hogan during this period. As heel, this relationship lent itself to his "macho" gimmick as a self-absorbed and jealous bully, (kayfabe) mistreating his manager Miss Elizabeth and threatening anyone who looked at her, including rebranding Hogan as the "Luster" in 1989.

For smart fans, it is Savage's performances, work, persona, and gimmicks that resonate. Fan comments on the *Old School Wrasslin* Facebook page (September 2, 2016) reflect this. For example, one fan notes, "Look up any promo of Macho Man especially 'the cream of the crop.' This is what wrestling lacks these days." Another recalls, "I will always remember the MACHO MAN!!!!!! Watched him as a kid every weekend!!!!" For context, Savage's "Macho Madness" gimmicks consisted of signature poses, sequined robes, sunglasses, as well as the intensely strained spoken delivery of his "Oh Yeaaaah!" catchphrase. Fan responses praise Savage for his ability to embody the persona, exude the character, and "own" the gimmicks that collectively make him a memorable WWF icon. For example, on *WWF Golden Years* (September 2, 2016) one fan asserts Savage is "the GREATEST world champ ... just my opinion!!" Another is enthralled by his gimmicks: "flying drop elbow ... the shades ... the cape ... the charisma.... OOOOHHHH YYYEEEEAAAAAHHHHHHH!!!," elements playfully picked by up by a third fan who added, "Ooooh Yea cream of the Crop Slim Jim Ooooh YEAH."

Smart fans are well-versed in recognizing good workers. Moreover, they also appreciate the salience of improvisation and the lack of choreographing or rehearsing that underpinned WWF-era performances. Mazer observes that "success is determined by a perception of charisma and stage presence rather than by any sort of athletic point system"[63] and, arguably, it is the smart fans' ability to read matches and evaluate performances that sets them apart from marks. For smart fans, critical appraisals tend to gravitate towards assessments of the character and accompanying gimmicks, the combative excitement and/or technical dimensions, as well as the work provided within the ring and in delivering promos outside of it.

Simply Ravishing: Rick Rude

Alongside Randy Savage, Ted DiBiase and the Honky Tonk Man, the heel that seems to garner the most critical reception is Ravishing Rick Rude. The campy yet provocative Rude taunted crowds through his (homo)erotic and sexualized displays. Upon entry to the ring, he would address and insult the crowd. Male audiences were told that they were fat and out of shape before being instructed to "keep the noise down while I show the ladies what a real sexy man looks like" as he took his robe off in a mock strip tease routine. His other gimmicks included a "rude awakening," which was both a finishing move and the occasional post-match kissing of attractive female audience members. Blurring homo- and hetero-sexual readings,[64] these "rude awakenings" allegedly rendered both opponents and females unconscious. A fan on *Old School Wrasslin* (September 5, 2016) recalls one such instance which triggered a feud: "I'll never forget the time he chose Sheryl [sic] Roberts to smooch on. Jake the Snake's wife. Back when wrestling was awesome." Other notable gimmicks included Rude continuously posing and gyrating his hips at the jeering crowd, while he often wore spray-painted images of his opponents on his tights. As two fans succinctly remarked on *Old School Wrasslin* (September 3, 2016), "Best on the microphone before his match starts" and "Best tights 'EVER."

Contemporary online smart fans are glowing in their praise for Rude and yearn for him to receive greater recognition as a top performer since his death in 1999. As one fan notes on *Old School Wrasslin* (September 3, 2016), "See how current heels take a page out of the Rick Rude hand book? Because he was a legend." Another fan adds, "Damn. He rewrote the book on how to be a great heel. May he rest in peace." For other fans on the thread, his status is beyond reproach. As one fan asserts, "Best natural heel ever along with the Million Dollar Man," which is further supported by another fan's contention that he is "one of the top 5 heels of all time." Two other fans hold him in the highest esteem: "He's on my Mt. Rushmore of pro wrestlers. One of the best to ever step into the wrestling ring. R.I.P." A different post, also on the same day on *Old School Wrasslin* (September 3, 2016), has a fan comment, "The man was literally not only one of my favorite heels ever but one of my personal favorite wrestlers PERIOD. R.I.P Ravishing."

While adhering to similar sentiments, other smart fan comments also hint at the power dynamics (and the indirect roles of Hogan and the Warrior) that limited his potential and impact in the WWF. Comments from *Old School Wrasslin* (September 4, 2016) reflect these aspects. One fan notes, "Put Rude in the Hall of Fame already. He easily could've been booked as a World Champ if Hogan wasn't scared to put him over." Another comments, "Rude's tights were always dope.... He should've won more gold" which yields the response that "in today's world, he probably would have, but the belts just didn't change as much back then, especially to heels" and a brief assertion that "Rick Rude was ahead of his time." Another fan on *Old School Wrasslin* (July 31, 2016) is more forthright in his opinion, stating, "The greatest wrestler to NEVER win the World title in the WWF.... RUDE could have carried that organization instead of guys like Hogan or the Warrior. Badly misused." Collectively, while endorsing Rude, these comments also reflect the perspective of many smart fans. WWF smart fans seek broader knowledge of backstage politics and developments that shape how wrestlers and angles are presented to the public. In the case of Rude, although he was inducted into the WWF Hall of Fame in 2017, smart fans remain critical of perceived poor treatment and the alleged privileging and safeguarding of major WWF faces at his expense.

Concluding Remarks

This essay has shown the remarkable durability and enduring passion among fans for a particular era of professional wrestling. The WWF's expansion into territories, onto network television, and into forms of popular culture in the 1980s and 1990s arguably made wrestling mainstream for the first time. In turn, this exposed WWF events and stars to broader, more diverse audiences. Of course, many of these fans were marks, who have either long since forgotten or moved away from wrestling, or rely on hazy and populist-informed accounts to celebrate the top faces of the era. In contradistinction, this essay revealed a greater complexity to professional wrestling, to the dynamics of how the WWF operated, and to the collective performances, work, personas, and gimmicks of its stars.

Through official sources and pre-packaged, commercialized formats, the WWF remains accessible for interested audiences to review and replay the events that transpired. However, it is the affective labor of smart fans and their passionate engagements that enliven, re-energize, and recreate the archival record. Through their knowledgeable investments and undertakings, smart fans reflect upon and reveal insider information by probing the inner workings of the WWF. Hence, tinged with nostalgic memories and yearnings, smart fans take pleasure in discussing the WWF, evaluating its stars and elevating the events that matter, while breathing new life into its halcyon days.

Notes

1. Better known as World Wrestling Entertainment (WWE) since 2002.
2. Nicholas Sammond, ed., *Steel Chair to the Head: The Pleasure and Pain of Professional Wrestling* (Durham: Duke University Press, 2005), 343.
3. Bobby Newman, "Professional Wrestling—Stereotypes, Not Only Archetypes: A Reply to Polizzi," *The Humanistic Psychologist* 21 (1993), 121–22.
4. Robert E. Rinehart, *Players All: Performances in Contemporary Sport* (Bloomington: Indiana University Press, 1998), 65.
5. Henry Jenkins, "Never Trust a Snake: WWF Wrestling as Masculine Melodrama," in Nicholas Sammond, ed., *Steel Chair to the Head: The Pleasure and Pain of Professional Wrestling* (Durham: Duke University Press, 2005), 42–62.
6. Ted Butryn, "Global Smackdown: Vince McMahon, World Wrestling Entertainment, and Neoliberalism," in David Andrews and Michael Silk, eds., *Sport and Neoliberalism: Politics, Consumption, and Culture* (Philadelphia: Temple University Press, 2012), 283.
7. Fiona McQuarrie, "Breaking Kayfabe: 'The History of a History' of World Wrestling Entertainment," *Management & Organizational History* 1, no. 3 (2006), 232–33.
8. Sharon Mazer, "The Doggie Doggie World of Professional Wrestling," *The Drama Review* 34, No. 4 (1990), 97.
9. Jenkins, "Never Trust a Snake," 34–35.
10. Mazer, "The Doggie Doggie World," 97.
11. Jenkins, "Never Trust a Snake," 34–35.
12. Mazer, "The Doggie Doggie World," 97.
13. "Wrestlemania VII," Wikipedia, https://en.wikipedia.org/wiki/WrestleMania_VII (accessed July 25, 2016).
14. McQuarrie, "Breaking Kayfabe," 234–35.
15. Damion Sturm and Andrew McKinney, "Affective Hyper-Consumption and Immaterial Labors of Love: Theorizing Sport Fandom in the Age of New Media," *Participations* 10 (2013), 357–62.
16. Garry Crawford, *Consuming Sport: Fans, Sport and Culture* (London: Routledge, 2004).
17. Annette Hill, "Spectacle of Excess: The Passion Work of Professional Wrestlers, Fans and Anti-Fans," *European Journal of Cultural Studies* 18, no. 2 (2015), 174–89.
18. Lawrence McBride and Elizabeth Bird, "From Smart Fan to Backyard Wrestler: Performance, Context, and Aesthetic Violence," in Jonathan Gray et al., eds., *Fandom: Identities and Communities in a Mediated World* (New York: New York University Press, 2005), 169.

19. McBride and Bird, "From Smart Fan," 169–70.
20. McBride and Bird, "From Smart Fan," 169.
21. Dan Fleming and Damion Sturm, *Media, Masculinities and the Machine: F1, Transformers and Fantasizing Technology at Its Limits* (New York: Continuum, 2011), 113–147.
22. Sturm and McKinney, "Affective Hyper-Consumption," 358–59.
23. Matt Hills, *Fan Cultures* (London: Routledge, 2002).
24. Cornel Sandvoss, *Fans: The Mirror of Consumption* (Cambridge: Polity Press, 2005).
25. McBride and Bird, "From Smart Fan," 169–70.
26. Henry Jenkins, "Rethinking 'Rethinking Convergence/Culture,'" *Cultural Studies* 28 (2014): 267–97.
27. Costantino Oliva and Gordon Calleja, "Fake Rules, Real Fiction: Professional Wrestling and Videogames," *The Proceedings of DIGRA 2009 Brunel University* (2009), 1–9, www.digra.org/dl/db/09287.48172.pdf (accessed August 10, 2016).
28. McBride and Bird, "From Smart Fan," 169–70.
29. Hill, "Spectacle of Excess," 174–89.
30. Damion Sturm, "Playing with the Autoethnographical: Performing and Re-Presenting the Fan's Voice. *Cultural Studies <=> Critical Methodologies* 15, no. 3 (2015), 215.
31. Fleming and Sturm, *Media, Masculinities and the Machine*.
32. Sturm and McKinney, "Affective Hyper-Consumption," 360–61.
33. Daniel Schulze, "Debating with Fists: Professional Wrestling: Sport, Spectacle and Violent Drama," in Katherine Dashper, Thomas Fletcher, and Nicola McCullough, eds., *Sports Events, Society and Culture* (London: Routledge, 2014), 54–56.
34. Roland Barthes, "The World of Wrestling," *Mythologies*, trans. Annette Lavers (New York: Hill and Wang, 1972 [1957]), 15.
35. Barthes, "The World of Wrestling," 19.
36. Schulze, "Debating with Fists," 53.
37. Barthes, "The World of Wrestling," 15.
38. Sturm, "Playing with the Autoethnographical," 219.
39. Jenkins, "Never Trust a Snake," 36–42.
40. Jenkins, "Never Trust a Snake," 39.
41. Jenkins, "Never Trust a Snake," 41–42.
42. Henry Jenkins, "Afterword, Part II: Growing Up and Growing More Risqué," in Nicholas Sammond, ed., *Steel Chair to the Head: The Pleasure and Pain of Professional Wrestling* (Durham: Duke University Press, 2005), 319–20.
43. McBride and Bird, "From Smart Fan," 169–70.
44. Jenkins, "Never Trust a Snake," 41.
45. Newman, "Professional Wrestling," 123–25.
46. Jenkins, "Never Trust a Snake," 41–43.
47. Mazer, "The Doggie Doggie World," 102.
48. Rinehart, *Players All*, 66–67.
49. Dalbir Sehmby, "Wrestling and Popular Culture," *Comparative Literature and Culture* 4, no. 1 (2002), 11.
50. Michael Atkinson, "Fifty Million Viewers Can't Be Wrong: Professional Wrestling, Sports-Entertainment, and Mimesis," *Sociology of Sport Journal* 19, no. 1 (2002), 49–50.
51. Mazer, "The Doggie Doggie World," 97.
52. McBride and Bird, "From Smart Fan," 166.
53. Oliva and Calleja, "Fake Rules, Real Fiction," 3.
54. Nicholas Sammond, "Introduction: A Brief and Unnecessary Defense of Professional Wrestling," in Nicholas Sammond, ed., *Steel Chair to the Head: The Pleasure and Pain of Professional Wrestling* (Durham: Duke University Press, 2005), 11.
55. Sehmby, "Wrestling and Popular Culture," 8.
56. Sehmby, "Wrestling and Popular Culture," 8.
57. Laurence de Garis, "Experiments in Pro Wrestling: Toward a Performative and Sensuous Sport Ethnography," *Sociology of Sport Journal* 16, no. 1 (1999), 70.
58. Laurence.de Garis, "The 'Logic' of Professional Wrestling," in Nicholas Sammond,

ed., *Steel Chair to the Head: The Pleasure and Pain of Professional Wrestling* (Durham: Duke University Press, 2005), 210–11.
  59. Sammond, "Introduction," 12.
  60. Sehmby, "Wrestling and Popular Culture," 7.
  61. de Garis, "Experiments in Pro Wrestling," 68.
  62. Mazer, "The Doggie Doggie World," 99.
  63. Mazer, "The Doggie Doggie World," 98.
  64. Mazer, "The Doggie Doggie World," 117.

Origins of the
Rock 'n' Wrestling Connection

SETH BOVEY

Even though rock music and professional wrestling are two different kinds of enterprise, one artistic and the other athletic, they have much in common. Roland Barthes describes wrestling as a "spectacle of excess," a description which could apply equally well to most rock concerts. Both forms of spectacle rely heavily on charismatic, flamboyant personalities, and outrageous behavior to get the audience emotionally involved in the show. The performers in both arenas also inhabit a seedy show-biz world apart from ordinary bourgeois existence, causing both types of spectacle to be considered low-brow entertainment. Moreover, both kinds of spectacle excite and release primal emotions in their followers, resulting in a catharsis of sorts. Given these parallels, the idea that the rebelliousness of rock could complement the rowdiness of wrestling seems obvious, and the practice of wrestlers using rock and roll songs as entrance music has become so commonplace that no one would imagine things being otherwise.

At one time, however, rock music and wrestling were worlds apart, each one appealing to a different core audience. Long before most wrestling fans could even stomach rock and roll, and a couple of decades before The Fabulous Freebirds became the first wrestlers to use a rock song as their entrance music,[1] wrestlers began cutting their own records as a way of promoting themselves. A Memphis-area wrestler named Sputnik Monroe was the first to do so in 1959, right at the tail end of the rock and roll craze that had swept the country and established rock as the music of choice for the youth culture that had developed after World War II. By that time, the 45 rpm single in the form of a seven-inch vinyl disc had also become the medium of choice for selling songs to record-buying youngsters, mainly because 45s were less breakable, more affordable, and more portable than ten-inch 78-rpm records.[2]

There was a growing demand for novel new sounds, and small, independent recording studios had sprung up in towns throughout America to record the efforts of aspiring hit-makers. Sputnik Monroe and other wrestlers who followed him tried to take advantage of this set of circumstances and the popularity of 7-inch vinyl records as a new medium for promotion, but it would be some time before wrestling fans were ready to embrace rock and roll. In the meantime, rock musicians looked to the world of pro wrestling for new song material; the first to do so were The Novas, a garage band in Minnesota, who recorded a song in 1964 to pay homage to The Crusher, their favorite wrestler, and created a template for mixing wrestling with rock music. A decade or so later, wrestlers began recording their own low-rent rock songs again as a means of establishing their public personas and promoting their wrestling characters, paving the way for the well-known "rock and wrestling" explosion of the 1980s.

It seems fitting that the first rock and wrestling connection was made in Memphis, the birthplace of rockabilly music and home of early rock and roll. Sputnik Monroe recorded his "compositions" at Peak Records, a label run as a side business by the Lansky Brothers, who were clothiers known mainly for outfitting musicians such as Elvis Presley with their hepcat clothes. It was located at Second and Beale Streets, not far from Ellis Auditorium, where Monroe wrestled regularly.[3] The A side of the single, "Sputnik Hires a Band," is more of a musical joke than a true song. It consists of Sputnik trying out one musician after another, spewing insults at each one and running them off. All told, Sputnik tries out some horn players, a pianist, two guitarists, a drummer, and a bassist. The closest that this skit gets to rock and roll is the part when the first guitarist plays the twangy guitar intro to "Raunchy," a rock and roll instrumental by Bill Justis and Sid Manker. Sputnik cuts him off and tells him sarcastically to play some rock and roll to dance to, not music to read comic books by. What makes this bit so amusing is the knowledge that "Raunchy" *is* a rock and roll song; people at the time would have been familiar with "Raunchy" because it was a smash hit just two years before, shooting up to number two on the Pop charts and number one on the R&B charts. What makes this part doubly funny is the knowledge that Bill Justis was from Memphis, so when Sputnik puts down "Raunchy" by suggesting that it is music for teenyboppers to read comic books by, he is tweaking the noses of Justis, his band, his fans, and all Memphisonians who were proud of their native son and hit-maker. Why would Monroe want to poke fun at something these people held near and dear? The answer to this question, as Chris Stacey and others have observed, is that Monroe was a "heel" (villain) wrestler who wanted to generate heat among the local population and motivate them to come to his wrestling matches to see him get his butt whipped.[4] When Monroe's wife, Midge Thompson, asked him who would buy the record, he said, "Nobody, but it might help the wrestling business ... any kind of exposure is better than none."[5] In other words, Monroe saw his novelty record as a promotional device, not a work of art, and he and his wife ended up giving many copies away to friends.[6]

Other Memphis-area wrestlers followed his lead and cut records of their own, but these songs were invariably country and Western, not rock and roll. In the early 1960s, for instance, Len Rossi recorded "A Wrestler's Prayer" and Jackie Fargo released "Champ of Champs,"[7] both of which are lugubrious, schmaltzy laments that have to do with legendary wrestlers of the past going to "that wrestling arena in the sky." This state of affairs seems curious, given the fact that Memphis was such an important center for early rock and roll. Memphis was the home of Sun Records, where Johnny Cash, Roy Orbison, Carl Perkins, Jerry Lee Lewis, and Elvis cut some of their greatest songs under the tutelage of Sam Phillips. Moreover, the King himself was a huge fan of wrestling. He not only enjoyed watching matches and socializing with wrestlers; he even dated a female wrestler named Penny Banner for a while in 1956, and played some charity shows in Ellis Auditorium.[8] Nonetheless, his involvement in wrestling was not enough to endear wrestling fans to his style of music. The wrestling crowd in Memphis during this time appears to have mainly been rural, working-class folk who preferred country to rock and roll, and the other wrestlers who made records during the 1960s catered to their more traditional tastes.

The resistance of wrestling fans to rock and roll was largely based on the genre's close association with African Americans. After all, a moralistic and racist backlash against rock and roll occurred in the South during the mid-fifties on the grounds that this new music was corrupting the morals of white teenagers. Asa "Ace" Carter of the White Citizens Council of Birmingham, Alabama, argued that "the basic, heavy-beat music of the Negroes" appealed to "the base in man, [bringing] out animalism and vulgarity." Here, Carter expresses the fear of many Southerners that white youngsters—especially white girls—would degenerate morally after being brutalized by rock and roll and get involved in miscegenation. Subsequently, Carter argued that rock and roll was part of an NCAAP plot "to mongrelize America," and he urged that all rock and roll music be removed from local jukeboxes and record stores.[9] Later, Carter's Citizen's Council protested a rock and roll show that featured black and white performers and the Birmingham city commissioners told the manager of the Municipal Auditorium not to book any more events that involved mixed-race performers. Elsewhere in the South, Elvis performed at a show in 1956 in Jacksonville, Florida, and found a judge waiting offstage to arrest him if he put on a "vulgar performance."[10] Examples such as these show that denunciations of rock and roll were couched in racist and moralistic terms.

Another view of these attitudes comes from Jim Dickinson, a Memphis-based pianist and rockabilly singer who recorded at Sun Records, played with Ry Cooder, and did session work with the Rolling Stones.[11] Dickinson talks about the ambivalence that rockabilly artists themselves felt when it came to playing a form of music with its roots in black rhythm and blues. On the one hand, rockabillies were inspired by the music of black artists, but, on the other hand, they shared the racial attitudes of other white Southerners and were uncomfortable associating with black culture.[12] These musicians also knew that rockabilly had a terrible reputation among upstanding members of Southern society, who saw this bastardized hybrid of country music and black R&B as abrasive, cacophonous, rebellious, hedonistic, morally debasing, and racially tainted. These morally-uptight citizens also viewed rockabilly as "the devil's music," for any music that fails to express the glory of God is worldly and not morally uplifting, and rockabillies felt that they were being sinful by playing it and corrupting others.[13] Given the ambivalence that Southern rockabilly artists felt toward their own music, one can imagine how ordinary, God-fearing Southerners felt about it, and, by extension, straight rock and roll, which was even more similar to black R&B and lacked the country element of rockabilly.

Given these attitudes, it should come as no surprise that the first wrestler to create a true rock and roll record was an African American who moved North to escape the South. Sometimes billed as "The Black Gorgeous George," Sweet Daddy Siki left Texas and relocated to Toronto in 1961. Unlike Sputnik Monroe, Siki could actually sing, and he has recorded several country-and-western albums (his preferred genre), which mostly feature covers of songs by artists such as Merle Haggard and Buck Owens. He has also done of his share of performing in dance halls and nightclubs, so one could say that Sweet Daddy was a semi-professional musician who played music between wrestling bouts. However, Sweet Daddy tried his hand at writing and recording rock and roll in the early '60s, cutting "Rock and Roll Shimmy Shimmy Partner" and "Momma Gimme Your Permission" with Pearl Reaves and the Paul Farano Trio as his backing band. Released on the Pearlsfar label as single number 107 in 1962,[14] this single was undoubtedly the first rock and roll record released by a wrestler. In a TV interview conducted in 1962, Sweet Daddy explains that he had wanted to put out a record for a long time because his wrestling fans had been asking him about his singing. He also points out that he used to sing in Canada quite a bit, and that he recorded the A side, "Shimmy Shimmy Partner," with a "good beat" so that it would appeal to teenagers.[15] Finally, the interview ends with Sweet Daddy saying, "I'm looking for a great success with this record."[16] As one can see, Sweet Daddy's attitude toward his record was very different from Sputnik Monroe's. He wanted to have as much success in the music business as he enjoyed in the wrestling business, and this interview was an attempt to promote his music as opposed to his career as a wrestler. Unfortunately, the record failed to make much of a splash, but Sweet Daddy Siki continues to sing with his band and work as a karaoke emcee for The Duke, a restaurant and bar in Toronto.[17]

The next step in creating the rock and wrestling connection was taken by a rock band, not a wrestler, because rock musicians in the 1960s were far more interested in wrestling than the wrestling crowd was interested in rock and roll. In 1964, a garage band from Edina, Minnesota, called The Novas wrote a rock and roll tribute to their favorite wrestler, Reginald Lisowski, aka The Crusher. Lisowski was a beer-swilling, barrel-chested tough guy who dyed his hair blonde and worked as a heel (villain) in the American Wrestling Association (AWA), based in Minneapolis, Minnesota. Known for his brawling, mauling style, Lisowski's gimmick was to take an incredible amount of punishment in the ring and still come back for the win. His main catchphrase was, "How 'bout dat?" and he took pleasure in calling his opponents "turkeynecks," a term that would be put to good use in The Novas' song.[18] The Novas were active in Minneapolis' thriving garage-band scene, but the acknowledged rulers of this scene were The Trashmen, who had hit it big in 1963 when their tune "Surfin' Bird" went to number four on the Billboard singles chart. Thus, The Novas wrote their paean to Lisowski in the style of The Trashmen and recorded it at Dove Studios in mid–1964. This first version was a primitive, eight-minute long basher with raunchy lyrics; when local promoter Sam Cerami heard the tape, he encouraged the boys to take out the obscenities and cut the song down to two-and-a-half minutes. They complied and re-recorded it, and "The Crusher" was picked up by Parrot Records and released as a single with "Take 7," The Novas' surf instrumental, on the flip side. By January 1965, "The Crusher" was a hit, climbing to number 88 on the Billboard Hot 100 chart and selling 250,000 copies.[19]

What makes this slab of rock and roll insanity so powerful is that it imitates Lisowski's wrestling persona to deliver a song about a new teen dance called—naturally—The Crusher. Vocalist Bob Nolan sings from the point of view of The Crusher himself, mimicking Lisowski's gravelly voice despite being only 1717 years old at the time. Nolan tells the listener how to do the dance by putting a couple of Lisowski's wrestling moves on his partner, mainly the hammerlock and the eye-gouge. At one point, Nolan even tells the listener to put his hand on his hip and squeeze his partner's neck until her face turns blue, in essence telling teenagers to abuse their dance partners. Moreover, the lyrics refer to listeners condescendingly as "turkeynecks," expressing the disdain that The Crusher had for scrawny, non-wrestling folk. Depending upon one's point of view, one can either see this song as incredibly humorous or amazingly perverse, but there is no denying its power to arouse interest in the listener. Its appeal is evident in the fact that the song continues to be relevant to rock fans even today; it still shows up on compilation CDs of garage music or novelty songs, appearing on at least half a dozen since the 1980s, and the song has been covered by many rock bands, most notably by The Cramps in the late '70s. Evidently, it also met the approval of the real-life Crusher, who was tickled pink by the tribute when someone played the single for him.[20]

Not surprisingly, The Novas' hit spawned an immediate knock-off called "King Krusher," a song recorded by another group of garage musicians from Minneapolis. This recording was sponsored by businessman George Garrett, who owned a record store and recording studio and who was also responsible for releasing The Trashmen's "Surfin' Bird."[21] In the words of drummer Ray Peters, Garrett "was always looking for a new sound to make a buck off of," and "The Crusher" seemed to be the start of a new trend, so he invited Ray Peters' band to record another song about the wrestler. Peters, guitarist Tony Caire, and bassist Doug Spartz did just that, calling themselves King Krusher and the Turkeynecks. The result is a much heavier rock song than the Novas' original number, with an added emphasis on making The Crusher roar in his gravelly voice so that he sounds more like King Kong than a person. In the middle of the song, Peters even breaks two drumsticks to simulate the sound of a turkey neck breaking![22] Unfortunately, "King Krusher" lacks the perverse charm and conceptual clarity of the Novas' hit, so it failed to make a national splash and ended up being an obscure garage tune that was reissued on a couple of compilation albums devoted to Minnesota bands.[23]

Back in Memphis, some other intriguing connections between garage rock and pro wrestling were made in the 1960s, but they failed to bear fruit until much later on. First, the renowned wrestling manager and personality Jimmy Hart got his start in a garage band called The Gentrys, for whom he, Larry Raspberry, and Bruce Bowles worked as vocalists. Their second single, "Keep on Dancing," rose to number four on the Billboard charts in October 1965, and the group appeared on TV dance shows such as *The Lloyd Thaxton Show, Hullabaloo, Where the Action Is*, and *American Bandstand*. The Gentrys became a top-drawing act in the South and placed five more singles on the Billboard charts, but Raspberry felt that the band was in a rut, so he left in May 1969. Hart took over leadership of the band and kept it going well into the 1970s; all told, The Gentrys released 21 singles and four albums. In the mid-'70s, Hart began working with independent music producer Jim Blake, helping to produce records by wrestler Jerry Lawler and backing up several other singing wrestlers on their recordings. Eventually, Hart would give up the band and go into wrestling himself, becoming the infamous megaphone-toting "Mouth of the South," a heel manager.[24] In the 1980s, however, he continued working in the realm of music, composing entrance themes for many wrestlers so that their sponsors could avoid paying royalties for pre-existing songs.[25]

Another amusing connection between Memphis garage bands and wrestling involved Jerry Phillips, son of Sam Phillips, the guiding light of Sun Records. Sam and Sputnik Monroe cooked up a scheme to generate more heat for Monroe, taking advantage of Jerry's unusually muscular build for a 12-year-old boy. After having Jerry train with some midget wrestlers for a while, Monroe began taking him to restaurants and bars in the Memphis area with a cigar hanging out of his mouth, claiming that Jerry was a midget.[26] Billed as "The World's Most Perfectly Formed Midget," Jerry began wrestling with real midgets on a circuit that included Arkansas and Mississippi; he was accompanied by a buddy of his named Johnny Dark, who played his Jimmy Hart–type manager.[27] The scheme worked for about three years until a crazed fan in Bentonville, Arkansas, pulled a knife on Monroe and Jerry, causing Jerry's parents to retire him from the wrestling business.[28] After that, Jerry joined a garage band named The Escapades, whose rivals were The Jesters; when both bands broke up, the leader of The Jesters reformed the band with several former members of the Escapades, including Jerry Phillips on guitar. In 1965, the band cut a single called "Cadillac Man" at Sun Studios. Instead of using their regular vocalist, The Jesters' leader brought in the aforementioned rockabilly singer Jim Dickinson as the vocalist in order to get a rawer vocal. The single had a pre–Beatles rock and roll sound and received some local airplay, but it failed to succeed nationally, so the band soldiered on for a couple more years before breaking up.[29]

The various wrestling-related songs by '60s garage bands failed to give birth to a long-term relationship between rock and wrestling until the 1970s, when the climate was right for the wrestling crowd to accept rock and roll as an expression of their own anti-establishment attitudes. The next wave of singing wrestlers was led by Beauregarde, a heel in the Pacific Northwest region who recorded the first full-length LP by a wrestler in 1970.[30] Beauregarde (aka Larry Pitchford) got his start by wrestling as a babyface (hero) named Eric the Golden Boy in Hawaii and the Philippines. A wrestling partner suggested that he adopt the name "Beauregarde" because it sounded aristocratic and arrogant, and a heel was born. Beauregarde proved to be a highly creative and effective heel; he would dress up in period costumes and imitate famous historical figures such as Napoleon, speaking to audiences in such a haughty, disdainful manner until they were whipped into wrathful fury.[31] The wrestler's creativity and verbal wit are fully evident in the songs on *Beauregarde* (F-Empire, 1971). On "I'm Talkin' Time," a slow, grungy blues song that begins with howling wolves and creepy horror-movie sound effects, Beauregarde sings about the concept of time and the impermanence of life. Another standout number is "Super Star Super Star," a slow, melancholy blues meditation on the drug-induced deaths of Janis Joplin and Jimi Hendrix. Musically, the other songs on the LP range from raucous blues rock to funky soul tunes with horn parts, with the tasteful guitar parts being played by Greg Sage, a 17-year-old whiz kid who would go on to form The Wipers, an influential punk/alternative rock band from Portland, Oregon.[32] While the music on this album sounds dated now, Beauregarde stands head and shoulders above other singing wrestlers because he actually has a decent singing voice and sings about topics other than his own macho self.

A few years later, in 1975, another heel, "Classy" Freddie Blassie, lent his vocals to a tune called "Pencil Neck Geek." Its lyrics originated from Blassie's experiences working with a "geek" in a St. Louis carnival whose neck was supposedly as skinny as a "stack of dimes," and they also refer to his favorite insult and catchphrase, "You pencil-neck geek!"[33] The song was written by California rockabilly revivalist Johnny Legend and Pete Cicero with Blassie's persona and catchphrase in mind. Legend had wanted to collaborate musically with wrestlers for some time, and it took him a couple of years to get Blassie into the recording studio.[34] The lyrics do a good job of embodying wrestling's physical ethos, oozing with contempt for people with slimmer builds. In one verse Blassie describes the pencil-neck geek as a freak that eats grit, sucks scum, and has a pea-head as well as a lousy physique, which is as slender as that of a pipe cleaner or a buggy whip.[35] Blassie goes on to promise that he will rid the world of this breed of freak by stomping their heads into the ground, dealing out the braggadocio typical of such songs. Ron Hall suggests that the attitude in this song came from Sputnik Monroe,[36] but I would suggest that it also owes something to "The Crusher." To be sure, Blassie's singing voice is no better than Monroe's, and the tune is more of a harmonica-wailing Western song than a rock and roll number, but it is very catchy, and the song gets its rock credits from the backing band that includes rockabilly maniac Johnny Legend and guitarist Billy Zoom of the punk band X. Blassie's masterpiece went on to become a hit on Dr. Demento's Radio Show, a nationally syndicated novelty-song show that was carried by most major-market FM radio stations during the 1970s and '80s. Moreover, "Pencil Neck Geek" continued to be heard after being reissued on several Dr. Demento "greatest hits" albums.[37]

In the South, rock music had to be appropriated by rednecks before it could become acceptable to a wrestling audience. During the early 1970s, bands such as Lynyrd Skynyrd showed young Southerners that they did not have to be hippies to be rockers, that they could grow their hair long and still be Southern rebels. In the late '70s, a long-lived a genuine rock and wrestling connection was made when independent record producer Jim Blake formed a label called Barbarian Records and released a number of singles by Memphis wrestlers, most notably by Jerry Lawler. As a wrestler, "The King" based his heel persona on a subversion of Elvis Presley's speech and mannerisms, turning Elvis' sneer into a leer and whipping crowds into a hateful frenzy with a barrage of crude, tasteless remarks.[38] His musical efforts, however, display a far gentler and more fun-loving persona. His "90 Pound Weakling," produced by Jim Blake and Jimmy Hart in 1977,[39] sounds like a Beach Boys pop song with female backing vocals and horns; this harmless bit of rock and roll is so slickly produced that it has none of the menace of "The Crusher" or "King Krusher." Nevertheless, it continues the wrestling tradition of melding braggadocio with contempt for skinny physiques. Lawler sings of going to the beach with his girl and getting sand kicked in his face by a couple of 210-pound bullies, after which he resolves to start lifting weights so that he can build up his body and beat up the bullies. The flip side of the single features "The Ballad of Jerry Lawler," another light-hearted rock and roll song that has Lawler bragging about being a better singer than Johnny Cash and a better wrestler than NWA heavyweight champion Jack Brisco. Although the record features a wrestler singing about himself to build a particular public image, it presents Lawler as a jocular, good-natured guy, not a brawler like The Crusher who wanted to take peoples' heads off. Lawler even released an LP called *Jerry Lawler Sings*, on which he is backed up by the Memphis Horns, guitarist James Burton, and a crew of other professional musicians from Memphis, and Lawler definitely holds his own as a singer.[40]

The same cannot be said of "Handsome" Jimmy Valiant, who had a gravelly, tuneless voice, but Valiant was the first wrestler to record a rock song that actually helped him to "get over" with the fans in his territory.[41] Working with Sam Phillips and Jimmy Hart, Handsome Jimmy lent his vocals to a song that Hart had written and recorded with The Gentrys called "Ballad of Handsome Jimmy." Hart evidently wrote the song with Valiant in mind, but he recorded his own version of the song and released it as a 45 rpm single on June 15, 1979, on the Fretone record label as single No. FR 052.[42] Using the same backing track, which is a generic blues-guitar shuffle done in the style of Foghat or any number of '70s rock and roll bands, Hart had Handsome Jimmy record his vocals on the song, which was renamed "Son of a Gypsy" and released on September 3, 1979, as Fretone single No. FR 053.[43] In the lyrics, Valiant's cocky persona claims to be a rock and roller and ladies' man raised by a gypsy. Valiant has trouble singing in time with the rhythm of the song, but that didn't matter to wrestling fans who loved Handsome Jimmy's swaggering, loud-mouthed character. Indeed, Valiant had been brought into the Memphis territory to work as a flashy, arrogant heel from New York City who would feud with Jerry Lawler and arouse some Southern anger in the fans against a Yankee upstart. However, the plan backfired; fans fell in love with Valiant's "Son of a Gypsy" persona, so Valiant was turned into a babyface (hero) by Memphis bookers.[44] His popularity in the Memphis territory was greatly enhanced by his rock and roll record, which Valiant sold at his matches and used as his entrance theme. In the meantime, Hart had been pushing his own single at area radio stations and receiving massive regional airplay, thereby promoting

Valiant's persona to a wider audience with a higher-quality recording of the same song.[45] More significantly, Handsome Jimmy's declaration that he was a rock and roller signaled that rock and wrestling had finally formed a partnership that would prove to be economically beneficial to wrestling.

These two decades of cross-pollination culminated in the well-known *Rock 'n' Wrestling Connection* that Vincent K. McMahon cooked up in the 1980s after WWF heel manager "Captain" Lou Albano met pop singer Cyndi Lauper on a flight to Puerto Rico.[46] On a lark, Albano appeared in Lauper's music video for "Girls Just Want to Have Fun," and by Spring 1984, the video was receiving heavy play on Music Television (MTV), the new epicenter for youth culture. McMahon saw an opportunity to expand his audience for wrestling by appealing to fans of MTV, so he and Lauper's management wrote a storyline in which Lauper and Albano feud over the heel manager's supposedly sexist attitudes. McMahon built the feud into a huge wrestling event in 1985 that pitted Wendi Richter (Lauper's proxy) against Fabulous Moolah (Albano's proxy); the match drew the largest audience in MTV's existence. The cross-promotion also helped to sell six million copies of Lauper's album and pushed the WWF into mainstream American culture.[47] McMahon expanded his audience even further by creating *Hulk Hogan's Rock 'n' Wrestling*, a Saturday morning cartoon that turned thousands of youngsters into wrestling fans and consumers of Hulk Hogan-themed merchandise.[48] Running from September 1985 to October 1986, the show often included music videos along with the adventures of Hulk Hogan, Captain Lou Albano, Andre the Giant, and other "good guy" wrestlers.[49] Another music-related project was *The Wrestling Album* (1985), a collection of novelty songs featuring the vocals of WWF wrestling personalities such as Hillbilly Jim, Junkyard Dog, "Rowdy" Roddy Piper, and Captain Lou Albano. David Wolff, Cyndi Lauper's husband and manager, came up with the album concept, and Rick Derringer produced most of the tracks, with Lauper producing the track by her partner-in-crime Albano. *The Wrestling Album* only rose to number 84 on the Billboard Top 200, but it spawned many follow-up recordings and imitations, including *Piledriver: The Wrestling Album 2* (1987), *WrestleMania: The Album* (1993), *WWF Full Metal* (1996), and *WWF The Music, Vol. 2* (1997). As a result of the album's influence, the recording of songs and music videos by wrestlers became almost obligatory after the mid–1980s, and the use of rock songs as entrance music became a de rigueur part of the wrestler's performance.[50]

Obviously, McMahon's *Rock 'n' Wrestling Connection* succeeded in a far more spectacular way than previous attempts to mix rock and roll with wrestling, but McMahon had several advantages that most people in wrestling lacked before his time: first, he had access to a nationwide television audience; second, the time was right for the wrestling crowd to embrace rock and roll and all that it represented; and third, McMahon could observe and learn from earlier attempts by others to combine rock with wrestling. The rock bands and wrestlers of the 1960s and '70s who recorded rock-and-wrestling novelty songs had to rely on record sales and radio airplay to promote their wares, and they were subject to the same elements of chance that ruled the efforts of other artists who tried to create hit records. Yet these experimenters in the marketplace of popular music also benefited from the openness of the music industry to new records during the 1960s and 1970s. Anyone with an idea for a song, some willing musicians, and access to a local recording studio could record some rock and roll and press up a few hundred copies of a 45 rpm single, which was the equivalent of today's YouTube video. Marketing the record was the hard part, but many in the record-buying public were eager to spend their money to hear a crazy new tune. In this atmosphere, the wrestling industry could exploit rock and roll music and the 7-inch *Rock 'n' Wrestling Connection* vinyl record as a new medium for promotion, and rock bands could exploit the colorful world of wrestling for material to sing about on their own records.

Notes

1. The Freebirds began using Lynyrd Skynyrd's "Free Bird" as their entrance theme in 1979. See "The Fabulous Freebirds," WWE.com, http://www.wwe.com/superstars/fabulous-freebirds (accessed July 12, 2016).

2. David P. Szatmary, *Rockin' in Time: A Social History of Rock-and-Roll*, 6th ed. (Upper Saddle River, NJ: Prentice Hall, 2007), 26.

3. Bill Dies, "'Clothier to the King' Lansky's Back on Beale," *Memphis Daily News*, July 21, 2014, http://www.memphisdailynews.com/news/2014/jul/21/clothier-to-the-king-lanskys-back-on-beale.

4. Chris Stacey, "'I Couldn't Carry a Tune in a Bucket': Music and the Transformation of Southern Politics and Culture in Professional Wrestling, 1959–1987," unpublished manuscript, 7.

5. Quoted in Sara Hoover, "Sputnik Monroe Wrestler … and Troubadour," *WKNO FM*, May 23, 2013, http://wknofm.org/post/sputnik-monroe-wrestler-and-troubadour-0#stream/0.

6. Hoover, "Sputnik Monroe Wrestler … and Troubadour."

7. Ron Hall, *Sputnik, Masked Men & Midgets: The Early Days of Memphis Wrestling* (Memphis: Shangri-La Projects, 2009), 100–2.

8. Hall, *Sputnik, Masked Men & Midgets*, 25, 112.

9. Altschuler, *All Shook Up*, 38–39.

10. Altschuler, *All Shook Up*, 39–40.

11. Craig Morrison, *Go Cat Go! Rockabilly Music and Its Makers* (Urbana: University of Illinois Press, 1996), 5.

12. Morrison, *Go Cat Go!*, 49.

13. Morrison, *Go Cat Go!*, 50.

14. Marv Goldberg, "Pearl Reeves/Reeves," Marv Goldberg's R&B Notebooks, 2009, http://www.uncamarvy.com/Concords/concords.html.

15. I have not been able to locate an audio file of this record, but record lists describe it as a mid-tempo rocker with a saxophone break.

16. Television interview with Sweet Daddy Siki, YouTube, February 12, 2013, https://www.youtube.com/watch?v=s31q5P5dMhs.

17. David Grossman, "Wrestling Legend Sweet Daddy Siki Singing a New Tune—Literally," InsideToronto.com, October 21, 2014, http://www.insidetoronto.com/news-story/4925035-wrestling-legend-sweet-daddy-siki-singing-a-new-tune-literally/.

Part IV. Wrestling and Media

18. "Reginald Lisowski," *Wikia*, http://prowrestling.wikia.com/wiki/Reginald_Lisowski (accessed July 13, 2016).
19. Billy Miller, Liner Notes, *The Novas: "The Crusher,"* Norton Records EP 075, 1999, vinyl EP.
20. Miller, Liner Notes, *The Novas*.
21. Jim Oldsberg, "Have Skins, Will Travel! The Ray Peters Story," *Lost and Found* 2 (1993), 116–17.
22. Oldsberg, "Have Skins, Will Travel!" 115.
23. Oldsberg, "Have Skins, Will Travel!" 116.
24. Ron Hall, *Playing for a Piece of the Door: A History of Garage & Frat Bands in Memphis 1960–1975* (Memphis: Shangri-La Projects, 2001), 67–68.
25. "Amazing But True …," *WWE Magazine*, July 2007, 23.
26. Jim Cornette and Mark James, *Rags, Paper and Pins: The Merchandising of Memphis Wrestling* (CreateSpace Independent Publishing Platform, 2013), 311.
27. Hall, *Playing for a Piece of the Door*, 86–87.
28. Cornette and James, *Rags, Paper and Pins*, 311.
29. Hall, *Playing for a Piece of the Door*, 86–87.
30. See "Beauregarde," onlinewrestling.com, http://www.onlineworldofwrestling.com/bios/b/beauregarde/ (accessed April 12, 2017).
31. See "Beauregarde and His Pro Wrestling History," zenorecords.com, http://www.zenorecords.com/beauregarde/history.htm (accessed April 12, 2017).
32. "Beauregarde and His Pro Wrestling History," zenorecords.com; see also Vernon Joynson, *Fuzz, Acid, and Flowers Revisited: A Guide to American Garage, Psychedelic and Hippie Rock (1964–1975)* (London: Borderline Productions, 2004), 64.
33. Freddie Blassie with Keith Elliot Greenberg, *"Classy" Freddie Blassie: Listen, You Pencil Neck Geeks* (New York: Pocket Books, 2003), 17. See also "Freddie Blassie," WWE.com, http://www.wwe.com/superstars/freddieblassie (accessed July 14, 2016).
34. Freddie Blassie with Keith Elliot Greenberg, *Listen, You Pencil Neck Geeks*, 202.
35. Freddie Blassie with Keith Elliot Greenberg, *Listen, You Pencil Neck Geeks*, 204.
36. Hall, *Sputnik, Masked Men & Midgets*, 101.
37. Freddie Blassie with Keith Elliot Greenberg, *Listen, You Pencil-Neck Geeks*, 204.
38. Hall, *Sputnik, Masked Men & Midgets*, 5.
39. Hall, *Sputnik, Masked Men & Midgets*, 98.
40. Hall, *Sputnik, Masked Men & Midgets*, 99.
41. Stacey, "'I Couldn't Carry a Tune in a Bucket,'" 13.
42. "Jimmy Hart and the Gentrys: 'Ballad of Handsome Jimmy' 1979 'B' Side," YouTube, September 22, 2014, https://www.youtube.com/watch?v=3kuBG2xYzKE.
43. "Handsome Jimmy Valiant: 'Son of a Gypsy' 1979 'A' Side," YouTube, September 22, 2014, https://www.youtube.com/watch?v=Z0iP3ZT8aw4.
44. Scott Bowden, "Anatomy of an Angle: Mercy, Daddy! Handsome Jimmy Valiant Cuts Record, Turns Heel," Scott Bowden Presents Kentucky Fried Rasslin, July 8, 2010, http://kentuckyfriedwrestling.com/theword2/?s=handsome+jimmy+valiant.
45. "Jimmy Hart and the Gentrys: 'Ballad of Handsome Jimmy' 1979 'B' Side," YouTube, September 22, 2014, https://www.youtube.com/watch?v=3kuBG2xYzKE.
46. Lillian Ellison with Larry Platt, *The Fabulous Moolah: First Goddess of the Squared Circle* (New York, Harper Collins, 2002), 166–77.
47. Scott M. Beekman, *Ringside: A History of Professional Wrestling in America* (Westport, CT, Praeger, 2006), 125.
48. Beekman, *Ringside*, 126–27.
49. "*Hulk Hogan's Rock 'n' Wrestling*," tv.com, http://www.tv.com/shows/hulk-hogans-rock-n-wrestling/ (accessed September 5, 2016).
50. James Montgomery, "'The Wrestling Album' at 30: The Inside Story of a Record That Started a Revolution," *Rolling Stone*, November 18, 2015, http://www.rollingstone.com/sports/features/the-wrestling-album-at-30-the-inside-story-of-a-record-that-started-a-revolution-20151118.

About the Contributors

Keiko **Aiba** is a member of the Faculty of International Studies at Meiji Gakuin University in Tokyo. She has researched gender inequality in the Japanese workplace, the body and gender, and how femininities and masculinities are constructed through the body.

Andrew **Baerg** is an associate professor of communication in the School of Arts & Sciences at the University of Houston–Victoria. His primary research interest involves the sports video game's relationship to culture.

Seth **Bovey** is a professor of English at Louisiana State University–Alexandria, where he teaches freshman composition, American literature, the novel, and film. His interests include literature and film about the American West, literary naturalism and realism, and popular culture, especially film and popular music.

André Mendes **Capraro** is a professor of physical education and supervises masters and doctoral students at Federal University of Paraná (Brazil). He coordinates the Group of Combat Sports, Fights and Martial Arts Studies (GESHECLAM)—UFPR.

Elizabeth **Catte** is a co-owner of the historical consulting company Passel and a historian-writer and consulting public historian. Her scholarly interests focus on LGBTQ+ history, public memory, and Appalachian politics and identity.

Justin D. **García** is an assistant professor of anthropology at Millersville University of Pennsylvania. His research interests include U.S. immigration, the anthropology of sports, social constructs of race and ethnicity, and urban anthropology.

Christiana Molldrem **Harkulich** is a scholar, director, producer, lighting designer, and actor. Her research has focused on indigenous performance in North America after the end of the Indian wars. She has also been published on USHistoryscene.com.

Kevin **Hogg** teaches at Mount Baker Secondary School in Cranbrook, British Columbia. His research interests include sports history, dystopian literature, and world religions.

Aaron D. **Horton** is an associate professor of history at Alabama State University. His research interests include transnational culture and sport, with an emphasis on comparative studies, publishing on North Korea in the 2010 World Cup and refugees and stereotypes, among other topics.

Josh **Howard** is a co-owner of the historical consulting company Passel and a consulting public historian. His scholarly interests center on sport and gaming history, public memory, and Appalachian history.

Riqueldi Straub **Lise** is a doctoral candidate in physical education at Federal University of Paraná (Brazil). He is a researcher in the Group of Combat Sports, Fights and Martial Arts Studies (GESHECLAM)—UFPR.

Jean-François **Loudcher** is a lecturer at University of Franche–Comté (France). His interests include the history of physical education in France, body techniques (Mauss, Foucault, Vigarello), image analysis, violence, the Olympics and sport history (including studies of France, United Kingdom and Switzerland).

Frédéric **Loyer** teaches physical education and is a specialist in combat sports. His scholarly interests include the socio-historical study of physical practices and sports and entertainment (particularly professional wrestling) as a means of interpreting social issues.

Zara **Mirmalek** is a Fellow in the Program for Science, Technology & Society at Harvard University. Her research focuses on work culture, professional identity, and human-machine relationships in work environments where people work with remote presence tools (e.g., robots and digital media).

Evan Karl **Nagel** is a doctoral candidate in kinesiology at Western University in London, Ontario. His research interests include the history of minor league baseball, U.S. hockey, and the Olympics.

Tyson L. **Platt** is an associate professor of psychology at Alabama State University. He researches auditory perception (especially as related to music), student perceptions of psychology instructors, and the social functions of professional wrestling.

Ximena **Rojo de la Vega Guinea** is a translator and editor of Mexican digital media. She is working on a book of essays on lucha libre. Her main interests are cultural studies, gender studies, lucha libre, and translation.

Edward **Salo** is an assistant professor in the history department at Arkansas State University. He teaches historic preservation, the history of comic books, and public history courses.

Natasha **Santos** is a doctoral candidate in physical education at Federal University of Paraná (Brazil). She is also a researcher at the Center for Research in Sports, Leisure and Society (CEPELS) at UFPR.

Hendrik **Snyders** is the heritage manager at the South African Rugby Union. His research focuses on race, sport, masculinity, memory, heritage and public history as well as colonialism in South Africa.

Christopher L. **Stacey** is an associate professor of history at Louisiana State University–Alexandria. His areas of expertise include colonial/19th-century American history, the Civil War, slavery, and the Atlantic World.

Damion **Sturm** is a senior lecturer in the School of Events, Tourism & Hospitality at Leeds Beckett University (UK). His research interests are in global media cultures (sport, celebrity, fan, and material), including Formula One, cricket, and rugby as mediated sporting events.

Index

AAA *see* Asistencia Asesoría y Administración (AAA)
Abdullah the Butcher 95–96
Adonis, Adrian 141–142, 145
African Political Organization (APO) 57–58
Akbar, Skandor 96
Akeem "The African Dream" *see* Gray, George
Albano, "Captain" Lou 151–152, 221, 298
Ali, Muhammad 4, 96, 249
Al-Kaissie, Adnan 98
All Japan Pro Wrestling (AJPW) 83
American Wrestling Alliance (AWA) 4
André the Giant 96, 99, 194
Angle, Kurt 48, 260
apartheid 62–67
Armstrong, Bob 32
Armstrong, Scott 29, 32
Asistencia Asesoría y Administración (AAA) 5, 42
Asuka 88–89
Austin, "Stone Cold" Steve 44, 102–103, 192, 238, 240–241, 245
AWA *see* American Wrestling Alliance (AWA)

Baba, Ali "The Terrible Turk" 94
Baba, Shohei "Giant" 83–84
Backlund, Bob 103
Banks, Sasha 148, 158–159
Barr, Art 42–43
Barthes, Roland 26, 110–112, 149–150, 154, 179–180, 213, 276–277, 289
Bayley 148
Bella Twins 157
Berman, Aaron (South African politician) 59
Big Boss Man 100
Billy and Chuck 142–144
Blassie, "Classy" Freddie 81, 296
Blue Demon 117
Boesch, Paul 94

Brakus 79
Brazo de Plata 116
Brisco, Jack 98
Brown, Dave 225
Bruns, Bobby 182
Burns, Martin "Farmer" 2

Candido, Chris 27
capoeira 165
Carwin, Shane 258–261, 263–264
Cassandro 113, 115–116
Castle, Dalton 144
catch-as-catch-can 211–213
Cena, John 46, 150, 183–185
Chyna 43, 155–156, 159
CMLL *see* Consejo Mundial de Lucha Libre (CMLL)
Cold War 26, 35, 80, 93, 95, 97–98, 150, 193
Colón, Carlos 40
Colter, Zeb *see* Mantell, Dutch
Combat Zone Wrestling (CZW) 5
Consejo Mundial de Lucha Libre (CMLL) 116
Continental Wrestling 221–222, 230–231
Coordinating Committee for International Recognition (CCIR) 62–63
Cornette, Jim 24, 26–27, 30–32
Couture, Randy 251, 255–256, 261
Crush 102
CZW *see* Combat Zone Wrestling

D-Generation X 102, 155, 238
Danielson, Bryan 189
Darsow, Barry 97
Davis, Bobby 96
Davis, Gardenia 1, 112–114
Del Rio, Alberto 7, 37, 39, 42, 49–52; and racism in WWE 51–52; and social class in Mexico 50
The Destroyer (Dick Beyer) 182
DiBiase, "The Million Dollar Man" Ted 229, 271, 280–281, 284

305

Dirty White Boy 25, 27, 30; and Southern identity 33
Divas Revolution 8, 157–159
Dreamer, Tommy 189
Dynamite Kid 6

ECW *see* Extreme Championship Wrestling (ECW)
Edge 150, 157
Elizabeth, Miss 152–153
El Patron, Alberto *see* Del Rio, Alberto
El Santo 5, 42, 115, 117
EMLL *see* Empresa Mexicana de Lucha Libre (EMLL)
Empresa Mexicana de Lucha Libre (EMLL) 4; *see also* Consejo Mundial de Lucha Libre (CMLL)
Evolve 193
Extreme Championship Wrestling (ECW) 5, 27, 32, 41, 88

The Fabulous Freebirds 222, 228–229, 289; *see also* Hayes, Michael
Fargo, Jackie 225, 291
Fatu 101, 103
Fédération Internationale de Lutte Amateur (FILA) 162
FILA *see* *Fédération Internationale de Lutte Amateur* (FILA)
Flair, Charlotte 158–159
Flair, "Nature Boy" Ric 4, 188
Flowers, May 115–116
FMW *see* Frontier Martial Arts Wrestling (FMW)
Foley, Mick 245–246
Frazier, Stan 99
Frontier Martial Arts Wrestling (FMW) 5, 86
Fytch, Tammy 25, 34; entry into wrestling 27–28; feminism 28–29; and male insecurities 29–31

Gagne, Verne 4, 77
Galento, Mario 230
The Gangstas 25, 27, 31; inflammatory behavior 31–32; and racial stereotypes 31–32
Gaviota, Miss 117–118
GLAAD (Gay and Lesbian Alliance Against Defamation) 143–145
Goldberg, Bill 188
Goldberg, Mike 254
Goldust *see* Runnels, Dustin
Gorgeous George 1, 4, 27, 95, 114, 137–140, 145, 249; challenging gender norms 138–139
Gotch, Frank 2
Gotch, Karl 83, 184
Gracie, Helio 249
Gracie, Royce 250

Graham, "Superstar" Billy 40
Gray, George 100
Great Depression 93–94
Great Kabuki 84, 102
Great Muta 84, 102
Greco-Roman wrestling 2, 11, 80, 162; in Brazil 166–173, 175; in France 6, 206, 213–217; regulation of in France 200–202, 214–215; in South Africa 56–58; transition from shooting to working in France 207–208
Griffin, Marcus 3
Guerrera, Juventud 41
Guerrero, Chavo, Jr. 41–42
Guerrero, Eddie 7, 37, 39, 41–48, 156
Gulf War 100

Hackenschmidt, George 2, 57, 207
Hall, Scott 40–41, 101
Hansen, Stan "The Lariat" 83, 187, 190
Hardy, Matt 150
Hart, Bret "Hitman" 6, 145, 275–276
Hart, Jimmy "The Mouth of the South" 224–225, 297–298; as member of the Gentrys 294
Hart, Owen 102
Hart, Stu 6
Hassan, Muhammad 104
Hayes, Michael 183; *see also* The Fabulous Freebirds
The Headshrinkers 101, 103
Hefer, Bull 65–68, 70
Henry, Mark 143
Herring, Heath 253–255, 260–264
Hijo del Santo 115
Hogan, Hulk 4, 9, 84–85, 99–100, 102, 152, 183–184, 194, 252, 270–272, 274–280, 283, 285, 298
Honky Tonk Man 271, 278, 282
Horner, Tim 26, 33

Ibushi, Kota 88
immigration: Mexican 37–39, 42, 46, 48–50
Inoki, Antonio 83–84, 184
Iranian Revolution (1979) 14–17
Iron Sheik 6, 12–14, 17, 39, 89, 98, 103, 279–280; as "Colonel Mustafa" 100; personal appearance 18–20
Ishii, Tomohiro 189
Itami, Hideo 87–88

Jacqueline 154
Jarrett, Jerry 99
JBL *see* Layfield, John Bradshaw (JBL)
Jericho, Chris 26, 32
Jim Crockett Promotions 4
jiu-jitsu 165, 210–211
Johnson, Duane "The Rock" 103, 184
Jordan, Orlando 145
Joshi puroresu (Japanese women's pro wrestling): body image 126–127, 131–132;

Index   307

challenges to gender norms 133; misperception of gender 128–129, 132–133; perceived benefits of training 122–126, 129–131
Junkyard Dog 181, 183

Kader, Abdul 69–70
Kai, Leilani 152
Kaientai 86
Kamala 99
Kamala #2 *see* Frazier, Stan
Kana *see* Asuka
Kanyon, Chris 144
kayfabe 38, 48, 100, 175, 221, 225, 229–231, 270, 272–276, 278–281, 283
KENTA *see* Itami, Hideo
Kimura, Masahiko 182
Kingston, Kofi 104
Kirchner, Corporal 98
Koloff, Ivan 97
Koloff, Nikita 97
Konnan 5
Kruschev, Krusher *see* Darsow, Barry
Kwang *see* Rivera, Juan

Lauper, Cyndi 9, 11, 151–152, 221, 223, 298
Laurer, Joanie *see* Chyna
Lawler, Jerry 99, 103, 154–155, 225–227, 231, 241, 296–297
Layfield, John Bradshaw (JBL) 46, 49
Layla 157
Lee, Brian 27, 30, 33
Lesnar, Brock 9, 46, 249–264; early career 250–251; entry into UFC 253; rematch with Frank Mir at UFC 100, 256–258; versus Randy Couture at UFC 91, 255–256
Levesque, Paul *see* Triple H
Lewis, Ed "Strangler" 3, 94
Lewis, Evan "Strangler" 80
Lisowski, Reggie "The Crusher" 290, 293–294
Lita 150–151, 155–157, 159, 245
Londos, Jim 3, 61, 76, 94
lucha libre 41, 109; origins 110; significance of masks 111–112
El Luchador fenómeno (*The Phenomenonal Wrestler*, 1952) 113
Luger, Lex 85
Lutteroth, Salvador 4, 110
Lynch, Becky 158–159

Maharaj, P.J. 68–69
Maivia, Rocky *see* Johnson, Duane "The Rock"
Mantell, Dutch 50–51
Marella, Santino 143
Marlena *see* Runnels, Terri
masculinity: Mexican/Chicano 37–39, 41–45
Máximo 116
McCool, Michelle 157
McDaniel, Wahoo 98

McMahon, Stephanie 156, 158, 245
McMahon, Vincent J. 78
McMahon, Vincent K. 3, 40–41, 141, 145, 221–223, 225, 228–229, 232, 271–272, 298
Meltzer, Dave 31–32, 93
Mendes, Rosa 145
Mexican Revolution (1910–1920) 109–110
Michaels, Shawn 102–103, 155, 238–240, 245
Mid-South Wrestling 183
Mil Máscaras 40, 49
Mir, Frank 252–253, 256–259, 261, 263–264
Mr. Fuji 82, 85, 101
Mr. Moto 81–82
modernization: in Brazil 163–164
Monday Night RAW 4, 44, 51, 142–143, 151, 154, 238–243, 245
Monday Nitro 4, 41, 155, 238–239
Mondt, Joe "Toots" 3, 180
Monroe, Sputnik 222–224, 289–292, 295–296
Monsoon, Gorilla 96, 280
Moolah, Fabulous 151–152
Morales, Pedro 40, 181
Morishima, Takeshi 189
Morton, Ricky 188
MTV 9, 11, 151–152
Muldoon, William 2, 81, 180
Munn, "Big" Wayne 3
Mysterio, Rey, Jr. 5, 7, 37, 39, 41–42, 46–50; and transnational identity 47–48

Nakamura, Shinsuke 88–89
Nakano, Bull 5
Nash, Kevin 188
Nation of Domination 102–103
National Wrestling Alliance (NWA) 3, 40
Neidhart, Jim "The Anvil" 103
New Japan Pro Wrestling (NJPW) 5, 83, 85, 87–88, 193
New World Order (nWo) 102–103
Nitro see Monday Nitro
NJPW *see* New Japan Pro Wrestling
NOAH *see* Pro Wrestling NOAH
NWA *see* National Wrestling Alliance
nWo *see* New World Order (nWo)
NXT 86, 88–90, 148–149, 157–158

Okada, Kazuchika 87, 185, 193, 195
Okerlund, "Mean" Gene 151
One Man Gang *see* Gray, George
Onita, Atsushi 5
Onoo, Kazuo "Sonny" 85–86
The Orient Express 101
Ortiz, Tito 249, 251, 254
Orton, Randy 48
Overeem, Alistair 261, 263–264

Parker, Dan 3
The Patriot (Del Wilkes) 103
Patterson, Pat 138, 144–145

308 Index

Paz, Eugène 203
Peixoto, José Floriano 170–172
Peixoto, Marshal Floriano 163
Peña, Antonio 5
physical culture: in Brazil 164–165, 168, 175; and education in France 203, 205; in France 209–210
Pillman, Brian 103
Piper, "Rowdy" Roddy 9, 99–100
Pons, Paul 166–169, 205
Pro Wrestling NOAH 193
Psichosis 5, 41

Raven 189
RAW see Monday Night RAW
RAW Is WAR see Monday Night RAW
Razor Ramon *see* Hall, Scott
Rhodes, Dustin *see* Runnels, Dustin
Rhodes, Dusty 142
Richter, Wendi 151–152
Rikidozan 5, 83, 182, 186
Ring of Honor (ROH) 88, 193
Rivera, Juan 102
Roberts, Jake "The Snake" 271, 276, 280, 284
The Rock *see* Johnson, Duane "The Rock"
ROH *see* Ring of Honor (ROH)
Ross, Jim 186, 241, 246
Rossi, Len 291
Roth, Ernie "The Grand Wizard" 95–96, 145
Rude, "Ravishing" Rick 271, 276, 278–279, 284–285
Runnels, Dustin 137–138, 142, 145
Runnels, Terri 155
Rusev 150
Russell, Lance 225, 230–231

Sable 148, 154–156
Sakata, Harold *see* Tosh Togo
Sammartino, Bruno 39, 78, 82, 89, 96–97, 181
Samoa Joe 87
Sandow, Damien 150
Santana, Tito 40
Savage, "Macho Man" Randy 152–153, 193, 271, 273–274, 278, 280–281, 283–284
Schmidt, Hans 77, 95
Segreto, Paschoal 167–169, 173–174
Sgt. Slaughter 100, 103, 279
Shamrock, Ken 249, 251
The Sheik 95–96
Shibata, Katsuyori 189, 195
Shimmer Women Athletes 193
Simmons, Ron 102
Smith, "British Bulldog" Davey Boy 103, 239, 276
Smoky Mountain Wrestling (SMW) 6, 24–34; closing 34; founding 26–27
Smothers, Tracy 25, 27, 32, 34
SMW *see* Smoky Mountain Wrestling (SMW)
Sorakichi Matsuda 80–81

South African National Wrestling Control Board (SANWCB) 62–65, 68–69
South African Sports Association (SASA) 63–64
Stampede Wrestling 6, 82
Stardom 193
Starr, Ricki 139–140
Steamboat, Ricky 82–83
Steele, George "The Animal" 152
Storm, Lance 26
Stratus, Trish 151, 155–157, 159, 245
Street, "Exotic" Adrian 139–140, 227
Strongbow, "Chief" Jay 7, 98
Sullivan, John L. 180
Sullivan, Kevin 27
Suzuki, Hiroko 87
Suzuki, Kenzo 87
Swagger, Jack 50–51
Sweet Daddy Siki 292–293
Sytch, Tammy *see* Fytch, Tammy

Tanahashi, Hiroshi 185, 193
Tanaka, Toru 82
Tatanka 98
Thesz, Lou 3, 5, 77, 83
TNA *see* Total Nonstop Action (TNA)
Tosh Togo 82, 95
Total Divas 157
Total Nonstop Action (TNA) 87
Toyota, Manami 5
Triat, Antoine-Hippolyte 202
Triple H 52, 102, 155–156, 158, 241–242, 245
Turner, Ted 4

UFC *see* Ultimate Fighting Championship (UFC)
Ultimate Fighting Championship (UFC) 9, 249–264; origins 250–251
The Ultimate Warrior 271, 274–276, 278
Uncle Elmer *see* Frazier, Stan
The Undertaker 99, 188, 238, 240, 245–246, 279
Union des Sociétés Françaises de Sports Athlétiques (USFSA) 209
Universal Wrestling Federation (UWF) 221–222, 229–231
UWF *see* Universal Wrestling Federation (UWF)

Vachon, Maurice "Mad Dog" 79
Valiant, "Handsome" Jimmy 226–227, 297–298
Vega, Savio *see* Rivera, Juan
Velasquez, Cain 259–261, 263
Ventura, Jesse 141, 280
Ville, Léon 205, 213
Volkoff, Nikolai 18, 97–98
Von Erich, Fritz 77–79, 95–96
Von Erich, Waldo 78, 95
Von Hess, Karl 77–79, 95

Von Poppenheim, Kurt 95
Von Raschke, Baron 78–79

Wagner, "Gorgeous" George *see* Gorgeous George
Watts, "Cowboy" Bill 229
WCCW *see* World Class Championship Wrestling (WCCW)
WCW *see* World Championship Wrestling (WCW)
West Hollywood Blondes 143–144
White, Dana 255, 258, 261
Wippleman, Harvey 102
World Championship Wrestling (WCW) 4, 24, 27, 41, 101–103, 143–144, 155, 188, 228, 234, 239, 244–246
World Class Championship Wrestling (WCCW) 78
World Wide Wrestling Federation (WWWF) 40, 66, 78, 82, 97–98, 141, 181, 271
World Wrestling Entertainment (WWE) 38, 42, 42–52, 92, 141, 193, 234, 238–247; depiction of homosexuality 142–145; *see also* World Wrestling Federation (WWF)
World Wrestling Federation (WWF) 4, 11–12, 24, 27, 140–141, 150–152, 154–156, 192–193, 221, 227–229, 270–278, 280–286, 298; racial stereotypes 35; *see also* World Wrestling Entertainment (WWE)
Wrestlemania 18, 98–99, 238, 271–272, 274–275; *Wrestlemania* (1985) 40, 152; *Wrestlemania III* (1987) 194; *Wrestlemania XIII* (1997) 103, 152, 155; *Wrestlemania 32* (2016) 159
Wright, "Das Wunderkind" Alex 79
Wright, Ron 30, 33–34
WWE *see* World Wrestling Entertainment (WWE)
WWE '13 (video game) 8, 234, 236–237; depictions of the "Attitude Era" 237–247
WWF *see* World Wrestling Federation (WWF)
WWWF *see* World Wide Wrestling Federation (WWWF)

Yokozuna 85, 102
Young, Darren 137, 144–145
Young, Silas 193

Zbyszko, Stanislaus 3, 213
Zhukov, Boris 98

www.ingramcontent.com/pod-product-compliance
Ingram Content Group UK Ltd.
Pitfield, Milton Keynes, MK11 3LW, UK
UKHW041925140426
5217IPUK00014B/314